The altarpiece in the Renaissance

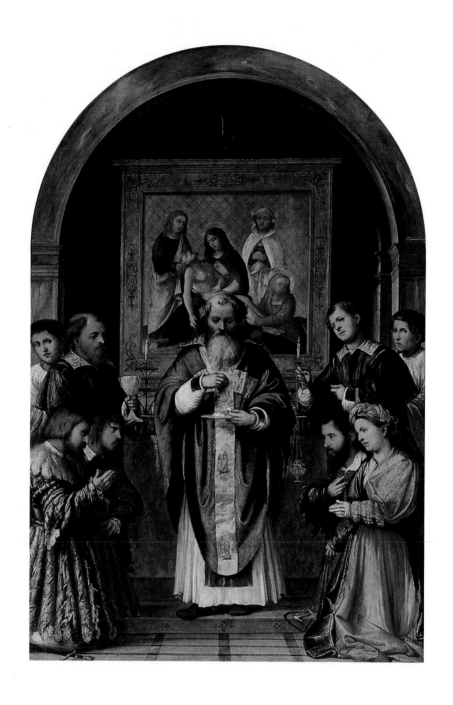

Gerolamo Romanino, *Mass of St Apollonius*, Brescia, Santa Maria Calchera

THE
ALTARPIECE
IN THE
RENAISSANCE

EDITED BY

Peter Humfrey

AND

Martin Kemp

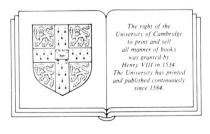

*The right of the
University of Cambridge
to print and sell
all manner of books
was granted by
Henry VIII in 1534.
The University has printed
and published continuously
since 1584.*

CAMBRIDGE UNIVERSITY PRESS

Cambridge
New York   Port Chester
Melbourne   Sydney

Published by the Press Syndicate of the University of Cambridge
The Pitt Building, Trumpington Street, Cambridge CB2 1RP
40 West 20th Street, New York, NY 10011, USA
10 Stamford Road, Oakleigh, Melbourne 3166, Australia

First published 1990

Printed in Great Britain by The Bath Press, Avon

British Library cataloguing in publication data
The altarpiece in the Renaissance.
1. Europe. Churches. Altarpieces, history
I. Humfrey, Peter   II. Kemp, Martin
755'.2'094

Library of Congress cataloguing in publication data
The altarpiece in the Renaissance/edited by Peter Humfrey and Martin
Kemp.
p. cm.
Includes bibliographical references.
ISBN 0-521-36061-7
1. Altarpieces, Renaissance. 2. Christian art and symbolism –
Modern, 1500 – I. Humfrey, Peter, 1947–   . II. Kemp, Martin.
N7862.A48   1990
726'.5296–dc20 89-17416 CIP

ISBN 0 521 36061 7

Contents

v

Illustrations

Figures

Acknowledgements

Most of the essays presented here are based on papers given at a conference of the Society for Renaissance Studies held at the Warburg Institute and Birkbeck College in London on 20–21 March 1987. The conference was organised by Peter Humfrey, and Martin Kemp took the chair in one of the sessions; the other three sessions were chaired by Julian Gardner, Francis Ames-Lewis and John White, all of whom made important contributions to the success of the occasion. We are grateful to the following organisations for providing financial assistance for speakers coming from abroad: the British Academy, the British Council and the National Endowment for the Humanities. We are also grateful for the help and advice provided by Malcolm Baker and Mauro Lucco.

SOURCES

Antwerp, Koninklijk Museum voor Schone Kunsten, plates 29, 37
Brescia, Basilio Rodella, frontispiece
Brussels, A. C. L., plates 22, 23, 24, 25, 26, 30, 31, 36
Castle Barnard, the Bowes Museum, plate 11
Chicago, Art Institute, plate 131
Dessau, Evangelisches Pfarramt, plate 27
Edinburgh, Tom Scott, plate 19
Florence, Alinari, plates 9, 15, 18, 20, 78, 79, 80, 81, 83, 86, 91
    Soprintendenza per i Beni artistici e storici di Firenze, plates 12, 14, 17
Graz, Landesmuseum Joanneum, plate 63
Leiden, Stedelijk Museum 'De Lakenhal', plate 21
London, Conway Library, plate 39
    National Gallery, plates 6, 60, 85
Madrid, Mas, plates 120, 127, 130, 132, 134
    Pandó, plate 125
Malibu, J. Paul Getty Museum, plate 38
Marburg, Bildarchiv Marburg, plate 4
Munich, Bayerische Staatsgemäldesammlungen, plate 67

New York, Metropolitan Museum of Art, plate 33
  Pierpont Morgan Library, plate 40
Paris, Brogi-Giraudon, plate 76
  Huralt, plate 69
  Réunion des Musées Nationaux, plates 34, 35
  Spadem, plate 123
Rome, Anderson, plates 88, 90, 92
  Gabinetto Fotografico Nazionale, plates 87, 136, 137, 138
Strasbourg, Museés de la Ville, plate 59
Turin, Chomon-Perino, plate 75
Utrecht, Rijksmuseum het Catharijneconvent, plate 32
Venice, Maria Ida Biggi, plates 112, 120
  Böhm, plates 111, 113, 114
  Fondazione Cini, plate 117
  Mark Smith, plate 140
  Soprintendenza alle Gallerie di Venezia, plates 16, 108, 115
Verona, Umberto Tomba, plate 77
Vienna, Alpenland, plates 54, 55, 56, 61
  Otto, plates 57, 58
Waddesdon Manor, National Trust, plate 41
Windsor, Royal Library, plate 89

Introduction The altarpiece in the Renaissance: a taxonomic approach

Martin Kemp

The study of a particular genre, genus, type, or category of art, such as the altarpiece, has distinct advantages. Sets of common features not only permit the analysis of what distinguishes a particular functional category of artistic product but also provide 'controls' or backgrounds against which variations in the genre appear in sharp relief. A broad range of questions about the function of images, how they come to embody meaning, about their commissioning and making, and about their effects and reception come into play. And, depending upon the chronological and geographical scope of the investigation, questions of development and regional characteristics can be brought into focus.

This is not say, of course, that the nature of any artistic genre is susceptible to easy, watertight and uncontestable definition, as we will have repeated cause to see in the case of the altarpiece. However, the term 'altarpiece' does refer in a widely accepted manner to a generally recognisable class of objects – in spite of intractable problems at the margins of the definition. Broadly speaking, we are referring to a structure containing a figurative image or complex of figurative images (almost invariably painted or sculpted) which is directly associated with an altar and comprises the upper part of the combined ensemble of the altar and its furnishings. It generally serves as a superstructure (either in a literally structural or in a visual sense) behind the table-top of the altar. The subject-matter of the image or images and the structural form of the altarpiece will be expected to bear some kind of relationship to its physical situation, with respect both to the altar and to the location of the altar itself within its own setting. For the most part we will be dealing with locations within churches rather than within purely private settings, and with permanent fixtures rather than temporary constructions.

The function of the altar is to provide a locus for the performance of the mass.[1] The climax of the mass is the elevation of the host, the symbolic wafer which is taken (at least at the start of our period) as embodying the True Presence of Christ. This is followed by the administering of the Sacrament of the Eucharist. A painting of the *Mass of St Apollonius* by the Brescian artist, Gerolamo Romanino (frontispiece), which is itself an altarpiece, neatly depicts the essential ingredients: the altar and

---

[1] For information on the mass, the role of altars and related liturgical matters See J. Braun, *Der christliche Altar in seiner geschichtlichen Entwicklung* (Munich, 1924); Braun, *Das christliche Altargät in seinem Sein und in seiner Entwicklung* (Munich, 1932), pp. 466–72; L. Eisenhofer, *Handbuch der katolischen Liturgik* (Freiburg, 1942); J. A. Jungmann, *The Mass of the Roman Rite* (New York, 1951); and J. G. Davies, ed., *A dictionary of liturgy and worship* (London, 1980).

the priest with the host, from which a fragment has already been broken for adminis-
tration to one of the kneeling congregation; and the chalice of wine, representing
Christ's blood, which is held by an attendant. The particular event represented here
involves the miraculous materialisation of a fully furnished altar to permit the saint,
who was Bishop of Brescia, to administer the Sacrament to a host of newly converted
Brescians. The altarpiece with which the miraculous altar has been adorned is of
an unusually simple kind and is placed in its most characteristic position. In this
instance, the image painted within the frame of altarpiece makes direct reference
to the Sacrifice of Christ, which comprises the central import of the mass. Such
an obvious directness of reference is, as we will see, relatively unusual.

The limiting of our investigation to the Renaissance, in this case defined as running
from *c.* 1400 to *c.* 1600, is arbitrary to a degree, but it does correspond to a period
in which the provision of altarpieces came to occupy a central role in the production
of many major artists and their workshops. Although painters in the Baroque and
later eras, such as Rubens, produced innovatory altarpieces in some numbers, the
prominence of the genre was undoubtedly less in the whole spectrum of artistic
production after 1600 than during the Renaissance. In the period 1400–1600, both
north and south of the Alps, many of the most significant questions of form and
content were rehearsed urgently and competitively in altarpiece design.

However, the immediate nature of the present collection of studies depends less
upon purely academic considerations of chronological and geographical scope than
upon the circumstances which gave rise to this collaborative effort. Most of the papers
in this volume were presented at a two-day conference on 'The altarpiece in the
Renaissance' held in March 1987 in London under the auspices of the Society for
Renaissance Studies. The programme was compiled by Peter Humfrey of the University of St Andrews, who has also played the major role in editing the papers for
publication and closely assisted in the preparation of this introductory essay. The
chronological scope was largely determined by the Society's remit. Perhaps its chief
disadvantage in presenting a rounded study of the altarpiece arises from the starting
date of 1400, which excludes detailed examination of the rise of the altarpiece as
a substantial genre during the thirteenth and fourteenth centuries. It is also apparent
that a conventionally defined historical period, like the Renaissance, does not necessarily correspond to what may be regarded as a distinct period in religious history.
The period 1400–1600, for example, is conspicuously ruptured by the Reformation,
but such conflicts of period definition between different historical disciplines can
encourage the asking of more varied questions than is facilitated by neater definitions
within each field of study.

The range of topics – geographical, thematic and chronological – was obviously
determined by the availability of research and researchers. The coverage of northern
European topics was distinctly thin at the conference, and the papers by Mark Evans
and Craig Harbison were subsequently solicited to give more balance in the published
volume. Peter Humfrey himself was also persuaded to include his paper on attempts
to co-ordinate sets of altarpieces in Venetian churches. We remain conscious, how-

ever, that the coverage cannot be comprehensive. For instance, post-Reformation images in northern Europe receive little prominence; and the French altarpiece remains unconsidered. The present introduction is not intended to rectify these shortcomings – nor to be unduly apologetic about what is a wide-ranging and intellectually varied collection of studies by significant researchers in the field – but rather to draw out some of the points which emerge from the reading of the essays as a whole. Many of these points were aired in the discussion which followed each session of papers.

Probably the most crucial problem which emerges – whether openly or implicitly – concerns the contexts of classification within which the images are to be considered and the kinds of evidence which are most germane for the historian within each context. Are we, for instance, to be primarily concerned with issues of form, style and expression, in as far as altarpieces relate to the broad category of images that we call 'art'? Or should we pay most attention to the particularity of an individual altarpiece in terms of the details of its commissioning and manufacture? When we turn to questions of meaning, do we conduct elaborate iconographical analyses of the content of altarpiece on the basis theological texts, within the category of religious images as a whole? Or should we be concentrating upon the particular liturgical functions of altarpieces as a specific category of object? Or should we limit ourselves austerely to the bare bones of the specific documentation of an individual altarpiece, which generally do little to flesh out the meaning of the images?

What clouds the arguments that ensue when such issues are raised in the general free-for-all of discussion at a conference is a failure to recognise the kind of question that is being asked in relation to the nature and level of the problem under investigation, and the kind of evidence that can and cannot be fruitfully brought to bear at each level. It is with this failure in mind that I propose to conduct my introductory review in terms of an investigation of a taxonomy of art, in which 'altarpiece' serves as a middle term. The taxonomy I am adopting is biological, but without intending to suggest that the products of artists can be handled precisely as if they were products of nature. As we will see, such a system of classification breaks down at key points. The biological taxonomy is simply used here as a way of categorising objects within a system that proceeds progressively from the general to the particular. The taxonomic classes I will be using are 'kingdom', 'family', 'genus', 'species' and 'individual'.

The kingdom: figurative images known as 'works of art'

The divinity of the science of painting considers works both human and divine, which are bounded by surfaces, that is to say the boundary lines of bodies.[2]

Any altarpiece can be discussed within the story of art without any acknowledgement that it belongs to the category of 'altarpiece'. In such a story, as conventionally told, the historical evidence relating to maker, date and place of origin will merely serve

---

[2] Codex Urbinas, Vatican, 12v in *Leonardo on painting*, ed. M. Kemp, trans M. Kemp and M. Walker, (New Haven and London, 1989), no. 89.

the function of historical location, and will be placed in the service of the autonomous history of those elements which are taken as the distinguishing features of 'art'. The kind of investigations in this volume might seem to be inimicable to such an enterprise. However, there are clear indications, above all in the paper by Evans, that questions of the development of an artist's work in relation to influence, evolution of style and artistic ambition can be examined productively through concentration upon the constraints of a particular genre. Moreover, as Ferino effectively shows, the period with which we are concerned was precisely that which saw the prizing of altarpieces outside their functional category – what she calls the transition from *Kultbild* to *Bildkult* (from images made to serve religious cults, to the cult of images as works of art).

Altarpieces are not alone in reflecting this transition. There is clear evidence that portraits, which had previously served their obvious functions, became valued as exemplars of an artist's style or of artistic excellence in general. The commissioning of a portrait of Giovanna of Aragon from Raphael as a gift from cardinal Bibbiena to Francis I is an early instance of the portrait as a work of art, since there is no evidence that Francis had any interest in Giovanna for personal or political reasons. She was an exemplar of Italian beauty as disclosed by the hand of a divine master. It is more surprising to find altarpieces – religious images made for specific locations – treated in this way. However, Francis also received gifts of altarpiece-type paintings from Raphael which were probably not executed for specific altars. The preservation of Leonardo's unfinished *Adoration of the Magi* by the Benci family – Leonardo had portrayed Ginevra de' Benci – may be a very precocious example not only of the appreciation of an unfinished painting but also of an altarpiece being treasured outside its intended context.

Artists in the period showed an increasing self-awareness that a major altarpiece could serve a broader role in establishing their credentials as producers of great 'works'. The famous letter of 1438 from Domenico Veneziano to Piero de' Medici provides vivid testimony of the artist's perception of the potential gains for both himself and the patron. It seems that Domenico was attempting to solicit the commission for the high altar of San Marco in Florence, a painting which was actually undertaken by Fra Angelico (plate 1):

> Just now I have heard that Cosimo [Piero's father] has decided to have made, in other words painted, an altarpiece *[tavola d'altare]* and wants a magnificent work, which pleases me very much . . . For if you knew the longing I have to do some famous work, and specially for you, you would be favorable to me . . . I promise that you will receive honour from my works'.[3]

Concentration on the meaning and functions of altarpieces tends to obscure the element of internal 'artistic' competition which favours the introduction of new formal and colouristic features. The experiments with spatial unification, which reached a peak around 1440 with Filippo Lippi's *Barbadori Altarpiece* (Paris, Louvre) and *Annun-*

---

[3] H. Wohl, *The paintings of Domenico Veneziano* (Oxford 1980), pp. 339–40, doc. 1 (trans. C. Gilbert, *Italian art 1400–1500* (Englewood Cliffs NJ, 1980), p. 5).

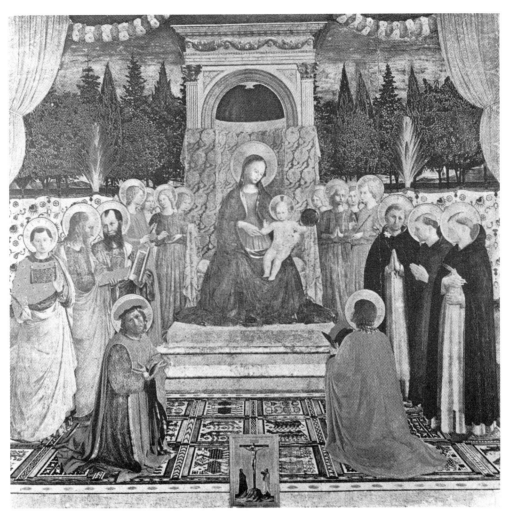

1 Fra Angelico, *Madonna, Child and Saints* (*the San Marco Altarpiece*)

ciation (Florence, San Lorenzo) and Fra Angelico's *San Marco Altarpiece*, do not seem to have been driven by theological or liturgical considerations but rather by an ambition to revivify the formal and emotional possibilities of a stock type in the light of new potentialities which were being developed across a range of genres by the pioneers of Renaissance art and architecture. At the same time as Masaccio and painters in his succession were exploiting new methods for the unification of space, Filippo Brunelleschi – who had himself been responsible for the invention of perspective – was attempting to impose an orderly system of harmonics on all aspects of church design. This system extended to the simplification of the fields of altarpieces within frames designed according to the geometrical precepts of his Renaissance style.[4]

---

[4] See C. Gardner von Teuffel, 'Masaccio and the Pisa polyptych: a new approach', *Jahrbuch der Berliner Museen*, 19 (1977), pp. 23–68; Gardner von Teuffel, 'Lorenzo Monaco, Filippo Lippi und Filippo Brunelleschi: die Erfindung der Renaissancepala', *Zeitschrift für Kunstgeschichte*, 45 (1982), pp. 1–30.

Sometimes it is difficult to know if form or meaning is the primary driving force in innovation – a question which Burckhardt had already recognised as a central problem.[5] The advent of major altarpieces after 1510 in which the Virgin is placed on high *in nubibus* and the figures are given a new freedom from their architectural confines – a development discussed by Chastel with respect to Fra Bartolomeo's *Carondelet Altarpiece* in Besançon (plate 69) – could be explained in Wölfflinian terms as the expression of a 'will' towards new formal grandeur and perceptual complexity in which the figures come to function as the architecture of the painting. However, we know that Raphael's *Madonna di Foligno* (plate 73), which challenges Fra Bartolomeo's painting as the first mature formulation of the new type, represents the revival of the ancient iconographical formula of the legendary vision of Augustus in Rome, which supposedly occurred on the Aracoeli, the site of the Church for which Raphael's altarpiece was destined.[6] Chastel alternatively suggests that Fra Bartolomeo might have been thinking of the imagery of the Immaculate Conception. We may also note that the visionary qualities of the Virgin *in nubibus* in Fra Bartolomeo's 1506 *Vision of St Bernard* (Florence, Accademia) – which was originally commissioned as a *Sacra Conversazione* and still manages to include the four required saints – corresponds in general terms to Savonarola's insistence on the depiction of the spiritual essence of the subject rather than the charming of the eye with irrelevant naturalistic and anecdotal detail. This becomes particularly apparent if Fra Bartolomeo's airborne vision is contrasted with the more anecdotal portrayal of the Virgin in Filippino Lippi's earlier version (Florence, Badia), in which Mary appears to have encountered the seated saint during a stroll in the countryside. The kinds of question raised by Chastel show that the natures of the motivating forces behind the new modes of depiction remain – almost a century after Burckhardt's death – susceptible to further clarification.

The family: religious images

> Do we not see pictures representing divine beings constantly kept under coverlets of the greatest price? And whenever they are unveiled there is first great ecclesiastical solemnity with much hymn singing, and then at the moment of unveiling the great multitude of people who have gathered there throw themselves to the ground, worshipping and praying to the deity, who is represented in the picture, for the repairing of their lost health and for their eternal salvation, exactly as if the goddess were there as a living presence.[7]

Altarpieces, by their very location and presentation, are devotional images *par excellence*, and raise questions about the legitimacy of images in Christian worship in the clearest manner. One valid context for their analysis is therefore the theological justification of images. The traditional and much-repeated justification of images,

---

[5] J. Burckhardt, *The altarpiece in Renaissance Italy*, ed. P. Humfrey (1988; Oxford, 1988), pp. 157 ff., 168–9.
[6] C. Gardner von Teuffel, 'Raffaels römische Altarbilder: Aufstellung und Bestimmung', *Zeitschrift für Kunstgeschichte*, 50 (1987), pp. 1–45.
[7] Codex Urbinas, 2v-3v; in *Leonardo on painting*, ed. Kemp, (as in note 2), no. 25.

codified at the post-Iconoclastic second Council of Nicea in 787, was threefold: to instruct in the faith, with images serving as 'the books of the unlettered'; to serve as reminders of the mystery of the incarnation and of the saints as exemplars, since visual images impress themselves on the memory more enduringly than words; and to stimulate devotion of the portrayed subjects, exploiting the special potency of visual representations.[8]

However, tensions remained, and suspicions of idolatory were never entirely dismissed. These tensions may be expressed in a mild form by the criticism of religious images in which art, naturalism and sensual beauty seemed to be cultivated more prominently than devotion. St Antoninus and Savonarola, both Florentine Dominicans, were deeply troubled by the overt display of secular skills and motifs in a Church context. Erasmus reacted in a similar manner to some of the religious art he saw in Roman churches. Decker shows in his paper how the tensions were reduced in German pre-Reformation altarpieces by various distancing devices, such as artificial framing and the use of regressive rather than modern styles. At other times, the charges of idolatory could emerge in their starkest form, as when some of the more extreme proponents of the Protestant Reformation began to advocate the total abolition of images from places of worship.

Of the three traditional justifications, the second (instruction in the faith) and third (the arousal of devotion) are obviously central to the functions of the altarpiece. Occasionally, as in the altarpiece by Romanino (frontispiece), instruction in the liturgical significance of the altar is explicitly available in the image. There is hardly an altarpiece that is not adapted to the arousal of devotion of the holy figures, particularly in relation to the cult of the Virgin and the cult of saints. In some of the complex carved and painted altarpieces in northern Europe, in which complete narrative cycles appear in a single altarpiece, the function of images as 'the books of the unlettered' is clearly satisfied, whatever more specific reference the subjects may make to the liturgy of the altar. However, altarpieces in Italy rarely serve this story-telling function in a direct or primary manner. When a narrative image does appear in the main field of an Italian Renaissance altarpiece it is generally in response to the dedication of the altar to the Annunciation or Assumption of the Virgin or some such event, and the image tends to assume a devotional rather than a story-telling air. A case in point is Filippino Lippi's *Annunciation* in the Carafa Chapel in Sta Maria sopra Minerva, Rome (plate 2). The Annunciation is set up virtually as a *Sacra conversazione* in which the Virgin is flanked by the Angel Gabriel and St Thomas Aquinas, who presents the kneeling figure of Oliviero Carafa. The arrangement reflects the joint dedication of the altar to the Virgin Annunciate and St Thomas, in what serves as a funerary chapel. The form and function of this altarpiece remind us that representations of the same narrative subject might have performed very different roles in their original contexts than we might assume nowadays simply by reading them as

---

[8] J. D. Mansi, *Sacrorum Conciliorum nova et amplissima collectio*, (Florence, 1759ff.), XIII, 377d ff. See J. Kollwitz, 'Zur Frühgeschichte der Bildverehrung', in J. Kollwitz and H. von Campenhausen, *Das Gottesbild im Abendland*, (Witten and Berlin, 1957), pp. 57–76.

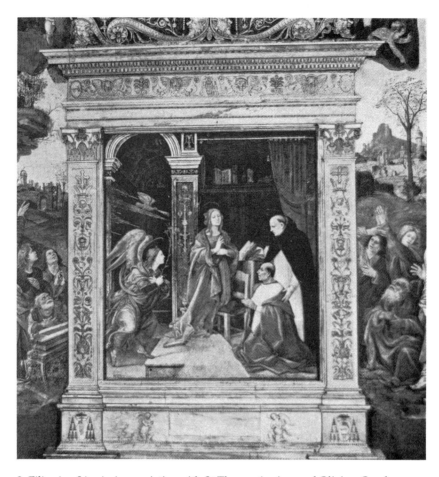

2 Filippino Lippi, *Annunciation with St Thomas Aquinas and Oliviero Carafa*

depicting the same story. The *Annunciation* painted by Fra Angelico at the top of the stairs to the monk's cells at San Marco (plate 3) is closely modelled on his altarpiece for San Domenico at Cortona, but its functional context is quite different. The inscription below the San Marco representation of the inviolate Mary enjoins the spectator not to neglect to say his 'hail Mary' – 'Virginis intacte cum veneris ante figuram pretereundo cave ne sileatur ave' – before moving on to the monastic cells or library.

The interpretation of the meaning of the images in altarpieces within the general family of religious images can cause problems. A major event in the Virgin's life such as the Annunciation had over the years been the subject of elaborate exegesis, not least by the Greek and Latin Fathers of the Church. There has been a tendency, particularly by iconographers who regard themselves as followers of Erwin Panofsky, to apply elaborate patristic exegesis to Renaissance narrative and non-narrative subjects, searching for elaborate symbolic meanings within the representation. There is no question that a standard symbolic language had developed and was accessible to artists. In the Annunciation, for example, the *hortus conclusus* – the 'enclosed garden' of the 'Song of Songs', which was taken as signifying Mary's virginity – became

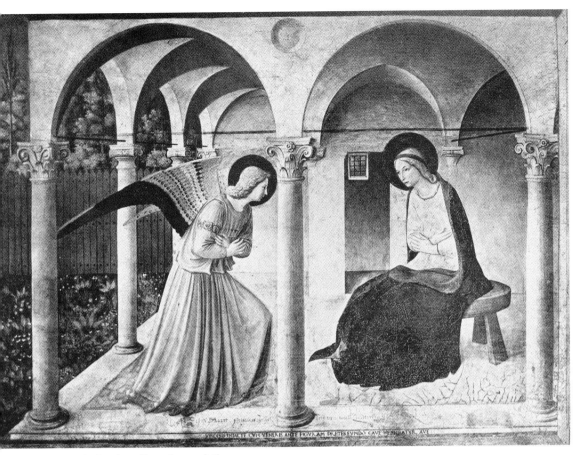

3 Fra Angelico, *Annunciation*

a standard feature, in such a way that the full panoply of textual exegesis did not have to lie directly behind the choice of this feature in each instance.

In some altarpieces iconographical schemes of astonishing intricacy had arisen, and textual explanations are obviously demanded. A notable example is provided by a series of German and south Netherlandish paintings, reliefs and tapestries which surprisingly merge the symbolism of the Annunciation with that of the unicorn hunt. The example illustrated here (plate 4) is the left wing of a damaged and dismembered altarpiece.[9] One of the legends of the unicorn was that it could only be captured by a virgin. This legend led to the identification of Christ with the unicorn – *sic et dominus noster Jesus Christus, spiritualis unicornis, descendens in uterum virginis* (in the words of the *Physiologus*) – and to the identification of Gabriel with the hunter. This particular image of the Annunciation is further packed with symbolic allusions. Some of these are signalled by banderoles. Gabriel's hounds are named as *pax, veritas,*

---

[9] H. G. Gmelin, *Spätgotische Tafelmalerei in Niedersachen und Bremen* (Munich, 1974), pp. 266–7, no. 70. For the iconography of the Virgin Mary and Maiden with a unicorn, see M. Freeman, *The Unicorn Tapestries* (New York, 1976), pp. 49ff.

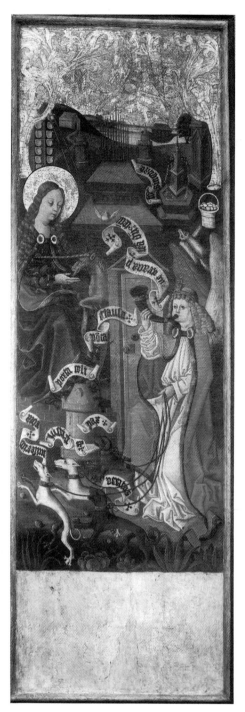

4 Anonymous South Netherlandish or German Master (*c.* 1500), *Annunciation (as the Unicorn Hunt)*

misericordia and *justicia*. The *porta celi* (the door of heaven) and *porta clausa* (the shut door, symbolic of Mary's virginity) are labelled, as is the *fons signatus* (the sealed fountain); while the Angel delivers her Biblical greeting, *'ave gratia plena dominus tecum'*. Amongst the unlabelled symbols are the enclosed garden, the rod of Aaron, the tower of David, the Ark of the Covenant and Gideon's fleece. Many of these symbols, though drawn from the Bible, are far from obvious as allusions to the Virgin, and considerable knowledge lies behind their being brought together in the first instance or instances of this type of Annunciation. And it would have required a sophisticated spectator to pick up all the allusions.

Generally, however, the symbolic language is less conspicuously signalled, and, indeed, one of the features of Renaissance naturalism was to absorb (or disguise) the possible symbolic references within the realism of the scene as a whole. It is this potential disguise of the symbolism which permits Panofskian iconographers their latitude. Any tree is likely to send an iconographer scurrying to look up *arbor* in the index to the *Patrologia Latina*. I am in agreement with those who advocate caution in this kind of analysis of meaning in religious paintings. Where the feature seems openly to invite explanation, like the repeated depiction of a walled or fenced garden in Annunciations, can we be reasonably confident that our search for textual explanation is justified. Any image in an altarpiece of one of the central mysteries, the Baptism for example, was *available* to contemporary and succeeding generations for patristic-style exegesis, but this is not the same as saying that these meanings were actively embodied in such images during their production.

The genus: the altarpiece

> If the event is of a devotional kind all the onlookers direct their eyes with various expressions of devotion towards the event, as when the host is displayed at the Sacrifice of the Mass.[10]

As van Os indicates in his paper, altarpiece is a 'functional category' within the family of religious images as whole. Yet in its association with an altar it was not functional in the same way as the Eucharistic chalice, which held the wine; and it did not have the status of the crucifix on the altar table, which had become virtually obligatory (particularly for a High Altar) even before its presence was specifically prescribed during the Counter-Reformation. An altarpiece was not prescribed as part of the altar either by canon law or by the liturgy, although the imagery in altarpieces could be closely associated with the liturgy of the mass, as has been stressed recently.[11]

There has been an increasing tendency amongst art historians to read the meaning of subjects in altarpieces in Eucharistic terms. In the relatively few examples of what

[10] Codex Urbinas, 115r-116v, in *Leonardo on painting*, ed. Kemp, no. 403.
[11] See particularly S. Sinding-Larsen, *Iconography and ritual: a study of analytical perspectives* (Oslo, 1984), with a good range of further bibliographical references.

may be called self-referential altarpieces – in which activities involving an altar and its furnishings are represented – this kind of interpretation is clearly appropriate. The Romanino altarpiece (frontispiece), which depicts a miracle that actually involved a miraculous altar and the administering of the Sacrament, is of this type, as is the work by Rogier van der Weyden discussed by Woods (plate 29). When a scene from Christ's passion is the subject of an altarpiece, a eucharistic interpretation may also seem appropriate. In the background of his altarpiece, Romanino depicted a *Lamentation*, as if to underscore the liturgical celebration in the foreground by showing Christ as a sacrificial victim. Yet recognition of the visual source for this particular image may also serve to remind us that the subject matter of altarpieces was determined at least as much by the devotional enthusiasms of the laity as by a clerical desire to expound doctrine. Romanino clearly based the central figure group of his fictive altarpiece on that of an earlier Brescian example, the *Lamentation over Christ*, painted in 1504 by Vincenzo Civerchio for the church of Sant' Alessandro (plate 5).[12] The choice of this subject for Civerchio's painting, the focus of which is Christ's sacrificial body, is explained by its commissioning for the chapel of the Scuola del Santissimo Sacramento. Although the subject is drawn from the story of Christ's Passion, as underlined by the crosses in the background, its depiction is removed from any predominantly narrative function by the anachronistic presence of persons not present at the event, including Saints Paul and Alexander. Their presence refers to the joint dedication of the altar to the 'most Holy Sacrament, Andrew the Apostle and the Conversion of St Paul' (as recorded in 1507) and to the dedication of the church as a whole to the Roman martyr, Alexander. However, the virtually naked figure cannot be identified as St Andrew, and appears to be the hermit saint, Onuphrius (rather than Adam, as Crowe and Cavalcaselle suggested). The surviving documentation fails to indicate why St Onuphrius (Onofrio) was preferred to St Andrew.

In the majority of altarpieces during the period preceding the Council of Trent such overt reference to the role and liturgical furnishing of the altar is rare. One of these rare instances occurs in Fra Angelico's *San Marco Altarpiece* (plate 1), where the small 'picture within a picture' of the Crucifixion seems to assume the role normally adopted by a free-standing crucifix on the table-top of the altar and may have rendered the presence of an actual crucifix unnecessary. Otherwise the familiar type of the Virgin with saints does not declare an obvious and open relationship to the liturgy. However, there has been an increasing tendency to regard the actual presence of Christ, particularly as a naked or semi-naked child, as carrying Eucharistic connotations. That Christ's body *could* have been read in this way is not in question, but the actual documentation of altarpieces featuring the Madonna and Child almost always indicates that Mary is the figure to whom devotion is primarily being directed, and that we might almost characterise the infant in these cases as the attribute of the Virgin. Rather than referring specifically to the liturgy of the mass, most altarpieces were tied into the liturgical functions of the church through the dedication of the

---

[12] For the documentation and critical history of the altarpiece, see R. Prestini, *La Chiesa di Sant' Alessandro in Brescia* (Brescia, 1986) pp. 111, 249–59; M. Marubbi, *Vincenzo Civerchio* (Milan, 1986), pp. 96–101.

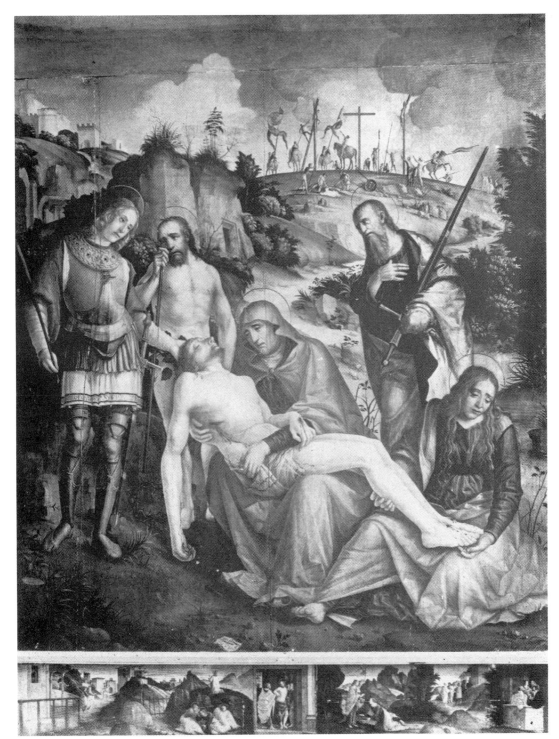

5 Vincenzo Civerchio, *Lamentation over Christ, with Saints*

altar or chapel to a particular cult, and to the celebration of that cult within the church calendar.

Far from being a compliant reflection of a rigidly established liturgy or cycle of devotions within a particular church, the commissioning of an altarpiece could itself modify the pattern of masses and celebration of feast days. If, say, a patron called Gerolamo took over the rights to a chapel dedicated to the Assumption of the Virgin in a Franciscan church, he might well decree that the altarpiece should depict the Virgin with Saints Jerome and Francis, and that the feast day of St Jerome (30 September) should be celebrated at his expense in suitably lavish manner, as well as providing finance for the conduct of masses for himself and his family.

The increasing exercise of this kind of patronage was a major factor in the rise of the altarpiece as a standard if non-canonical and liturgically inessential component in an altar's decoration. The patronage of chapels in Italian Renaissance churches, such as San Lorenzo in Florence, provides classic illustrations of the effect of local finance on the form and functions of the building.[13] The essays by Woods and Harbison give clear indications that a similar kind of patronage also exercised a major influence in northern Europe, even if the results looked rather different. Associated with the factor of patronage – and rivalling it for importance – were the new kinds of individual devotion fostered by the Mendicant orders. The new tendencies in devotion did much to encourage the kind of personalised relationship to religious images which was characteristic of an altarpiece in a family chapel or even in a more communal sense in a chapel patronised by a body of laymen. The presence of donors within the main field of the altarpiece clearly signals that a new kind of relationship exists and that a different form of decorum is being tolerated.

However, the rise of the altarpiece as a genus, for these and other reasons, does not mean that we are dealing with a self-contained category of image which presents no problems of definition. As the chapter by Hills makes clear, the formal and functional characteristics of Italian paintings associated with altarpieces, and of altarpiece-like paintings not placed directly over altars, are extremely varied. This variety precludes a watertight definition – a point underlined by Harbison's telling review of a wide range of northern European examples. The *Madonna and Saints* by Fra Angelico (plate 14), painted on a wall in the same first-floor corridor of San Marco as the *Annunciation* (plate 2), both looks like an altarpiece in formal arrangement and is executed in an *a secco* technique more akin to tempera on a panel rather than in the standard fresco technique for Florentine murals. Yet its location makes it most unlikely that it was associated with a functional altar. On the other hand, we know that altars were adorned with paintings that were not, strictly speaking, altarpieces. It was not uncommon for the processional banner of a confraternity, depicting for example the Madonna della Misercordia, to serve as the 'altarpiece' within their chapel for most of the year.

This untidiness of form and function tends to diminish as the period progresses.

---

[13] R. Gaston, 'Liturgy and patronage in San Lorenzo, Florence, 1350–1650', *Patronage, art and society in Renaissance Italy*, ed. F. Kent and P. Simons (Oxford, 1987), pp. 111–33.

The papers in this volume illustrate the general trend towards increasing prescription of the format and content of altarpieces during the sixteenth century. One of the pressures towards uniformity was already apparent in the previous century and appears to have arisen as a result of design considerations rather than religious requirements. I am referring to the desire by Brunelleschi and by architects in his succession to establish an invariable harmony of design in the building as a whole and in its components. Brunelleschi's own Florentine church of Santo Spirito even today shows signs of his attempt to establish a uniform format for the chapels and altarpieces; and the set of Sienese works in the Cathedral at Pienza, to which van Os has devoted such effective attention, provides perhaps the best of the surviving examples of co-ordinated altarpiece design from the earlier part of our period.[14] Humfrey shows how such design considerations were taken up in sixteenth-century Venice and were crucially reinforced by the Counter-Reformation desire to be more prescriptive about the content of sets of altarpieces within each church. However, his paper also illustrates the way in which the commissioners of altarpieces were characteristically reluctant to surrender their freedom of choice when faced with the attempted imposition of a uniform type.

There were also other factors which predisposed altarpiece designers to adopt a measure of standardisation. The success of any genre of devotional art relies upon certain standards of formality and familiarity, and, at the more profound level discussed by Rosand, upon the way in which the formal resonances of the composition are themselves carriers of meaning. Raphael's drawings for the *Disputa* show that he was from the first thinking of a 'hollow' composition, in which the lunette was treated much as the interior of a semi-dome, but found that a central focus was required. He accordingly introduced the altar as a way of bringing the format of his composition as a bearer of meaning into perfect harmony with the theological import of the gatherings of Christian authorities in the lower tier and the divine figures in the upper realm.

The increasingly strict control of meaning in Counter-Reformation and early Baroque Catholicism is well illustrated by both Davies and Wright. The kind of fixedly elaborate theological interpretations which we were reluctant to impose on earlier altarpieces now seem to be very much to the point. The relative free-for-alls which had characterised local liturgical practice and had given the patrons so much scope for shaping the forms and activities of their parish churches were subject to increasing control. No part of the functional or decorative furnishing of chapels and altars, or of the functions of liturgical spaces within the church as a whole, could expect to escape scrutiny. Considerable regional variations continued to persist – it is difficult to see El Greco's chapel decorations taking precisely the same form outside Toledo – but these variations were subject to detailed proscription by the Church hierarchy on both local and national bases to varying degrees. As Davies stresses, El Greco's library suggests that he was well capable on his own behalf of understanding the theological

---

[14] H. W. van Os, 'Painting in a house of glass: the altarpieces of Pienza', *Simiolus*, 17 (1987), pp. 23–38.

and liturgical implications of altarpiece design in a post-Tridentine context. The iconographical terms in which his works can be appropriately analysed seem different from those of a *quattrocento* altarpiece in San Lorenzo in Florence.

The species: types of altarpiece

> Leonardo di Ser Piero da Vinci has undertaken as of March 1480 to paint a panel for main altarpiece, which he is obliged to have completed in 24 or at the most 30 months.[15]

How we classify the species or types of altarpiece depends upon which criteria we deem to be important, and different criteria will produce different characteristics for the definition of species within a single genus. This, obviously, is where the biological system of classification becomes least directly applicable to our present endeavour. Leonardo's unfinished altarpiece of the *Adoration of the Magi* for San Donato could, for example, be considered within the category of paintings for high altars, or of altarpieces commissioned by private (posthumous) patrons, or of altarpieces with narrative subjects, or according to various regional and chronological categories. The list of categories could proliferate almost endlessly – and sometimes seems to do so, as researchers desperately cast around for a new angle on old material. It might be interesting to analyse altarpieces by cost, or by length of time for execution. Other possible categories, such as altarpieces in which Christ has curly hair, would not (or at least I hope not) seem to be worth investigating.

Hills argues that many of our categories for the analysis of altarpieces are our own mental constructs and do not correspond to categories that were used in the period itself. I do not think this should concern us too much, providing that we are clear what we are doing. Any historical investigation hinges upon the interaction between the criteria available within the period in question and the insights produced by fresh re-combinations and analyses of the material by creative historians. However, if our modern categories do not interact directly with the criteria of the period – as is the case with too many semiotic, structuralist and post-structuralist approaches – our analyses will be historically arbitrary and unavailable for refutation.

The authors in this collection of essays illustrate how different types of criteria for the 'species' of altarpiece can be brought to bear productively upon our understanding of their appearance in a historical context. Woods, for example, selects the species of 'Netherlandish carved altarpieces around 1500', and sharpens our awareness of formal characteristics in such features as framework shape as well as dealing with the meaning of the images. Evans, Ferino and Davies, by contrast, operate through a conventional classification of altarpieces by artist, but by bringing the considerations related to the individual artist into fruitful conjunction with other historical criteria they indicate to varying degrees what can happen when the study of an

---

[15] The contract for the high altar of San Donato a Scopeto, 1481, in L. Beltrami, *Documenti e memorie riguardanti la vita e le opere di Leonardo da Vinci* (Milan, 1919), pp. 7–8; trans. Kemp and Walker, in *Leonardo on painting*, ed. Kemp (as in note 2), p. 268.

artist's style moves beyond the obsession with individualism which has tended to dominate humanist art history. Indeed, Ferino lays bare one of the steps which has lead to the domination of art history by the cult of 'great' artists.

One of the purposes of a conference and one of the justifications for bringing the papers together in published form is to show how the mental ordering of related material by different scholars from different traditions can suggest new possibilities. It is not my intention in this, the briefest of the sections in my introduction, to enumerate the variety of species used explicitly or implicitly by our authors – and even less to expand upon their forms of classification – but rather to suggest that the reader remains creatively alert both to what is being accomplished and to the potentialities of categories which have not been exploited here.

The individual

> I made a picture representing a holy subject, which was brought by someone who loved it and wished to remove the attributes of its divinity in order that he might kiss it without guilt.[16]

To some extent it is true to say that the features that particularise an altarpiece, letting us distinguish it from closely related examples, are those which emerge most readily from the specific documentation of each example. Yet, within the range of causes specific to the production of an individual altarpiece, the operative events may be so eccentric and unsusceptible to historical analysis that they are better handled by the novelist than the historian. Leonardo's perverse patron probably falls into this category. A bewilderingly wide variety of historical imponderables, many of which lie outside the scope of any conceivable documentation, may be crucial for the involvement of any of the individuals involved – the patron, the artist, the prior of the monastery, or whoever might have made a direct input into the work.

The main body of available evidence which permits us to understand what is specific to a particular altarpiece consists of the contracts between patrons and artists, though documents relating to such questions as the dedication of altars may also be of considerable value. Contracts, as legal documents which were designed to serve a specific function, inevitably reveal certain aspects of the circumstances behind an altarpiece better than others. We will expect to find the names of the parties agreeing to the contract, including the artist or artists, and we might reasonably anticipate finding adequate details of price, stipulated materials, completion date and (less regularly) arbitration procedures. By contrast, information about the required subject-matter tends to be disappointingly minimal. Leonardo's contract with the monks of San Donato does not specify a subject at all, and leaves us with something of a puzzle, since the *Adoration of the Magi* is an unexpected choice for the high altar in a church dedicated to St Donatus. More often, contracts contain a bare listing of the subjects, typically naming the Virgin and specific saints but including no detailed iconographi-

---

[16] Codex Urbinas, 13v-14r; Ibid., no. 4.

cal instructions. Sometimes reference is made to a drawing submitted in advance by the artist (and occasionally appended to the contract), which obviously permitted approval of the iconographical details. However, where such drawings survive, the finished works seem not to adhere all that closely to the approved design. Alternatively, an existing altarpiece by the same or another artist may be prescribed as a model. Some contracts specify that the details of the portrayal are to be agreed with someone on the ground, such as the prior, but there is no indication that standard mechanisms existed for detailed control over the depiction of the subjects. It is clear that major masters were expected to know how to portray the saints and their stories 'in the customary manner', and that they exercised a good deal of discretion, particularly in the earlier part of our period. Again, I think it is true to say that the doctrinal rigidities of the Reformation and the Catholic response meant that detailed control was increased in the sixteenth century, but this control still seems to have fallen far short of placing a theologian at the artist's elbow on a day-by-day basis.

Rarely a document survives that gives an insight into the way in which a particular decision was taken – typically, as we may suspect, on the basis of the erratic to and fro of discussions and opportunistic choices rather than elaborate advance planning. A document of 1455 related to an altarpiece of the *Trinity with Saints* (plate 6), begun by Pesellino and finished after his death in Filippo Lippi's workshop, gives an entertaining account as to how one saint arrived in this picture.[17] The chamberlain of the Compagnia della Trinità in Pistoia wrote an unusually conversational minute of a meeting on 10 September, called to decide upon the commissioning of an altarpiece. The overall motivation for the commission was, characteristically for such organisations, that the Confraternity felt its honour to be diminished by the lack of an altarpiece, and the members decided by a narrow majority that the goodly sum of 150 to 200 florins should be spent. There then ensued 'an argument in the Compagnia as to the chief figures in the altarpiece':

> It was determined by agreement of all that in the middle should be the Trinity, since it is our insignia, and there should be two flanking saints. For one it was determined that it should be St James the Greater, because he is protector of the region, and the other should be St Zeno, who is likewise protector of all the priesthood in Pistoia, and the third should be St Jerome, and because the fourth was lacking, I, priest Piero di Ser Landi, humbly begged the Compagnia, seeing that I was devoted to the glorious saint messer Saint Mamas the martyr, that if they were willing that such a figure should be painted there, I would wish to make a great celebration each year for the said Compagnia and to leave in perpetuity for the said celebration six minas of grain.

Saint Mamas, a shepherd martyr of the seventh century whose feast day fell on 17 August, is an obscure figure whose presence in the altarpiece we would be hard-pressed to explain but for the unusual survival of Piero's minute. The opportunistic

---

[17] For the documentation of this altarpiece, see P. Bacci, 'La 'Trinità' di Pesellino della National Gallery di Londra', *Rivista d'Arte* (1904), pp.160–77. At the meeting Piero showed the other members a drawing for the proposed altarpiece which he had obtained from a painter in Florence. See also Gilbert *Italian art* (as in note 3), pp. 114–16.

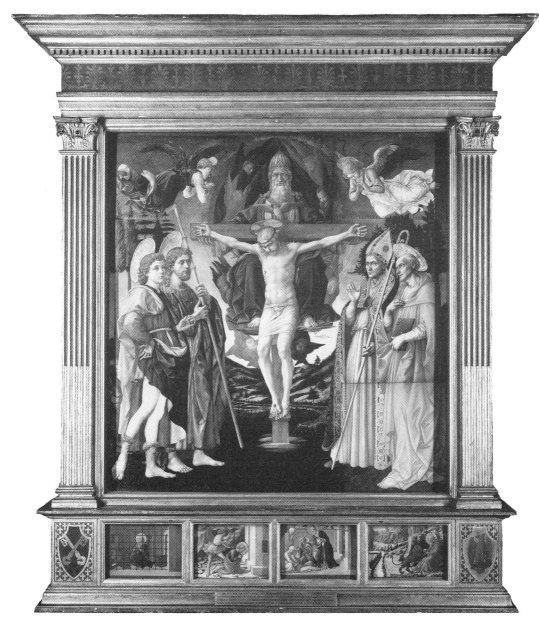

6 Pesellino (completed by Filippo Lippi), *Trinity with Saints*

move by the enterprising chamberlain is hardly likely to have been precisely mirrored in the conduct of many other commissions, but I suspect that the kind of individualistic factors that came into play in this Pistoian incident probably had a more powerful role in shaping the content of earlier Renaissance altarpieces than any elaborate devising of iconographical programmes on a theological or liturgical base.

The role of the individual artist in giving each altarpiece its particular character is rather more obvious, certainly with respect to those features classified under the broad heading of 'style'. There is good evidence that both patrons and artists became increasingly aware during the course of the period of the varied but 'equal excellences' of different masters' manners – and of the variation in each master's own style as his art 'developed'.[18] While this self-consciousness can first be clearly documented in Italy, it is certainly apparent at a relatively early date in the writings of Dürer and by implication in the works of Pacher. It is also difficult to believe that such an intellectual and aware painter as Jan van Eyck was unconscious of what distinguished his own particular manner. This heightened self-awareness of artistic individuality could not be better displayed at the very end of our period than by El Greco, who showed that even extreme idiosyncracies of individual style could be compatible with liturgical and theological meanings of a highly developed kind.

In conclusion I should like to suggest that it is part of the inexhaustible richness of our attempts to understand the past that the relatively straightforward re-grouping of material under different taxonomic headings can help stimulate new insights into the complex nexus of causes and circumstances that lie behind the production of works of art within a society. However, in undertaking our re-classifications we must be continually alert to the level and nature of the category with which we are working, to the assumptions behind the categories and to the way in which different kinds of written and visual evidence assume relevance in relation to our preferred taxonomy. The essays collected here show that the Renaissance altarpiece is such a rich and varied genus in its own right that it fully justifies the attention that it is now receiving from researchers.

[18] M. Kemp, ''Equal Excellences': Lomazzo and the explanation of individual style in the visual arts', *Renaissance Studies*, 1 (1987), pp. 1–26.

1 *Some thoughts on writing a history of Sienese altarpieces*

H. W. van Os

In 1893–94 Jacob Burckhardt initiated the study of altarpieces with a substantial essay later published as one of his *Beiträge zur Kunstgeschichte von Italien*.[1] He intended it as a contribution to a 'Kunstgeschichte nach Aufgaben', a new type of art history that he regarded at the end of his life as his legacy to the future. 'My legacy is to deal with art history according to *Aufgaben*'. Now *Aufgabe* is a German word for which there does not exist a precise English equivalent, and I shall use the words 'tasks' and 'challenges' in order to come as close as possible to what *Aufgabe* means in a given context. At times, however, I will have to retain the original German expression. Aby Warburg was one of the very few scholars of the next generation who confessed himself the heir of this legacy of Burckhardt. He wrote: 'We should not shrink from pursuing Jacob Burckhardt's path, however much we may feel daunted by his overpowering personality'. The result was Warburg's study of Florentine portraiture, which he published as a kind of appendix to Burckhardt's *Beiträge*.[2]

Shortly before his death H. W. Janson returned to Burckhardt's 'Kunstgeschichte nach Aufgaben' in his Gerson lecture of 1981, entitled *Form follows function – or does it?*[3] Janson argued that observations on iconography and patronage can be far better integrated into this type of art history than into the traditional history of style. But he discussed only isolated examples, including some sculptures by Donatello, the work of the eighteenth-century French sculptor Louis-François Roubiliac, and some Spanish still-lifes of the seventeenth century. He presented some fascinating case-studies. His remarks provide an accurate reflection of the current state of research on altarpieces. More and more careful reconstructions are being published. Much creativity is now invested in recreating the authentic architectural settings of altarpieces, and even more in tracing their donors. Much learned information has been amassed from the study of liturgy, theology and devotional practices. But what we still lack is what many of our paintings also lack: a proper frame.

How much sense does it makes to treat objects like altarpieces together in a historical process? Burckhardt does not provide unequivocal answers to this basic question. He gives a diachronic description of altarpieces from the thirteenth century down

---

[1] J. Burckhardt, 'Das Altarbild', in *Beiträge zur Kunstgeschichte von Italien* (Basle, 1898). Trans. as *The altarpiece in Renaissance Italy*, ed. P. Humfrey (Oxford, 1988). The quotations from Burckhardt that follow are taken from the English translation.

[2] N. Huse, ''Anmerkungen zur Burckhardts 'Kunstgeschichte nach Aufgaben''', in *Festschrift Wolfgang Braunfels*, ed. F. Piel and J. Träger (Tübingen, 1977), pp. 157–66.

[3] H. W, Janson, *Form follows function – or does it? Modernist design theory and the history of art* (Maarsen, 1982).

to the Baroque. In the course of this description the criteria for the development undergo a change. First he sketches the origins of the altarpiece as an adequate decor for the celebration of the Eucharist. Within this context 'adequate' is formulated in terms of size and iconography. Once polyptychs have been installed on altars, another *Aufgabe* becomes the norm of the development: what he calls 'das einheitliche Bild', a unified picture field and a unified pictorial space that enable the artist to develop a new kind of illusionism. When he comes to the sixteenth century Burckhardt proclaims 'the complete victory of the unified picture'.[4]

Once the challenge of the unified image has been met a new criterion for the development of the altarpiece is needed. In response to the new challenge Burckhardt postulates iconography as an artistic *Aufgabe*. He opens the last part of his essay with the sentence: 'If one is seeking to identify an important and characteristic task of a particular nation or period, then it would be difficult to find a more eloquent example than that of the representation of the Madonna and saints in fifteenth-century Italy.'[5] After the representation of the Madonna with saints he deals with the most important narrative and devotional themes of altarpieces. In Burckhardt's essay different criteria tend to be adopted according to different phases. The first phase, which could be called the genesis of the altarpiece, is the easiest to describe because the goal of the artist seems clear: the creation of an appropriate functional object called altarpiece. Once this *Aufgabe* is solved the next phases are more difficult to describe. Why? Because the criteria for the development are less clear. For one thing, there happen to be different ways of approaching the same *Aufgabe*. Let us compare for a moment the history of the altarpiece with that of another functional object such as the train. When dealing with the period in which a satisfactory design for a train had yet to be realised, the historian of trains is in the relatively comfortable position of having to describe all kinds of interconnected carriages on rails pulled by engines. His problems begin as soon as these odd combinations develop into functional trains, mainly because of the wide range of possible solutions. It would be too easy for the historian of trains to choose one model as the norm for evaluating all the others. If, for example, the German Intercity were to be taken as the normative model, it would become very much easier to discuss all the other trains in the world. This is exactly what Hellmut Hager did with regard to altarpieces when he chose Duccio's *Maestà* as the climax of the generative phase of the history of the altarpiece. If Duccio's monumental synthesis of Madonna, saints and angels is taken as the aesthetic norm, the fact that people did not adhere to that norm, but opted for polyptychs with separate figures in separate niches, can only be explained in terms of degeneration.[6]

For Burckhardt the aesthetic criterion of his second phase was 'das einheitliche Bild'. With the introduction of the 'tavola quadrata' in Florence the *Aufgabe* was fulfilled. We can see how normative this criterion had become when we see Trecento polyptychs forced with a kind of fanatical zeal into square frames with 'cholonne

---

[4] Burckhardt, *The altarpiece*, p. 60.
[5] Ibid., p. 110.
[6] Hager, *Die Anfänge des italienischen Altarbildes: Untersuchungen der Entstehungsgeschichte des toskanischen Hochaltarre-tabels* (Munich, 1962), p. 154.

a chanali da lato e architrave, fregio, chornicione e foglie di sopra' ('fluted columns at the sides, and architrave, frieze, cornice and foliage above'), to quote a passage in the *Ricordanze* of Neri di Bicci.[7] At the same time, there are certain disadvantages in taking 'das einheitliche Bild' as the only aesthetic norm for the development of the Renaissance altarpiece. In the first place, if we regard such polyptychs as no more than the precursors of the unified field, and of the unification of the composition within a single pictorial space, we risk creating a distorted view of the polyptych as a development in its own right. Secondly, other interesting innovations are reduced to the status of provincial developments. Burckhardt's norm of unification obscures other Renaissance inventions. As an example I would mention Vecchietta's altarpiece of the *Assumption* in the Cathedral in Pienza (plate 7). In the same church the 'tavola quadrata' was introduced into Sienese painting. Vecchietta's picture, which was the main altarpiece of the church, was not a 'tavola quadrata'; yet it remains a fascinating Renaissance altarpiece. Its tripartite structure was probably inspired by Mantegna (see plate 68), whose altarpieces Vecchietta must have seen on his trip to northern Italy, when he painted in Castiglione Olona. Burckhardt evidently got into trouble when he came to deal with these tripartite altarpieces, because they did not fit into his too narrow model for innovation. Hence he could only assign Mantegna's San Zeno altarpiece to a category apart.[8]

In the third and last part of his essay Burckhardt introduced yet another norm. For the late fifteenth and early sixteenth centuries he is primarily concerned with artistic invention in the presentation of specific scenes and images. This criterion presents us with another problem. Artistic invention was not, of course, restricted to altarpieces in any given period. Although Burckhardt obviously realised this, he still assigned to the producers of altarpieces the status of innovators of painting in general: 'The important point for us is that such influences were channelled above all through the church altarpiece, which became the most progressive genre in Italian painting.'[9] Hence he could not avoid the evaporation of the specific *Aufgaben* of altarpieces in a general description of stylistic change.

Following Burckhardt's thinking one becomes aware of the double status of the *Aufgabe*. It is the art historian who deduces the challenge from history. But the *Aufgabe* should be continually tested in terms of its historic validity. Burckhardt's too narrow definition of the *Aufgabe* in the second phase results in a somewhat distorted view of the historical process I would like to describe. If, on the other hand, the 'challenge' is formulated in much more general terms, as in his third part, we risk losing sight of the specific character of the functional object itself. The main problem of Burckhardt's approach is that by formulating different 'challenges' in the course of one historical sketch, he makes us look at the same objects from different angles. In fact, he wrote three essays on the history of altarpieces instead of one. The pursuit

---

[7] Neri di Bicci, *Le Ricordanze*, ed. B. Santi (Pisa, 1976), p. 33.
[8] Burckhardt, *The altarpiece*, p. 68
[9] Ibid., p. 81

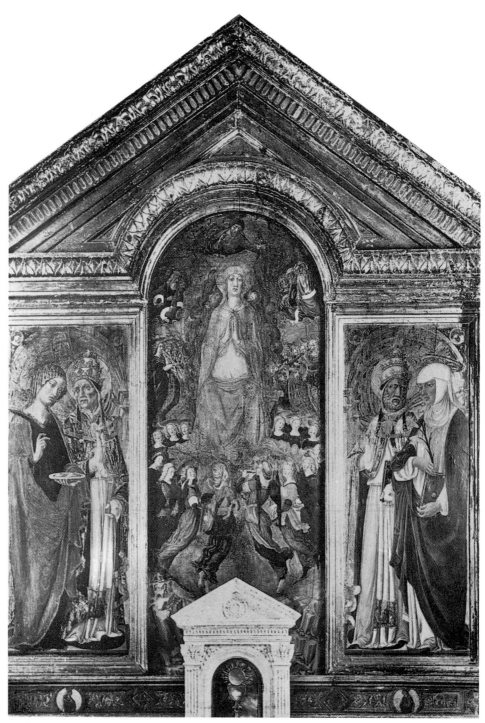

7 Vecchietta, *Assumption of the Virgin*

of 'Kunstgeschichte nach Aufgaben' is much more difficult than Janson implied when he presented some fascinating but isolated case studies.

Like Janson I would formulate *Aufgaben* in terms of function. Although 'function', no less than *Aufgabe*, is an ambivalent term, it is clear that in singling out a group of paintings that once served as altarpieces we must take account of the purpose they fulfilled in their original settings. 'Altarpiece' is a functional category, whereas 'fresco', for example, refers simply to the physical character of the painting. There are a number of frescoes that were meant to be altarpieces (plate 8). The next question would be 'purpose for whom?' I can see three categories of 'users' of an altarpiece. First, there is the clergyman who wanted a visual liturgical prop that was adequate in terms of form and content. He would have enjoyed an altarpiece as an embellishment of an altar of his church, and as an instrument for theological propaganda. Secondly, there are the faithful, who presumably enjoyed the splendour of their churches even more when it was enhanced by the golden shine of altarpieces. They would also have received instruction from the pious representations, which were normally concerned with themes related to the Eucharist, and with saints who were the main heroes of the church or the religious representatives of their specific religious community. In the third place, some of the faithful who had money and who saw some purpose in the presence of an altarpiece in a church, acted as donors of altarpieces. In the case of Siena, the most powerful donor was the Commune itself, which in the first half of the Trecento paid for many altarpieces in the Duomo and in other churches. During the second half of the century corporations became important as donors. These corporations also reflected the interest of powerful families. Private individuals also commissioned altarpieces as a way to serve the church and to communicate their name and pious intentions to future generations. Very often they commissioned altarpieces at the end of their lives. They were mostly buried in the chapel of their altarpiece, and thus in some way or other a funerary function was also expressed in the iconography of the altarpiece.

In a history of altarpieces, paintings are studied as means to ends. These ends are set by the liturgy and the architectural setting, by the demands of patrons and advisers, and by the creativeness and aspirations of artists. When we analyse how all these ends were met, we are dealing with the function of an altarpiece. If we were to separate the ends, we would be unable to delineate the changing emphasis on these different ends. We would no longer be able to grasp the emancipation of artistic invention within the framework of a history of art according to function. The quality of the means-to-ends analysis depends very much on how one manages to balance the ends. Fixation on just one of them might eventually lead to the most bizarre results. In addition to an awareness of the limitations of any functional approach, intellectual discipline and art-historical common-sense are needed here.

Two elements of the functional analysis of altarpieces should be singled out. The first is that of the liturgy. Again and again liturgical function has been stressed in recent research of altarpieces, including my own. But very often the meaning of 'liturgical function' within art history is not quite clear. It is certainly not always

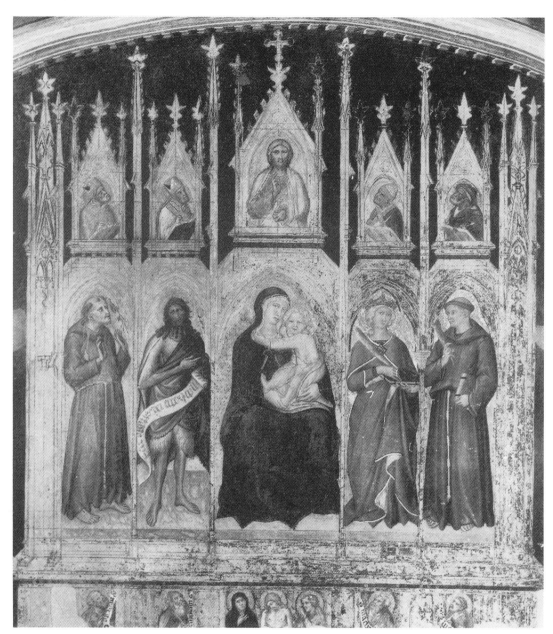

8 Lippo Vanni, *Virgin and Child with Saints*

a motor of change in the history of the development of altarpieces. Altarpieces change in periods when the liturgy remains the same. There are many examples of an altarpiece on a particular altar being replaced by another that retained the identical liturgical function. The opposite is also true: there are changes in the liturgy that do not lead to a new altarpiece. Liturgy is the basic condition for the very existence of altarpieces. No altarpiece without an altar. With regard to 'Kunstgeschichte nach Aufgaben', the statement that an altarpiece is a liturgical object is self-evident. This is not to say that the point is not worth stressing, however, since most modern viewers tend to look at an altarpiece exclusively as a work of art.

As to the relationship between iconography and liturgical texts, Staale Sinding-Larsen has very rightly remarked that one should be extremely careful not to fall into the trap either of over-interpretation or of under-interpretation.[10] In the present state of research I am much more afraid of the first trap than of the second, especially when dealing with altarpieces in relation to their liturgical function. To take an example: altarpieces contain Eucharistic symbolism as a matter of course. There is nothing special about this, because they were made for this purpose. Thus the conspicuous representation of a Man of Sorrows in an altarpiece does not necessarily indicate that the people who commissioned the painting had a special interest in the cult of the Corpus Domini. It merely constitutes an interesting variation of the existing symbolic repertoire. Every Madonna on an altar is related to the Eucharist because of the general liturgical symbolism of incarnation; every suffering Christ refers to the Eucharist because of the ritual of sacrifice. Liturgical function may be seen in most cases as a matter of routine. Of course these matters deserve investigation, but one should not go too far. I feel that over-interpretation is a shortcoming of certain recent studies on altarpieces, especially when traditional elements of their iconography are interpreted as references to a specific liturgical function.

Sinding-Larsen has introduced into our studies the very useful word 'message-efficiency' to create room for artistic invention in terms of iconography and ritual: 'Thus an artist might exploit functional requirements and work out a liturgical iconography in artistic terms without impairing its liturgical message.'[11] I could not agree more. But Burckhardt went further. He raised the possibility that the artistic terms might be frustrated by the requirements of the people who cared for the liturgical message: 'Since in certain periods the church altar provided the focus for some of the highest achievements in the visual arts, it would also be important to investigate how far liturgical practices in different countries and centuries might have stimulated or inhibited developments.'[12] Burckhardt's observation might also open our eyes to the fact that in the Renaissance 'liturgical practices' in some cases made the altarpiece obsolete. Redecoration of the high altar could imply an alternative for an altarpiece. New liturgical objects, such as the bronze ciborium by Vecchietta for the high altar of the church of Ospedale della Scala in Siena, were invented (plate 9). It was considered such an adequate solution that some thirty years later it was transferred to the Duomo to replace Duccio's *Maestà* on the high altar. No decoration at all was foreseen for the high altar of the Duomo of Pienza (plate 10). The huge window inspired by northern Gothic architecture in effect replaced the altarpiece. The question of whether an altarpiece constitutes the most adequate decoration for an altar forms an integral part of the history of the Sienese altarpiece in the second half of the Quattrocento.

[10] S. Sinding-Larsen, *Iconography and ritual: a study of analytical perspectives* (Oslo, 1984), pp. 33–53.
[11] Ibid., pp. 53–9
[12] Burckhardt, *The altarpiece*, p. 15

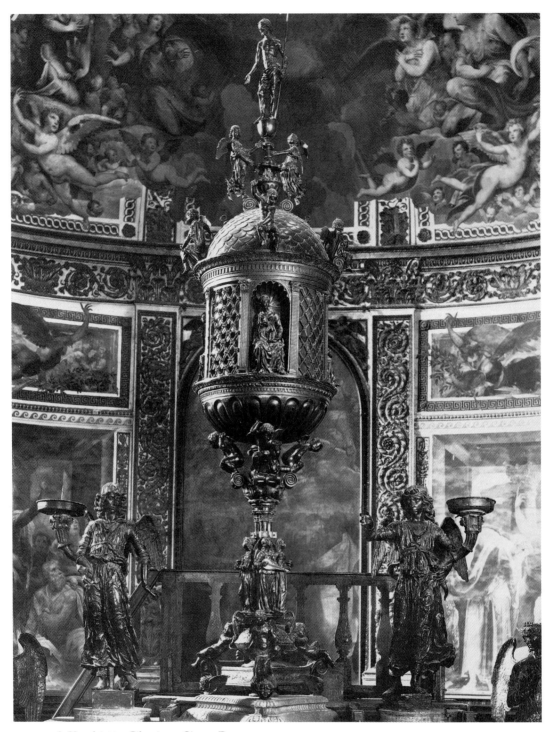

9 Vecchietta, Ciborium, Siena, Duomo

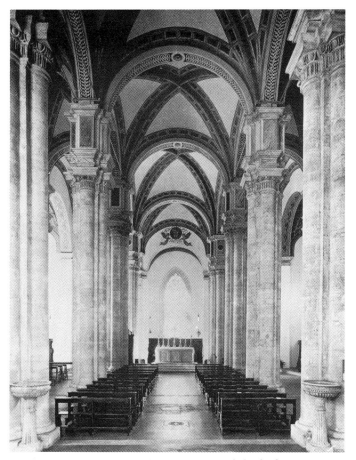

10 Pienza, Duomo, view of interior, towards high altar

The second element of a functional approach that deserves special attention is patronage. Even more than liturgy the study of patronage is 'à la mode'. One risks arousing the suspicion of being old-fashioned if one betrays even the slightest doubts about its significance for the visual aspects of works of art. Yet Burckhardt would not have accepted patronage as a dynamic factor in his 'Kunstgeschichte nach Aufgaben'. When discussing the complete victory of the unified image he writes: 'Although the more advanced painters would certainly have found the unified field congenial, their customers – whether clergy or laity, confraternities or individual donors – would very likely have long continued to prefer the traditional polyptych format.'[13] He focuses on the artist as the source of innovation. The patron is the one who needs art. Precisely for that reason the bourgeois could only be a restricting factor in the permanent process of artistic innovation. Perhaps Burckhardt would have chased out of the archives all those promising young scholars looking for documentation about the second grandson of the aunt of the donor of the altarpiece for a church in some Italian village. He might have sent them back to art and the artists.

[13] Ibid., p. 56

The great Sienese Renaissance Pope Pius II certainly does not fit into Burckhardt's conception of the role of patronage. But Pius was an exception in the Sienese tradition. He brought a Renaissance architect from Florence to the province of Siena to build his Pienza.

With Rossellino the Florentine modernisation of the altarpiece was introduced on Sienese soil. Here it is interesting to see the effect of this powerful patron on the further careers of the painters of Pienza. It shows how stable the milieu of commissioners of Sienese painters – the networks in which they functioned – must have been.

Even an exceptional patron like Pius II was not able to change the production of a Sienese workshop permanently. In Renaissance Siena painters were often employed within definable networks, as Gaudenz Freuler has recently shown in his thorough studies on Bartolo di Fredi in Montalcino.[14] A painter like Bartolo invented very original polyptychs. But his inventions were specific answers to specific questions. His unusual altarpieces remained isolated proofs of his creativity. Neither he nor his patrons brought about a general fashion in altarpieces. Even Pius did not provide the Sienese with an exclusive new norm for their production, despite the introduction of the 'tavola quadrata'. During the Renaissance pluriformity was paramount in Siena. Tradition persisted in the same region where fascinating innovations also took place. It was only at the end of the Quattrocento that the Gothic polyptych and its many variants disappeared completely. The Sienese example might serve to teach us that the patron's role can be very variable. It has to be defined from one case to another. A patron certainly cannot be considered a maker of change *per se*. Often he did no more than provide the money. Even the activities of patrons of quite exceptional power and wealth could have the effect simply of increasing the quantity of artistic production without improving its quality.

The rather complex concept of function may also cause one to lose a sense of priority in the basic organisation of the paintings concerned. What is the point of departure: the liturgy, the patron, the iconography, or the painter? Are works of art to become just pretexts for the writing of social history or the history of liturgical thought? In taking altarpieces apart I assumed that if I went for function I might gain fresh insights into the form and content of Sienese paintings; and I was certainly not disappointed. Over and over again I had to ask myself the question of how to thread the objects together. The thread leads me back to Burckhardt once again.

In the first sentence of his essay on the altarpiece he announced an *Aufgabe* not for painters but for art historians. Strangely enough he did not himself meet the challenge in the essay. This *Aufgabe* I would consider the most important challenge for us. 'It would be an important and instructive task to investigate the various forms that the decoration of the Christian altar has assumed in every country throughout its history.' We still do not possess an adequate typological system for the functional

---

[14] G. Freuler, 'L'altare Cacciati di Bartolo di Fredi nella chiesa di San Francesco a Montalcino', *Arte Cristiana*, 73 (1985), pp. 149–67; Freuler, 'Bartolo di Fredis Altar für die Annunziata-Kapelle in S. Francesco a Montalcino', *Pantheon*, 43 (1985), pp. 21–39.

object we are studying. We have studied local norms and forms, but we still do not have even the most basic phenomenology of the objects of our research at our disposal. In my experience the most adequate framework for our study is to be found in a typology according to shapes of altarpieces. This might sound disappointing, and I would be the first to acknowledge that this framework does not show many ornaments of intellectual sophistication. However, I feel that the longing for intellectual complication has been one of the main temptations of art historians since Panofsky. Functional objects like altarpieces are not ready-mades for intellectuals, and we need the modesty and the intellectual clarity of someone like Jacob Burckhardt to realise this.

In the bibliography of his stimulating study Sinding-Larsen added after the title of Hager's *Die Anfänge des italienischen Altarbildes*: 'Morphological; liturgical dimension absent.'[15] This remark does not do justice to Hager's innovative study. In his book the liturgical dimension is subordinate only to morphology. I am convinced that the only way one can write an art history of altarpieces is by accepting morphology as its framework. But such a morphology should be based on the kind of typology asked for by Burckhardt, if only to prevent the kind of oversimplification that led Hager to proclaim the *Maestà* as the ideal solution for an altarpiece. Our framework should also take account of what I have come to regard as one of the essential issues of the history of altarpieces: the relation between the altarpiece and architecture. For the last time I would like to quote Burckhardt, who already knew what we had to discover anew so many decades later:

> An altar of an early period ... could only survive the rebuilding of its church if it happened to be the focus of an ancient public cult ... Normally, however, each century regarded its own religious outlook as the only true one, and whenever a church was built or rebuilt, the decoration of its altars duly conformed with prevailing decorative tastes. In cases where the church fabric itself survived unaltered, new altar decoration might replace the older ones gradually, in a piecemeal fashion; or else as a result of a single decision or command, a whole group of old altarpieces might be replaced for the sake of symmetry by a matching set of new ones.[16]

In my work on Sienese altarpieces I have learnt that the history of building and rebuilding of churches and chapels has to be studied carefully in order to understand the dynamics of the history of the altarpieces that belonged to them. Christa Gardner von Teuffel has shown us the importance of the architect for the invention of the 'tavola quadrata'. Her studies, in which altarpiece and architecture form an inseparable whole, have provided us with the essential contours of the morphology I am talking about.[17] But there remains one big problem. One nearly always needs to

---

[15] Sinding-Larsen, *Iconography*, p. 201.

[16] Burckhardt, *The altarpiece*, p. 15

[17] C. Gardner von Teuffel, 'Iconographie und Archäologie: das Pfingsttriptychon in der Florentiner Akademie an seinen ursprünglichen Aufstellungsort', *Zeitschrift für Kunstgeschichte*, 41 (1978), pp. 16–40; Gardner von Teuffel, 'The buttressed altarpiece: a forgotten aspect of Tuscan fourteenth-century altarpiece design', *Jahrbuch der Berliner Museen*, 21 (1979), pp. 21–65; Gardner von Teuffel, 'Lorenzo Monaco, Filippo Lippi and Filippo Brunelleschi: die Erfindung der Renaissancepala', *Zeitschrift für Kunstgeschichte*, 45 (1982), pp. 1–30; Gardner von Teuffel, 'From polyptych to pala: some structural considerations', in *La pittura nel XIV e XV secolo: il contributo dell'analisi tecnica alla storia dell'arte*, ed. H. W. van Os and J. R. J. van Asperen de Boer (Bologna, 1983), pp. 323–30.

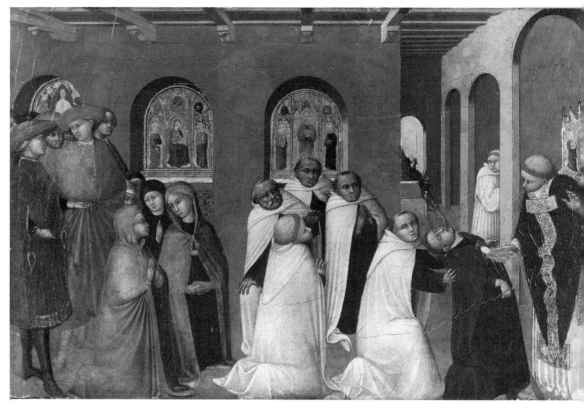

11 Sassetta, *A Miracle of the Sacrament*

reconstruct the original spatial settings, and all too often this is an impossible task. Even the side altars of Pienza with their 'tavola quadrata', although at first sight seeming to conform to their original arrangement, were in fact put in the wrong places, with their altarpieces mistakenly reconstructed, by the restoration architect.

Looking at Sassetta's predella painting of a miracle of the Sacrament in the Bowes Museum (plate 11), I realise how much is still lacking in our understanding of paintings within their architectural settings. Even the best reconstruction cannot evoke the original atmosphere in which these paintings functioned. Here we can see a polyptych standing on the high altar as a precious, rich, Gothic element that, with its shining presence, creates the sacral atmosphere within the choir chapel. We can also see lunette altarpieces, in the form of triptychs adapted to round-topped niches, in the side chapels. The high altarpiece is an autonomous object with its architectural forms creating its own space, while the side altarpieces have been transformed into wall decoration. A systematic inventory of the visual records such as this would be of great help in a modern morphology of altarpieces. Another inventory, comprising the rather small corpus of drawings artists made of altarpieces within their architectural settings, would also be very helpful. Such drawings often document the artistic challenge of painting within architecture – painting as part of the architecture, architecture as part of the painting – in most fascinating ways.

In his diary for 20 May 1942 Bernard Berenson wrote with characteristic bravura: 'Jacob Burckhardt was a real pioneer. After him it is easier for any instructed person to apply the same questions, to pose the same problems, to set up the same categories for any period of the past and with relatively modest gifts with satisfactory results. It is easy for these mediocrities to ignore their debts, and to be accepted as great scholars and interpreters.'[18] At least I have not made that mistake, and I have paid my debts.

---

[18] B. Berenson, *Rumor and reflection* (New York, 1952), p. 96.

2 *The Renaissance altarpiece: a valid category?*

Paul Hills

By publishing a volume of essays on the altarpiece in the Renaissance we are identifying the altarpiece as a subject of discourse, and, by implication if not by design, setting it apart from the other images and artefacts produced in the Renaissance. Looking at recent articles and books it is evident that the study of the altarpiece has become a growth sector in mediaeval and Renaissance studies; and to judge by the crowds drawn by recent conferences we are dealing with a fashionable or at least favoured subject. So it may be timely to ask, are we justified in isolating the altarpiece in the Renaissance as a category? And what are the consequences of doing so?

Works of art, like other artefacts, can be organised in different kinds of series and sequences. Titian's *Assunta* in the church of the Frari in Venice can be viewed as a masterpiece by Titian, a key work in the artistic development of the master; or it can be studied in the context of the building which houses it, alongside the other works of art, the furnishings and the architecture of that building. Or, devotees of iconography may place it in a series of paintings of the Assumption of the Virgin. Or, it may be studied as a stage in what is termed the development of the Venetian altarpiece. Or, could it be just high altarpieces? Or altarpieces of conventual churches? Or altarpieces over twelve feet high? We can multiply almost at will the categories or sub-categories into which it is slotted, and open new fronts for scholarly attack when old ones lose their charms. We like to imagine that the particular series we favour has an objective existence, and that what we are engaged upon is an act of reconstruction. But such series are not reconstructions but constructs – constructs of the inquiring mind. Any chosen series is a product of a frame of reference.

At this point the commonsensical student of the altarpiece will be wanting to get back to brass tacks, or better, to planks and dowels. If our categorisation is based upon the archaeologically precise study of the physical object, it is argued, then our method evades the taint of subjectivity. But this response is itself the product of an attitude or frame of reference. How can we study the physical object without some prior conception of which objects we are to go out and scrutinise? In the case of altarpieces it involves tricky questions of demarcation, particularly with regard to image, frame and setting. In the Renaissance, as in many periods, conceptual and physical frames do not always coincide. Consider, for example, Ghirlandaio's decoration of the Sassetti Chapel in S. Trinita (plate 12): do the portraits of Francesco Sassetti and Nera Corsi belong to the narrative cycle or to the altarpiece, or perhaps

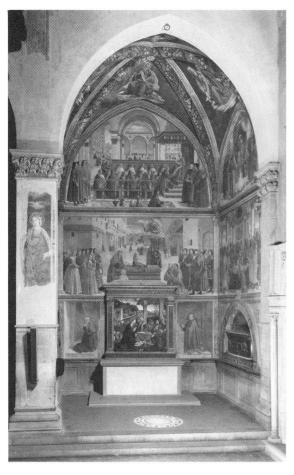

12 Florence, S. Trinita, View of Sassetti chapel with frescoes of life of St Francis and altarpiece of the *Adoration of the Shepherds*, by Domenico Ghirlandaio

to the tombs that flank them?[1] Structurally they cannot be considered part of the altarpiece; unlike the Adoration of the Shepherds, they are painted in fresco rather than on panel; and they are unambiguously positioned outside the carved frame. Any categorical isolation of altarpiece as class of object flies in the face of the fifteenth century's own very subtle deconstruction of the opposition between inside and outside.[2] In Masaccio's *Trinity* (plate 83), whether it is altarpiece or tomb, or both, this inversion of the logic of the frame is already at work: the function of the frame (in the *Trinity* the pilasters flanking the chapel) is to include what is outside it, namely the donors.[3] Once the notion of optical continuum was realized by Brunelleschi and Alberti no art-object could actually be isolated within the wider purview of vision. The entities that discourse, creed or dogma might keep separate, are joined by the

[1] See E. Borsook and J. Offerhaus, *Francesco Sassetti and Ghirlandaio at Santa Trinita, Florence* (Doornspijk, 1981).
[2] On the logic of the frame see J. Derrida, *The truth in painting*, trans. G. Bennington and I. Mcleod (Chicago and London, 1987), esp. pp. 37–82.
[3] For the role of light in joining outside to inside see P. Hills, *The light of early Italian painting* (New Haven and London, 1987), pp. 132–7.

eye. In this context the frame ceases to be an absolute barrier or limit, and becomes only the symbol of isolation or boundary. As symbol it will become open to inversion.[4] It is precisely because conceptual demarcations do not coincide with the more obvious demarcations between physical objects, that I think we should be wary of a Burckhardtian art history according to *Aufgabe* (for which see chapter 1 in this volume by H. W. van Os) inasmuch as this concentrates attention upon classes of objects at the expense of the relations between them. To borrow the language of literary theory, such an approach privileges paradigmatic relations (altarpiece as member of a class of objects) over syntagmatic relations (altarpiece as part of a larger whole – either the physical one of the chapel and church that houses the altarpiece, or the 'mental' one of contemporary needs, beliefs and attitudes). An art history that is to get beyond the stage of cataloguing needs to attend to both paradigmatic and syntagmatic relations, and it needs to be rather careful not to box itself within its own categories.

Like everyone else, I know, or think I know, perfectly well what is meant by the title of this volume. Walk through any church and it would seem we know what is an altarpiece and what is not. Walk through the National Gallery in London and we could probably recognise the types of paintings that are – or rather 'were' – altarpieces, though we might be undecided about one or two smaller works which might or might not have belonged to side altars or to the altars in domestic chapels. Most of us would not include Titian's *Holy Family with a Shepherd* in our mental image of an altarpiece, yet, in the absence of its early provenance can we be certain that it never stood over any kind of altar?[5] A number of Raphael's paintings, such as the *Holy Family of Francis I* (Paris, Louvre), are equally ambiguous as to whether or not they were intended to be positioned over altars.

Although we all make use of a mental image of what altarpieces look like, there are many ambiguous cases from the Middle Ages as well as from the Renaissance. The frescoes by Cimabue, Simone Martini and Pietro Lorenzetti, on walls behind altars in the Upper and Lower Church of San Francesco at Assisi, hardly prepare us for the strange case of Altichiero's *Crucifixion* which spreads across three bays behind the altar of the chapel of SS. Giacomo e Felice in the Santo at Padua (plate 13). Unlike the frescoed altarpieces at Assisi by Simone Martini and Pietro Lorenzetti, this makes no attempt to imitate the format of panel painting; in this respect it is far from anticipating the fictive devices adopted by Quattrocento painters, such as Benozzo Gozzoli,[6] when they disguised fresco as panel. In the way it fills the available wall surface, Altichiero's *Crucifixion* is much closer to Michelangelo's *Last Judgement*. It would seem that when Michelangelo destroyed Perugino's altarpiece of the Assumption, he replaced it by a vast reredos that is coterminous with the wall itself.

---

[4] For consideration of framing conventions see E. H. Gombrich, *Means and ends: reflections on the history of fresco painting* (London, 1976).
[5] National Gallery, London, no. 4; H. Wethey, *The paintings of Titian*, vol. 1 (London, 1979), pp. 94ff.
[6] For example, Gozzoli's altarpiece of St Sebastian in S. Agostino at San Gimignano. For reconstruction of the altar in the Chapel of SS. Giacomo e Felice in the Santo, D. Negri, 'Il nuovo altare della Cappella di San Felice', *Il Santo. Rivista Antoniana di Storia Dottrina Arte*, vol. 6 (Padua, 1966) pp. 366–8.

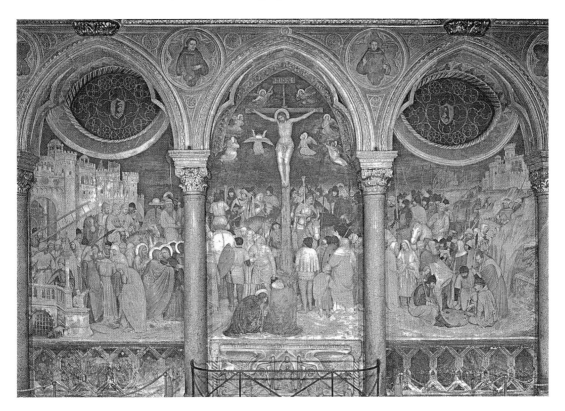

13 Padua, Basilica del Santo, View of chapel of SS. Giacomo e Felice with *Crucifixion* fresco
by Altichiero

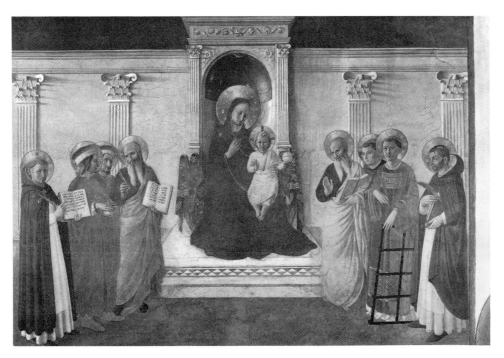

14 Fra Angelico, *Madonna and Child with Eight Saints*

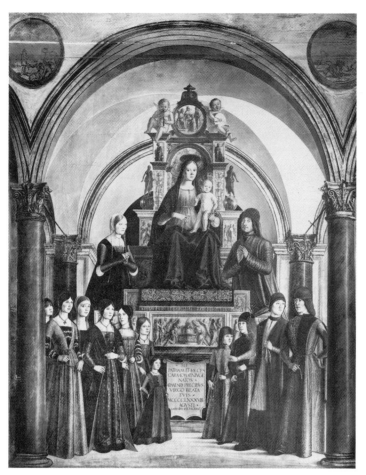

15 Lorenzo Costa, *Madonna and Child with Giovanni II Bentivoglio and his Family*

Just as there are paintings behind altars which hardly conform to preconceptions about altarpieces, so there are images that read as altarpieces because of their format or the way the sacred figures are presented and yet may not have been attached to altars. Fra Angelico's *Madonna and Child with Eight Saints* (plate 14) painted on a wall in the convent of S. Marco arouses expectations that, in spite of its position in a narrow upper corridor, an altar of some kind stood beneath it. It appears extremely unlikely that this was ever the case. Similarly, the marquetry of the east wall of the Sacrestia delle Messe in the Cathedral of Florence, with the depiction of three enthroned saints below and Annunciation above, reads like an altarpiece: although, in this sacristy, the function of such an iconic image as the three saints is closely related to the priest's preparations for the mass, it is not, strictly speaking, an altarpiece.[7] Sacristies may frequently have been repositories for altarpiece-like objects that were not placed directly above altars.

[7] See M. Haines, *The 'Sacrestia delle Messe' of the Florentine cathedral* (Florence, 1983), pp. 143–73. Haines argues that the lateral saints are intended to induce the right frame of mind in the celebrant preparing to say mass (p.150).

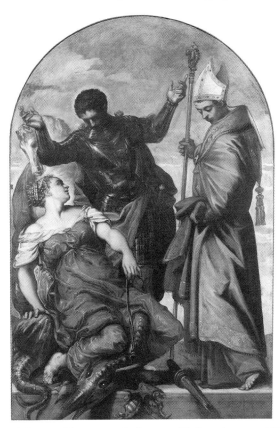

16 Jacopo Tintoretto, *St George with the princess and St Louis*

The Bentivoglio Chapel in the church of S. Giacomo Maggiore in Bologna has an altarpiece with a *Madonna Enthroned with Saints* by Francesco Francia; to its right, on the right-hand wall of the chapel, is a fresco by Lorenzo Costa which also shows an enthroned Madonna with Child (plate 15). The format of Costa's fresco is evidently modelled on Emilian altarpieces with their characteristically high thrones elevating the Madonna; in place of attendant saints we encounter a family gathering in the form of portraits of the donor, Giovanni II Bentivoglio, his wife and numerous children. When seen *in situ*, the fresco, situated at right angles to the altar and a short distance from it, is not mistaken for an altarpiece, and yet Costa has deliberately imitated the characteristic composition of an altarpiece in order to dignify his dynastic assembly.

The sixteenth century affords many examples of non-altarpieces looking deceptively like altarpieces. Two canvases by Tintoretto now in the Accademia might well be mistaken for smallish altarpieces. One shows *St George with the Princess, and St Louis* (plate 16), the other *St Andrew and St Jerome.* They were commissioned to furnish the Magistrato del Sal in the Palazzo dei Camerlenghi in Venice, an entirely secular office in which there is no evidence of altars.[8]

It is worth stressing that the distinction between iconic and narrative presentation

[8] R. Pallucchini and P. Rossi, *Tintoretto: Le opere sacre e profane* (Milan, 1982), cat. nos. 161–2, pp. 165–6.

offers no grounds for differentiating between altarpiece and non-altarpiece. That narrative altarpieces are commonplace is obvious, even if they may not have been designated *storia* before the sixteenth century.[9] It is also true that there are many situations in churches where saints are represented in isolation from narrative, in a mode that certainly recalls their presentation in altarpieces. Stained-glass windows had presented saints in this manner since the High Middle Ages, and many a Madonna and Child in stained glass – in the Upper Church at Assisi, for example – is as frontal and iconic as those in panel paintings. From that tradition it seems a logical progression to the situation in the Pazzi Chapel where the stained-glass window representing St Andrew appears – as others have pointed out – to do service as altarpiece.[10]

Particularly problematic as far as neat categorisation is concerned are the piers of churches and the pilasters that flank chapels. In the fourteenth century the flat faces of piers became the posts for tiers of saints in niches or sentry boxes – as in S. Croce in Florence and many other churches. Such tiers of saints, detached from the narratives that flank them, call to mind the communion of saints, the pillars of the Church Universal, not built by hands. In Orsanmichele saints were depicted on each of the four faces of the freestanding piers and the three faces of the wall-piers. Here the imagery is expanded to include a hexagon above, often showing the assumption of the saint, and a predella-like scene below (plate 17). Resemblances to altarpieces are reinforced by the gold backgrounds that enrich many of these frescoes; and it is noteworthy that in the late fifteenth century some of the frescoed images were actually replaced by paintings on panel. These thin panels, painted by masters such as Lorenzo di Credi and Jacopo del Sellaio, were neatly inset into the shallow recesses on the Trecento piers. Apart from that of St Anne, there were no altars abutting these piers, therefore, in spite of appearances, there is no justification for classifying the pier decorations of Orsanmichele as altarpieces.[11]

Renaissance churches were cluttered with images which did not belong either to narrative cycles or to altarpieces as we understand that term. Wackernagel reminds us of the 'numerous separate pictures that appeared here and there on exposed sections of wall, probably also frequently on the front side of nave piers without association with an altar; these were special donations occasioned by devotional or ex-voto purposes. Such separate pictures in the first half of the Quattrocento usually took the traditional form of a vertical rectangular or pointed panel'.[12] Though Wacker-

---

[9] I owe this point to Charles Hope, who kindly lent me the text of his paper before its publication (C. Hope, 'Altarpieces and the requirements of patrons', in *Christianity in the Renaissance*, ed. T. Verdon and J. Henderson (Syracuse NY, 1989). He argues that prior to the sixteenth century the term *storia* was almost exclusively used to describe the subjects of predellas and fresco cycles, and was not applied to the principal subjects of altarpieces; Hope refers to this again in 'Aspects of criticism in art and literature in sixteenth-century Italy', *Word and Image*, 4 (1988) pp. 1–10, esp. p. 1

[10] A. Luchs, 'Stained glass above Renaissance altars: figural windows in Italian church architecture from Brunelleschi to Bramante', *Zeitschrift für Kunstgeschichte*, 48 (1985), pp. 177–224.

[11] I owe this information about the absence of altars to the kindness of Diane Zervas who has undertaken a documentary study of Orsanmichele.

[12] M. Wackernagel, *The world of the Florentine Renaissance artist* (Princeton, 1981), p. 136. In his chapter, 'Northern altarpieces as cultural documents', Craig Harbison comments on the versatility and variety of panel paintings in the churches of northern Europe; see p. 54.

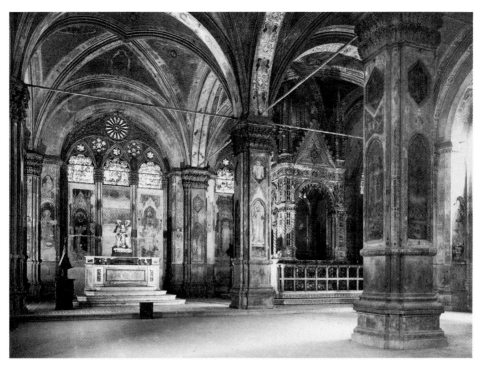

17　Florence, Orsanmichele, view of interior

nagel's assertion that such images were 'without association with an altar' is surely too dogmatic, it is certain that there were many sizable panel paintings in Renaissance churches which were not altarpieces.

Christa Gardner von Teuffel has made the pertinent observation that 'within the architectural revolution, initiated by Brunelleschi, new sacred spaces were designed and with them novel altarpiece settings. It is not too much to say that the setting of altar and altarpiece was one of the major functional requirements of Brunelleschian architecture'.[13] It may be added that what Brunelleschi provided with one hand, he took away with the other, like a Chancellor of the Exchequer. Brunelleschi's slender columnar architecture effectively acted as a prophylactic against the higgledy-piggledy erection of altars in front of piers or columns. Brunelleschi's columns, unlike Trecento piers, were too thin to act as backdrop or support to altars. In other words, Brunelleschian church design laid down a grid that controlled the siting of images. For Brunelleschi the fictive space of pictorial images ideally should not be allowed to disturb the axial perspectives of his churches. Once the sacred painting had become – to use Alberti's simile – like a window, then its siting became as much a concern of the architect as the siting of any other aperture, whether window, arch or door.

While Brunelleschi's churches embodied a new ideal of order, old habits died hard. Individual panels for piers, such as Botticelli's *St Sebastian* for Santa Maria Maggiore (now in Dahlem Museum, Berlin), were still being commissioned in the second half

---

[13]　C. Gardner von Teuffel, 'From polyptych to pala: some structural considerations', in *La pittura nel XIV e XV secolo: il contributo dell' analisi tecnica alla storia dell'arte*, ed. H. W. van Os and J. R. J. van Asperen de Boer (Bologna, 1983), p. 328.

of the fifteenth century, and even in the sixteenth. Vasari records in his own *Vita* that upon the cessation of the plague in 1528, 'my first work was a small picture [*tavoletta*] for the Servite church of S. Piero, Arezzo. It stood against a pilaster and represents St Agatha, St Roch and St Sebastian in half-length figures.'[14] Since *tavoletta* could either mean 'little altarpiece' or 'little panel', it is not clear from Vasari's terminology if his votive picture was or was not attached to an altar. Votive images, whether panels or wax figures, were wont to cluster in the vicinity of altars and shrines, only occasionally assuming the status of altarpiece.

The relative failure of Renaissance tidying up, whether aesthetically or liturgically motivated, is indicated by Carlo Borromeo's *Instructiones fabricae ecclesiasticae*, where he instructs that sacred images should not be permitted close to the ground or in damp or dirty places.[15] The decrees of his Provincial Council of Milan were even more draconian. The council of 1576 ordered that all *sacrae tabulae* and *imagines pictae* which were in an indecorous condition or position should be destroyed. Such decrees would have been otiose if sixteenth-century church interiors were models of order in the arrangement of images.

I hope that my remarks may have opened up questions as to what is or what is not an altarpiece in the Renaissance. Considering how a decision is reached, at least three possible grounds for categorisation suggest themselves. I will call these: intention, construction and use. Most art historians do not hesitate in selecting intention as the determining factor. If it can be ascertained that a painting or sculpture was commissioned to go over an altar – in other words, if the brief asked for an altarpiece – then that work is, from the moment of its inception and *sub specie aeternitatis*, an altarpiece. Caravaggio's *Death of the Virgin* (Paris, Louvre), commissioned as an altarpiece, placed briefly over an altar in Santa Maria della Scala in Rome, rejected as an altarpiece by the priests of the church, and acquired for his private gallery by the Duke of Mantua, is by most scholars still designated an altarpiece. When it comes to categorisation, original intention is privileged above use. One good reason for this is that it is original intention – the brief – which normally accounts for my second criterion, namely construction. Nevertheless, it is worth asking how far the genre 'altarpiece' is dependent upon intentionality, and the consequences of that dependence.

It has become an article of faith amongst well brought up art historians to consider the site or context for which a Renaissance work of art was commissioned or intended. To do our homework (or better, fieldwork) on this has become a badge of professionalism that sets apart the historian from amateurs, critics and aesthetes. For some, such badges are most earnestly to be sought, and thus the dominant image of any

---

[14] G. Vasari, *Le Vite de' più eccellenti pittori, scultori ed architetti*, vol. 7 ed. G. Milanesi (Florence, 1906), p. 651; trans. as *The lives of the painters, sculptors and architects*, vol. 4, ed. W. Gaunt, (London, 1963), p. 258.

[15] *Cap*. XVII, printed in P. Barocchi, ed., *Trattati d'arte del cinquecento fra manierismo e controriforma*, vol. 3 (Bari, 1962), p. 43. For the decrees of the Provincial Council see ibid., p. 442.

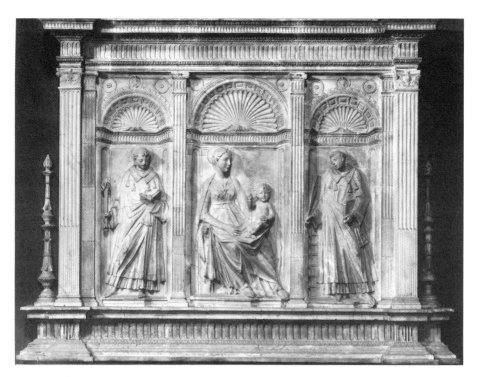

18 Mino da Fiesole, *Madonna and Child with Saints Lawrence and Leonard*

Renaissance altarpiece worth its salt has come to be an object planned for a specific location. If after a number of years an altarpiece is moved away from its intended location, and perhaps away from an altar, this tends to be discounted as an unfortunate aberration, an irrelevant part of its history. Driven by a melancholic and conservative nostalgia for an irretrievable past, it is origins and makers, the creative process, and the relation between patron and artist in that process, which absorb the attention of scholars of the Renaissance, whilst the life or after-life of the work of art is more or less taken for granted, or treated as fortuitous.

Yet perhaps the after-life or survival of the work of art – the uses to which it is put and the responses which it generates – may reveal aspects of the work which an obsession with origins conceals. Unlike the Forth Bridge, great Renaissance works of art were not infrequently dislocated, sometimes within a very short time of their creation, and yet they continued to be highly prized.

Consider Mino da Fiesole's *Madonna and Child with Saints Lawrence and Leonard* (plate 18), which is today mounted in a wall of the Badia in Florence out of striking distance of any altar. This marble altarpiece – Vasari calls it a *tavoletta* – was commissioned by Dietisalvi Neroni in about 1464 for his chapel, dedicated to St Leonard, in the church of S. Lorenzo in Florence.[16] When, very shortly afterwards, Dietisalvi was exiled, the monks of the Badia paid Mino to complete it, and in 1470 it was placed in the sacristy of their church. In its new location the flanking saints would

[16] Vasari *Le vite,* vol. 3, (as in note 14), p. 120.

have borne no dedicatory relation to the setting, yet the Benedictines seem to have been happy to pay Mino to complete the work. Their apparent lack of fastidiousness about the choice of saints to people their sacristy should make us pause.

The early history of Mino's *Madonna and Child with Saints Lawrence and Leonard* suggests that by the late fifteenth century the function of an altarpiece as an object to be positioned over a specific altar and to be viewed in the context of the liturgy may take second place to its power to inspire devotion simply as a beautiful religious image. Vasari's account of the exhibition of Leonardo's cartoon of the Madonna and Child with St Anne testifies to the symbiotic relationship between cult value and aesthetic value in the High Renaissance. Leonardo, who had been commissioned to paint the monumental, double-sided altarpiece for Santissima Annunziata in Florence, and granted lodgings there by the Servite friars, exasperated his patrons by failing to start work on the panels. Instead he made a cartoon, apparently unrelated to the altarpiece. By exhibiting the cartoon, Leonardo was in a sense setting up a rival ceremony to the unveiling of an altarpiece. Although, as Martin Kemp has pointed out, the inclusion of St Anne had specifically Florentine and therefore political overtones, according to Vasari, the procession of people flocking to view the work took on the character of a religious festival.[17] The focus of their gaze and source of their wonder was the beauty and expression of a human face, the face of Our Lady, because it displayed 'all the simplicity and beauty which can shed grace on the Mother of God, showing the modesty and humility of a Virgin contentedly happy, in seeing the beauty of her Son, whom she tenderly holds in her lap'. Such rapt attention was being paid to the human face at a pivotal period in the history of images. *A propos* of another, curiously analogous, pivotal period, the late nineteenth century, Walter Benjamin has written: 'In photography, exhibition value begins to displace cult value all along the line. But cult value does not give way without resistance. It retires into an ultimate retrenchment: the human countenance.'[18] Historians of the Renaissance have hardly begun to respond to the significance of the human countenance.

Perhaps the most famous example of evasion of intended context is Raphael's *Transfiguration* (see plate 99). This monumental altarpiece was commissioned by Cardinal Giulio de' Medici for his cathedral in Narbonne. After Raphael's death it was displayed for time in the Cardinal's palace, the Cancelleria, before being transferred, in 1523, to the high altar of S. Pietro in Montorio. Evidently there is some quality attaching to the work which allowed its function as altarpiece to be deferred by several years, and then for it to be installed – without apparent sense of impropriety – over an altar for which it was not intended. Of course, this is obvious; and Sylvia Ferino

[17] Ibid., vol. 4, p. 38–9; Gaunt, *The lives*, p. 164. For the political significance of the St Anne see M. Kemp, *Leonardo da Vinci. The marvellous works of nature and man* (London, 1981), p. 226. For analysis of Vasari's account of the exhibition see D. Summers, *The judgment of sense* (Cambridge, 1987), pp. 125–7.

An example of the loosening of the bond between an altarpiece and its intended site is Bronzino's *Pietà*, (now in Besançon, Musée des Beaux-Arts). Originally commissioned for the Chapel of Eleanora in the Palazzo Vecchio, it was given by Duke Cosimo as a diplomatic gift to a Spaniard, and Bronzino was ordered to paint a replica for the Florentine altar: See Vasari, *Le vite*, vol. 7, p. 597.

[18] 'The work of art in the age of mechanical reproduction', *Illuminations* (London, 1970), pp. 227–8.

Pagden's paper in this volume cites other examples of dislocation of altarpieces by Raphael. I raise the topic here in order to return to the question: what are the consequences of isolating the altarpiece in the Renaissance as a category for discourse? One danger, it seems to me, is that it accentuates those aspects of a work – frequently its most conventional features – which mark it off as belonging to the genre altarpiece, while it devalues or obscures those features which are not highlighted by this classification.

By attending, on the other hand, to the contingencies of history we may attain a deeper understanding of the work of art. As Theodor Adorno reminds us:

> Over time, great works reveal new facets of themselves, they age, they become rigid, and they die. Being human artefacts, they do not 'live' in the same sense as human beings. Of course not. To put the accent on the artefactual aspect in works of art seems to imply that the way in which they came to be is important. It is not. The emphasis must be on their inner constitution. They have life because they speak in ways nature and man cannot. They talk because there is communication between their individual constituents.[19]

To show, as I have tried to do, that the genre altarpiece has fuzzy edges where definition may be uncertain is not to deny the existence of a genre. Plenty of genres have fuzzy edges. But it does mean we should beware of closed categories. And while it would be a peculiar act of blindness to deny the existence of altarpieces, are we entitled to ask if altarpieces were identified as a topic for discourse in Renaissance Italy? For convenience, two broad groups of writers may be distinguished: on the one hand, theorists of art, on the other, theologians and preachers.

In Alberti's *Della pittura* there is no specific mention of altarpieces. Indeed it is striking that by adopting the term *historia*, Alberti avoids specifying, in the manner that earlier discourse had, either whether he is referring to a sacred or a secular subject, or whether he is referring to a painting on panel *(tavola)* or on the wall *(pictura)*. At the opening of Book III (para. 52) he makes a fleeting reference to the two varieties of support – 'tavola o parete' – but not to draw any distinction between them; and the Latin text omits the phrase altogether. In his *De re aedificatoria* he inveighs against the practice of crowding every place with altars, preferring the ancient rule of one altar in the middle of the temple. On altarpieces he is silent, apart from referring to the antique practice of placing statues of the deity in temples.

Moving into the sixteenth century, altarpieces as a category are not primary objects of discourse amongst art theorists. Ludovico Dolce opens his dialogue the *Aretino* in front of the *gran tavola*, Titian's *St Peter Martyr* (destroyed; formerly Venice, SS. Giovanni e Paolo).[20] When he compares Titian with Raphael or Michelangelo, there is no hint that like should be compared with like, altarpiece with altarpiece, fresco with fresco. And while Dolce invokes literary parallels to justify variety of *maniera*, he betrays no inkling that this variety might also derive from artefactual distinctions between altarpiece and non-altarpiece.

---

[19] *Aesthetic theory*, trans. C. Lenhardt (London, 1970), p. 6.
[20] L. Dolce, *Dialogo della pittura, intitolato l'Aretino* (Venice 1557), p. 1; reprinted in M. Roskill, *Dolce's 'Aretino' and Venetian art theory of the cinquecento* (New York, 1968), p. 84.

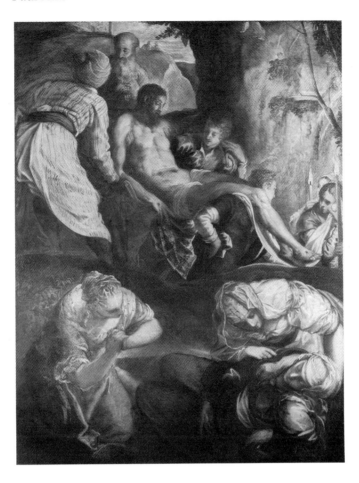

19 Jacopo Tintoretto, *The Deposition of Christ from the Cross*

As a tireless painter of altarpieces himself, it is hardly surprising that Vasari has more to say about them. Usually he refers to them as *tavole* rather than *tavole d'altare*. In his own *Vita* he describes many of the altarpieces that he had painted, including the one for Bindo Altoviti of which he made a replica 'in un piccolo quadro, quasi di minio' as a thank-offering to Bindo.[21] Here again we encounter a characteristic Renaissance undermining of the distinction between altarpiece and non-altarpiece. The replication in miniature is a picture of a picture ('la pittura di detta tavola', says Vasari). The larger object, the altarpiece, belongs to the public and to the religious domain; the smaller object is a derivative and a memento; it is a token of friendship that belongs to the private domain. Notionally the imagery of altarpiece and miniature is the same, but through replication in a radically different scale the sacred imagery is aestheticised. And as the memento is detached from any intended locus, it can the more readily be treated as an exemplar of artistic skill and a commodity of exchange amongst those who value such exemplars. The spread of engraving during the Renais-

[21] Vasari, *Le vite*, vol. 7, p. 669. For terminology in the north see Harbison, this volume, p. 52.

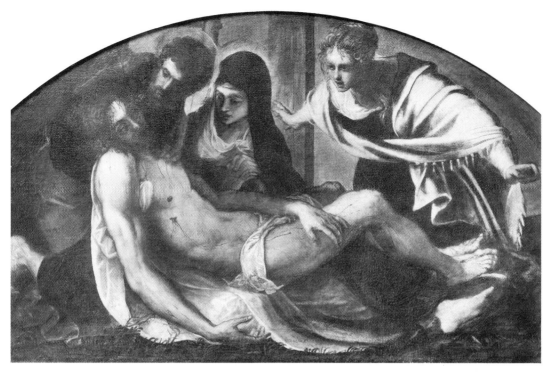

20 Jacopo Tintoretto, *Pietà*

sance presented another – and highly influential – means by which sacred imagery
was reproduced and thus given an existence separate from the cult object, whether
altarpiece or non-altarpiece. The engraving of Raphael's altarpieces soon after their
execution marks a significant stage in the post-medieval prising apart of the image
as artistic composition from its unique physical locus in the object.

Looking at the other class of writers to whom altarpieces ought to have been of
interest, namely theologians and preachers, it is striking that the category in which
they deal is the broad one of 'sacred images', *imagines sacrae*. Only rarely do preachers,
such as San Bernardino or Savonarola, specify altarpieces as such. Many of the miracle-working images of Renaissance Italy, such as the Madonna that gave its name
to S. Maria dei Miracoli in Venice, began life as simple tabernacles, shrines or ex-votos.
To the faithful it made little difference if a sacred image was an altarpiece or not
– as one may still observe in Catholic churches to this day.

Similarly, if we examine two canvases by Tintoretto, one an altarpiece, the other
not, we find no fundamental differences of religious feeling or implications of dogma.
The format of the *Deposition* (plate 19) signals that it was an altarpiece, and in fact
it comes from S. Francesco della Vigna. The *Pietà* (plate 20), on the other hand,
was painted for the secular setting of the courtyard of the *Procuratie*. The differences
between the two pictures flow from differences in format, not from any putative
distinctions between liturgical and non-liturgical contexts.

If we are interested in the history of religion there is nothing to be gained, and perhaps something to be lost, in separating altarpieces from the general class of sacred images.

Categories are useful as tools of inquiry as long as their limitations are recognised. There is a quality in Giovanni Bellini's canvas of *Doge Agostino Barbarigo presented to the Madonna and Child* (Murano, S. Pietro Martire) which allowed it to appear at home in Barbarigo's family palace while he lived, and in S. Maria degli Angeli at Murano, to which he left it in his will. By the end of the sixteenth century pictorial games of musical chairs must have become commonplace for they gave rise to the conceit of *quadri riportati*. The accounts of the Procurators of S. Marco in Venice record another, rather different, kind of *quadro riportato* from the those familiar to us from Annibale Carracci's ceiling of the Farnese Gallery: in 1571 a payment was made to Jacopo Tintoretto for 'uno quadro colla nativita del nostro signore se mete in chiesa di San Marco sopra l'altar grande da nadal' – a *quadro* of the Nativity of Our Lord for placing on the high altar of S. Marco on Christmas Day.[22] Structurally this cannot have been an altarpiece for in the same account books these are designated as *palle:* it was a temporary visual aid, put in place for Christmas alone, and removed when Christmas was over.[23] The work has not been traced. Perhaps such visual aids were not common. Could we call them seasonal altarpieces and admit them as another joker in our pack of pictorial categories?

[22] D. F. von Hadeln, 'Beiträge von Tintorettoforschung', *Jahrbuch der Preussischen Kunstsammlungen*, 32 (1911), Beiheft, p.54, doc. 5.

[23] One puzzle is the reference to Tintoretto's *tavola* in Raffaello Borghini, *Il Riposo* (Florence, 1584): 'Nella Chiesa di San Marco sopra l'Altar maggiore è la tavola della Nativita di Christo fatta da lui' (ed. M. Rosci, Milan, 1967, p. 557). It is evident from Francesco Sansovino, writing in 1580, that the *pala d'oro* was in place on the high altar, and still very much esteemed; the later editions of *Venetia città nobilissima et singolare* (Venice, 1663), make no mention of the Tintoretto (vol. 1, p. 100). Borghini, or his informant, appears to have mistaken a temporary arrangement for a permanent installation.

3 *The northern altarpiece as a cultural document*

Craig Harbison

Is it possible to make valid and interesting generalisations about northern European altarpieces? In today's scholarly climate, one would no doubt immediately feel the scepticism of one's colleagues greeting any such endeavour.[1] As so many of the studies in this volume attest, this is a time of contextual analysis, the careful study of particular circumstances. Even our sense of categorisation sometimes deserts us – is the altarpiece a valid category, asks Paul Hills?[2] All we seem certain of is the individual creation; all we seem attracted to is the way it fits into a uniquely determined situation.

I am enough of a nominalist myself to feel that there cannot be any absolute justification for making a generalisation, except that it seems, to the observer, both interesting and productive. I would certainly welcome the reader's scepticism about any of my generalisations – so long as it does not stem from a categorical rejection of such an endeavour. Historians do inevitably try to make some sense out of the past, give it some coherent shape or design. Certainly it is better to do this knowingly, to admit one's particular inclination to simplify a complex picture into certain agreeable patterns.

In his chapter in this volume, H. W. van Os has mentioned several perspectives which he would like to see applied to the overall evaluation of Italian Renaissance altarpieces. I was particularly intrigued by his advocacy of a typology based on shapes of altarpieces.[3] To my knowledge no scholar has raised this issue with northern altarpieces, especially over several centuries. A careful study along these lines might indeed produce very interesting results. I am thinking in particular of the rather sudden development, and then demise, of the elaborately scalloped shapes for altarpieces found in the second quarter of the sixteenth century (see plate 21); no doubt these bear an interesting relation to other aspects of art and culture at the time.[4] However, detailed consideration of a painting's shape falls outside the scope of this

My thanks to Jane Connell and Robert A. Koch for help in locating photographs and references, and to the Research Council, University of Massachusetts, Amherst, for assistance with photograph purchase.
[1] See chapter 1 by H. W. van Os in this volume.
[2] See chapter 2 by Paul Hills in this volume.
[3] See chapter 1 in this volume, pp. 30–2.
[4] Several things about these frames might be worth noting here. The first is the way they can give the painting a precious old-fashioned look – reliquary-like – recalling the early examples of the combination of oil painting and sculpture such as the Jacques de Baerze/Melchior Broederlam altarpiece in Dijon; this might be related to other archaisms found in northern painting in the first half of the sixteenth century. Secondly, in an example like that by Engebrechtsz, illustrated in plate 21, we can observe the way the painter makes creative use of the irregular shape in order to accommodate his growing narrative interests. This is certainly different from earlier examples like Broederlam.

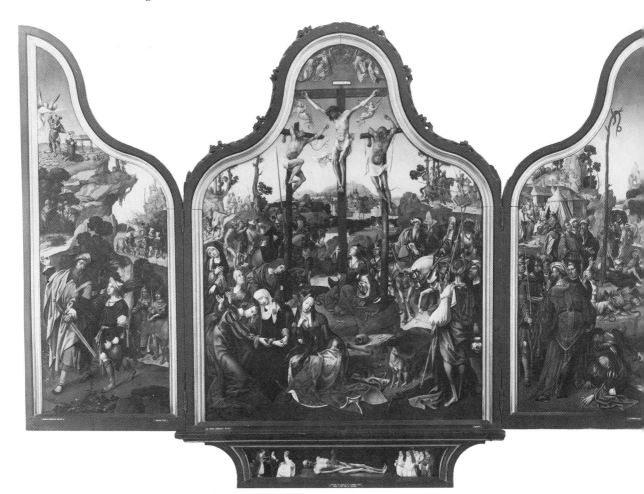

21 Cornelis Engebrechtsz, *Crucifixion Altarpiece*

chapter. I mention it in order to stress one thing: there are certainly avenues of approach to the problem of general tendencies in altar painting other than the one I have chosen. Mine derives to some extent from a need to respond to previous attempts in this area; as well as stemming from some of what I perceive to be my own and others' basic reasons for studying, and thus hoping to learn from, this material.

Examination of the meaning and function of northern Renaissance altarpieces has been governed in large measure by two seemingly divergent points of view. The first of these seeks to elucidate the religious significance of, especially, fifteenth-century paintings by reference to traditional Church practice; this is thought to be contained in the form of the liturgy used at the performance of sacraments and in the prayers prescribed by the breviary for various feasts as well as for the canonical hours of the day.[5] Religious meaning thus embodies the consensus of opinions voiced by official Church spokesmen; it is institutional and bookish, as well as intended above all to be understood and practised communally. This critical position might be seen as idolatrous, in its rather worshipful attitude, and in the way that it attributes literal and unvarying meaning to religious imagery.

On the other hand, especially in dealing with later fifteenth- and early sixteenth-century products, some scholars have taken a different stance. They have found the novel thrust of religious art at this time in the increasing attention to 'secular satisfactions'.[6] What one critic has called the 'underground wishes of men'[7] are thought of as coming to the surface of consciousness and eventually breaking off from institutional church expression, to find release in the secular production of more personal imagery, portraits, still-lifes and fleshly cabinet pieces, to name a few. Here we find what might be seen as the art historical equivalent of iconoclasm: acceptance of the notion that secularising impulses are somehow inimical to true religious expression and therefore demand to be siphoned off from it. (In trying to explain such secularising tendencies, other scholars have claimed that seeming new themes in sixteenth-century art are in fact just disguised presentations of traditional Church teachings, especially of a rather ascetic Christian–Protestant or Catholic–morality.[8])

This brief characterisation of these two critical interests – symbolist versus secularist, we might for convenience call them – is admittedly exaggerated. Scholars who favour a traditional symbolic reading of religious art certainly recognise how much personal devotion plays a part in this imagery;[9] and those who argue for the distinctiveness of 'secular satisfactions' acknowledge the difficulty we have today in determining just how sharp contemporary thinking might have been on such matters.[10] My initial simplified characterisation was, however, meant to suggest an interesting parallel in thinking. Although one person's institutional propriety may be another's institutional abuse, the fact remains that in this case both tend to accept the notion that religious meaning is properly characterised as conventional, and that one risks

[5] The following studies are important, although they differ in the kind of liturgical evidence they use, as well as in the care with which they use it: B. Lane, *The altar and the altarpiece: sacramental themes in early Netherlandish painting* (New York, 1984); C. Purtle, *The Marian paintings of Jan van Eyck* (Princeton, 1982); and L. B. Philip, *The Ghent altarpiece and the art of Jan van Eyck* (Princeton, 1971), especially pp. 61–78, 'The eternal mass'. Other authors who have made important contributions to this way of thinking include M. B. McNamee and Carla Gottlieb; see the references cited in Lane's bibliography.
[6] See, for instance, M. Baxandall, *The limewood sculptors of Renaissance Germany* (New Haven and London, 1980), esp. pp. 78–93.
[7] M. Schapiro, '"Muscipula Diaboli," the symbolism of the Mérode altarpiece', *Art Bulletin*, 27 (1945), p. 187.
[8] This is the way several authors interpret the secular work of the mid-sixteenth-century Flemish artist, Pieter Aertsen; see J. A. Emmens, '"Eins aber is nötig" – zu Inhalt und Bedeutung van Markt – und Küchenstücken des 16. Jahrhunderts', *Album Amicorum J. G. van Gelder* (The Hague, 1973), pp. 93–101; and K. M. Craig, 'Pieter Aertsen and *The Meat Stall*', *Oud-Holland*, 96 (1982), pp. 1–15; and Craig, '*Pars Ergo Marthae Transit*: Pieter Aertsen's "inverted" paintings of *Christ in the House of Martha and Mary*', *Oud-Holland*, 97 (1983), pp. 25–39.
[9] This is true for instance in the work of C. Purtle, *The Marian paintings* (as in note 5).
[10] See Baxandall, *The limewood sculptors* (as in note 6), p. 78: ' It seems almost as if the Reformation decade may have concretely analysed out a mixture of functions within pre-Reformation sculpture: the major devotional function having been extracted, minor residual functions are being precipitated as separate minor genres.
'This is difficult to think about because it must be very much a question about the eye of the beholder, about whether people were disposed to look for and see certain extrinsic qualities in the image.'

(or gains) a secularist heresy by breaking out of institutional control. In my view, the Reformation may represent a response to the loss of a sense of religious community felt by many western Europeans. But the main response to that sense of loss was not in turn the later institutionalisation of a more purely secular sphere of art.

One purpose of this chapter is to suggest an alternative to this dichotomy, an alternative which is hopefully more fruitful and more appropriate for the early modern period.

We have surprisingly little illuminating documentary evidence about the terminology applied to, and the physical use and situation of, fifteenth-century northern European altarpieces. The specifically denotative contemporary term for an altarpiece – *autaer tafel* – is rarely used in fifteenth-century documents. We find it employed, for instance, when Tommaso Portinari is trying to recover the *Last Judgement* altarpiece by Hans Memling which Hansa merchants had stolen, along with Portinari's ship, and taken to Danzig;[11] perhaps the use of the term in these documents is meant to stress the sanctity of the object and therefore the sacrilegious nature of the theft. But more often, even when we are certain that a painting was intended as an altarpiece, no special term is applied, other than the word *tafel*, which is used indiscriminately for all paintings.[12] This is the case, for instance, with Dirk Bouts' *Holy Sacrament* altarpiece, commissioned by the Confraternity of the Holy Sacrament in Louvain for their altar in the church of St Peter (plate 22); for this painting, at least until the Second World War, we had good contemporary documentation, including the original contract between painter and confraternity; but nowhere was the work referred to as an 'altarpiece'.[13]

To my knowledge, no fifteenth-century document mentions the manner in which a painting, particularly a folding triptych or polyptych, could or should be used during a religious ceremony.[14] Fully articulate public altar paintings are rarely, if ever, shown within fifteenth-century panels. If a painting is portrayed within another painting, it is likely to be a simple panel viewed in the private context of the home.[15] No fifteenth-century drawings exist which might give us a helpful overview of the

[11] See J. Bialostocki, *Les musées de Pologne*, Les primitifs Flamands, Corpus de la peinture, 9 (Brussels, 1966), pp. 104–5.

[12] I have checked all the fifteenth-century documents published so far in the *Corpus* of Flemish primitives (see note 11 above), in addition to other miscellaneous sources, such as Schöne mentioned below in note 13.

[13] See W. Schöne, *Dieric Bouts und seine Schule* (Berlin/Leipzig, 1938), pp. 240–1 (documents 55–63, dating from 1464–86).

[14] My own observations in this regard are supported by the findings of James Marrow, who plans to publish a study analysing several hundred contemporary references to works of art, mostly from devotional literature. My thanks to Professor Marrow for responding to this matter prior to the publication of his study.

[15] Based on a survey of the corpus of illustrations in the English translation of M. J. Friedländer's *Early Netherlandish painting*, I made a similar point in 'Visions and meditations in early Flemish painting', *Simiolus*, 15 (1985), p. 116. Kim Woods treats the very different issue of painted representations of sculpted altarpieces in chapter 4 of this volume.

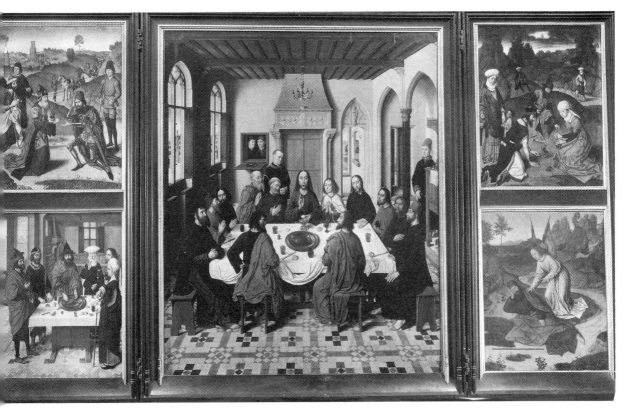

22 Dirk Bouts, *Holy Sacrament Altarpiece*

way an altarpiece was planned, how it was meant to work, what sort of contemporary framework or surrounding it was given, and so forth.[16]

A representative selection of altarpiece paintings done throughout the century shows how seemingly fragmentary our knowledge is. The Ghent Altarpiece, presumably finished by the van Eycks in 1432, is the largest and most famous religious ensemble executed in Flanders in the fifteenth century. But it still is not clear if this work was meant from the start to be seen as it is today; and, even if it was, whether

---

[16] The only fifteenth-century drawn altarpiece designs which exist either show the most elementary frameworks or are likely to be later copies. The most indicative, and virtually the only, examples are found in the Louvre: a *Christ carried to the Tomb*, school of Roger van der Weyden (inv. 20.666); a *Crucifixion Triptych with Scenes from the Life of St Eloi*, also circle of Roger (inv. 20. 654); and *Scenes from the Life of St Barbara*, attributed to the Master of the Legend of St Barbara (inv. 20.665) all illustrated and described in Frits Lugt, *Musées du Louvre, Inventaire général des dessins des écoles du nord, Maitres des anciens Pays-bas nés avant 1550* (Paris, 1968), pp. 9–10, cat. nos. 16 and 17, plates 10–11; and p. 19, cat. no. 55, plate 28. A survey of the published catalogues of the following collections produced no important additional examples: London, British Museum, Dutch and Flemish drawings; Oxford, Ashmolean Museum, Netherlandish and German drawings; Oxford, Christ Church, Netherlandish and German drawings; Edinburgh, National Gallery of Scotland, Netherlandish drawings; Amsterdam, Rijksmuseum, fifteenth- and sixteenth-century Netherlandish drawings; Antwerp, Plantin-Moretus Museum, Dutch and Flemish drawings; Paris, Louvre, Netherlandish, German and Swiss masters born before 1550; Paris, Bibliothèque Nationale, northern European drawings; Cologne, Wallraf-Richartz-Museum, Netherlandish drawings; Erlangen, Universitätsbibliothek, German and Netherlandish drawings; and Vienna, Albertina, German and Netherlandish drawings. K. G. Boon, *Netherlandish drawings of the fifteenth and sixteenth centuries*, Rijksmuseum Amsterdam (The Hague, 1978), text vol. 203 says that designs for painted altarpieces are a rarity in the Netherlands.

it was given a single consistent meaning relating to the altar over which it hung.[17] A triptych with the *Martyrdom of St Hippolytus* in the Cathedral of St Sauveur in Bruges was apparently executed by several artists, one doing the historical scenes, the other the contemporary donors (plate 23); but just why this might be is uncertain.[18] Also telling for our purposes is the fact that this work, apparently begun as a personal devotional one, ended up serving as the only painting, presumably over the altar, in the chapel of the Guild of Lime Porters at St Sauveur.[19] And, finally, Gerard David's large triptych with the *Baptism of Christ*, painted in 1502–07, is replete with sacramental implications especially evident in the impressive figure of the vested angel (plate 24).[20] Yet during the donor's lifetime this work remained a private one, only hung over a public altar in 1520 after the patron's death, and then to be accompanied by carefully specified masses for his soul.[21]

One provisional conclusion to be drawn from such widely scattered examples is that fifteenth-century religious paintings, whether used constantly over an altar or not, were very versatile items. As the simple term *tafel* most often applied to them at the time implies, they were just that – *panels*, readily adaptable to a wide variety of contexts and meanings, both private and public.

At first glance, this rather indeterminant situation in the fifteenth century appears to become more explicit in the sixteenth. Terminology applied to altarpieces seems both more specific and more consistent. In contrast to the situation found in the case of the Dirk Bouts altarpiece mentioned above, Pieter Pourbus' *Holy Sacrament* altarpiece, commissioned by the Confraternity of the Holy Sacrament in Bruges in 1559 (plate 25), is called an *oultaertafel* in the first surviving sixteenth-century document referring to it (1569).[22] Although they are still not numerous, more sixteenth-century northern European drawings survive which are helpful in showing the total conception or plan of an altarpiece.[23] This is the case, for instance, with a remarkable series of at least five double-sided drawings, complete with folding wings, which the Elder

---

[17] The relevant scholarly literature for this work is of course quite large, and includes the work of L. B. Philip mentioned in note 5 above. The most recent and careful analysis of the polyptych in light of eucharistic theology is by D. R. Goodgal, *The iconography of the Ghent Altarpiece*, Phd. dissertation, University of Pennsylvania, 1981.

[18] L. Devlieger, *De Sint-Salvators Katedraal te Brugge, Inventaris*, Kunstpatrimonium van West-Vlaanderen, deel 8 (Tielt, 1979), pp. 169–71, voices the usual opinion that Dirk Bouts began the work and that after his death Hugo van der Goes was asked to complete the unfinished panel which represents the donors. But it is also quite possible that the centre and right panels were executed by a Bouts follower or assistant. And in either case – whether the work was begun by Bouts or a follower – one might well still wonder why it was not completed in a stylistically consistent manner. See also the discussion of the various proposals about authorship in *Flanders in the fifteenth century, art and civilisation*, exhibition catalogue, Detroit Institute of Arts (1960), pp. 108–12, cat. no. 19.

[19] See the two references cited in the preceding note, especially the Detroit catalogue.

[20] See C. Harbison, 'Some artistic anticipations of theological thought', *Art Quarterly*, n.s. 2 (1979), pp. 67–89, esp. pp. 79–83.

[21] See the documents published in A. Janssens de Bisthoven, M. Baes-Dondegne and D. De Vos, *Stedelijk Museum voor Schone Kunsten, Brugge*, Les primitifs flamands, Corpus de la peinture, 1, revised edition (Brussels, 1981), pp. 152–6.

[22] See Devlieger, *De Sint-Salvators Katedraal* (see note 18), pp. 179–80; also P. Huvenne, *Pierre Pourbus, Peintre Brugeois, 1524–1584*, exhibition catalogue (Bruges, 1984), pp. 160–6, cat. no. 6.

[23] There are relevant, but still not particularly helpful, works in London, Amsterdam, Antwerp, Erlangen and Vienna.

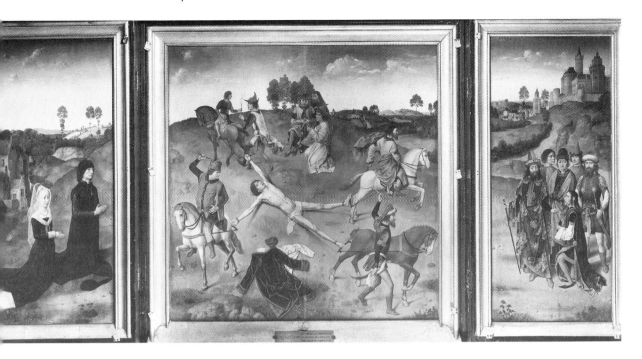

23 Dirk Bouts and Hugo van der Goes, *Martyrdom of St Hippolytus Triptych*

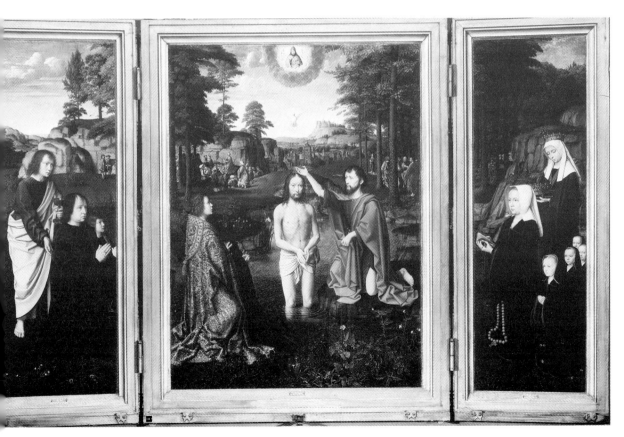

24 Gerard David, *Baptism of Christ Triptych*

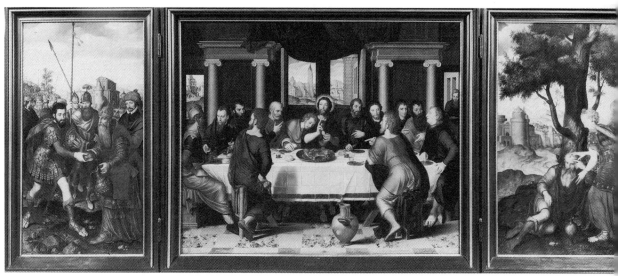

25 Pieter Pourbus, *Holy Sacrament Altarpiece*

Cranach executed around 1515–20.[24] In ways like these – naming and planning – the sixteenth century exhibits a more conscious play with the notion of an altarpiece, thinking through and specifying its use.

This trend also seems to be evident in two additional areas: the subjects or central themes of altarpieces and the portrayal of altar paintings in other works of art, especially in other paintings. In both Catholic and Protestant circles in the sixteenth century, altarpieces are enlisted in the promotional schemes of the Church. For Catholics, this sometimes means a focus on the sacraments (as in the case of the Pourbus work just mentioned)[25] or on the Virgin or on martyrdoms of the saints. The number of representations of martyrdoms in Flemish altarpieces of the early Counter-Reformation is quite remarkable – and clearly propagandistic in nature – these are exemplary images of steadfast adherence to the true and Catholic faith (plate 26).[26]

Lutherans also focused on their interpretation of the sacrament of communion. An interesting sixteenth-century example is Lucas Cranach the Younger's 1565 panel for the castle church in Dessau (plate 27); here the apostles have been transformed into the various Protestant Reformed leaders – Luther, Melanchthon, etc. – whom the donor, Joachim von Anhalt, clearly supports.[27] The Protestant emphasis on the

[24] The Cranach drawings are today in the Louvre, Paris; Schlossmuseum, Weimar; Kupferstichkabinett, Berlin; and Museum der Bildenden Künste, Leipzig. For all of these, see J. Rosenberg, *Die Zeichnungen Lucas Cranachs d.A.* (Berlin, 1960), pp. 20–2, cat. nos. 29, 30, 31, 36 and 37.

[25] Infrequently represented in the fifteenth century, the Last Supper becomes one of the most popular subjects in sixteenth-century religious art, whether Catholic or Protestant.

[26] See D. Freedberg, 'The representation of martyrdoms during the early Counter-Reformation in Antwerp', *Burlington Magazine*, 118 (1976), pp. 128–38, esp. pp. 136f.

[27] See for instance *Kunst der Reformationszeit*, exhibition catalogue, Staatliche Museen zu Berlin, DDR (Berlin, 1983), p. 370, cat. no. F1, and colour plate p. 392; also O. Thulin, *Cranach-Altäre der Reformation* (Berlin, 1955), pp. 96–110. A sober but monumental commemoration of the Last Supper continued to be found over some Lutheran altars into the seventeenth century, when an unknown Dutch artist executed the influential sculpture still located above the altar of the Oslo Cathedral.

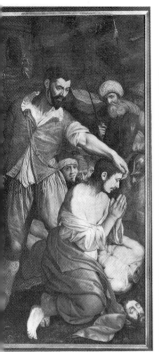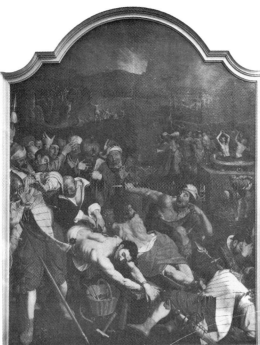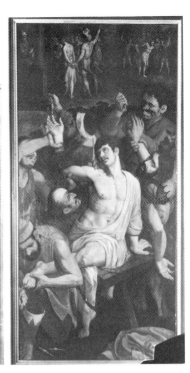

26 Ambrosius Francken and workship(?), *Martyrdom of Saints Crispin and Crispinian*

Word could and did often spell destruction for (or at least lack of commission of)
painted images. In some intriguing cases the pulpit itself was inserted as the central
panel into a kind of triptych still placed over the altar (plate 28).[28] The previous
single function of the altar – as location for the saying of the mass – was thus overlaid
with the newly primary dispensation of the Word.

Toward the end of the sixteenth century a type of painting which is helpful for
our purposes was taken up in earnest: images of church interiors. Fully articulated
church interiors, peopled with numerous human actors, are extremely rare in fifteenth-century northern European panels (see plate 29).[29] In the late sixteenth and
throughout the seventeenth centuries there is, in Catholic examples, an elaborate
display of Church ritual, especially centering around the rapidly multiplying number
of altars (plate 30); by contrast, in Protestant works, there is a conscious lack of

[28] See K. Lankheit, 'Dürers ''Vier Apostel'' ', *Zeitschrift für Theologie und Kirche*, 49 (1952), pp. 238–54, especially
pp. 250–2. The work illustrated in plate 28 is discussed in detail by K. Reissmann, *Die Kunstdenkmäler der Provinz
Brandenburg, VII, 3, Stadt-/und Landkreises Landsberg (Warthe)* (Berlin, 1937), pp. 47–50 and figs. 109–11, p. 151.
[29] In Flanders Roger van der Weyden's propagandistic *Seven Sacraments* altarpiece is exceptional; see Harbison 'Visions
and meditations', esp. p. 89 and note 9; and the reference made there to S. Koslow, *The Chevrot Altarpiece*,
Phd. dissertation, New York University, 1972. In Germany, the painting of the *Miracles of St Bruno* (1489) commissioned by the Emperor Frederick III for the Carthusian monastery in Cologne (now in the Wallraf-Richartz-Museum)
is also extremely unusual; see A. Stange, *Deutsche Malerei der Gotik*, (rpt. Nendeln, 1969) Vol. 5, fig. 114, and
p. 57. Kim Woods' chapter in this volume discusses examples of sculpted altarpieces represented within paintings
found especially in manuscripts.

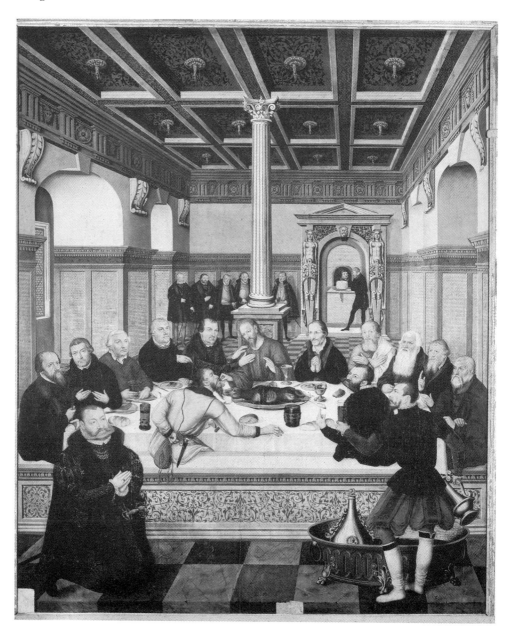

27 Lucas Cranch the Younger, *Last Supper*

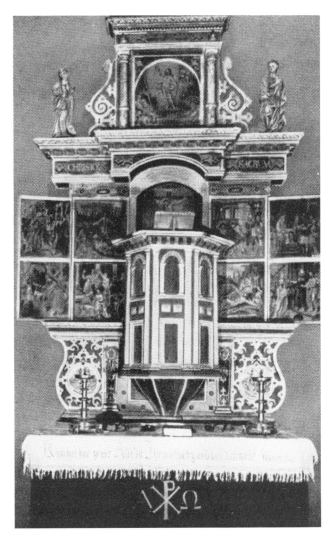

28 'Thomas Maler' (Master TB), *Scenes from the Passion of Christ c.* 1500 (altered to present form, overpainted and attached to pulpit, *c.* 1605)

display, a positive elimination of altarpieces in the serene, newly whitewashed structures (see plate 32).[30]

The situation of the altarpiece, its status within the Church, can in some ways be said to be clarified by these images. The development of confessional differences brings a new sense of purpose and dedication to the Catholic use of altarpieces – and a drastic limitation or change to Protestant attitudes. But should this lead us

[30] Good examples of Catholic church interiors are found in the Musées Royaux des Beaux-Arts de Belgique in Brussels (plate 30); others are today in the Kunsthistorisches Museum, Vienna, and in the Prado in Madrid. Works like these seem consciously to focus on a series of new, co-ordinated altarpieces moving down the nave of the church. One motive behind such images in the north might be related to the ideal which Peter Humfrey treats in Renaissance Venice (see his chapter in this volume). Contemporaries probably felt that there was something special about these newly elaborated – and harmoniously co-ordinated – Counter-Reformation interiors which needed to be recorded. Representative Protestant examples are covered in the recent survey by W. Liedtke, *Architectural painting in Delft* (Doornspijk, 1982).

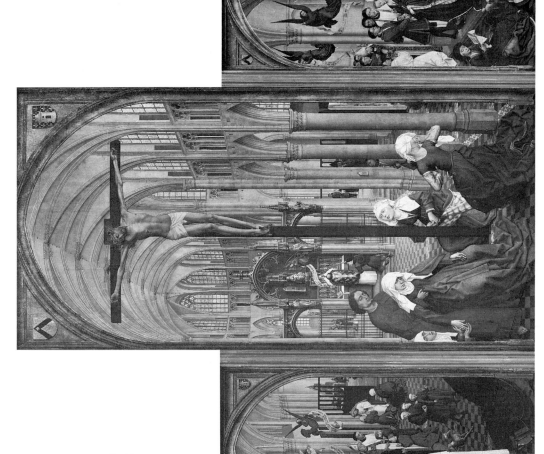

29 Roger van der Weyden and workshop (?), *Seven Sacraments Altarpiece*

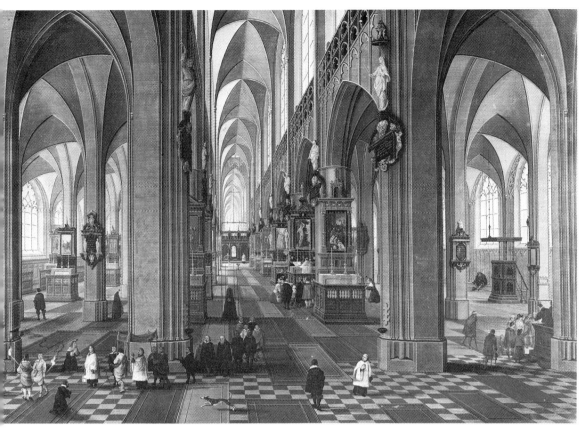

30 Peeter Neefs, *Antwerp Cathedral Interior*

to believe that, from the mid-sixteenth century on, contemporaries really had a rather straightforward and clearly defined view of what an altarpiece was – or at least should be?

Not surprisingly, the notion that later sixteenth- and seventeenth-century northern altarpieces become clearer and more straightforward in their content and use must be treated with caution, if not strongly qualified. Surely it was possible in an initial period of reform for some patrons and artists on both sides to adopt what seemed like new and relatively simple ideas about the use of imagery over Christian altars? A judicious selection of sixteenth-century works might encourage one to believe that the period's chief impulse was toward clarification of the meaning and function of altarpieces. It is equally plain that individual patrons and artists, and particular social, economic and political situations would make virtually impossible the maintenance of a single prescribed attitude toward altarpieces. Many interesting experiments in altar painting continued to be carried out by artists like Jan van Scorel and Maarten van Heemskerck.[31] Pieter Aertsen's post-1550 altarpieces could also be taken as indi-

---

[31] See especially the recent treatment of these artists in the exhibition catalogue *Kunst voor de Beeldenstorm, Noordneder-landse kunst 1525–1580*, Rijksmuseum (Amsterdam, 1986); two instructive examples discussed there are Scorel's three altarpieces executed for the Benedictine Abbey in Marchiennes *c.* 1538 (pp. 228–31, cat. nos. 109–10); and Heemskerck's 1538 two-tiered altarpiece painted for Alkmaar and now in Linköping (discussed and illustrated in the introductory text volume for the Amsterdam exhibition, pp. 68–9, figs. 109–10).

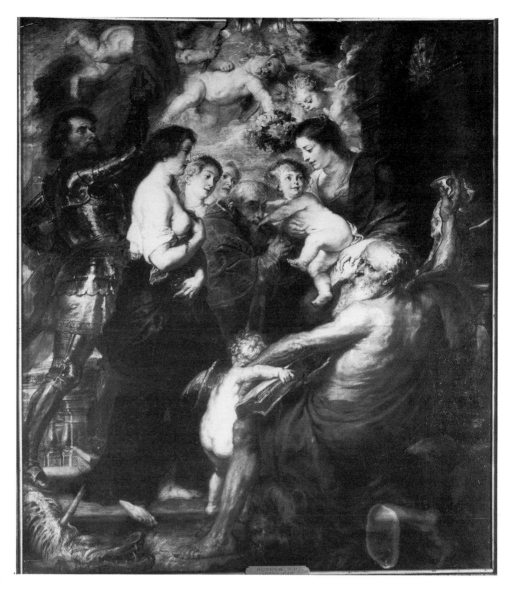

31 Pieter Paul Rubens, *Madonna and Child with Saints*

cative, covering a range of impulses both old and new, mundane and dogmatic.[32]

Moreover, the richness of reference lives on, or is alluded to, in prominent seventeenth-century examples. It may be true that many Catholic altarpieces of this time sought to proclaim the power and perseverance of the Counter-Reformation church.

[32] Examples include the Amsterdam *Adoration of the Magi* triptych fragments with many details drawn from the early Netherlandish tradition (illustrated and discussed in the Amsterdam *Beeldenstorm* catalogue (see note 31), pp. 349–51, cat. nos. 230–1); and the continued mariolatry of the Leau altarpieces of the *Seven Joys* and *Seven Sorrows of the Virgin* (discussed and illustrated by D. Kreidl, 'Die Religiöse Malerei Pieter Aertsens als Grundlage seiner Künstlersichen Entwicklung', *Jahrbuch der Kunsthistorischen Sammlungen in Wien*, 68 (n.f. 32 (1972), esp. pp. 82–8).

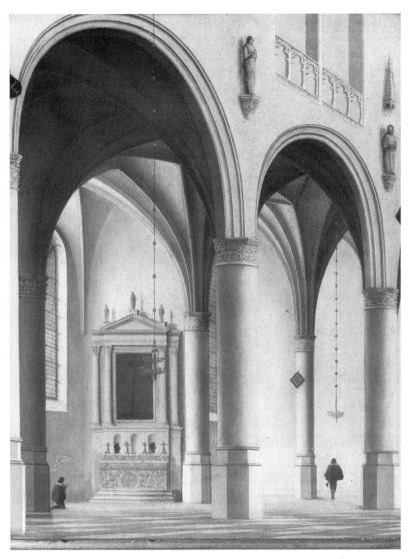

32 Pieter Saenredam, *Interior of St Lawrence's, Alkmaar*

One of the Church's great practitioners in this vein was Peter Paul Rubens. But Rubens' work can also embody a new sense of intimacy in personal devotion,[33] as well as a strong feeling for the family, the old and young, men and women, the generations together in a congenial family context. This latter quality, often taken as especially evident in Dutch Protestant imagery, is found throughout Rubens' works, but is perhaps nowhere more fully exhibited than in his painting of the *Madonna and Child with Saints* which was, by his own instructions, placed over the altar in

[33] See D. Freedberg, 'A source for Rubens's Modello of the *Assumption and Coronation of the Virgin*: a case study in the response to images', *Burlington Magazine*, 120 (1978), pp. 432–41.

the chapel where he was buried (plate 31).[34] Rubens certainly thought that altarpieces should operate on multiple levels – both personal and institutional.

On the other side of the confessional divide, Pieter Saenredam's church interior paintings are often taken as the epitome of Reformist restraint in church decoration. Yet in several of his neatly limned, recognisable if not archeologically accurate, interiors, Catholic altarpieces have been reinserted into the now Protestant edifices. And worshippers have – blasphemously, according to strict Calvinists – removed their hats as they kneel in silent prayer before the images (plate 32). Why did Saenredam introduce such seemingly antithetical details into his spare interiors? Was he being idealistic, projecting a view of simple and direct Catholic piety which might appeal even to the Dutch Protestant, and thus appealing for tolerance?[35] Or was he simply opportunistic, bowing to the wishes of an underground Catholic patron in the northern Netherlands? Probably, as was the case with many of his Dutch contemporaries, Saenredam was both idealistic and opportunistic – a combination which certainly did not foster the creation of a simple and straightforward attitude, in this case toward the use of altar paintings.

Any attempt which the Reformation or Counter-Reformation Churches made to clarify and simplify the use of altarpieces was inevitably complicated, even confused over time. And if this was the case in the sixteenth and seventeenth centuries, how much more was it true in the hundred or hundred and fifty years before and leading up to the eventual split and attempted reform? Even the fact that the initial thrust of Reform and Counter-Reform seems to have been one of clarification can, I think, legitimately lead us to conclude that earlier imagery was anything but simple and straightforward in the manner in which it dealt with the relation of the altar and the altarpiece.

I have argued that very little clear and consistent evidence survives about the meaning and function of the altarpiece in fifteenth-century northern Europe. At this point I would say further that I do not think that this is accidental: it is not simply a question of losses in the historical record, or of our inability to find or interpret the evidence in a simple or consistent fashion. Attempts have been made to interpret fifteenth-century altar paintings according to a rather narrow set of guidelines though to embody 'the attitude of the teaching church'.[36] These are inadequate to the task, I think, because the altarpiece is a much more complicated phenomenon than that point of view suggests. Numerous historical studies have shown that the Catholic Church in the fifteenth and early sixteenth centuries did not exercise the tight control over its faithful which a narrowly defined religious meaning in art would either require or suggest. Many were the complaints from the clergy about the behaviour of lay

---

[34] Rubens' painting of the *Madonna and Child with Saints* is still in the artist's burial chapel in St Jacques, Antwerp. See S. Alpers, 'A taste for Rubens', *Art in America*, 66 (1978), pp. 64–72, especially p. 72 n. 6, who refers in turn to a 1976 Master's Thesis at the University of California, Berkeley, by Celeste Brusati.

[35] Cf. E. Jane Connell's thesis, 'The Romanisation of the Gothic Arch in some paintings by Pieter Saenredam: Catholic and Protestant implications', *Rutgers Art Review*, 1 (1980), pp. 17–35. Connell's belief in Saenredam's expressive distortion of architectural features is disputed by R. Ruurs, *Saenredam: the art of perspective* (Amsterdam, 1987), p. 99, note 53.

[36] Purtle, *The Marian paintings*, p. xvi.

parishioners.[37] The large number of lay patrons for works of art, especially in Flanders, certainly suggests a more broadly based point of view.[38]

At one extreme we might therefore want to look for unorthodox, even heretical, attitudes in altarpieces. The works of Hieronymus Bosch would usually be cited in this respect. It is usually assumed that none of Bosch's works were intended for church altars; but that does not mean that they did not refer, in a critical manner, to the various unorthodox views on the sacrament of the altar then circulating in the Netherlands.[39] Some more radical proposals that Bosch had contacts with the Adamites, or was an avid follower of alchemical learning, also need to be considered seriously.[40] Bosch's imagery has proved evocative to many artists since the early sixteenth century;[41] it certainly does suggest free-thinking, if not outright heresy. He and other artists may very well have meant to refer to unorthodox ideas without being totally negative or disapproving. As is the case with Bosch's contemporary, Gerard David (plate 24), there may have been an element of wishful thinking in these artists' vision of alternative worlds or ideas.[42] Such paintings may not have been intended, from the start, to serve as public altarpieces; but the fact that artists chose a format and, often, a subject matter associated with altarpieces is important. It suggests that they or their patrons wanted to present religious ideas within a framework that was well understood and also thought to be versatile enough to accommodate original thinking or imagery.

There is much to be said for looking at altarpieces closely with a view to discovering their unofficial theological positions. This would still be only one aspect of what I believe are intentionally complex, multi-purposed creations. This may seem self-evident: such an important and widespread type of painting must have attracted,

---

[37] See especially Jacques Toussaert, *Le sentiment religieux en Flandre à la fin du moyen âge* (Paris, 1963); also in general, E. de Moreau, *Histoire de l'Eglise en Belgique*, Vol. 4, (Brussels, 1949); E. Delaruelle, E.-R. Labande and P. Ourliac, *L'Eglise au temps du Grand Schisme et de la crise conciliaire (1378–1449)* (Paris, 1964); F. Rapp, *L'Eglise et la vie religieuse en occident à la fin du moyen âge* (Paris, 1971); and J. Pelikan, *Reformation of Church and Dogma (1300–1700)* (Chicago, 1984) (esp. chapter 1, 'Doctrinal pluralism in the later Middle Ages'). For Germany, see for instance B. Möller, 'Frömmigkeit in Deutschland um 1500', *Archiv für Reformationsgeschichte*, 76 (1965), pp. 5–30 (English translation in *Pre-Reformation Germany*, ed. G. Strauss (New York, 1972) pp. 13–42).

[38] A survey of several thousand German images of the time shows the same number of lay donors as clerical (certainly a change from the Middle Ages); in Flanders the change is more dramatic: lay donors outnumber clerical by more than two to one. See C. Harbison, 'Symbol and meaning in northern European art of the late middle ages and early Renaissance: response to James Marrow', *Simiolus*, 16, (1986), esp. p. 171 and note 12.

[39] See Harbison 'Some artistic anticipations' (see note 20), esp. pp. 68–75.

[40] The classic discussion of Bosch and the Adamites is by W. Fraenger, *The millenium of Hieronymus Bosch* (Chicago, 1951); Fraenger's thesis, although disputed by almost all other scholars, is supported by P. Reuterswärd, *Hieronymus Bosch* (Stockholm, 1970). It is not true, as is often claimed, that the Adamites had died out by Bosch's time; see N. Cohn, *The pursuit of the millenium*, rev. ed. (New York, 1970), pp. 178–86. For Bosch and alchemy see most recently the series of studies by L. S. Dixon: *Alchemical imagery in Bosch's Garden of Delights*, PhD. dissertation, Boston University, 1980 (published Ann Arbor, 1982); 'Bosch's Garden of Delights Triptych: remnants of a "Fossil Science"', *Art Bulletin*, 63 (1981), pp. 96–113; 'Water, wine and blood – Science and liturgy in the *Marriage at Cana* by Hieronymus Bosch', *Oud-Holland*, 96 (1982), pp. 73–96; and 'Bosch's *St Anthony Triptych* – an apothecary's apotheosis', *Art Journal*, 44 (1984), pp. 119–31.

[41] Relevent for my purposes here is the use of doodles resembling Bosch's paintings as an enticement left by a free-love heretic in Marguerite Yourcenar's historical novel set in the mid-sixteenth century, *The Abyss*, translated from the French by G. Frick, New York, 1976.

[42] Cf. Charles De Tolnay's interpretation in *Hieronymus Bosch*, trans. M. Bullock and H. Mins (New York, 1966). Also relevant is Gerard David's *Baptism* triptych with its reference to the notion that unbaptised children might still be saved by God; this possibility is discussed in Harbison, 'Some artistic anticipations' (see note 20), pp. 79–83.

over the course of a century, many sorts of messages. My contention about the multi-faceted meaning of altarpieces is more specific than that: for a number of years, starting in the fifteenth century, altarpieces became a popular means of communication because they were perceived at the time as both versatile and multiple in their meaning, allowing them to become the records of personal religious experience in the broadest sense. This versatility did not, initially, seem like a bad thing. How is this evident in the works themselves? How can we uncover such meaning today? As the iconographical method has developed in the last fifty years, art historians have tended to assume that meaning in Renaissance imagery could be uncovered with the use of learned contemporary texts. More recently it has become apparent that we can and should expand our concept of a painting's reference system. A image can certainly shape and/or reflect the time in which it was produced in many ways – not only by encoding bookish philosophical discussion into disguised symbols. How do what we see in a painting – physical relationships, temporal, spatial and emotional relationships, objects, textures, portrayed effects of light and colour – lead us on, to speculate on further meaning and intention?

We should always be alert to the vitality of fifteenth-century altarpieces in dealing with basic human issues of sexuality and, in particular, marriage. In Italian art, Michael Taylor has suggested the way images from the life of St Nicholas might relate to contemporary problems in providing women's dowries;[43] while Diane Owens Hughes has probed the purposes of family portraits, including donor portraits on northern altarpieces.[44] In general terms, the studies of a social historian like Natalie Zemon Davis might prove useful in alerting art historians to possible social/sexual inroads into visual thinking.[45] In the case of northern altarpieces, it is perhaps not accidental that Roger van der Weyden was favoured in commissions given by women or particularly important to them;[46] while for Jan van Eyck's surviving work we find only male patrons, and this despite the fact that van Eyck's imagery is largely devoted to the Virgin Mary. Wary of exaggerating such a distinction, we still might consider more fully the way these artists' appeal to contemporaries could have been distinguished along gender lines.

Many years ago, Meyer Schapiro made initial observations on the issue of sexuality in the Mérode Triptych (plate 33);[47] subsequently, Jozef de Coo connected the work

[43] See M. D. Taylor, 'Gentile da Fabriano, St Nicholas and an inconography of shame', *Journal of Family History*, 7 (1982), pp. 321–32.

[44] See D. O. Hughes, 'Representing the family: portraits and purposes in early modern Italy', *Journal of Interdisciplinary History*, 17 (1986), pp. 7–38, esp. pp. 15–18 (with further references).

[45] See the collection of Davis' essays, *Society and Culture in Early Modern France* (Stanford, 1975); and especially her paper 'Some tasks and themes in the study of popular religion', in C. Trinkaus and H. A. Oberman, eds., *The pursuit of holiness in late medieval and Renaissance religion*, (Leiden, 1974), pp. 207–36. The essays of Christine Klapisch-Zuber are important for Italian art in a similar way: *Women, family and ritual in Renaissance Italy*, trans. L. Cochrane (Chicago, 1985).

[46] I am thinking here of the Braque triptych, probably commissioned by Catherine de Braque (for which see S. N. Blum, *Early Netherlandish triptychs: a study in patronage* (Berkeley, 1969), chapter 3, pp. 29–36); and the Beaune *Last Judgement*, part of a hospital patronage extremely important to Nicolas Rolin's wife, Guigone de Salins (for this see N. Veronee-Verhaegen, *L'Hotel Dieu de Beaune*, Les primitifs flamands, Corpus de la peinture, 13 (Brussels, 1973), esp. pp. 48–50).

[47] See Schapiro, '"Muscipula Diaboli"' (note 7 above), esp. pp. 185–7.

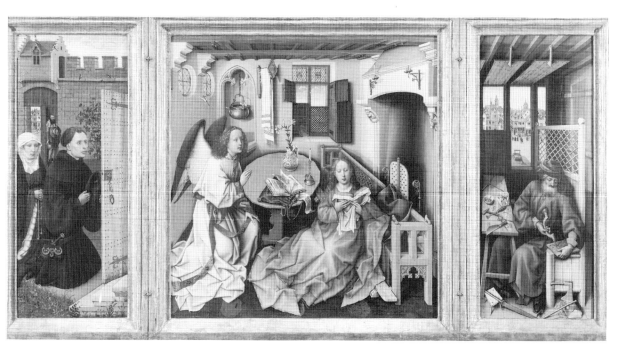

33 Robert Campin, *Mérode Triptych*

with the couple's desire for offspring and more recently Cynthia Hahn has presented an interpretation of it as a full-blown theological discussion of the family.[48] These are appealing speculations, especially in light of the obvious personal nature of the triptych, which has also made Hahn reluctant to call it an altarpiece. Uncovering such meaning in these works may seem to necessitate, at least for the moment, their change from 'altarpiece' to 'triptych' status. That is largely a temporary technical problem, since I do not think that in the long run it will seem that such meanings are improbable in public altarpieces.

In a more purely religious sphere, there are also many ways that we might open up our investigations of these works. Certainly these images can be fruitfully related to the ceremonies, especially that regarding the Eucharist, that took place on the altars beneath them.[49] But as Henk van Os points out in chapter 1 of this volume, altarpieces are not ideal liturgical objects;[50] unlike ciboria, they were not created

[48] See J. de Coo, 'A medieval look at the Mérode Annunciation', *Zeitschrift für Kunstgeschichte*, 44 (1981), pp. 114–32; and C. Hahn, ' ''Joseph will perfect, Mary enlighten and Jesus save thee'': the Holy Family as marriage model in the Mérode Triptych', *Art Bulletin*, 67 (1986), pp. 54–66.
[49] See the references cited in note 5 above.
[50] See pp. 25–7 of this volume.

for a closely defined liturgical purpose.[51] Artists, patrons and viewers did not always follow traditional church teachings with regard to the liturgy. Lay men and women were obsessed during the fifteenth century with the notion of the Real Presence of Christ in the eucharistic wafer, a vision of the miracle of transubstantiation which did not necessitate partaking of the physical elements of the sacrament itself. It was enough to see the blessed transformed host which had miraculously become the body of Christ. This phenomenon, already chronicled by social and religious historians,[52] has recently been implicated in the study of art in different ways by Leo Steinberg and Carolyn Bynum.[53] Steinberg's male/sexual perspective and Bynum's female/sacramental one may come together in some of the altarpieces of Flemish painters,[54] especially in some of the paintings of Jan van Eyck. In van Eyck the minutely detailed sexuality of the Christ Child is offered to donor and/or spectator by the red-robed priest/altar/Virgin. The Chancellor Rolin's dramatic personal vision is not a mere symbol of the sacrament of communion: the Chancellor has a vision of the body of Christ, its sexuality and humanity, which penetrates the symbolism of the ritual by means of a potent vision of physical reality (plate 34).[55] It might also be noted that at this climactic moment the Chancellor does not have a sign of his earthly wealth, his money bag, hanging at his side. Although initially planned, that is an element in the painting which was apparently deemed unnecessary, perhaps indecorous, in the final product.[56] Here certainly are all the makings of a complex personal narrative.

Participating in the sacrament of the altar is in such works embedded in the wider perspective of lay prayers and meditations, imitating saints and holy figures, and even, if necessary, conflicting with learned advisers.[57] Just as paintings not found over an altar can refer to things which might take place there,[58] so altarpieces can and do allude to a range of religious activities taking place beyond the confines of the altar precinct. Many donors of altarpieces are shown piously fingering rosary

---

[51] In attempting to document a liturgical purpose for the development of the winged altarpiece in Germany, Donald Ehresmann concludes that 'the variety of liturgical purpose served by [the] early winged altarpieces ... reflects the extensive freedom allowed by the late medieval Church in liturgical matters'; see D. Ehresmann, 'Some observations on the role of liturgy in the early winged altarpiece', Art Bulletin, 64 (1982), pp. 359–69, esp. p. 368.

[52] See for instance P. Browe, Die Eucharistischen Wunder des Mittelalters (Breslau, 1938); Browe, Die Verehrung der Eucharistie im Mittelalter (Rome, 1967); and Toussaert, Le sentiment religieux (see note 37), esp. 122–204.

[53] L. Steinberg, The Sexuality of Christ in Renaissance Art and Modern Oblivion, New York (1983); and C. W. Bynum, 'The body of Christ in the later Middle Ages: a reply to Leo Steinberg', Renaissance Quarterly, 39 (1986), pp. 399–439.

[54] Paintings which might be mentioned in this connection include the Aix-en-Provence Madonna in Glory attributed to Robert Campin; Roger van der Weyden's Bladelin triptych (Berlin); and Hugo van der Goes' Portinari altarpiece and Berlin Nativity.

[55] Scholarly literature on the Rolin Madonna is voluminous; among the works which might be mentioned are J. Snyder, 'Jan van Eyck and the Madonna of Chancellor Nicolas Rolin ', Oud-Holland, 82 (1967), pp. 163–71; and H. Adhémar, 'Sur la Vierge du Chancelier Rolin de Van Eyck', Bulletin de l'Institut Royal du Patrimoine Artistique, Bruxelles, 15 (1975), pp. 9–17.

[56] See E. Dhanens, Hubert and Jan Van Eyck (New York, n.d.), esp. p. 279 and fig. 173 (p. 276).

[57] See Harbison 'Visions' (as in note 15). An important study of this topos in late medieval art is F. O. Büttner, Imitatio Pietatis, Motive der christlichen ikonographie als Modelle zur Verähnlichung (Berlin, 1983) with an impressive corpus of illustrations.

[58] See for instance the Calvary of Hendrik van Rijn, reproduced and discussed by P. Vandenbroeck, Catalogus Schilderijen 14e en 15e Eeuw, Koninklijk Museum voor Schone Kunsten, Antwerpen (Antwerp, 1985), pp. 25–8 (no. 519). The inscription at the bottom of the panel states that van Rijn founded 'that altar (over there)' and that the spectator should 'pray for him'.

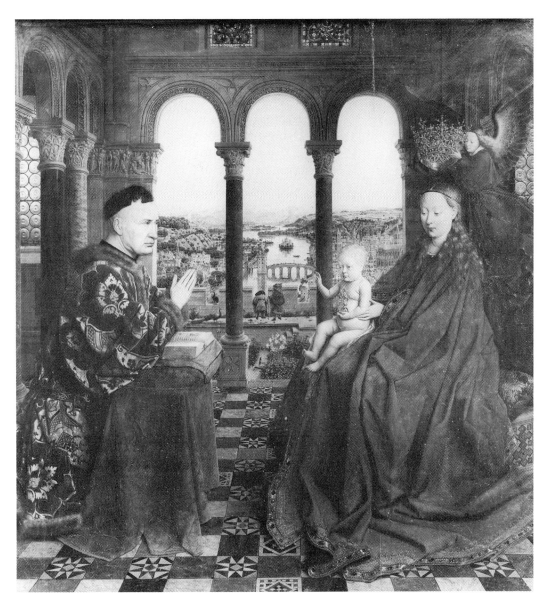

34 Jan van Eyck, *Nicolas Rolin Adoring the Virgin*

beads or reading in prayer books, as in Roger van der Weyden's *Columba* altarpiece (Munich, Alte Pinakothek). These lay people can be understood as carrying out the pious duties imposed upon them by priests during penance or confession. The growing emphasis on confession and penitential rites at this time has been chronicled by historians;[59] it should equally be correlated with the portrayed habits of the altarpieces' patrons.

Pilgrimage and procession were an important part of fifteenth-century religious life. Richard Trexler has shown how these and other popular religious rites activated interest in religious imagery in Renaissance Italy.[60] The same could be done in northern Europe. Jan van Eyck was sent on a pilgrimage by the Duke of Burgundy;[61] the duke himself visited the miracle-working image of the Virgin at Notre-Dame de Boulonge at least thirteen times during his life.[62] Roger van der Weyden went on a jubilee year (1450) pilgrimage to Rome;[63] and Tournai authorities sentenced Robert Campin to make an expiatory pilgrimage to Saint-Gilles in Provence.[64] In past scholarship these pilgrimages have been studied for the stylistic impact they might have had on the artists' careers.[65] They must have had an impact on artists' religious attitudes as well. Already a popular form of religious activity, pilgrimages could be and were, increasingly in the fifteenth century, carried out in the mind.[66] In effect, one journeyed mentally to the holy site and experienced the final vision of the miraculous image in one's imagination. This process might help us understand the impact and use of some contemporary imagery. The painting over the altar might

[59] See H. Lea, *A history of auricular confession and indulgences in the Latin Church*, vol. 2 (Philadelphia, 1896); P. Michaud-Quantin, *Sommes de Casuistique et manuels de Confession au moyen age (xii-xvi siècles)* (Louvain, 1962); T. C. Price Zimmerman, 'Confession and autobiography in the early Renaissance', *Renaissance Studies in Honor of Hans Baron*, ed. A. N. Molho and J. Tedeschi, (Dekalb IL, 1971), pp. 123–40; T. N. Tentler, *Sin and confession on the eve of the Reformation* (Princeton, 1977); L. G. Duggan, 'Fear and confession on the eve of the Reformation', *Archiv für Reformationsgeschichte*, 75 (1984), pp. 153–75; and in general, Toussaert *Le sentiment* (see note 37) pp. 104–22; and J. Bossy, 'The social history of confession in the age of the Reformation', *Transactions of the Royal Historical Society, London*, 5th series, 25 (1975), pp. 21–38.

[60] See R. C. Trexler, 'Florentine religious experience: the sacred image', *Studies in the Renaissance*, 19 (1972), pp. 7–41.

[61] See W. H. J. Weale, *Hubert and John van Eyck, their life and work* (London, 1908), xxxi–xxxii, document of 26 August 1426.

[62] See A Benoit, 'Les pèlerinages de Philippe le Bon à Notre-Dame de Boulogne', *Bulletin de la Société d'Etudes de la Province de Cambrai*, 37 (1937), pp. 119–23.

[63] See for instance T. H. Feder, 'A reexamination through documents of the first fifty years of Roger van der Weyden's life', *Art Bulletin*, 48 (1966), esp. p. 430.

[64] See for instance M. Davies, *Roger van der Weyden* (London, 1972), p. 191; and in general for Campin's biography, P. H. Schabacker, 'Notes on the biography of Robert Campin', *Mededelingen van de Koninklijke Academie voor Wetenschappen, Letteren en Schone Kunsten van België, Klasse der Schone Kunsten*, 41 (1980), no. 2, pp. 3–14. For judicially rendered pilgrimages such as Campin's, see in general Etienne van Cauwenbergh, *Les Pèlerinages expiatoires et judiciaires dans le droit communal de la Belgique au moyen âge* (Louvain, 1922).

[65] For Roger, see P. H. Jolly, 'Rogier van der Weyden's Escorial and Philadephia *Crucifixions* and their relation to Fra Angelico at San Marco', *Oud-Holland*, 95 (1981), pp. 113–26; also A.M. Schultz, 'The Columba Altarpiece and Roger van der Weyden's stylistic development', *Münchner Jahrbuch der Bildenden Kunst*, ser. 3, 22 (1971), pp. 63–116. For Campin, see G. Troescher, 'Die Pilgerfahrt des Robert Campin, Altniederländische und Südwestdeutsche Maler in Südostfrankreich', *Jahrbuch der Berliner Museen*, 9 (1967), pp. 100–34; with corrections by C. Sterling, 'Etudes Savoyardes I: Au temps du duc Amedée,' *L'Oeil*, 178 (October 1969), pp. 2–13.

[66] See J. Sumption, *Pilgrimage, an image of medieval religion* (London, 1975), esp. pp. 257–302; B. Dansette, ''Les pèlerinages occidentaux en Terre Sainte: une pratique de la 'Devotion Moderne' à la fin du Moyen Age? Relation inedite d'un pèlerinage effectué en 1488'', *Archivum Franciscanum Historicum*, 72 (1979), pp. 106–33, 330–428; and J. van Herwaarden, 'Geloof en geloofsuitingen in de late middeleeuwen in de Nederlanden: Jerusalembedevaarten, lijdensdevotie en kruiswegverering', *Bijdragen en Mededelingen betreffende de geschiedenis der Nederlanden*, 98 (1983), pp. 400–29; and in general Toussaert, *Le sentiment* (as in note 37), pp. 267–79.

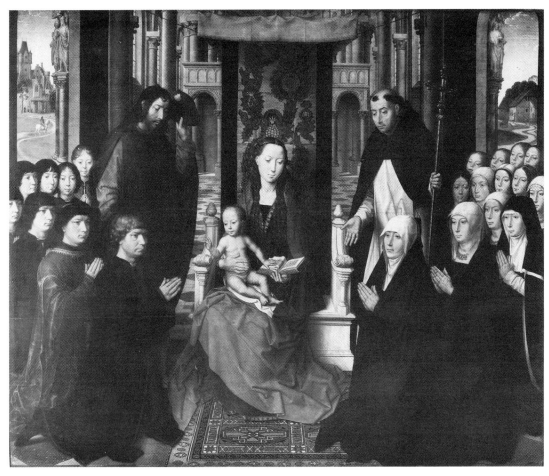

35 Hans Memling, *Virgin and Child with Jacob Floreins, his family and Saints James and Dominic*

very well be meant to stimulate the viewer to enact a mental pilgrimage or remember the results of a real one (plate 35).[67]

Only one important early Netherlandish panel painter – Roger van der Weyden – ever portrayed the contemporary enactment of the sacrament of the altar.[68] In

[67] This might also be an interesting way to interpret the fact that in some copies of van Eyck's *Madonna in a church* the donor is placed in a landscape (see Purtle, *The Marian paintings*, fig. 66: version by Jan Gossaert). Here the landscape can be seen as a reference to the physical experience of a pilgrimage, while the image of the Virgin is the equivalent of the miracle-working icon/sculpture found at the pilgrim's destination, the ecclesiastical shrine. Compare the elaborate interpretation of fifteenth-/and sixteenth-century northern landscapes as representing a pilgrimage ideal by R. L. Falckenburg, *Joachim Patinir: the landscape as an image of the pilgrimage of life* (Amsterdam, 1988). Other fifteenth-century works which might be usefully related to the notion of pilgrimage visions include: the Aix-en-Provence *Madonna in Glory* attributed to Robert Campin; Roger van der Weyden's Florence *Entombment*; an *Adoration* scene like that on the Boutsian Pearl of Brabant triptych in Munich; and Hugo van der Goes' Portinari altarpiece.

[68] I am excluding here archetypal or non-historical representations of the sacrament, such as the Mass of St Gregory, found in fifteenth-century panels by or around such artists as Robert Campin (version in Brussels, Musées Royaux des Beaux-Arts, inv. no. 6298), discussed and illustrated in the Detroit exhibition catalogue (as in note 18), pp. 84–7, cat. no. 10. Another interesting example of this theme executed by a Utrecht artist *c.* 1460 shows a crucifixion in the central panel, St Christopher on the right wing, and the Mass of St Gregory on the left; now in the Centraal Museum, Utrecht (illustrated in Friedländer, *Early Netherlandish painting*, vol. 3 (Leiden, 1968), no. 38, pl. 56).

Roger's unique *Seven Sacraments* altarpiece, a propagandistic work executed for the beleaguered bishop of Tournai,[69] we see a contemporary layman assisting at the centrally placed, and centrally important, communion ceremony (plate 29). In addition, inscribed banderoles contain various Biblical and patristic passages justifying the Church's sacramental theology. Banderoles and other inscriptions are found occasionally throughout fifteenth-century northern art, in panels and in reproductive works such as woodcuts and engravings;[70] never to my knowledge do they tie a painting directly and specifically to ceremonies performed on the altar in front of the panel.[71] (It is curious to note that inscriptions on non-altar paintings *can* refer specifically to the altar.[72]) It does seem an odd disclaimer – for altar paintings not to take advantage of such an opportunity to be literally altar-related. In the case of some early Flemish works, like Roger's Bladelin triptych in Berlin, we know that inscribed banderoles were contemplated, only to be painted out as the work progressed.[73] This process certainly does not suggest a general desire to correlate imagery and particular Church ceremony or theology. Rather, the absence of banderoles/inscriptions allows the meaning of the work to become less attached to any one passage or exegesis, less restricted and more open in its thrust.[74]

Fifteenth-century northern European culture demanded a flexible means of artistic expression. The period witnessed constant social change. A bourgeois middle-class rose to prominence and made increasing demands on artists.[75] Philip the Good, Duke of Burgundy, drew from this group to create a powerful and influential new bureaucracy. These courtly functionaries can be credited with consistent promotion

---

[69] See the references in note 29 above. Even this focused, didactic image can tell a complex story: for instance, about the bishop of Tournai (see Koslow, *The Chevrot Altarpiece* (as in note 29); about the inclusion of assorted contemporary portraits (see R. H. Marijnissen and G. van de Voorde, 'Een onverklaarde Werkwijze van de Vlaamse Primitieven, Aantekeningen bij het werk van Joos van Wassenhove, Hugo van der Goes, Rogier van der Weyden and Hans Memling', *Mededelingen van de Koninklijke Academie voor Wetenschappen, Letteren en Schone Kunsten van België, Klasse der Schone Kunsten*, 44 (1983), no. 2, pp. 41–51); and about social prerogatives in an ecclesiastical setting (see Vandenbroeck, *Cataglous* (as in note 58), pp. 153–8).

[70] See L. Lebeer, 'Le dessin, le gravure, le livre xylographique et typographique', in *Bruxelles au XVe Siècle* (Brussels, 1953), pp. 187–217 for an introduction to this topic.

[71] Here I take issue with the implications of Barbara Lane's work to the effect that there is, in early Netherlandish art, some direct reference from image to liturgy; see *The altar and the altarpiece*, esp. chapter 3, 'The Eucharistic Rite and the Easter Liturgy' and the references to other studies contained there.

[72] See for instance the *Calvary* of Hendrik van Rijn referred to in note 58 above.

[73] See R. Grosshans, 'Infrarotuntersuchungen zum Studium der Unterzeichnungen auf den Berliner Altären von Roger van der Weyden', *Jahrbuch Preussischer Kulturbesitz*, 19 (1985), pp. 137–77, esp. pp. 154ff. The presumably Spanish copy of Roger's work in the Metropolitan Museum in New York preserves the original design with banderoles; see T. Rousseau, 'A Flemish altarpiece from Spain', *Metropolitan Museum of Art Bulletin*, 9 (1950), pp. 270–83.

[74] I do not think that over the course of the fifteenth century there is a consistent enough move away from banderoles to say that the overriding impulse was to become more realistic, that the banderoles were felt to interfere with the panels' creation of a convincing illusion. There are in general too many qualifications on early Flemish panels' realism for that development to be seen as a totally determining force. In the case of banderoles, some other considerations, such as that connected with achieving a more generalised meaning, must have played a part in their elimination. See also note 79 below.

[75] See the interesting if somewhat extreme interpretation of B. Zülicka-Laube, 'Die "flandrische Manier" und die Eindeckung der bürgerlichen Welt der Städte', *Wissenschaftliche Zeitschrift der Karl-Marz-Universität Leipzig*, 12 (1963), pp. 429–44. L. Campbell, 'The art market in the Southern Netherlands in the fifteenth century', *Burlington Magazine*, 118 (1976), pp. 188–98, esp. pp. 192–3, published a document in which a patron ordered a work with details to be executed in the manner found in homes of the local bourgeoisie.

of early Flemish panel painting (see plate 23).[76] Still recovering from the time of the Avignon papacy, the Catholic Church continued to be faced by a crisis pitting Pope against council. In the midst of these tensions in Church leadership, the lay population was encouraged to broaden and deepen its own ideas of personal religious experience. Civic organisations – guilds and confraternities – were important political forces, as well as patrons of the arts. The economic situation of many potential patrons was good, but clearly not equal to that of the old nobility or clerical elite. In many cases, these latter groups continued to favour works of art executed in materials more costly than oils – gold, silver or tapestry.[77] But, for the majority of middle- and upper-middle class patrons, panel painting, and in particular altarpieces, seemed the appropriate artistic medium. These were also the patrons for whom a sense of self, worldly and eternal fame, was a new experience, and one to be celebrated with visual means.

Altarpieces provided a versatile means of expression to satisfy simultaneously a great number of needs and demands. The perfection of the northern oil glaze tech- nique allowed the illusionistic incorporation of almost any material substance into a panel-enamelwork, glass, metal, tapestry and, of course, stone or wood sculpture. The framework of painted images, the variety of shapes and sizes, the number of panels which could be incorporated into a single whole, made them effective in many ways. Different types of objects from different environments could be specified by patrons; such objects could clearly have multiple meanings for the individual and the society for which they were produced. Painted environments could unite different times in the same space. Such visionary worlds could also be produced by emotional expression of uncanny psychological depth. Altarpieces in the fifteenth century were almost constantly being called upon to do something new or different, to test the limits of decorum in religious art which they inherited.[78] There are images which direct the viewer solely to adore the host presented in a monstrance (see plate 36), thereby accepting an institutional definition of religious faith.[79] The restlessness of religious/social/economic and political boundaries at the time did not often favour such a device. Rather, altarpieces became a prime forum for the experimental appro- priation of ideas from one aspect of society to another, from one aspect of one's life to another.

---

[76] On the functionaries in general, see the important work of J. Bartier, *Legistes et gens de finances au XVe siècle, les conseillers des ducs de Bourgogne Philippe le Bon et Charles le Téméraire* (Brussels, 1955); and P. Kauch, 'L'apparition d'un nouveau groupe social aux Pays-Bas bourgignons: celui des fonctionnaires', *Revue de l'Institut de Sociologie Solvay*, 15 (1935), pp. 122–9. For the interest of these individuals in the visual arts, see Bartier, esp, pp. 27–82; and W. Blockmans and W. Prevenier, *The Burgundian Netherlands* (Cambridge, 1986), pp. 328–9.

[77] For an interesting case of this phenomenon, see Duke Charles the Bold's gift of a gold reliquary of himself and St George (in imitation of van Eyck's painted van der Paele *Madonna*) to the city of Liège after the duke had pillaged the town and slaughtered many of its inhabitants; discussed and reproduced in the Detroit catalogue referred to in note 18 above, pp. 298–300, cat. no. 133 (with colour illustration).

[78] One might make an analogy here with Mikhail Bakhtin's concept of the novel, the literary form which is meant to reveal the limits of the genre, which is always stretching the limits of convention and understanding placed upon it by a previous generation. See for instance, M. Bakhtin, *Problems of Dostoevsky's Poetics*, ed. and trans. C. Emerson (Minneapolis, 1984).

[79] The inscribed banderoles in this work hail the host as source of life and truth through which all offerings are completed; see Vandenbroeck, *Catalogus* (as in note 58), pp. 35–8 (no. 224).

The preceding two paragraphs present a large number of only partially justified generalisations. Not least among these is the notion that it is altarpieces in particular which respond to the need for a novelistic and personal form of visual expression. Does the need for artistic versatility have something to do with the altarpiece in particular? The answer seems to be both yes and no. Yes, in the sense that the sacrament acted out at the altar was crucial both theologically and as an artistic reference point. (There are a relatively small number of fifteenth-century religious images which do not make some reference to Christ's sacrificial mission.) Yes also in the sense that the altarpiece is the most elaborate movable form of Christian art produced at the time, and therefore the most physically capable of telling a complex story. And yes in the way that a crucial component of contemporary thinking about art was the patron's wish to appropriate or assume various public *personae* (see plates 34 and 35). But no, individual stories might still be told most fully in the arena of a private work of art.

No one has yet produced a systematic study of all fifteenth-century works that we know were intended from the start as altarpieces, trying to determine exactly what these documented altarpieces were doing and how they were accomplishing it. It is perhaps all too easy, as I have to some extent done here, to mingle demonstrable altarpieces together with works that may only distantly, if deliberately, refer to the altar and the altarpiece.[80] The evidence we have does not suggest that such a functionally restricted survey would produce conclusive results about attitudes toward the altarpiece; nevertheless it should be undertaken. And until it is done we must recognise that present generalisations may need eventually to be revised.

Study of a representative corpus of fifteenth-century northern religious paintings does suggest that about half are public, in most cases altar, paintings, and the other half, private devotional works, which in a few cases may have hung over house altars.[81] Significantly, these two groups of paintings seem at this point equally interesting and novel in the way that they deal with content and ideas, in the way that they inevitably present complex personal stories about contemporary morals and manners. At present it would be very difficult to attribute either to the altar panel, or to the private devotional image, the decisive or exclusive power of inspiration or purpose which characterises the period as a whole. Time and again we find this to be true in northern religious art: in the use of terminology, preparatory designs, overall content or meaning, the art seems for the most part intentionally fluid, non-specific. One has the feeling that a lack of easy categorisation is itself significant.

All art may eventually submit to multiple interpretations, or be shown to result from multiple sources of inspiration. Fifteenth-century northern religious art is more specifically and intentionally multiple in its message, however, than that generalisation implies. It is not just a matter of there being a variety of impulses behind successive

---

[80] This is a problem pointed out by C. Purtle in her review of Lane, *The altar and the altarpiece*, in *Art Bulletin*, 69 (1987), esp. p. 652.

[81] Here again I am to some extent depending on illustrations in the English translation of Friedländer's *Early Netherlandish painting* and Stange's *Deutsche Malerei der Gotik* (see above notes 15 and 29).

images; but that within any one image there is both subtlety and openness to a variety of meanings, simultaneous and intentional diversity of motive. It was important to relate experience, not yet to define controversial issues or dogma. This was a time before the divisive distillation of views found to some extent in the sixteenth century (and which certainly affected some of the art produced then), a time before the Protestant Reform and Catholic Counter-Reform became bent on crushing their own more liberal and experimental wings. The challenge which fifteenth-century northern European altarpieces present to historians is one that we rarely accept. We are too likely to look for a single, specific meaning for an apparently specific form of art; or, if other meanings seem to arise, to see the way they become supposedly separate, discrete categories of art in their turn. But perhaps the object was *not* to separate out the various strands of meaning found in a fifteenth-/or early sixteenth-century altarpiece – but to observe their fertile interaction. Discovering that original heterogeneity in the early modern period may help us unravel some of the cultural cliches which we have, at times unconsciously, inherited.[82]

[82] This chapter is dedicated to Bob Koch on his retirement.

4 *The Netherlandish carved altarpiece c. 1500: type and function*

Kim Woods

During the fifteenth and early sixteenth centuries, Netherlandish carved wooden altarpieces were popular works of art, in considerable demand both at home and abroad. Although about 300 of these altarpieces survive, very few are dated or documented. Fewer still may be identified with any certainty as products of less prolific centres of altarpiece production, such as Ghent. The original functions of the altarpieces have never been satisfactorily explored, and the reasons for their popularity are unclear. From the mid-fifteenth century to the mid-sixteenth century, carved wooden altarpieces are occasionally represented in Netherlandish paintings, manuscript illuminations and prints. These representations, although never very numerous, provide a valuable insight into altarpiece type and function, and it is from this specific source that this chapter derives its information.

Some altarpieces appearing in visual sources seem to have been flights of fancy on the part of the artists. Others are identifiable as archaic rather than contemporary altarpieces, or more recent but still old-fashioned types. For these reasons visual representations of carved altarpieces serve only to confirm rather than prove conclusively the date or authenticity of an altarpiece type, or indeed the date of the source in which they appear. Many representations could be of painted rather than carved altarpieces. The indications that an altarpiece was intended to be carved rather than painted are firstly the illusion of three dimensions which, unfortunately, is seldom very marked; secondly the representation of three-dimensional architectural tracery above the scenes, invariably a vital component of a carved altarpiece but not a painted one; and thirdly the brown and gold colouring. Just as in grisaille paintings artists represented unpainted stone statues that would in fact have been coloured, so they represented carved altarpieces, which would invariably have been polychromed, as unpolychromed wood with only gilded decoration. Those altarpiece representations securely identifiable as carved are very often to be found in paintings, manuscript illuminations or prints with an ecclesiastical theme such as the mass, consecration scenes or the Vision of St Gregory, but also occasionally in coronation scenes. Unlike paintings or individual carved images, carved altarpieces are never illustrated in a domestic setting, except in a private chapel.

Among the altarpiece representations which obviously relate to surviving altarpiece types is the inverted T shaped altarpiece in a painting entitled the *Adoration of the Holy Sacrament* (plate 36) by an anonymous painter almost certainly from Brussels,

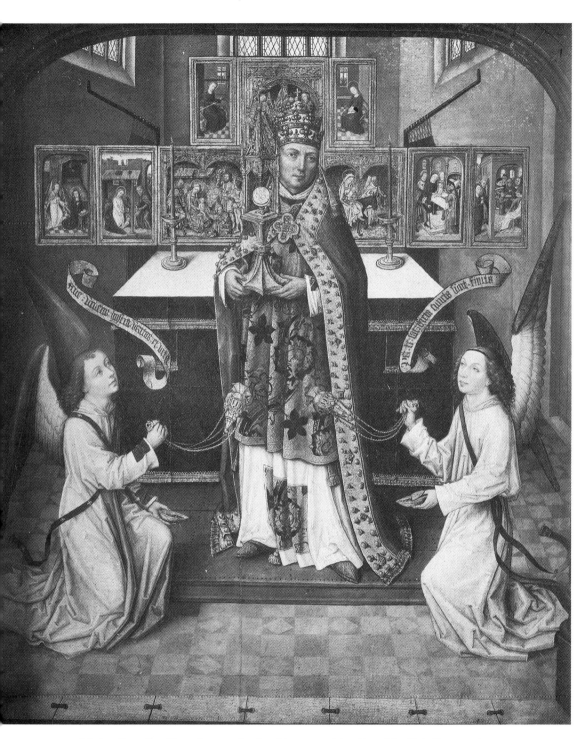

36 Attributed to Vrancke van der Stockt group, *Adoration of the Holy Sacrament*

and datable to the 1480s.[1] Here the monstrance is displayed by a Pope attended by two angels swinging censers and dressed in albs. The altarpiece stands fully open on the altar behind, displaying scenes from the Infancy of Christ: the Annunciation and Nativity on the painted shutters to the left, the Adoration of the Magi and the Flight into Egypt in the lateral carved scenes and the Presentation in the Temple and the Child Christ in the Temple with the Doctors of the Law on the right painted shutters. All that may be seen of the central section is the figure of God the Father with two angels, suggesting that the hidden scene was perhaps the Death and Assumption of the Virgin.[2] The altarpiece serves to confirm the Brussels authorship of the painting, for the scenes recall Rogier van der Weyden's Columba and Baldelin triptychs (Munich, Alte Pinakothek and Berlin, Dahlem Museum), while the format of the altarpiece clearly resembles Brussels carved altarpieces such as the Nativity altarpiece in the Musée Departemental, Rouen, *c.* 1480, or the Passion altarpiece in the church of St Dymphna, Geel, *c.* 1490, which also demonstrates the impact of Rogier's designs, particularly in the *Descent from the Cross*.[3] The carved body of the altarpiece in the painting completely fills the width of the altar, the wings extending beyond; the curtains drawn back behind the wings could be extended to enclose the altar precinct when the altarpiece was closed.

The altarpiece representation is as significant for its function as for its type and setting. The artist has represented the climax of the ceremony of the Benediction, the display of the monstrance; inscriptions on the banners held by the angels proclaim the living host and the complete sacrifice of Christ. The altarpiece so prominently displayed tracing the infancy of Christ is evidently intended to complement and augment the liturgical ceremony.

A second carved altarpiece appears in the miniature representing a mass scene, f. 9 of the *Traité sur l'oraison dominicale* for Philip the Good, dating from 1457–67 (Brussels, Bibliothèque Royale, ms. 9092).[4] Philip the Good kneels at a prie-dieu adjacent to an altar on which stands a poorly drawn altarpiece of the inverted T shape with scenes of Christ carrying the Cross, the Crucifixion and the Descent from the Cross. As Delaissé observed, the representation of three dimensions, or indeed of spatial recession, was not the artist's strong point, but the altarpiece is apparently intended to be carved rather than of metal as Delaissé believed. The altarpiece type is similar to that of the *Adoration of the Holy Sacrament*, and is comparable to Brussels altarpieces such as the one from Rieden (Stuttgart, Landesmuseum) and a second from the House of the Poor Clares, Megen, Brabant (East Berlin, Staatliche Museen),

[1] P. Vandenbroek *Catalogus schilderijen 14e en 15e eeuw* (Antwerp, 1985), pp. 35–8, no. 224, fig. 19.

[2] Surviving Nativity altarpieces with a central Death of the Virgin scene include the Antwerp altarpiece in the Leonarduskirche, Frankfurt; the Antwerp altarpiece formerly in the church at Ophoven, West Germany; and the altarpiece in the Victoria and Albert Museum in London.

[3] R. H. Randall, 'A Flemish altarpiece made for France', *Journal of the Walters Art Gallery*, xxxiii (1970–71), p. 17, fig. 8; *Flanders in the fifteenth century* exhibition catalogue, Detroit Institute of Arts (1960), pp. 240–4, nos. 74–7.

[4] The text of the treatise was translated for Philip the Good in 1457, and it was presumably complete by 1467, the date of the Duke's death; see L. M. J. Delaissé, *Miniatures medievales* (Brussels, 1959), plate 40

both of which may date from the same period.[5] Although the altarpiece has small painted upper shutters, oddly there are no large wings; instead the altarpiece is framed by the altar curtains, which are drawn, forcing a bystander to peep round them in order to observe the scene. In this miniature the association between the scenes from the Passion of Christ in the altarpiece and the death of Christ as commemorated in the mass celebrated at the altar is clear.

The altarpiece which appears in the *Mass of St Gregory* after the Master of Flémalle (versions Brussels, Musées des Beaux-Arts and New York, Aquavella Galleries)[6] has also been thought to be gilded metal, but judging by the altarpiece format and the complex tracery it appears more likely that the artist intended it to be carved. Here the altarpiece contains five scenes: Christ before Pilate, the Flagellation, the Crucifixion, Entombment and Resurrection. There are no shutters, and again the work is framed by drawn curtains. Although there are many examples of comparable altarpieces dating from *c.* 1480, such as the Passion altarpiece probably made in Brussels now in the town hospital of Stassfurt, East Germany,[7] there are none from before *c.* 1440 when the original painting was presumably done. Nevertheless, the extant carved stone altarpiece carved by Claus de Werve for Bessy-les-Citeaux in 1430 with seven carved scenes, and documentary evidence such as the contract for a carved altarpiece containing eight scenes for Flines Abbey in 1448[8] are evidence that a more complex carved altarpiece was being produced earlier in the century; this suggests that the altarpiece here may have been devised by the Master of Flémalle from a current type. The altarpiece is again associated with the mass, here the ceremony which produced a vision of Christ.

Several prominent representations of carved altarpieces contain not narrative scenes but images. Although altarpieces early in the fifteenth century followed this format, for example the altarpiece in the Reinoldikirche, Dortmund, of *c.* 1420,[9] this type forms only a tiny minority among surviving works later in the century. The Savigny altarpiece in Trier Cathedral, dated 1493, comprises five statues within an inverted T shaped frame.[10] A mediocre artist might have chosen to represent a non-narrative altarpiece rather than a narrative one because it was easier to draw; nevertheless, the frequency with which the non-narrative format occurs in visual sources suggests that artists may instead have been recording a type which in fact persisted throughout the fifteenth century.

Probably the best-known representation of a non-narrative carved altarpiece is the one appearing in the central section of the *Seven Sacraments* altarpiece by Rogier van

---

[5] T. Müller, *Sculpture in the Netherlands, Germany, France and Spain: 1400–1500* (Harmondsworth, 1966), p. 94, plate 109; M. Voegelen, 'Die Gruppenaltäre in Schwäbisch Hall', *Münchner Jahrbuch*, 13 (1923), p.142.

[6] M. J. Friedländer, *Early Netherlandish painting*, 14 vols (Leiden 1967–76), vol. 2, plate 100; H. T. Musper, 'Die Brüsseler Gregormesse', *Bulletin des Musées Royaux des Beaux-Arts de Belgique*, 1 (1952), pp. 89–94; *Flanders in the fifteenth Century* (as in note 3). pp. 84–7, no. 10.

[7] E. Linsse, 'Ein Niederländisches Schnitzkunstwerk der Spätgotik in Stassfurt', *Bildende Kunst*, 12 (1961), pp. 809–18.

[8] A. Pinchart, *Archives des arts, sciences et lettres: documents inédits*, 1 (Ghent, 1860), pp.42–9.

[9] Müller, *Sculpture in the Netherlands* (as in note 5), pp.23, 29f, 93, plate 19; J. Steyaert, *Sculpture of St Martin's, Halle and related work* (PhD., University of Michigan, 1974, authorized facsimile, Ann Arbor, Michigan, 1980), pp.134–7.

[10] *Aspekten van de Laatgotiek in Brabant*, exhibition catalogue, Stedelijk Museum (Louvain, 1971), catalogue AB 15.

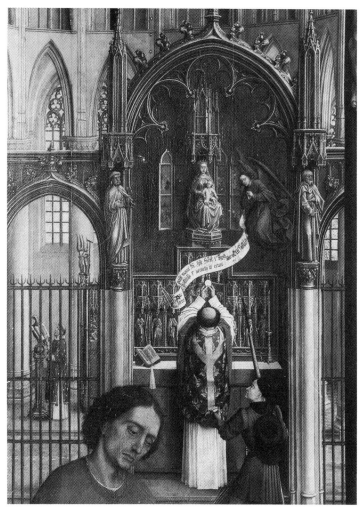

37 Rogier van der Weyden, *Seven Sacraments* altarpiece (detail)

der Weyden, probably dating from the late 1440's (plates 29, 37).[11] Three standing figures, presumably saints, are placed beneath tracery to either side of a raised central section, the carvings of which are hidden by the officiating priest. The altarpiece again has no wings and it is difficult to imagine how wings could possibly have been attached in the confined setting within the screen. On top of the altarpiece case rests a wooden statue of the Virgin and Child set within a tabernacle with tracery and wings. In this way, the depth of the case is employed almost like a shelf or cupboard, and the raised central section serves to emphasise the elevated statue which it bears. This arrangement is frequently found in visual representations of carved altarpieces, and it is clear that the iconographic scheme of the altarpiece itself could be complemented or expanded by the statues it supported.

The altarpiece forms part of the celebration of the Eucharist; the artist chooses

[11] Friedländer *Early Netherlandish painting* (as in note 6), vol. 2, plate 34.

the moment of the elevation of the host, and the representation of Christ on the Cross in the foreground illustrates for the viewer the significance of the Sacrament. Perhaps the hidden central section of the altarpiece contained a carved representation of the Crucifixion as does the Reinoldikirche altarpiece; be that as it may, the presence of the statue of the Virgin and Child above the central section is significant. It serves to honour the Virgin, the mother of Christ, to remind the participant of the birth of Christ even at the commemoration of his death and forms a focus for prayers to the Virgin so often included in the mass. A similar arrangement is to be found in a rather later painting, *c.* 1480, *Henry II fighting the Infidel* by the St Barbara Master (Münster, Landesmuseum).[12] Here Henry receives the blessing before an altarpiece with a central Crucifixion placed under tracery, two lateral images to right and left and with a statue of the Virgin and Child resting on the raised central section.

Examples of this non-narrative altarpiece format are to be found as late as *c.* 1500, suggesting that the type was not superseded by the narrative altarpiece as surviving works might suggest. For example an altarpiece of this type appears in the miniature of the *Martyrdom of St Thomas à Becket* in the Breviary of Isabella the Catholic (London, British Library, Ms. Add. 18851, f. 314);[13] the manuscript dates from 1497, close to the surviving Savigny altarpiece, which shows that the artist could plausibly have been recording a current rather than an old-fashioned altarpiece type.

The *Mass of St Gregory* by the Master of the Legend of St Catherine, apparently a Brussels artist, dates from *c.* 1480 and exists in two versions, one in Granada, the second in a private collection in Gelderland.[14] The latter includes what appears to be an inverted T shaped carved altarpiece with lateral statues and what might be a central crucifix, though not a full narrative Crucifixion. In the Granada version the altarpiece, conversely, is divided into three round-headed sections, the central section raised, containing a central statue of Christ as the Salvator Mundi with lateral images apparently of St Peter and St Paul. The artist appears to be drawing a parallel between the vision of Christ and the Salvator Mundi and between Pope Gregory and the founding fathers of the Church, St Peter and St Paul, a parallel lost in the second version; this, together with the less conventional altarpiece type, might suggest that the Granada version is the original.

A few altarpieces survive which have round-headed raised central sections and flat-topped lateral sections: the Brussels Passion altarpiece in the Museum Mayer van den Bergh in Antwerp and the Brussels altarpieces in Ytter-selö and Skänela in Sweden, the Ytter-selö work containing statues rather than narrative scenes.[15] This altarpiece type appears relatively frequently in visual representations by artists from several areas of the Netherlands but most notably from Ghent or Bruges and

[12] Ibid., vol. 4, plate 61.
[13] P. Dearmer, *Fifty pictures of Gothic altars* (London, 1910), plate xl.
[14] Friedländer *Early Netherlandish painting* (as in note 6), vol. 4, plate 56; R. van Schoute, *La chapelle royale de Grenade*, Les Primitifs Flamands, Corpus I/6 (Brussels, 1963), pp. 111, 115–17.
[15] J. de Coo, *Museum Mayer van den Bergh catalogus*, 2 (Antwerp, 1969), p. 195, no. 2244–6; A. Andersson, *Medieval wooden sculpture in Sweden*, 3 (Stockholm, 1980), figs. 136–7.

from the north Netherlands. It occurs, for example, in the prints representing the Mass of St Gregory by Master IAM of Zwolle.[16]

The altarpiece type with three round-headed sections is more unusual, one of the few surviving examples being the altarpiece in the church of Grip, Norway, which, like the work in the Granada Mass of St Gregory, contains three statues.[17] Interestingly enough, the altarpiece is thought to be north Netherlandish, though the attribution is tentative. In visual sources most altarpieces of this type are to be found in Ghent/Bruges manuscripts, for example the one on f. 14v of the Hours of Mary of Burgundy (Vienna, Oesterreichische Nationalbibliothek, cod. 1857),[18] which contains four statues placed under tracery. The Hours may date from the 1470s. A far later example occurs in the Spinola Hours of *c.* 1520,[19] where the illumination of the funeral mass (plate 38) includes a gilt-coloured altarpiece with tracery above, a carved frieze below, and containing two lateral saints and a central Virgin and Child.

Visual representations are sufficiently numerous to suggest that the round-headed altarpiece format was a recognised type of the fifteenth and early sixteenth centuries. Although its appearance in Ghent/Bruges manuscripts could be seen simply as an example of the re-use of patterns for which the manuscript group is well known, it is tempting to suggest that some of the many carved altarpieces produced in Ghent, none of which is identifiable today, might have been of this type, as were some painted altarpieces, the most important prototype probably being the upper wing panels of Van Eyck's Ghent altarpiece. Perhaps this type was particularly associated with Ghent and Bruges, but the demands of the export market which Ghent and Bruges painters and manuscript illuminators alike supplied do not obviously account for the distinctive altarpiece format. Although altarpieces of this shape were to be found in Italy, for example, they were neither common nor obviously accessible to Netherlandish carvers, and there is no evidence to suggest that they formed a source for Netherlandish altarpiece design. This altarpiece format might instead have been conceived in emulation of the past. A few Mosan reliquaries are of this shape and the twelfth-century Mosan retable of the Pentecost (Paris, Musée de Cluny) has a round-headed central section and very long, flat-topped lateral sections not unlike the format of the surviving Mayer van den Bergh altarpiece.[20] The unusual round-headed shape of the *Entombment* triptych by the master of Flémalle (London, Courtauld Institute Galleries) is also thought by some to be based on Romanesque precedents.[21] Some painters could have wished to introduce a sense of the past into their work by the inclusion of a historical rather than contemporary altarpiece; rep-

[16] F. W. Hollstein, *Dutch and Flemish etchings, engravings and woodcuts* c. 1450–1700, (Amsterdam, 1949–69), 12, pp. 273–5.

[17] E. S. Engelstad, *Senmiddelalderens kunst i Norge* (Oslo, 1936), pp. 252f, no. 61, plate 180; J. Leeuwenberg, 'Een nieuw facet aan de Utrechtse beeldhouwkunst III: Vijf Utrechtse altaarkasten in Noorwegen', *Oud Holland*, 74 (1959), pp. 79–102.

[18] O. Pächt, *The Master of Mary of Burgundy* (London, 1948), plate 12.

[19] A. von Eeuw and I. M. Plotzek, *Catalogue of the Ludwig collection, 2* (Cologne, 1982), no. 18.

[20] *Rhin-Meuse: Art et civilisation 800–1400*, exhibition catalogue, Musées Royaux d'Art et d'Histoire and Wallraf-Richartz Museum (Cologne, 1972), p. 251.

[21] B. Lane, 'Depositio et elevatio: The symbolism of the Seilern triptych', *Art Bulletin*, 57 (1975), pp. 21–30.

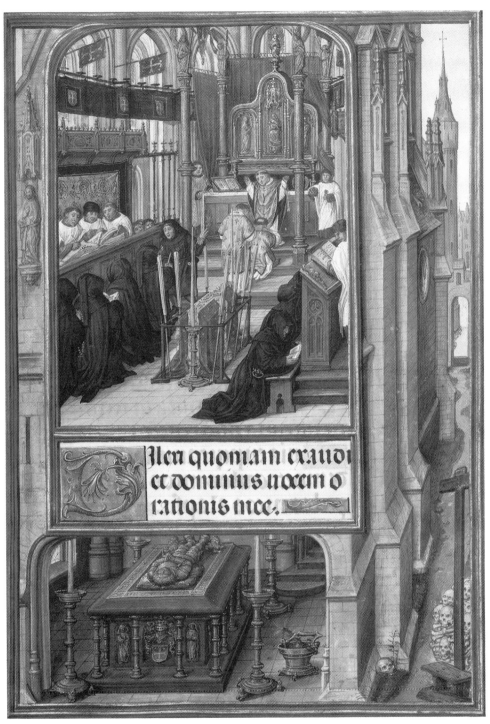

38 *Funeral service* from the Spinola Hours, f. 185r

resentations very like the twelfth-century *Pentecost* altarpiece which could be painted, carved or metal appear in numerous manuscript illuminations throughout the fifteenth century. It is possible that it was this archaic shape that survived in fifteenth-century carved altarpiece design, or was even consciously revived, perhaps because it was different and therefore more exotic or because it evoked a sense of the past.

The altarpiece in the illumination of the mass scene, f. 31v in the Prayerbook of Albert of Brandenburg, has a raised central section resembling an ogee arch.[22] This miniature comes closest to representing one of the commonest Antwerp altarpiece types illustrated by the altarpiece in the Church of St Lawrence, Bocholt, which dates from around the same time as the Brandenburg Prayerbook, *c.* 1515.[23] Nevertheless, the two altarpieces are not identical. It seems likely that the artist was presenting a variation on the round-headed altarpiece type rather than one of the current Antwerp carved altarpieces, which were, in any case, invariably narrative works, and first appear significantly later than earliest similar representation in Ghent/Bruges manuscripts.[24] The absence of the distinctive Antwerp carved altarpieces in visual representations is conspicuous, and the most obvious explanation is not that artists were refusing to record authentic current altarpiece types but that almost none of those responsible for visual representations came from Antwerp.

In most of the examples seen so far, the carved altarpiece as it appears in visual sources is closely associated with the mass celebrated at the altar. Where this is not the case, the altarpiece appears invariably to have been included for a specific reason. An inverted T shaped carved altarpiece appears on an altar, the carved wings fully open, in the background of the *Annunciation to Zachariah* by the Master of the St John Altarpiece (Rotterdam, Museum Boymans-van Beuningen);[25] the artist has been supposed to be north Netherlandish, and the altarpiece is of interest since the fragments of the 1475–7 s'Hertogenbosch piece by Adriaen van Wesel represent the only evidence of north Netherlandish carved altarpiece types. The altarpiece has carved rather than painted wings and a predella, rare for *c.* 1490, the conjectural date of the painting; the s'Hertogenbosch altarpiece seems also to have had both carved wings and a predella. The carved scenes which the altarpiece contains are difficult to decipher; the central scene may be the Betrothal of the Virgin, highly relevant to the theme. Be that as it may, it forms part of the ecclesiastical setting in which the Annunciation to Zechariah took place, a scene to which the artist pays unusual attention.

The spectacular, polychromed Passion altarpiece in the *Consecration of St Augustine* by the Master of the the Legend of St Augustine (New York, Cloisters) lends religious

[22] A. W. Biermann, 'Miniaturehandschriften Albrechts von Brandenburg', *Aachener Kunstblatter*, 46 (1975), p. 128.

[23] 'Retabels', *Openbaar Kunstbezit in Vlaanderen*, 47/1 (1979), pp. 28f.

[24] One of the earliest representations of an altarpiece of this type in Ghent/Bruges manuscripts occurs in the Mass scene, f. 16 of the so-called Voustre Demeure Hours, Berlin 78B13, dating perhaps from the 1480s, about 30 years before the earliest similar Antwerp altarpieces were made; see G.I. Lieftinck, *Boekverluchters uit de omgeving van Maria van Bourgondie*, Verhandelingen van de Koninklijke Vlaamse Academie, Klasse der letteren, 21 no. 66 (Brussels, 1969), 2, plate 152.

[25] Friedländer, *Early Netherlandish painting* (as in note 6), vol. 5, plate 25.

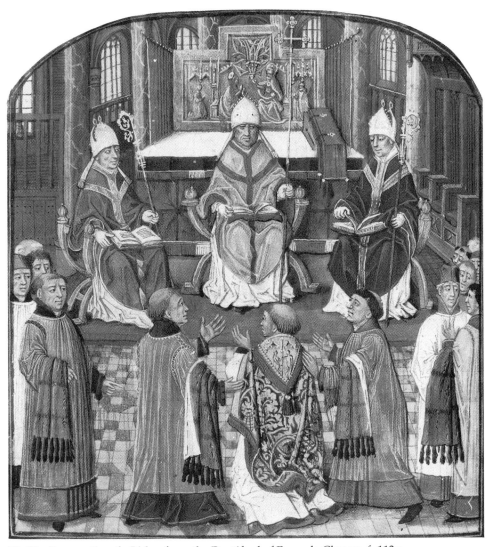

39 *The Consecration of a Bishop* from the Pontifical of Ferry de Clugny, f. 113v

authority to the event.[26] The artist of the Pontifical of Ferry de Clugny represented a carved altarpiece in his miniature of the Consecration of a bishop (plate 39) containing the scene of the Virgin enthroned interceding to God the Father, drawing an obvious parallel with the consecration and the priestly office. The *Presentation of the Child Christ in the Temple* in the Hours of Nicholas Firmian, dating before Firmian's death in 1510 (Sotheby's, 10.12.80, f. 43v), includes a carved altarpiece with Abraham about to sacrifice Isaac, a type for the pending sacrifice of Christ. Although these examples may simply show that artists were adopting Eyckian methods to extend the message of their works, they suggest that an altarpiece almost invariably related to the theme

---

[26] Ibid., vol. 6b, plate 240.

of the visual source in which it appears was as closely associated with the major theme of its altar setting, that is the mass and the wider liturgy of the Church.

In the Netherlandish Church carved altarpieces had no practical function, since they accommodated neither the Reserved Sacrament nor relics. Insofar as their function has been considered, scholars have suggested that they served as a Bible for the poor.[27] Conversely the evidence of visual representations suggests that the carved altarpiece had a liturgical function proper to its place on the altar of a church or chapel. The Passion of Christ and the Nativity cycle, the two major themes of the mass, form the most popular subject-matter in both visual representations and surviving altarpieces, and are often found together through the use of statues balanced on the altarpiece case. For example, the altarpiece of the Virgin and Child which appears in the frontispiece of the Breviary of Eleanor of Portugal (plate 40) is complemented by a statue of Christ as Salvator Mundi at the apex of the case.[28] In the Hours of Philip the Good the illumination of the mass (Cambridge, Fitzwilliam Museum, ms. 3–1954, f. 253)[29] shows the priest elevating the Host before the crucified Christ represented in the carved altarpiece on the altar; some surviving carved altarpieces also include a Last Supper as the central predella scene.[30] In this way the altarpiece could visualise the events celebrated in the mass almost as in the central panel of Rogier van der Weyden's *Seven Sacraments* triptych.

The altarpiece setting, as represented in visual sources, suggests an even closer association of ceremony and image; in the mass scene of the Prayerbook of Albert of Brandenburg a column is placed at each corner of the altar and on each is placed the figure of an angel bearing one of the instruments of the Passion. This is one of numerous examples dating from as early as the 1440s; for example the Rogerian *Exhumation of St Hubert* (London, National Gallery) contains a painted altarpiece with a similar arrangement, and documentary evidence makes it clear that this sort of altar complex was common.[31] Therefore the mass was enhanced not only by the altarpiece but by the statues around the altar.

Given the strong liturgical associations of the carved altarpiece, it is tempting to suppose that these works of art reflect an ecclesiastical hegemony, a sort of didactic clerical programme designed to augment the power and rituals of the Church. Patterns of patronage alone would contest this view, for many altarpieces were commissioned by lay individuals or by church wardens on behalf of a congregation rather than

---

[27] F. Prims, 'Altaartafels als schoolgerief', *Antwerpiensia*, 19 (1949), pp. 54–7; J. van Herck, 'De Vlaamse gebeeldhouwde altaartafelen der laat-gotiek (1)', *Bijdragen tot de Geschiedenis* (Jan-Feb, 1930), p. 70. A recent article, however, maintains the liturgical importance of German carved altarpieces: D. L. Ehresmann, 'Some observations on the role of liturgy in the early winged altarpiece', *Art Bulletin*, lxiv (1982). pp.359–69.

[28] P. de Winter, 'A Book of Hours for Isabella the Catholic', *Bulletin of the Cleveland Museum of Art* (Dec. 1981), fig. 7.

[29] L. M. J. Delaisse: *La miniature flamande à l'epoque de Philippe le Bon* (Milan, 1956), plate 56; see forthcoming article by Anne van Buren in *Scriptorium*.

[30] For example the Netherlandish carved altarpieces in the parish churches of Jäder, Ljusdal and Vadstena in Sweden and Orsoy, Vreden and Affeln in Germany.

[31] In 1460 Cleerbout van Westervelde of Ghent undertook to polychrome for the church of Aspere not only the altarpiece but the 'Vier engelen die boven an den autaer staen up vier pilaeren', here evidently of wood rather than of metal; see C. L. Dierix, *Mémoires sur la ville de Gand*, vol. 2. (Ghent, 1815), p. 255.

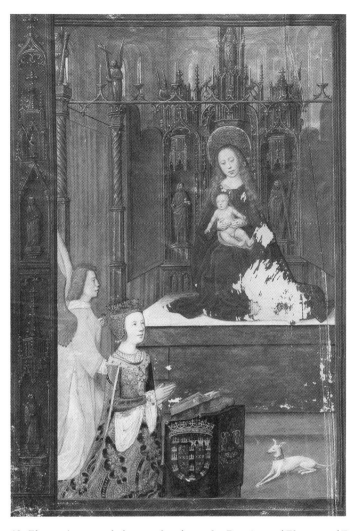

40 *Eleanor in prayer before an altar* from the Breviary of Eleanor of Portugal, f. 1v (frontispiece)

by the clerical hierarchy. The programme of most surviving altarpieces is simple, even popularising, and without great didactic potential. The fact that entire altarpieces were copied, let alone individual scenes or patterns, might suggest not only pot-boiling but also a response to the demand for a fixed type of church furnishing, appropriate to the main themes of church ceremonial. Secondly the populace, whom the church hierarchy would have wished to influence, were rarely given prominent place in representations of the ceremony of the mass. For example in the mass scene of a Book of Hours in Waddesdon Manor (plate 41) it is the clergy serving before the altar who dominate;[32] the view of the few bystanders present is even obscured by the wings of the altarpiece which are only half open, stressing the private, clerical

---

[32] L. M. J. Delaissé, J. Marrow and J. de Wit, *James A. Rothschild collection at Waddesdon Manor: illuminated manuscripts* (Fribourg, 1977), ms. 31, cat. 26. It is no accident that this miniature, with its Nativity altarpiece, precedes the Mass of the Virgin in the Book of Hours.

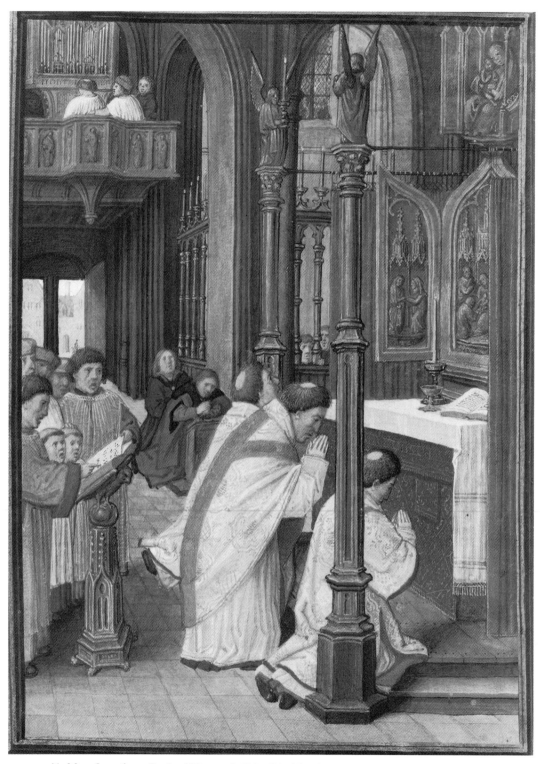

41 *Mass Scene* from Book of Hours, f. 154v (Waddesdon Manor)

nature of the mass rather than the public ceremony. The public mass in the *Mass of St John the Evangelist* by an anonymous master named after the painting (Novi Ligure, Coulant Peloso col.) is the exception that proves the rule, and here the Meeting of Abraham and Melchisedek, a type for the mass of the sort commonly used in efforts to instruct the unlettered, forms the highly unusual subject matter of the carved altarpiece.[33]

Visual sources confirm the contention of scholars like Toussaert who claim that by the fifteenth century the mass was essentially a clerical affair, with the congregation reduced to the status of bystanders; that the climax of the ceremony was not the reception of the mass (almost never represented in visual sources) but the Elevation of the Host (frequently represented) where the real presence of Christ was proclaimed; that public participation was guaranteed only at the high church festivals of Christmas and Easter, the themes which form by far the most frequently found subject matter of carved altarpieces, while normal parish mass was neglected; that the pious church-goer's experience of the mass consisted of observation and private devotions.[34] The frontispiece of the Breviary of Eleanor of Portugal (plate 40) suggests the form that private devotions might have taken, for here Eleanor is represented kneeling at a prie-dieu, attended by an angel, regarding a vision of the Virgin and Child, apparently the central section of the altarpiece come to life; Master IAM of Zwolle used a similar device in his prints of the Mass of St Gregory. Church reformers might have regarded this sort of devotion as superstition and this sort of celebration of the mass as nothing more than an exclusive rite in which the congregation connived rather than participated. They would surely have disapproved of the close association between the altar images, and particularly the altarpiece, and the liturgical ceremonies which dominated church practice. Perhaps, therefore, visual representations casts a little light on why Netherlandish carved altarpieces went out of fashion quite so abruptly around the middle of the sixteenth century.

---

[33] Friedländer, *Early Netherlandish painting* (as in note 6) vol. 6b, plate 267.

[34] G. Dix, *The shape of the liturgy* (Glasgow, 1947), chapter 15; J. Toussaert, *La sentiment religieux en la Flandre à la fin du Moyen Age* (Paris, 1960); T. Klauser: *A short history of the Western liturgy* (London, 1969), chapter 3; while resisting the interpretation of developments in the mass as a symptom of religious decline, John Bossy draws attention to the effective elimination of the congregation from parts of the service: J. Bossy, 'The mass as a social institution 1200–1700', *Past and Present*, 100 (1983), pp. 29–61.

5 Reform within the cult image: the German winged altarpiece before the Reformation

Bernhard Decker

It is well known that the Reformation in Europe was hostile towards the cult of images as traditionally practised within the Catholic Church. In their attempt to return to the apostolic origins of the Christian faith, many reformers regarded the use of images as little more than a relic of pagan superstition. Yet this hostility also developed out of a long process of self-criticism and self-reformation within the medieval image-cult.[1] Indeed, the official arguments of the reformers against the use of pictures in churches did not differ greatly from the official pronouncements on the subject from Rome since the time of Pope Gregory the Great. Both positions accorded with the central educational postulate that images were *adiaphora*: in other words, dispensable aids to piety for those unable to read the holy scriptures.[2] Officially, therefore, there was no disagreement on the matter. Although the reformers' intentions were radical, their statements on this subject were not particularly original.

The point at issue was not so much that of religious images in general, even though reformers were well aware that any image was liable to be corporeally identified with the holy person represented. The main issue, rather, was that of the direct association of images with the rites of Christian worship. In fact, dissent about images focused on altar images, especially those occupying the liturgical centre of a church, namely the high altar.[3] This controversy may be seen as a response to a specifically German tradition of treating cult images as a special kind of art, especially in the form of the carved and winged altarpiece, a type that flourished between *c.* 1300 and 1530. The fact that most of the important German winged altarpieces from this long period have polychromed carvings rather than paintings in the *corpus*, or main central section, illustrates the direct connection that existed between sculpture and the idea of cult representation in medieval Germany. By virtue of the very medium habitually employed, the cult of images in medieval Germany was subject to constant reform, and this in return brought about constant change in the character of cult images. For a better understanding of the enormous change that took place in the use of cult images one should recall the kind of image that existed before the winged altarpieces took over the liturgical centre of churches.

---

[1] Some of the issues addressed in this paper are discussed in a more detailed form in B. Decker, *Das Ende des mittelalterlichen Kultbildes und die Plastik Hans Leinbergers* (Bamberg, 1985).

[2] M. Stirn *Die Bilderfrage der Reformation* (Gütersloh, 1977); C. Christiansen, *Art and the Reformation in Germany* (Athens OH, 1979).

[3] Ostensibly the criticism was directed against supposedly idolatrous subjects such as the Coronation of the Virgin. But there is convincing evidence that the attack on false iconography was in fact concentrated on the 'false' medium of sculpture, and in particular on the sculpted figures of the winged altarpiece.

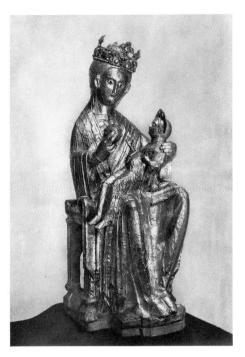

42 *Golden Madonna, c. 1000*

As far as is known, the first sculpted cult images make their appearance in Ottonian times (see plate 42).[4] They consisted of a wooden nucleus with a gold-plated surface that was often covered with jewels. These small-scale sculptures symbolised the isolated 'majesty' of the enthroned patron, whether Virgin with Child or some other saint. They were located behind, above or beside the mensa in a tabernacle, but they never stood on the altar itself. After the celebration of mass, they were not permitted to remain in place but were removed, because of both their material value and their function as idols. They all contained relics considered to be the three-dimensional representatives of holy persons. This fact makes Ottonian cult images all the more interesting, for they contain within themselves a fundamental conflict between, on the one hand, the existence of Christian cult images with an idolatrous function and, on the other, an official denial of the theological legitimacy of such images. Officially neither cult images nor idolatry existed; and what were in effect cult images were officially subsumed under the category of ecclesiastical decoration.[5] This position enabled the Church to declare the widespread practice of idolatry to be an abuse, but at the same time to dismiss it as a purely marginal phenomenon. By analogy with the medieval discussion of miracles, the dictum of St Paul could

[4] H. Keller, 'Zur Entstehung der sakralen Vollskulptur in der ottonischen Zeit', in *Festschrift für Hans Jantzen* (Berlin, 1951), pp. 71ff; H. Schrade, 'Zur Frühgeschichte der mittelalterlichen Monumentalplastik', *Westfalen*, 35 (1957), pp. 33ff.

[5] J. Braun, *Der chirstliche Altar in seiner geschichtlichen Entwicklung* (Munich, 1924); J. Sauer, *Symbolik des Kirchengebäudes und seiner Ausstattung in der Auffassung der Mittelalters*, (2nd ed. 1924; reprint Münster, 1964). For the actual use of cult images, see H. Bredekamp, *Kunst als Medium sozialer Konflikte: Bilderkämpfe von der Spätantike bis zur Hussitenrevolution* (Frankfurt 1975).

be applied to the discussion of the medieval ideal of images: 'Signa data infidelibus, non fidelibus' ('a sign given not to them that believe, but to them that believe not') – in other words the truly faithful had no need of images.[6] Historical discussion gains little by repeating accusations that the Church engaged in trickery or hypocrisy in this area. It is far more important to understand the significance of cult representation. It is well known that ordinary people often regarded these wooden and gilded Ottonian majesties as possessing miraculous powers. In combination with relics, the sculptures represented the celestial authority of the saints on earth, and stood in a very direct sense as a tangible surrogate for the holy person himself. In this way, they were able to neutralise the arbitrariness of the real feudal lord.[7]

Traditionally, then, sculpture had played a role of central importance in the context of cult representation in Germany. Its role then became even more crucial in the carved and winged altarpieces that after 1300 came to replace the golden 'majesty' figures, which were abolished and removed from the cult stage. While the older figures had often threatened the Church's authority by inspiring idolatry, the winged altarpieces no longer presented the holy figures in a way likely to prompt acts of physical adoration, such as touching and kissing. Set within their new framework, the sculptures lost their miraculous powers. It becomes more understandable, therefore, that sculpture was now for the first time allowed to remain on the altar, and – even more significantly – to be connected with the mensa itself (see plate 43).[8] Numerous statues – often in the symbolic numbers of twelve or twenty-four – were now displayed as a celestial chorus to the saints enshrined in the *corpus*. Wings were also introduced to help guard against abuses in the veneration of images. The wings were opened on holy days, in other words, exceptionally; during most of the church year they remained closed, in a way that again reflects a cautious attitude towards cult images. The winged altarpiece thus combines two approaches: the periodic tolerance of cult images, and the fear of idolatry. With them, the Church begins to demonstrate its newlyfound self-confidence as a heavenly representative on earth. Although altarpieces sometimes continued to contain relics as part of the furnishing or ecclesiastical ritual, these were no longer emphasised as surrogates for a holy person; and altarpieces served rather to demonstrate the legitimacy and authority of the glorious *Ecclesia* itself, especially by means of representation of a Mystical Marriage of the Virgin with the Son of God in the central *corpus*. It is here that the *Ecclesia Spiritualis* celebrates its role as lord protector of the alliance of heaven and earth. Hence we may regard the winged altarpiece as a kind of 'arca novi testamenti', an ark of the new covenant in which an institutional mystery rather than

[6] See I Cor. 1:22, 14:22; see also E. Demm, 'Zur Rolle des Wunders in der Heiligkeitskonzeption des Mittelalters', *Archiv für Kulturgeschichte*, 57 (1975), p. 303.

[7] M. Warnke, *Bau und Überbau: Soziologie der mittelalterlichen Architektur nach den Schriftquellen* (Frankfurt, 1976), pp. 70ff.

[8] One of the most interesting examples of the transitional phase in the development of the winged altarpiece is the high altar of St Elisabeth in Marburg, consecrated in 1290. This wingless retable also served as a treasure-house for relics, including the golden shrine of St Elizabeth, which was intended to be displayed on the evidently incomplete stone stage set above the stone archtecture of the altar. This example provides indirect evidence that the winged altarpiece of the future contradicted the tradition of the ostentatious display of relics. See D. Ehresmann, 'Some observations on the role of liturgy in the early winged altarpiece', *Art Bulletin*, 64 (1982), pp. 359–69.

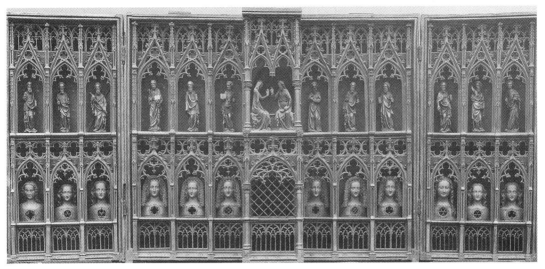

43 Marienstatt, Cistercian Abbey, former high altar, before 1350

a personal one is worshipped.[9] Quite apart from its imagery, the form of the winged altarpiece simultaneously reflects both a prohibitive and restrictive attitude towards images in Christian worship, and a departure from this principle by means of a carefully controlled use of images in direct relationship with the liturgy.

Seen from the perspective of reform, the winged altarpiece of the fourteenth century should be interpreted as an attempt to avoid idolatry. In this sense it may be related to contemporary efforts at monastic reform, and in particular to the ideals of the Cistercian order, which aimed to dispense with the luxury of figurative representation altogether. But the place traditionally occupied by images in the church had always been precarious, and their use had always been carefully controlled and subject to reform. At the very least, medieval cult images had always been set within an architectural frame – a niche, a pedestal, a tabernacle, or simply a tracery surround – in a way that served to emphasise the character of the image as a representation. This kind of framing, consisting of architectural forms echoing those of the church in which the image was set, may be seen as a necessary precondition for the acceptability of the cult image. Until the end of the period in which cult images were used in Germany, the niche-bound structure of the sculpted figures was preserved.

Up to now I have not mentioned the specific forms employed for the individual cult image. It is no coincidence that the recognition of the validity and worth of cult images was linked with the development of altarpiece wings and of the architectural framework. The first step towards a formal structuring of cult value, in the sense of a canonical order of formal beauty, was taken in about 1400, with the consciously programmatic style of the International Gothic, one of the most characteristic products of which was the so-called *Schöne Madonna*.[10] With its overt beauty, this

---

[9] B. Decker 'Die spätgotische Plastik als Kultbild; *Jahrbuch für Volkskunde*, n.s. 8 (1985), pp. 92–106.

[10] *Schöne Madonnen*, exhibition catalogue, Salzburger Domkapitel (Salzburg, 1965); C. H. Clasen, *Der Meister der Schönen Madonnen* (Berlin and New York, 1974).

new type of Madonna (plate 44) provided the first explicit expression of the worth and value of the sculpture itself, a medium that became the most important locus of the reform of cult images up to the time of the Reformation. Although not a cult image in the strict sense of the term, the *Andachtsbild* (private devotional image) of the *Schöne Madonna* was nevertheless very important as a predecessor of what later developed into a *Gnadenbild* (a miraculous image, usually associated with public devotion). Exported from a few centres in the east such as Prague or Breslau, ideal models of the type were reproduced and disseminated throughout the German-speaking countries. Only a very few of these sculptures are known to have served as the central cult element within a winged altarpiece, one of them being the Madonna of Weildorf (Bavaria), dating from as late as 1429. In general, they were isolated images, located far away from the cult centre of a church, since their popularity was in conflict with the officially restricted status of cult images.

Towards the middle of the fifteenth century, a strange phenomenon may be observed. Certain winged altarpieces started either to integrate older International Gothic sculpture into the *corpus*, or to refer directly by form and iconography to originals of that period. The first known altarpiece to show this retrospective attitude seems to be the high altar dating from 1469 of the former collegiate church at Tiefenbronn (Swabia), which incorporates an International Gothic *Pietà* (plate 45). But even the most important masters, such as Michael Pacher, were apparently involved in this movement, as we can see in the high altar of St Wolfgang (Austria), completed in 1481 (plate 46; see also plates 54–6). Not only does Pacher return to the two-figured group of the Coronation of the Virgin (in other words, to the fourteenth-century iconography of this theme), but he also refers to an International Gothic form represented by a relief in northern France from the late 1390s at the castle of La Ferté-Milon (Aisne) (plate 47).[11] Both works show the same two-storied construction, with the main scene located above and the scene with the assistant angels in the area below. A very similar derivation from the past can be seen in the Cracow altarpiece by Veit Stoss, dated 1489. Here the central group of the Death of the Virgin follows an earlier type of this theme, surviving examples of which may be seen in the main portal tympanum of Regensburg Cathedral, and in an epitaph by the same sculptor of about 1420 in the church of St Emmeram, Regensburg. A different way of integrating earlier sculpture is adopted in the altarpiece of the *Coronation of the Virgin* in St Elisabeth, Marburg (Hesse), dating from around 1518. Here an older *Pietà* group – one of the finest examples of the type – is placed in the predella of the altarpiece to form what is almost an additional *corpus* in its own right.

All these examples clearly pay homage to the older sculpture, both for their historical value and as canonical exemplars of holiness. I believe that the retrospective character of altarpieces of this type may be seen as a phenomenon parallel to the use of Byzantine forms in the West in the Middle Ages. The difference between the two phenomena is a historical one: while the exotic-seeming Byzantine art was believed to reproduce

[11] See B. Decker, 'Zur geschichtlichen Dimension in Michael Pachers Altären von Gries und St Wolfgang', *Städel Jahrbuch*, 7 (1977), pp. 293–318; also the chapter by M. Evans in this volume.

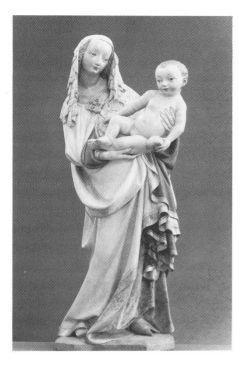

44 *Schöne Madonna, c.* 1390–3

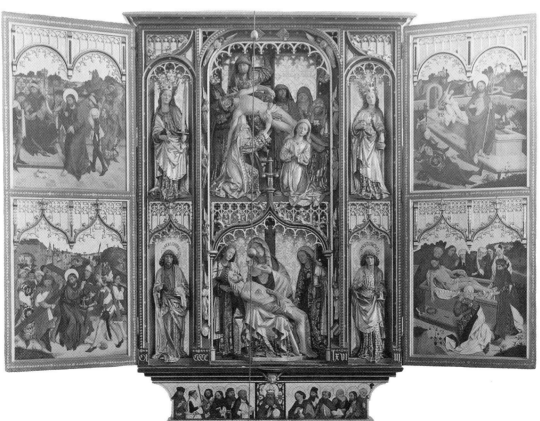

45 Tiefenbronn (Swabia), former collegiate church, high altar, dated 1469

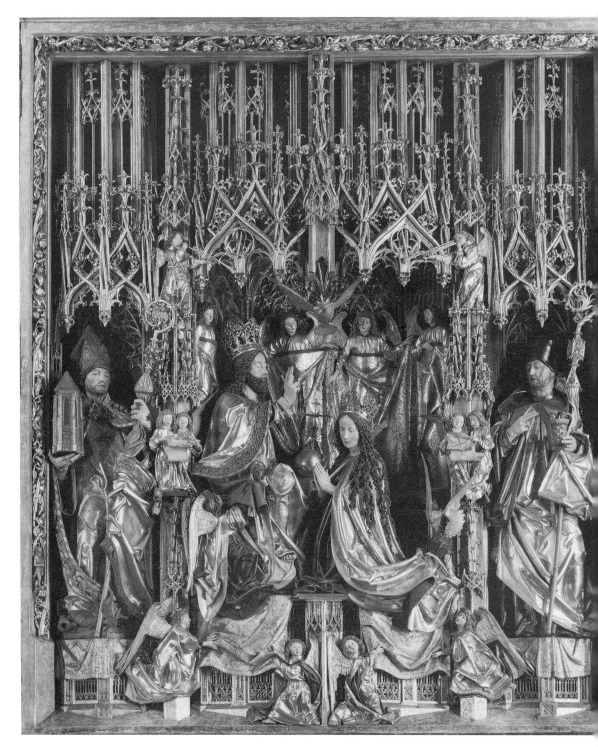

46 Michael Pacher, Shrine of St Wolfgang altarpiece, completed 1481, St Wolfgang (Austria), parish church

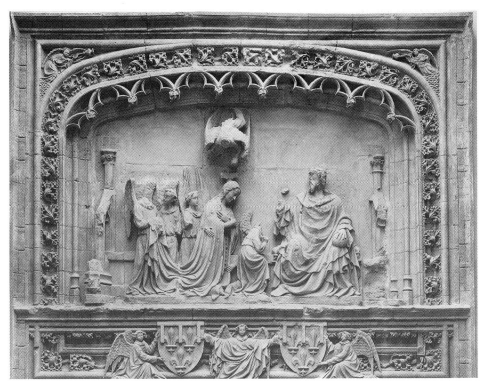

47 *Coronation of the Virgin, c.* 1400, portal relief Castle of La Ferté-Milon (Aisne), France

Early Christian, and – with its legendary origins in St Luke – even apostolic patterns of a universally valid Christian art,[12] the uniformity and conformity of International Gothic was 'home-made' art, just a few generations old, and a topical matter of vivid and continuous veneration within western religious civilisation. It seems reasonable to conclude that the practice of adapting International Gothic images to the next context of the winged altarpiece only makes sense if it is acknowledged as an attempt at self-reform within cult images, and as an attempt to validate the cult image through the establishment of trustworthy and examinable roots.

The keyterms of uniformity and conformity that I have used to describe the style of the International Gothic are intended to express a sense of proportionality between God and the likeness of God. This means that through retrospection or revival, these mystical and scholastic formal ideals took on a far more demonstrative character than they had previously had. The interaction between the old forms and the new naturalistic art within the same *corpus* enhances both categories in terms of purity, originality and apostolic, or Early Christian, virtue.

By the end of the fifteenth century, the Christian cult image came increasingly under pressure. Under the conditions of a naturalistic and empirical art, cult images were accused of having become profane and secular. Geyler von Keysersberg, for example, said of the altarpieces of his time: 'St Catherine, St Barbara, St Agnes and

[12] H. G. Beck, *Von der Fragwürdigkeit der Ikone*, Bayerische Akademie der Wissenschaften, philosophisch-historische Klasse, Sitzungsberichte 7, 1985 (Munich, 1985).

St Margaret are all painted nowadays as if they were noblewomen or common girls – their clothes, in fact, are just like those of noblewomen and whores.'[13] Hence new arguments were needed to justify church images. These could only be found in the use of forms that appeared idealised in relation to the profane world, and which avoided the realistic representation of fashionable luxury. Confronted with the fundamentalist arguments of the opponents of images, the Christian cult image had to demonstrate its conformity with the Gospel by the innocence of its form. This supposition is supported by Michael Baxandall's discovery of some interesting patterns in contemporary stage instructions about figures described as 'prophetalis', 'patriarchisch', and 'zwelffbottisch' (apostolic).[14] Images of holy persons were expected to convey dignity by means of neutral garments.

The sculptures produced in Hans Leinberger of Landshut deserve particular attention in this context.[15] His works provide an outstanding example of the way in which different types could be used in the process of reforming the cult image. In style and inconography, Leinberger combined two traditions: first, the *Schöne Madonna* of the International Gothic, and secondly, the Byzantine concept of the Madonna of St Luke; and on the basis of this combination, he produced images such as the Madonna in the Moosburg altarpiece, erected *c.* 1511–15 (plates 48–9). The same relationship between the renewal of the cult image and the revival of earlier styles may be seen still more directly in Albrecht Altdorfer's small engraving of a Madonna in Glory, obviously portraying a model of a *Schöne Madonna* of *c.* 1400 (plate 50),[16] and in his icon painting in the *maniera greca*, created in 1519 for the pilgrimage chapel of the *Schöne Madonna* in Regensburg.[17] The duality in the concept of reform that lies behind the images of Leinberger and others thus clearly reveals an ambivalence of attitude towards the concept of the cult image during the period. This is especially apparent in the way that, in order to make it acceptable within the devotional context of the early sixteenth century, the cult image was made to approximate to earlier historical types, and to formal ideals that were the ancestors of the images currently in use.

The purification of the cult image had another significant artistic and aesthetic aspect. In an attempt to make cult images less vulnerable to idolatry, artists began drastically to reduce the brightness of the coloured and gilded sculptures, and even to paint them in a wood-coloured monochrome. The use of this technique seems to be another direct reaction to the attacks on luxury, and to the general hostility towards the inclusion of three-dimensional sculpture in altarpieces. Although monochromy had been used in Netherlandish altar painting since the time of Jan van Eyck, and a strong tradition had developed for painting the exteriors of altarpiece

---

[13] 'Sant Katharin, sant Barbara, sant Agness od sant Margredt, malen sie ietz nit anders weder die edlen weiber gond und die gemeinen düren, dann zwischen edlen weiber unn hüren ist kein underscheid der cleid halb'. Geyler von Keysersberg, *Evangelia mit usslegung*, (Strasbourg, 1517), fol. CLXXIV.

[14] M. Baxandall, *The limewood sculptors of Renaissance Germany* (New Haven and London, 1980), pp. 202, 236, note 42.

[15] G. Lill, *Hans Leinberger: der Bildschnitzer von Landshut* (Munich, 1942).

[16] F. Winzinger, *Albrecht Altdorfer: Graphik* (Munich, 1969), no. 119.

[17] A. Hubel, 'Die schöne Maria von Regensburg', in *850 Jahre Kollegiatstift zu den hll. Johannes Bapt. und Johannes Ev. in Regensburg, 1127–1977*, ed. P. May (Munich and Zurich, 1977).

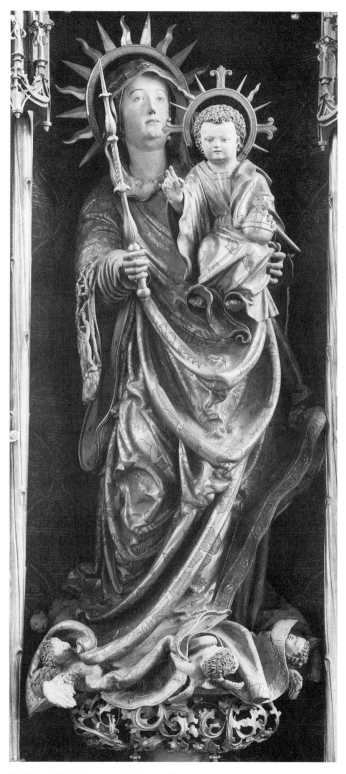

48 Hans Leinberger, *Madonna* from the high altar of St Castulus, Moosburg, Bavaria, 1511–14
(photograph of *c*. 1920)

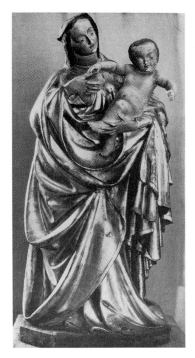

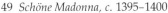

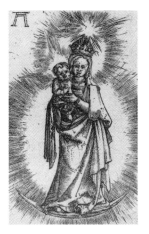

49 *Schöne Madonna, c.* 1395–1400   50 Albrecht Altdorfer, *Schöne Madonna, c.* 1515–20

wings in grisaille,[18] the technique had no influence at the time on interior sculpture. The first carved altarpiece to show a totally monochrome surface is probably the Münnerstadt altarpiece of 1492 by Tilman Riemenschneider;[19] and even this move towards reforming the image was by no means generally accepted, since a few years later, in 1504–5, Veit Stoss of Nuremberg painted the work with colours, and 'completed' it according to the orders of the Münnerstadt authorities. However, Riemenschneider successfully applied his monochrome ideal to other works, as in the famous Altar of the Holy Blood in Rothenburg, or the Altar of the Assumption in Creglingen. And although it is Riemenschneider who is particularly associated today with virtuoso carved figures with a monochrome surface, there are many monochrome altarpieces by other contemporary sculptors on the Upper and Lower Rhine, and in Swabia and Austria, which indicate that monochromy became one of the most common ways of depicting the reformed cult image. Veit Stoss – the artist responsible for painting the formerly monochrome altarpiece at Münnerstadt – himself later produced some of the finest monochrome sculptures the world had ever seen, prompting even Vasari to praise his understanding and his masterly art.[20]

Stoss is not known to have produced a monochrome altarpiece before 1520, when although advanced in years, he was commissioned to carve the high altar of the

[18] M. T. Smith, 'The use of grisaille as a Lenten observance', *Marsyas*, 8 (1957–9), pp. 43–54.
[19] H. Krohm and E. Oellermann, 'Der ehemalige Münnerstädter Magdalenaltar von Tilman Riemenschneider und seine Geschichte', *Zeitschrift des deutschen Vereins für Kunstwissenschaft*, 34 (1980), pp. 45ff.
[20] G. Vasari, *Le vite de' più eccellenti pittori, scultori ed architettori*, vol. 1 (1568), ed. G. Milanesi (Florence, 1878), p. 167; see also J. Rasmussen, ''' . . . far stupire il mondo'': Zur Verbreitung der Kunst des Veit Stoss', in *Veit Stoss: die Vorträge des Nürnberger Symposions*, ed. R. Kahsnitz (Munich, 1985), pp. 107ff, especially 121.

Carmelite church in Nuremberg (plate 51), of which his son, Andreas Stoss, was prior.[21] This altarpiece, which was later transferred to Bamberg Cathedral, is of special interest. Although in bad condition, it still provides a striking demonstration of the significance of monochromy in relation to the cult image. The Carmelite prior Andreas gave detailed instructions that illustrate the high esteem in which it was held. He ordered the strict observation of the liturgical calendar by having the wings closed after the services on feast days; he wished to reduce the amount of candlelight to a minimum, so as to keep the carved wooden surface clean; and finally, he instructed that the altarpiece should never be painted 'carelessly' with colours ('Nullus prior faciat eam coloribus pingere faciliter'). The reason for this, he continued, would be clear to all masters of this art. Some years later, Andreas stated to the Nuremberg City Council that the altar had been made by his father's hands alone, and that it was a work of art that praised and beautified itself ('es lobt sich und schoent sich selbst'). This testimony has normally been interpreted in purely aesthetic terms, but since we know that Andreas was a leading representative of the Catholic Reform in Nuremberg, his words also imply that the beauty of the monochromy was especially appropriate to the liturgical dignity of the altarpiece.

Together with the elaborate technique of wood-carving, monochromy may thus be regarded as the outstanding expression of the movement to legitimise cult images towards the end of their history. In this, one can see an analogy to what Erasmus of Rotterdam and others had said about the piety of the woodcuts and engravings of Dürer, which – monochrome as they were – were praised for their 'unfleshly' colourlessness.[22] In this way, monochromy was seen to symbolise purity and innocence. Because grisaille painting had been used for the outside of altarpiece wings, this more or less 'grey' exterior had previously been regarded as the 'Lenten garment', in contrast to the splendour of an altarpiece's interior. With its correspondingly greater effect of asceticism, being veiled in a garment of repentance inside as well as out, the completely monochrome winged altarpiece is entirely appropriate as a symbol of the reform of images.

Finally, these issues should be discussed in terms of the external format of altarpieces. For a long time, scholars thought that the obvious changes within German altarpieces of the pre-Reformation period had been caused by the increasing influence of the 'welsch' – in other words, of Italian Renaissance art. Assuming such a dependence on Italian models, some writers have seen monochrome wood sculpture, for instance, as an imitation of bronze sculpture. A very similar question arises over the presumed Italian origins of certain altarpiece shapes, such as the trefoil arched top or the lunettes of the Bamberg altarpiece by Stoss (plate 51). This was also assumed in the case of Dürer's wingless Landauer altarpiece (Vienna, Kunsthistorisches Museum), the original frame of which survives in Nuremberg (Germanisches National

---

[21] R. Hausherr, 'Der Bamberger Altar', in ibid., pp. 207ff, especially p. 213.

[22] See H. Rupprich, 'Das literarische Bild Dürers im Schrifttum des 16. Jahrhunderts', in *Festschrift für Hans Kralik* (Horn, Austria, 1954), p. 2320; see also Rupprich, *Dürer: Schriftlicher Nachlass*, vol. 3 (Berlin, 1969), pp. 466ff.

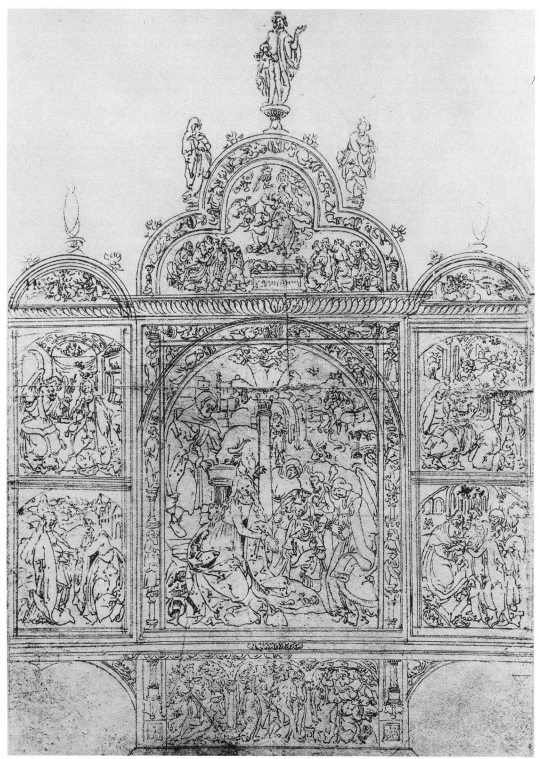

51 Veit Stoss, model drawing for the former high altar of the Carmelite church in Nuremberg,
   1520

museum).[23] The salient point here concerns the columns: did Dürer want to create a wingless altarpiece in the shape of an Italian *pala* because wings of the German type did not fit together with columns of the Italian type? But the St John the Baptist altar in the Teyn church, Prague (plate 52) – a monochrome wood-carving of the 1520s by the monogrammist I.P. – provides us with an altarpiece in which wings and columns may be seen combined. Everything here seems Italianate, inspired by the 'welsch'. Yet the wooden columns are used as rod-hinges for the wings, and rotate with them, in a way that is totally un-Italianate. Leinberger's Moosburg altarpiece (plate 48), dating from a decade earlier, is also relevant to this question. The form of the missing wings that housed the surviving reliefs has not been reconstructed, because although the rod-hinges are still *in situ*, they have not been recognised as such on account of their highly unusual form and technique. Unlike the Italianate columns of the Prague altarpiece, the rod-hinges in Moosburg consist in a typically Late Gothic fashion of twisted rods. In my view, Italian Renaissance models were not the source for this form of construction, but rather small-scale Byzantine triptychs. There is a beautiful example in bronze of such a triptych, dating from *c*. 1150, in the Victoria and Albert Museum in London; another, tenth-century example is in Berlin (Dahlem Museum, Skulpturengalerie). Another similar combination of Renaissance and Byzantine forms may be recognised in a small German altarpiece of the early sixteenth century also now in Berlin (plate 53). If we interpret the late Roman and Byzantine triptychs as representing a framework for the Epiphany of God – an idea that was adapted from the cult of Caesar – we might then see the use of some of the features of certain Late Gothic altarpieces, such as those on Prague and Moosburg, as an attempt to redefine the Christian Epiphany in cult images. Altarpieces were no longer regarded either as a shrine or as an ark of the new covenant, but rather as a simple medium of visionary appearance analogous to Byzantine models, which were in turn believed to follow Early Christian models. In this way, the modified form of the reformed altarpiece of the pre-Reformation period represents not a stylistic shift, but rather a change in the concept of the sacred image.

Almost all German altarpieces of this kind were made after 1510. There is a single example (in Regensburg) dating from as early as 1505; but it is most unlikely that this was the first. Could it perhaps have been Dürer who introduced the new type of construction into the art of the winged altarpiece? Some of his early altarpieces would become much more understandable if they were reconstructed in this manner, including the Paumgartner altarpiece of *c*. 1500 (Munich, Alte Pinakothek). The same would apply to his Heller altarpiece of 1509 (central section lost; copy in Frankfurt, Historisches Museum), with its additional wings by Matthias Grünewald.[24]

The form of the medieval cult image came to an end because of the inner contradiction that had always been present within Christian cult images. The era for representation by images was over, and the social background for it had changed. But in

---

[23] For important corrections of the traditional interpretation of the altar frame, see J. Rasmussen, *Die Nürnberger Altarbaukunst der Dürerzeit* (Hamburg, 1974), pp. 20ff.
[24] B. Decker, 'Notizen zum Heller-Altar', *Städel-Jahrbuch*, 10 (1985) pp. 179ff.

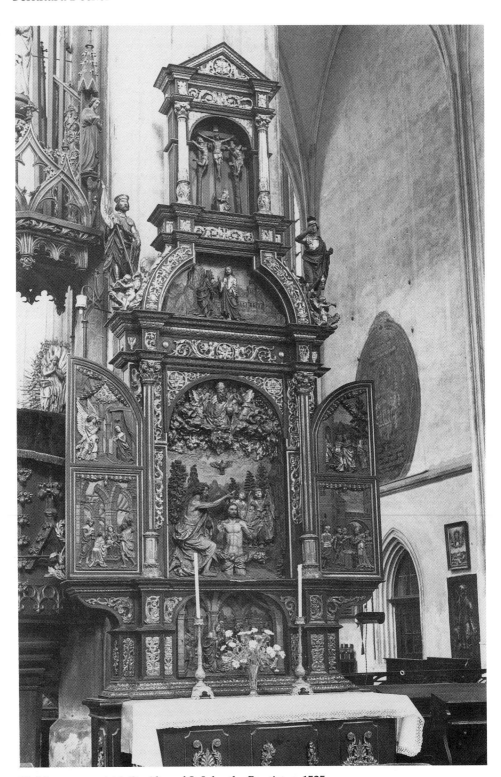

52 Monogrammist I. P., Altar of St John the Baptist, *c.* 1525

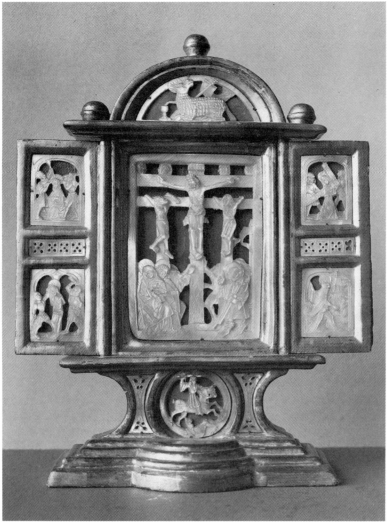

53 Private altarpiece, South German, early 16th century

the period immediately before this change an attempt was made to legitimise the medieval cult image by way of the modifications that I have outlined: first, by the retrospective use of the canonical forms and iconography of the International Gothic; secondly, by a reduction of colour, until the central *corpus* had become completely monochrome; and thirdly, by the adoption of a Byzantine, portal-like form for the altarpiece frame. This use of the 'epiphanic' frame, probably introduced by Dürer, then signalled the abandonment of cult representation in favour of a type of image that served rather as some kind of apparition. The post-Reformation experience was then to show that there is much truth in Hegel's dictum that, in contrast to Greek sculpture, Christian art was not the medium best fitted to represent the true image of God.

6　*Appropriation and application: the significance of the sources of Michael Pacher's altarpieces*

Mark Evans

Any study of artistic borrowings, whether of style or motif, must take full account of the purpose of such borrowings, and of the altered physical and cultural contexts in which they were put to work. The altarpieces of Michael Pacher, consisting of complex assemblages of painting and sculpture within an architectural framework, provide a particularly clear illustration of this. As is well known, Pacher was exceptionally broad in his artistic horizons, and he borrowed extensively from the art of Italy and the Netherlands, as well as from that of his native Germany. But still insufficiently appreciated is the extent to which he sought to integrate the knowledge and experience gained on his travels within a strong regional tradition of altarpiece design.

Passage of time and changes in taste have afflicted most of Pacher's retables. The biggest of them all, that in Salzburg parish church (1484–98), was almost entirely destroyed in the eighteenth century.[1] Only the central figure of the Virgin and some fragmentary shutter paintings survive from his altarpiece in St Lorenz im Pusteral (begun *c.* 1462–63; plates 57–8) and only two painted panels remain from his approximately contemporary retable dedicated to St Thomas.[2] (See plate 63.) That in Gries near Bolzano (*c.* 1471–88) has lost its pinnacles and nearly all of its shutters,[3] and the painted *Fathers of the Church* altarpiece in Munich (*c.* 1479–82) is bereft of decorative carvings, having been removed from its original site at Kloster Neustift.[4] (See plate 67.) Pacher's only work to survive unscathed in its intended location is the high altarpiece in the parish church of St Wolfgang near Salzburg (1471–81).[5] (See plates 54–6.) Over eleven metres high with twenty-three paintings, six large statues and a host of smaller carvings, this single ensemble comprises nearly a half of Pacher's extant sculpture and three-quarters of his surviving paintings. It is central to the following discussion.

Such retables were semi-architectural undertakings, requiring an establishment of joiners, gilders, carvers and painters. The staff of Pacher's business included, at times, his brother or cousin Friedrich, his son Hans, and the artist known as the

---

This essay is largely based upon chapter 5 of my doctoral dissertation, *Northern painters and Italian art from the mid-fifteenth to the early sixteenth centuries* (University of East Anglia, 1983). I should like to acknowledge the advice of my former supervisor, Professor A. H. R. Martindale.

[1] N. Rasmo, *Michael Pacher* (London, 1971), pp. 185–93, 234, 239.
[2] The dating of these works has been debated. See ibid., pp. 20–8 and M. L. Evans, *Northern painters*, pp. 91–2.
[3] Rasmo, *Michael Pacher*, pp. 61–72, 230–3, 239, 247.
[4] The dating of this work has been debated. See ibid., pp. 101–2 and M. L. Evans *Northern painters*, pp. 93–4.
[5] Rasmo *Michael Pacher*, pp. 133–84, 233–4, 248 and, especially, M. Koller and N. Wibiral, *Der Pacher-Altar in St Wolfgang* (Vienna, 1981).

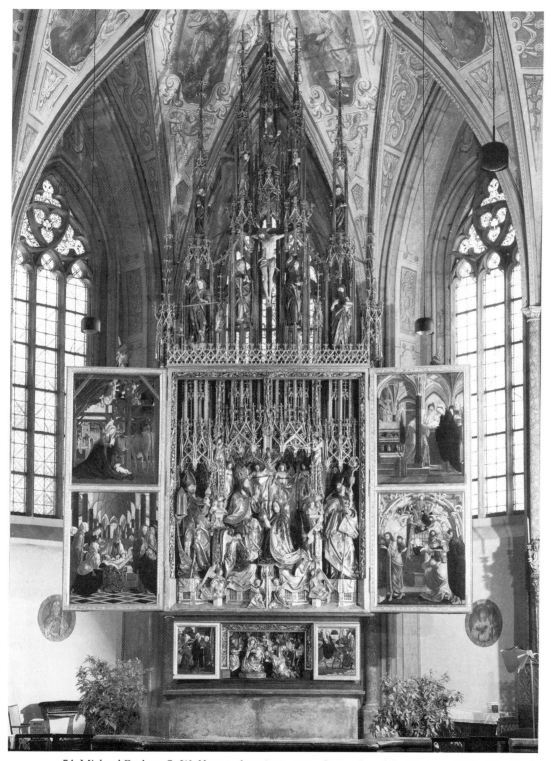

54 Michael Pacher, St Wolfgang altarpiece open, *Coronation of the Virgin* and *Life of the Virgin* shutters

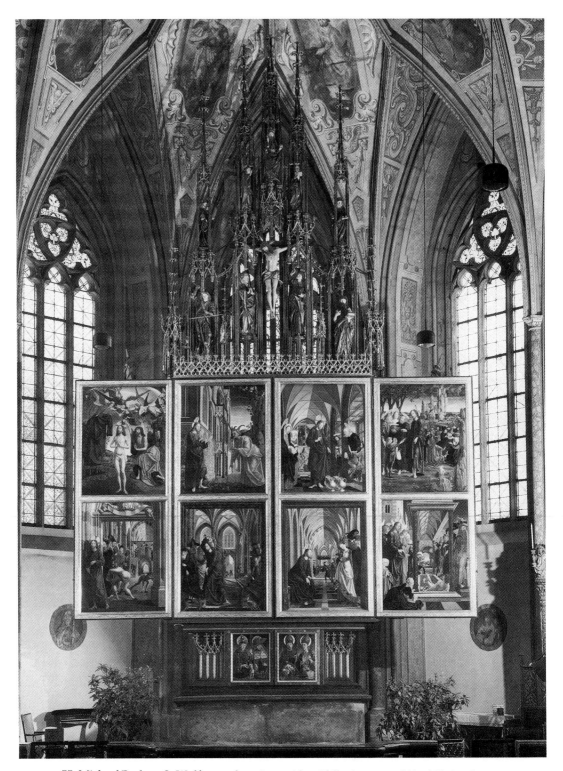

55 Michael Pacher, St Wolfgang altarpiece with middle tier open, *Life of Christ* shutters

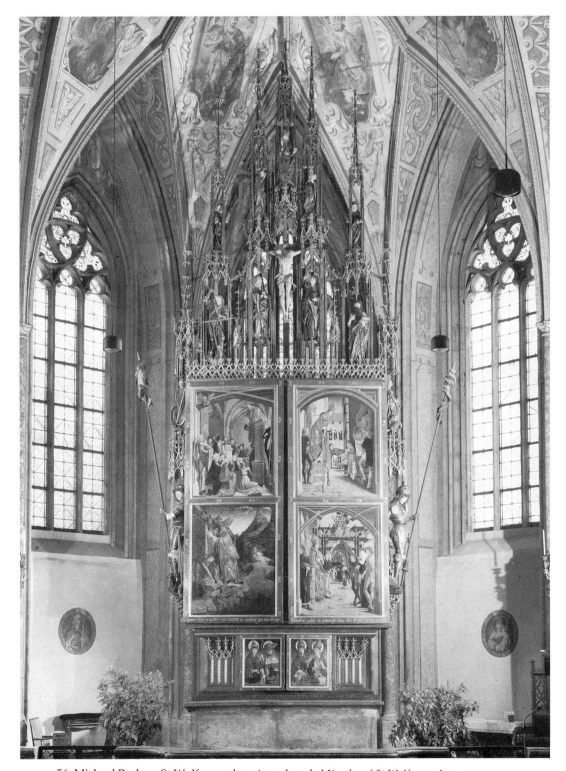

56 Michael Pacher, St Wolfgang altarpiece closed, *Miracles of St Wolfgang* shutters

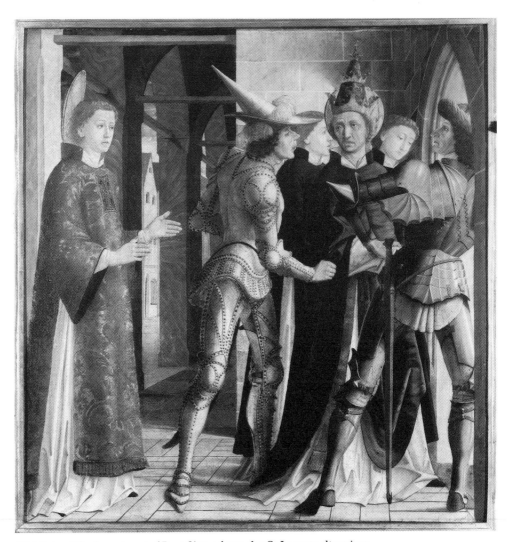

57 Michael Pacher, *Arrest of Pope Sixtus* from the St Lorenz altarpiece

Master of Uttenheim, all of whom worked in a style derived from his own.[6] The painters of the backs of the altarpieces at Gries and St Wolfgang had quite different styles, indicating that Pacher sometimes sub-contracted less important work to outsiders.[7] Accordingly, specific motifs in his altarpieces may reflect the experiences of assistants, as well as those of the head of the *atelier*. Pacher's painted and sculptural *oeuvre* retains a very distinctive identity. That the scale of his undertakings required collaboration should not mislead us to assume, however, that he was merely the designer of the works which bear his name.[8]

[6] Rasmo, *Michael Pacher*, pp. 193–210. See also A. Ronen, *The Peter and Paul Altarpiece and Friedrich Pacher* (Jerusalem, 1974); Koller and Wibiral, *Der Pacher-Altar*, p. 220.

[7] Rasmo, *Michael Pacher*, pp. 63, 134. Earlier, Multscher had also sub-contracted the painted wings of the Sterzing altarpiece to an outsider; M. Tripps, *Hans Multscher: seine Ulmer Schaffenzeit 1427–1467* (Weissenhorn, 1969), p. 127.

[8] This is implied by M. Baxandall, *The limewood sculptors of Renaissance Germany* (New Haven and London, 1980), p. 253.

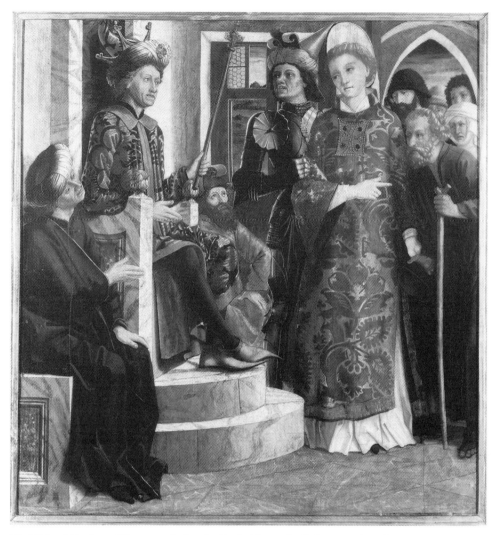

58 Michael Pacher, *St Lawrence before the Prefect* from the St Lorenz altarpiece

Pacher remained a citizen of his native town of Bruneck throughout his life, but all of his documented works were commissioned by patrons from other cities, as far to the south as Bolzano and as far to the north as Salzburg and St Wolfgang. This reflects the geography of the Tyrol, a mountainous region with few individual centres of sufficient size to provide a constant demand for large and expensive altarpieces. That Pacher should travel frequently was in the nature of his employment. As we shall see, on at least two occasions he travelled far beyond the Alpine regions where he customarily lived and worked.

As a mature artist in 1471 Pacher was contractually required to follow the dimensions as well as the approximate iconography of Hans von Judenberg's Bolzano altarpiece of 1422.[9] It is nevertheless difficult to discern a direct relationship between Pacher's

[9] Rasmo, *Michael Pacher*, pp. 233, 247; T. Müller, *Sculpture in the Netherlands, Germany, France and Spain 1400–1500* (Harmondsworth, 1966), pp. 44–5.

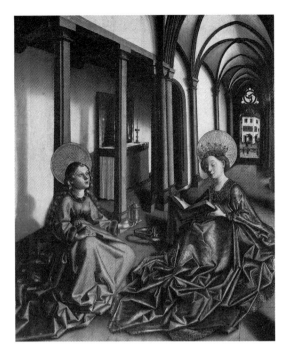

59 Konrad Witz, *St Mary Magdalene and St Catherine in a Church*

work and the late 'International Style' still prevalent in local workshops during his youth. In 1458–9 the distinguished sculptor Hans Multscher of Ulm was based at Sterzing, some forty kilometers from Bruneck, where he assembled and completed his high altarpiece in the parish church.[10] Pacher's familiarity both with the design of this work and with Multscher's monumental and angular style was such[11] that it seems likely that he worked at Sterzing as a journeyman during the completion of this altarpiece. His taste for exotic costume and, particularly, headgear may have been informed by that of Konrad Laib, established at Salzburg since 1449, whose pictorial style derived directly from those of the Master of Flémalle and Jan van Eyck.[12] The skill in the control and depiction of multiple dramatic light sources already apparent in Pacher's early paintings (plate 63) is foreshadowed in the pictures of Konrad Witz of Basel (plate 59).[13] Compositions by Witz could also have provided the source for the numerous vistas down church interiors which appear in the scenes from the St Wolfgang altarpiece wings (plate 55). Pacher's familiarity with the facial types and drapery configurations of the itinerant Dutch sculptor Nikolaus Gerhaert had been noted.[14] The decorative profusion and the emotive contrast between light

[10] Baxandall, *The limewood sculptors*, p. 246.
[11] Müller, *Sculpture* (as in note 9), pp. 120–1; Rasmo, *Michael Pacher*, pp. 64, 30; and Koller & Wibiral, *Der Pacher-Altar*, pp. 222–3.
[12] For Laib see A. Stange, *Deutsche Malerei der Gotik*, vol. 10 (Munich and Berlin, 1960), pp. 20ff. and *Spätgotik in Salzburg-Die Malerei 1400–1530* (Salzburg, 1972), pp. 84–91.
[13] The stylistic similarities between Pacher's paintings and those of Witz were stressed by O. Pächt, *Osterreichische Tafelmalerei der Gotik* (Augsburg, 1929), pp. 44ff., 51ff., who wrongly saw the Master of Uttenheim as an intermediary. Rasmo, *Michael Pacher*, p. 34 casually dismisses the striking similarities without analysis.
[14] See ibid., pp. 68–70 and Baxandall, *The limewood sculptors*, pp. 16, 248–50, 253.

and shade which so distinguishes the shrine of the St Wolfgang altarpiece are distinctly suggestive of works by Gerhaert and may reveal Pacher's knowledge of his lost *chef d'oeuvre*, the retable of 1465–7 at Constance Cathedral.[15] Various motifs in the Gries and St Wolfgang altarpieces also indicate Pacher's familiarity with the engravings of the Master E.S., which diffused Gerhaert's sculptural style throughout South Germany.[16]

With the above comparisons I have sought to locate the origins of Pacher's style within the *avant-garde* circle of painters and sculptors trained in the Netherlands which was transplanted to the Alpine regions between the late 1430s and the early 1460s. As Pacher was a master painter by 1467, he was probably born around the turn of the third and fourth decades of the century and trained during the 1440s or 1450s.[17] In this period the Netherlands was a magnet for artists from many parts of western Europe. The Catalan Luis Dalmau was there as early as 1431 and Dürer's father had travelled from Hungary and spent 'a long time with the great artists in the Netherlands' before he arrived at Nuremberg in 1455.[18] As Pacher was responsive to the work of Multscher and Gerhaert, it is feasible that he sought to acquire a first-hand knowledge of Netherlandish art, the better to compete with such outsiders.

Similarities have been pointed out between the *Coronation of the Virgin* from St Wolfgang (plate 54) and a relief of the same subject at La Ferté-Milon near Paris (plate 47), the work of a Netherlandish trained sculptor dated 1392–1407.[19] It has also been noted that the closest precedents for the prominent cheek-bones, pouting lips and heavily lidded eyes of several of the painted angels from the background of the Gries shrine are to be found in the pictures of Hugo van der Goes.[20] The Netherlandish iconography of the Virgin kneeling before the Christ Child in the St Wolfgang *Nativity* panel (plate 54) could derive from engravings by the Master E.S., but a graphic source could not have suggested the careful portrayal of the Child as the source of illumination in this nocturne. An anonymous panel painting and a miniature are thought to reflect a lost *Nativity* by Hugo van der Goes, set at night with the Virgin kneeling before a luminous Christ Child under a raftered roof with a group of angels illuminated from beneath by the divine light (plate 60).[21] Hugo's lost original may have informed the St Wolfgang *Nativity*. In the same altar-

---

[15] Some hints as to the appearance of this altarpiece may be provided by Gerhaert's deeply undercut tomb of Frederick III in Vienna, dated 1469–73. For the latter and the 'subtle play of light and shade' in Gerhaert's wood sculpture see Müller, *Sculpture*, pp. 82, 107.

[16] M. L. Evans, *Northern painters*, p. 98. The derivation of the engraved *Madonna of Einsiedeln* from a fresco above the tomb of Otto III von Hachberg in Constance Cathedral indicates that the master E.S. was very probably at Constance, presumably in Gerhaert's immediate circle, in 1465–6. See *Meister E.S. Ein oberrheinischer Kupferstecher der Spätgotik* (Munich, 1986), pp. 44–6.

[17] See Rasmo, *Michael Pacher*, pp. 15–6, 247, where it is argued with a rather unrealistic precision that he was born in 1430–5 and trained in 1445–50.

[18] C. R. Post, *A history of Spanish painting*, vol. 7, *The Catalan School in the late Middle Ages* (Cambridge Mass, 1938), pt. 1, p. 12; and H. Rupprich, ed., *Dürer Schriftlicher Nachlass*, vol. 1 (Berlin, 1956), p. 28.

[19] B. Decker, 'Zur geschichtlichen Dimension in Michael Pachers Altären von Gries und St Wolfgang', *Städel-Jahrbuch*, 6 (1977), pp. 313–14; and 'Reform within the cult image: German winged altarpieces before the Reformation', in this volume, pp. 90–105.

[20] Rasmo, *Michael Pacher*, p.68.

[21] E. Hempel, *Michael Pacher* (Vienna, 1931), pp. 5–6; F. Winkler, *Das Werk des Hugo van der Goes* (Berlin, 1964), pp. 119–26, 141–54.

piece the *Death of the Virgin* panel (plate 54) incorporates a foreshortened bed and a small hovering figure of Christ with angels, both motifs which appear in Hugo's famous version of this theme, a work which impressed other foreigners including Schongauer and Bermejo.[22] The semi-circular carved diaphragm arch before Pacher's *Death of the Virgin* may also derive from Netherlandish pictures, such as the *Nativity* by Petrus Christus (Washington, National Gallery of Art).[23] Analogies can also be drawn between the pairs of Evangelists from the back of the St Wolfgang predella (plate 61) and Marinus van Reymerswaele's later pictures of *Two Tax Gatherers* (plate 62). These may not be accidental if Marinus' compositions indeed derive from a lost Eyckian painting of two half-length men with books, as has been proposed.[24] These comparisons suggest that Pacher may have visited the Netherlands, probably not earlier than 1467, the year in which Hugo van der Goes entered the Ghent painters guild,[25] and perhaps during the period March 1469–May 1471, when he is undocumented in the Tyrol.[26] Pacher's works reveal few if any points of comparison with the pictures of Rogier van der Weyden, but a strong attachment to the tradition of Jan van Eyck, which had previously impressed Konrad Witz and Konrad Laib.

Historians have stressed the commercial links between south Germany and north Italy, for which the comparatively low Brenner Pass served as a crucial gateway.[27] Pacher's home town of Bruneck was situated south of the Brenner and slightly to the east of the main trade route through Brixen, Bolzano, Trent and Verona to the Veneto.[28] That he utilised this highway early in his career is indicated by his first known work, the lost altarpiece at Bolzano, signed and dated 1465.[29] There is documentary evidence that several German painters and sculptors were active in the Veneto, at Padua and Treviso as well as Venice itself, during the Quattrocento.[30] These considerations elucidate the context of Pacher's visit to the Venetian *terraferma* which, though undocumented, is clearly attested to by motifs to be found in his earliest surviving paintings.

The abrupt foreshortening in the *Martyrdom of St Lawrence* from his St Lorenz altarpiece and the *Funeral* from his retable dedicated to St Thomas would be incomprehensible without reference to Mantegnesque prototypes, such as the martyred St James and

---

[22] Rasmo, *Michael Pacher*, p. 142. For the early dating of Hugo's painting and the derivation from it of Schongauer's engraving and Bermejo's panel painting in Berlin see D. De Vos, *Stedelijke Musea Brugge Catalogus Schilderijen 15de en 16de Eeuw* (Bruges, 1979), pp. 210–13.

[23] For the latter, and related works, see E. Panofsky, *Early Netherlandish painting*, vol. 1 (Cambridge MA, 1953), pp. 314–15.

[24] By M. J. Friedländer, *Early Netherlandish painting*, vol. 1, *The Van Eycks and Petrus Christus* (Leyden and Brussels, 1967), p. 68. See also L. Silver, *The paintings of Quentin Massys* (Oxford, 1984), pp. 210, 213–14.

[25] For Hugo's chronology see M. J. Friedländer, *Early Netherlandish painting*, vol. 4, *Hugo van der Goes* (Leyden and Brussels, 1969), pp. 11–13.

[26] For Pacher's documentation see Rasmo, *Michael Pacher*, p. 247.

[27] For instance, F. Braudel, *The Mediterranean and the Mediterranean world in the age of Phillip II*, vol. 1 (London, 1972), pp. 202–11.

[28] The route traversed by Antonio de Beatis in May 1517 and Michel de Montaigne in October 1580. See *The Travel Journal of Antonio de Beatis*, ed. J. R. Hale (London, 1979), pp. 59–62 and *Montaigne's Travel Journal*, ed. D. M. Frame (San Francisco, 1983), pp. 46–53.

[29] Rasmo, *Michael Pacher*, pp. 61, 234.

[30] M. L. Evans, 'Northern artists in Italy during the Renaissance', *Bulletin of the Society for Renaissance Studies*, 3: 2 (Oct. 1985), pp. 14–18.

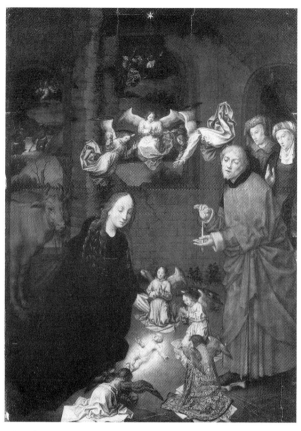

60 After Hugh van der Goes, *Nativity at night*

St Christopher from the Ovetari Chapel frescoes of the Eremitani Church in Padua.[31] Pacher's *Murder of St Thomas* composition (plate 63) reads like a 'mirror image' of Mantegna's Eremitani *St James Baptising Hermogenes* (plate 64), from which the attitude of St James has been transformed into that of the murderous knight. The parquet-type flooring of alternate series of diagonal strips, no longer visible in Mantegna's double fresco of the *Execution of St Christopher* but clearly apparent in an old copy after it in Paris, may also be seen in Pacher's *Arrest of Pope Sixtus* from the St Lorenz altarpiece (plate 57).[32] Pacher's *Lion of St Mark* and *Ox of St Luke* on the reverses of the St Thomas panels have been shown to derive from another important Paduan monument, Donatello's Santo altarpiece.[33] The groupings of monks, mouths agape, craning forward over each other's shoulders from the *Murder* and *Funeral of St Thomas* may also have been appropriated from the crowds of onlookers in Donatello's Santo reliefs of the *Miracle of the Mule*, the *Miser's Heart* and the *Penitent Son* (plate 65).[34]

[31] For the dating of the latter see G. Fiocco, *L'Arte di Andrea Mantegna* (Venice, 1959), pp. 83–92 and R. Lightbown, *Mantegna* (Oxford, 1986), pp. 387–400.
[32] The bottom part of the fresco is almost entirely obliterated. The copy, which appears to be exact, is in the Musée Jacquemart-André, Paris.
[33] By F. Winkler, *Altdeutsche Tafelmalerei* (Munich, 1941), p. 237.
[34] Rather than from lost frescoes by Fillippo Lippi, as proposed by Rasmo, *Michael Pacher*, pp. 24–6.

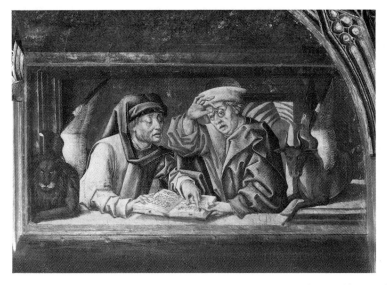

61 Michael Pacher, *St Mark and St Luke*, back of predella of St Wolfgang altarpiece

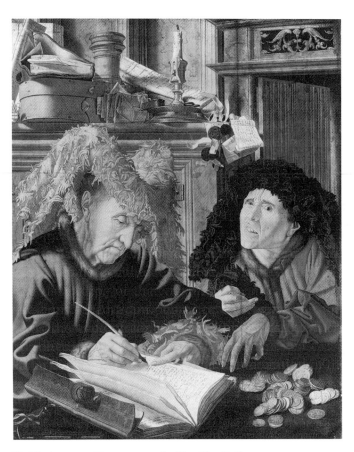

62 Marinus van Reymerswaele, *Two Tax Gatherers*

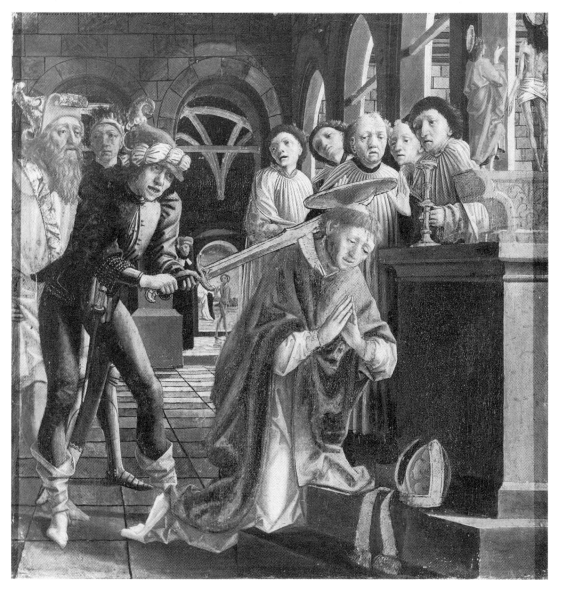

63 Michael Pacher, *Murder of St Thomas* from the St Thomas altarpiece

As neither the St Thomas nor the St Lorenz paintings include low viewpoints, such as appear in Mantegna's frescoes of *St James led to Martyrdom* and the *Martyrdom of St James*, both probably added to the Ovetari Chapel after 1453, it has been proposed that Pacher visited Padua before they were painted, and that the pictures with low viewpoints which appear in the St Wolfgang (plate 55) and the *Fathers of the Church* (plate 67) altarpieces are evidence of a second visit to the city.[35] This hypothesis is unconvincing on account of the fragmentary state of Pacher's early *oeuvre*, his subsequent use of both high and low viewpoints and the presence of the latter in

[35] Ibid., pp. 22–4, 104–8.

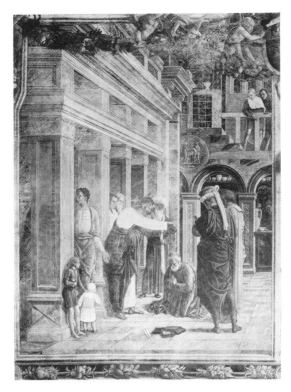

64 Andrea Mantegna, *St James Baptising Hermogenes*, fresco

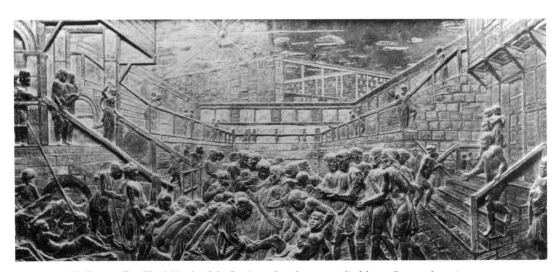

65 Donatello, *The Miracle of the Penitent Son*, bronze relief from Santo altarpiece

the Santo reliefs by Donatello, which he already knew. The primary stylistic evidence that Pacher returned a second time to north Italy, probably in *c*. 1475–6, is the striking similarity between the architectural background of the *Disputation with the Devil* from the shutters of the *Fathers of the Church* altarpiece and that of Antonello da Messina's *St Sebastian* (Dresden, Gemäldegalerie), painted during that artist's own visit to Venice.[36] Whilst it is not impossible that Pacher made such a journey at a time when he was heavily engaged upon the St Wolfgang altarpiece (completed 1479–81), Pächt's attribution of the *Disputation with the Devil* to Friedrich Pacher[37] may have an important bearing on this issue. Friedrich's single signed and dated work, his *Baptism of Christ* of 1483 (Munich, Frauenkirche), depicts the scene behind a diaphragm arch on the threshold of which are a couple of small birds, a fruit and peacock. It has been noted that this motif closely reflects Antonello's *St Jerome in his Study*, (London, National Gallery), in Venice from an early date.[38] In the central panel of the St Catherine altarpiece at Neustift, attributed to Friedrich, is an abruptly fore-shortened figure of a dead executioner with one leg bent.[39] The pose of the latter is unlike any in Michael's known work and its most direct prototype is none other than the recumbent soldier in Antonello's *St Sebastian*. Also, whilst Michael entirely eschewed Renaissance architectural detail, a building with rusticated brickwork appears in the scene of the *Disputation with the Philosophers* and a chapel with a shell niche may be seen in that of *St Catherine refusing to adore the Idol*, both from the shutters of the St Catherine altarpiece. The above interpretation permits the reduction of Michael Pacher's proposed visits to the Veneto to a single journey and dispenses with any necessity for dating this prior to *c*. 1460. The contract for the lost Bolzano altarpiece, dated 1465, may have been drawn up in the course of this sojourn.

Having sought to outline the range of Pacher's sources, we may proceed to evaluate their significance by examining the way in which he applied them in his altarpieces. Both the general compositional layout of the *Murder of St Thomas* (plate 63) and the foreshortened bier in the scene of his *Funeral* reveal a debt to Mantegna, but the emotional impact of either composition is dependent less upon spatial configurations than the complex scheme of lighting, reminiscent of those utilised by Witz (plate 59). In each scene, a primary light source from the right foreground and two subordinate ones from the right and rear envelop the events in pools of light and dark, criss-crossed by long shadows and beams of illumination. Similarly, in the *Martyrdom of St Lawrence* the sanctity and pathetic vulnerability of the tortured saint are emphasised by the abrupt contrast between his pallid body and the shadowy huddle of his executioners. Much of the dramatic force of the *Arrest of Pope Sixtus* (plate 57) depends upon the strong fall of light through the doorway to the right, which throws

[36] Ibid., p. 108. For Antonello's *St Sebastian* see *Antonello da Messina,* Museo Regionale (Messina, 1981), pp. 165, 182–4.

[37] Pächt, *Osterreichische Tafelmalerei,* p. 79 An architectural background related to that in the *Disputation with the Devil* appears in the *Annunciation to Joseph* from an altarpiece dedicated to the Virgin in Innsbruck, attributed to Friedrich Pacher, for which see Stange, *Deutsche Malerei,* p. 187 and plate 291.

[38] By Ronen, *The Peter and Paul Altarpiece,* p.7 and note 24.

[39] Stange, *Deutsche Malerei,* pp. 182, 186 and plate 290.

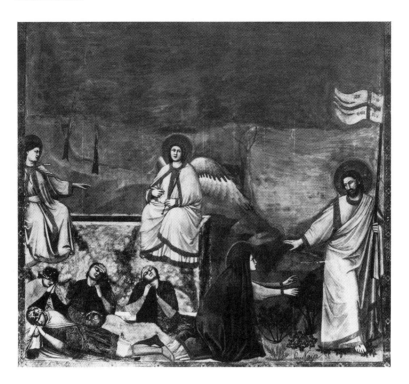

66 Giotto, *Noli Me Tangere*, fresco

the pontiff's face into half shade, contrasting violently with the evenly lit features of the soldiers and deacons.

Both this work and *St Lawrence before the Prefect* (plate 58) portray complex narratives. In the *Arrest*, pope and saint look beseechingly at one another, the other deacons submissively accompany their captors and one soldier glances thoughtfully back at St Lawrence. In *St Lawrence before the Prefect* the judge and his advisers look questioningly at the saint, who tilts his head respectfully and points in answer to the poor crowded anxiously behind.[40] Witz had previously made similar use of expression, glance and gesture to establish the dialogue in scenes from the *Heilspiegelaltar*, but Pacher's compositions portray a sequence of linked psychological responses more reminiscent of Giotto's Scrovegni Chapel frescoes. As in Giotto's famous *Noli Me Tangere* fresco (plate 66), the isolation of Pacher's St Lawrence from his captive superior is established by the devices of futilely outstretched hands against a background of empty space and of the contrast between an immobile pose and a figure which turns back but continues to move purposefully away. Other Giottesque analogies in the *Arrest* are the attitude of the backturned soldier, reminiscent of that of the hooded figure who tugs at St Peter's mantle in the Scrovegni *Kiss of Judas*, and the

---

[40] The Prefect (or the Emperor Decius) demanded the treasures of the Church, which had been entrusted to the saint, from Lawrence, who had distributed them to the sick and needy. See L. Réau, *Iconographie de L'art Chrétien*, vol. 3, pt. 2 (Paris, 1958), pp. 787–92.

group of heads hemming in the Pope which, it has been pointed out,[41] recalls the threatening crowd in Giotto's fresco.

As in the St Thomas and St Lorenz compositions, the figure groupings in the cycle of the life of the Virgin from the innermost shutters of the St Wolfgang altarpiece (plate 54) are generally confined to a narrow foreground space. In the last of these, the *Death of the Virgin*, the figures are primarily arrayed in depth, rather than across the picture plane. This new concept of compositional articulation is developed more fully in the scenes of the life of Christ from the middle tier of shutters (plate 55). The compositions of the *Attempted Stoning of Christ, Christ Cleansing the Temple, Christ and the Woman taken in Adultery* and the *Marriage at Cana* run first across the foreground and thence through the middle distance to the extreme background.

A number of motifs in these panels which emphasise pictorial depth are of Paduan origin. In *Christ Cleansing the Temple* the chancel stairs mounted by figures recalls the Santo relief of the *Penitent Son* (plate 65) and the money-changers peering from the arcade are probably derived from Mantegna's *St James Baptising Hermogenes* (plate 64). This fresco may be the source of the figures looking down from the landing in the *Marriage at Cana*, where those looking round columns have precedents in the Santo reliefs. The resurrected man in the St Wolfgang *Raising of Lazarus* (plate 55) is Mantegnesque and his tomb canopy is a Gothic reinterpretation of the triumphal arch in the Ovetari Chapel *St James led to Martyrdom*. In the *Death of the Virgin*, the *Attempted Stoning of Christ* and *Christ Cleansing the Temple* the figures advancing before the diaphragm arches have precedents in Mantegna's Ovetari frescoes of the *Assumption of the Virgin* and the *Martyrdom of St Christopher*. A more problematic device is that of the pair of similarly posed figures viewed from the front and the back in the *Attempted Stoning of Christ* (plate 55) which have been compared with the archers in the London *Martyrdom of St Sebastian* (London National Gallery) by the Pollaiuolo brothers.[42] As this is the only apparently Florentine motif in Pacher's *oeuvre*, its most likely source would be a print or drawing.[43]

Pacher may have known lost Paduan or Veronese paintings by Jacopo Bellini, whose sketchbooks include several compositions arrayed into perspectival depth. However, there is a marked tendency in Jacopo's known works for the main narrative to become lost in the middle ground or far distance. It is more likely that the St Wolfgang life of Christ scenes (plate 55) owe more to Donatello's relief of the *Penitent Son* (plate 65) and Mantegna's *Martyrdom of St Christopher*, each of which portrays a complex and lucid narrative with the major emphasis in the foreground and a sequence of subsidiary figures continuing the story vertically upon raised levels and backwards into space. The vivid lighting contrasts and the sweeping architectural backdrops in Pacher's scenes derive from the Eyckian tradition.

Despite his use of such perspectival appurtenances as foreshortened figures, receding arcades and tiled floors in the St Thomas and St Lorenz altarpieces, Pacher's

---

[41] By Rasmo, *Michael Pacher*, p. 32.
[42] Ibid., p. 144.
[43] At least one drawing of nudes by Pollaiuolo was circulating in Padua by 1474. See M. L. Evans, 'Pollaiuolo, Dürer and the Master IAM van Zwolle', *Print Quarterly*, 3: 2 (June 1986), pp. 111–12.

early handling of one-point perspective was unsure. In the *Murder of St Thomas* (plate 63) most of the lines of floor tiles converge to a common point but the orthogonals of the altar come together in a quite different location beyond the extreme left of the composition and the tie bars running through the arcade do not align exactly. The lines of the flooring tiles in the *Funeral* scene (the pattern of which may derive from a lost work by Filippo Lippi)[44] are bent where they are interrupted by the furthermost support of the bier and the legs of the man standing beyond it. Pacher came increasingly to grips with the one-point system in the St Lorenz panels, even resorting to a perspectival grid superimposed with diagonal lines masquerading as the pattern of the floor tiles in *St Lawrence before the Prefect* (plate 58). Whilst most of the main orthogonals in the St Lorenz paintings adhere to a common vanishing point, some minor lines such as those of the window embrasures in the *Annunciation* and *St Lawrence before the Prefect* remain unsubordinated to the overall schemes. Only in *St Lawrence Distributing Alms* does there appear a true one-point system with an unemcumbered vanishing point.

Lacking the painted shutters of the Gries altarpiece, it is impossible to examine Pacher's treatment of pictorial space between the St Lorenz and St Wolfgang retables. In the shutters of the latter he used the one-point system with increasing fluency, and jarring solecisms such as the discrepancy in scale between the man mounting the staircase and the figures seated upon the bench in the background of the *Marriage at Cana* are few. In the St Wolfgang altarpiece Pacher began to realise the additional potential of perspective visually to unite the constituent parts of his ensemble. The horizon lines of the *Circumcision* and the *Death of the Virgin* from the lower register of the inner shutters (plate 54) correspond both to one another and to the platform upon which the statue of the Virgin is kneeling in the central shrine.[45] In the upper register, the horizon line of the *Presentation* is significantly lower. The compositions and viewpoints of the life of Christ paintings from the second tier of shutters were arranged with distinct perspectival logic (plate 55). The compositions in its lower register are united by a horizon common to all save the *Raising of Lazarus*.[46] The centre of this group is firmly anchored by two frontal vistas set within similar diaphragm arches, which are flanked by a pair of compositions angled slightly inwards to the right and left. Like the composition of the *Presentation*, those of the central upper scenes from the second tier are foreshortened from a rather lower viewpoint. The top right and top left paintings are landscapes, whose viewing points are not clearly definable. In the outer shutters with the Miracles of St Wolfgang (plate 56), the two upper scenes share a common horizon line lower than that of the bottom right composition. The viewing point of the bottom left landscape, once again, is indistinct. Pacher seems to have been working towards the idea that the compositions in the St Wolfgang shutters should be foreshortened as if viewed from a single point. Jan van Eyck, in the exterior shutters of the Ghent altarpiece, had begun to grasp

---

[44] Rasmo, *Michael Pacher*, pp. 22–6.
[45] Koller and Wibiral, *Der Pacher-Altar*, fig. 19a.
[46] Ibid., fig. 19b.

the notion that the upper components of a multi-tier polyptych could be represented as though from a lower angle than those beneath, but the application of a single systematic viewpoint to an assemblage of pictures remained a dramatically novel idea. Even at the Ovetari Chapel it was imperfectly and even contradictorily realised. Pacher's use of the systematic viewpoint probably depends on slightly later works by Mantegna where it appears in a more fully developed form, such as the St Luke altarpiece of 1453–4 (Milan, Brera), formerly at S. Giustina, Padua.[47]

Pacher's preoccupation with perspective reached its ultimate development in the *Fathers of the Church* altarpiece (plate 67). At the sacristy in Kloster Neustift where the altarpiece was housed, its subject-matter is continued in the frescoes of the Virgin and the four Fathers on the vault above. As in Pizzolo's *tondi* portraying analogous figures in the apse of the Ovetari Chapel, the churchmen are depicted as though viewed through openings cut into the vault.[48] When open, all three panels of the altarpiece are firmly linked by a unified perspectival scheme with an eyepoint at a low level on the centreline of the composition. Not as low as that in Mantegna's late Ovetari frescoes, this viewpoint is more like that in the San Zeno altarpiece in Verona (plate 68), which Pacher could have viewed on his way through the city from the Tyrol to Padua. Like the *Fathers of the Church* altarpiece, Mantegna's polyptych has distinct sculptural associations, as it was partly inspired by Donatello's Santo altarpiece.[49] The three identically sized panels of the San Zeno altarpiece depict a single scene, viewed from the centre, just above the bottom edge of the frame. As in this work, the pseudo-architectural divisions of the compartments of the Fathers of the Church polyptych are continued into the perspectival setting of the composition, illusionistically emphasising the painted architectural background. The foreshortened cloths of honour behind the saints in the wings of Pacher's altarpiece continue behind those in the central panel, defining the rectangular space of the cells which the four inhabit.[50] This motif serves an analogous function to the colonnade which delimits the chamber within which Mantegna's *Sacra Conversazione* is set. The canopies above the heads of Pacher's saints project forwards, slightly before the architectural setting, like the swags and the lamp hanging beyond the foremost plane of Mantegna's painted lintel. Similarly, the foreshortened forms of the lecterns and the little accessory figures in the *Fathers of the Church* altarpiece project to the limit of the painted space in the bottom foreground, as do the figures of St Peter, the tiny mandolin-playing angels and St John in the San Zeno altarpiece.[51]

The formal similarities between these two altarpieces and their complete variance in architectural and decorative detail epitomise Pacher's attitude to his Italian sources.

[17] For which see Fiocco, *L'Arte di Andrea Mantegna*, pp. 96–7 and Lightbown, *Mantegna*, pp. 401–3.

[48] These figures are not, however, foreshortened as though viewed from beneath, as were Pizzolo's in the Ovetari Chapel. Foreshortening more reminiscent of these Paduan prototypes appears in the much damaged frescoes in the tabernacle at Monguelfo, which are attributed to Pacher. See Rasmo, *Michael Pacher*, pp. 102, 114, 233.

[49] A. Venturi, *Storia dell'Arte Italiana*, vol. 7, pt. 3 (Milan, 1914), pp. 146–54.

[50] But Pacher's *Fathers of the Church* are seated in a series of cells, separated from one another by party walls, rather than in a single continuous space.

[51] For the disposition of the scenes from the exterior of the *Fathers of the Church* altarpiece, disturbed in *c*. 1890 but apparently without a common viewpoint, see G. Goldberg, 'Zu Michael Pachers Kirchenväteraltar in der Alten Pinakothek', *Pantheon*, 38: 3 (1979), pp. 263–7.

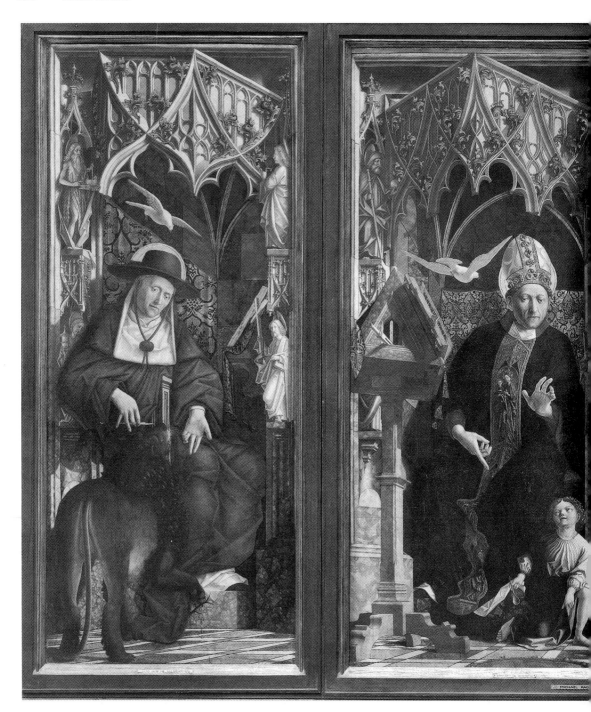

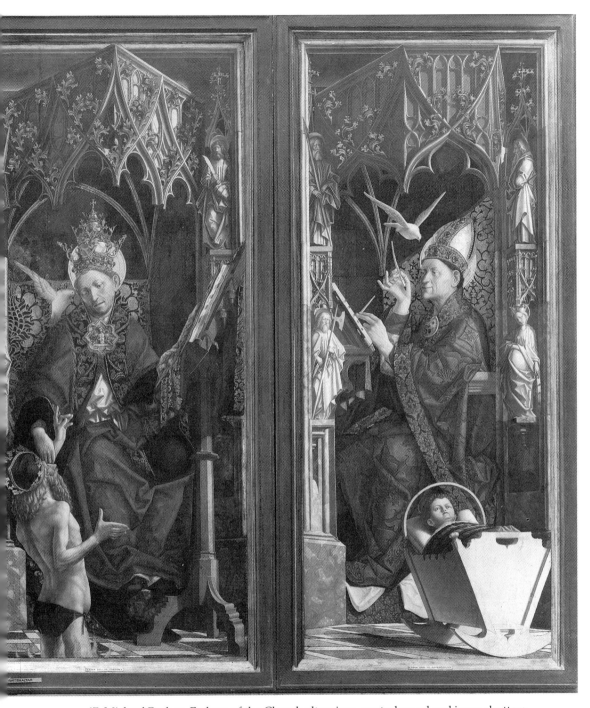

67 Michael Pacher, Fathers of the Church altarpiece, central panel and inner shutters

With the sole exception of the costume of the soldier at the left of the St Lorenz *Arrest of Pope Sixtus* (plate 57) whose cuirass with moulded musculature and pendant skirts probably derives from Mantegna's reconstructions of Roman armour, Pacher unceremoniously rejected the antique vocabulary of the Paduans. When he copied the general structure of settings from Italian works, as in the *Murder of St Thomas* (plate 63), their style of decoration was transformed into northern Gothic. His most specific 'architectural' borrowings from Italian sources, the floor tiles in the *Funeral of St Thomas* and the *Arrest of Pope Sixtus*, are of such an inconspicuous nature that their origins are not immediately apparent. Given the taste for the exotic which is exemplified by the fanciful costume which appears in many of his paintings, this rejection of the antique must have been a deliberate decision. This was not simply a case of satisfying the expectations of conservatively minded patrons, like those at Gries, who considered an altarpiece of 1422 to be a suitable model for a work in prospect in 1471.[52] A freestanding altarpiece like that at St Wolfgang (plate 54) was, in effect, a particular species of wooden architecture, the design and construction of which required a detailed knowledge of architectural and decorative forms and the capacity to draw complex ground plans and elevations. Had Pacher accepted classicising costume and architectural devices in his paintings, he would either have had to similarly modify his sculptures and decorative carvings (as Dürer actually did in his design of 1508 for the frame of his *Adoration of the Trinity* altarpiece)[53], or to tolerate a stylistic disjunction between the two. Moreover, the flamboyant Gothic forms to which he remained faithful echoed the architectural settings in which his altarpieces stood.[54] Even in Padua, the classicising repertory of Donatello and Mantegna was not applied to buildings on a significant scale until long after Pacher's return home. By contrast, the clear narrative configurations of the Italians could be sensitively adapted and their foreshortening, one-point perspective and low viewpoints were enthusiastically accepted for their potential to reconcile pictorial with plastic values.

The central characteristic of Pacher's altarpieces is the co-ordination of sculptural, decorative and pictorial elements. At St Wolfgang the tracery on the head of the bed in the *Death of the Virgin* (plate 54) deliberately echoes the patterns on the plinths beneath the main statues, just as the interleaved ogives on the upper canopy of the balcony in the background of the *Temptation of Christ* (plate 55) recall the forms of the shrine canopies. Diaphragm arches seek to mediate between painted settings which draw the eye into pictorial space and the real architectural forms which frame the shrine sculpture. The perspectival depth of the St Wolfgang pictures was increas-

---

[52] It has been argued that such antiquarian exercises in German sculpture of the later fifteenth and early sixteenth centuries reflected a conscious intention to reform religious images by a return to earlier models. See B. Decker, 'Reform within the cult image: German winged altarpieces before the Reformation', in this volume, pp. 90–105.

[53] P. Humfrey, 'Dürer's Feast of the Rosegarlands: A Venetian altarpiece', *Bulletin of the Society for Renaissance Studies*, 4: 1 (April 1986), pp. 32–4.

[54] It has been argued that the congruity between the decorative architectural framework of the altarpiece and the architectural forms of the church in which it was located sought to emphasise that the image was merely a representation and thus to avoid any stigma of idolatry. See B. Decker, 'Reform within the cult image' in this volume.

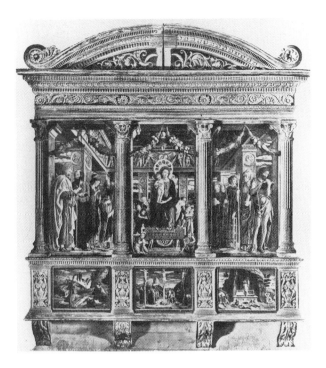

68 Andrea Mantegna, San Zeno altarpiece

ingly stressed at the same time as the full depth of the shrine box was exploited[55] to make the central sculpture a more truly 'three-dimensional' tableau. Spatial correspondences between the former and the latter could be established by the application of a viewpoint common to both. The swelling shapes of drapery forms borrowed from Gerhaert and the Master E.S. allowed a simpler and grander conception of form, whilst their multiple folds and creases accentuated contrasts between light and shadow which emphasised their plasticity. In paintings, analogous effects were achieved by dramatic Eyckian lighting; major sources establishing a dominant accent which was mitigated by secondary schemes. At Kloster Neustift Pacher went further in this breaking down of the barriers between different media, reaching the verge of illusionism with the *Fathers of the Church* altarpiece (plate 67) standing, like a simulation of a carved and polychrome retable, beneath the fictive perforations on the sacristy vault.

'Welsch' and 'Deutsch', Italianate and Germanic, were recognised stylistic options in early sixteenth-century German art[56] and it would be surprising if Pacher was entirely ignorant of this antithesis. He utilised one-point perspective with a verve and daring equal to that of Mantegna, but his indifference to the classical repertory of his Italian contemporaries could hardly have been greater. For costume details,

[55] Baxandall, *The limewood sculptors*, p. 254.
[56] Ibid., pp. 135–42.

drapery types and figure groups, to say nothing of schemes of light and shading, he referred to the Netherlandish *avant garde* and their German followers. His appropriation of ideas and motifs was explicitly conditioned by the context within which these would be applied: the south German altarpiece.

7 Fra Bartolomeo's Carondelet altarpiece and the theme of the 'Virgo in nubibus' in the High Renaissance

André Chastel

The *pala* by Fra Bartolomeo in the Cathedral in Besançon (plate 69) is not mentioned by Vasari in his life of the painter and it has not been much commented upon since. Far from his native land, the *pala* was reserved for visitors to the main city of Franche Comté, for it was unknown to engravers. Its importance was only realised when it was exhibited in Paris in 1935, and especially when it was shown again in 1965.[1]

The origin of the work and its vicissitudes have already received some consideration. In 1511 the archives of the convent of San Marco in Florence mention the commission of a 'picture that went to Flanders, ordered by messire Ferrino' – in other words, Canon Ferry Carondelet, imperial ambassador, who passed through Florence in that year on his way to the court of Rome. Three hundred and twenty gold ducats were paid for this great creation, destined for export, on which Fra Bartolomeo was assisted by Mariotto Albertinelli.[2]

The work was ordered for the funerary chapel of the Carondelet family in the Cathedral of Saint-Etienne, where the canon held the position of archdeacon. As was noted more than a century ago, the *pala* subsequently underwent certain modifications. Following the construction of the citadel in 1676, the *pala* was transferred to the new cathedral; and an unfortunate accident at that time required the amputation of the lunette representing the *Coronation of the Virgin*, the area generally recognised as the contribution by Albertinelli. The central part of the lunette, as well as the figure of an angel that had previously been cut away, are both now in the Staatsgalerie in Stuttgart. An old copy in a local collection gives a sense of the total composition (plate 70), although on a much smaller scale (70 x 40 cm). But it is odd that in the copy the figure of Mary Magdalen replaces that of the canon in his red robe. The same iconographic difference occurs on two other copies of the central part of the altarpiece, one at Chantilly (Museé Condé) and the other in the Soane Museum, London. In 1971 Lodovico Borgo suggested an explanation for this: 'Between 1519 and 1676 the altarpiece was displayed in the chapel of Mary Magdalen in the cathedral of Saint Stephen.'[3] This is correct, but it does not answer the question, and the testimony needs to be tempered somewhat. In 1674 the former imperial city was conquered by the armies of Louis XIV. A commemoration of the ambassador

[1] *Exposition de l'Art italien de Cimabue a Tiepolo* (Paris, 1935); *Le seizième siècle européen* (Paris, 1965).
[2] See V. Marchese, *Memorie dei più insigni pittori, scultori e architetti domenicani*, vol. 2 (Bologna, 1879), pp. 79–80.
[3] L. Borgo, 'The problem of the Ferry Carondelet altar-piece', *Burlington Magazine*, 113 (1971), p. 366 note 13.

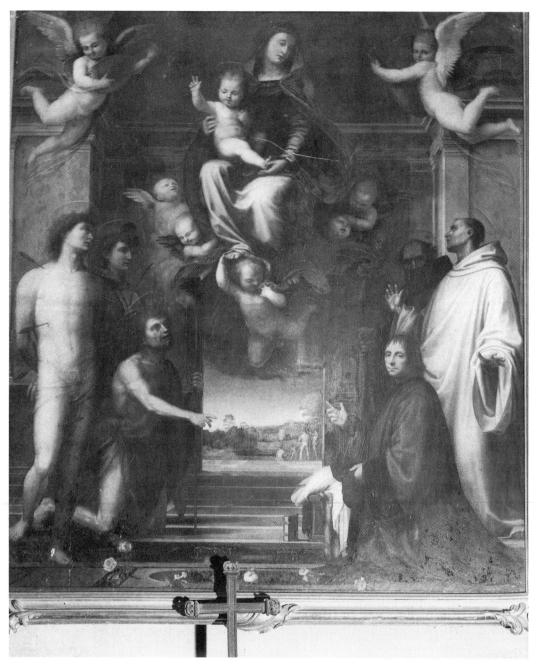

69 Fra Bartolomeo, Ferry Carondelet altarpiece

of Maximilian I and Charles V was not opportune. The painting was thus probably reworked between 1674 and 1676, or a bit later, perhaps around 1719. But it remains to be discovered at what moment the image of Mary Magdalen was in turn effaced, revealing once more the sly but powerful features of the donor. We may assume

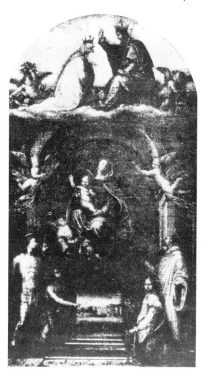

70 Copy after the Carondelet altarpiece

that it happened in the nineteenth century, when the province demonstrated a new pride in its unique history.

The structural layout of the *pala*, according to our reconstruction, has a dissatisfying quality that perhaps betrays some disagreement between the partners, Baccio and Mariotto. Even when one has taken account of differences of style, the three registers of figures do not appear perfectly co-ordinated. The immense but never finished *St Anne* altarpiece (Florence, Museo di San Marco), which was undertaken by Fra Bartolomeo in 1510, has neither a supplementary composition at the top nor a landscape opening below. The symmetrical grouping of the saints, forming what we rather ambiguously call a *Sacra Conversazione*, is perfectly coherent. In the Carondelet *pala*, the celestial region forms a separate scene at the summit of the apse, similar to that in Albertinelli's *Annunciation* (plate 71). But in the latter work the relation between God and the Virgin justifies the disembowelling of the structure, while in the *pala* of Besançon the two zones are superimposed without being physically connected. There may, however, be a symbolic connection, in the sense that the *pala* may be intended to express the traditional opposition of heaven, where the Virgin is exalted, and earth, the locus of original sin. This is a possibility to which I shall return later.

There is no problem with the choice and distribution of the saints: in keeping with tradition, they look either at the Madonna or at the spectator; and all but one raise their eyes towards the celestial scene at the top. The attitude of the Baptist

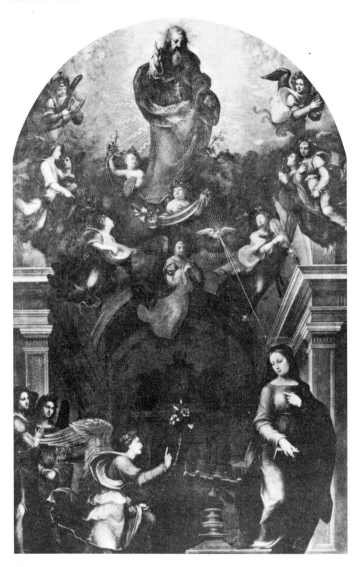

71 Albertinelli, *Annunciation*

kneeling in the foreground cannot, however, be interpreted in the same way. He looks *sursum*, towards the crowned Virgin in the apex, presenting the donor to her, and not, as has been suggested, indicating the strange scene that appears below the floating Madonna. The disposition of the centre of the composition bothered Wölfflin a great deal. Occupied by a Madonna on clouds, *sulle nuvole* or *in nubibus*, it does not convey the powerful impression of majesty that he considered indispensable for compositions in the Grand Manner. Here are his words:

> Another point about the picture is the subject, for the Madonna floats on clouds enclosed within an architectural interior from which the open air is seen only through a door in the background. This is idealisation of a new kind: Bartolomeo may have wanted a dark background with half-light effects in depth, but he also created a

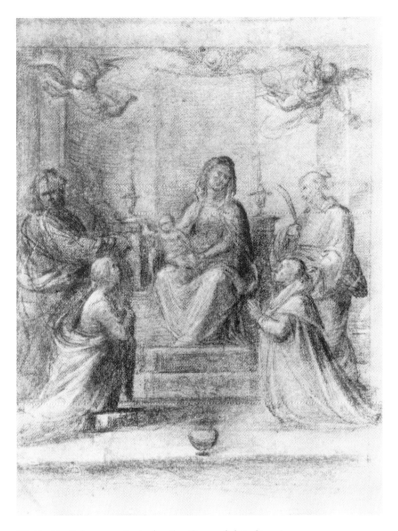

72 Fra Bartolomeo, study for the Carondelet altarpiece

new kind of spiritual contrast with the saints who stand on the ground. The spatial effect is adversely affected, however, and the open door contracts rather than increases it.[4]

The slightly confused character of the work is the result of a series of compromises. The preparatory drawings point in this direction. A study in Rotterdam (Boymans-van Beuningen Museum) generally attributed to Albertinelli is rather close to the general composition, with the Madonna (whose pose is admittedly totally different) floating between two pairs of saints above a vague landscape, and the donor placed on the right. In a study incontestably by the hand of Bartolomeo (plate 72), the donor is on the right, but is placed before an enthroned Virgin framed in an architectural structure. In the *pala*, we find the traditional apsidal articulation but not the throne, as well as a *veduta* opening under the floating group, the lozenge-shape of which

[4] H. Wölfflin, *Classic art*, trans. P. and L. Murray (1899; London, 1952), p. 146.

is formed by the angels and the Madonna. Thus two entirely different conceptions are brought together in the final composition.

Serious conflicts must have plagued the workshop in the convent, for the partnership between Mariotto and Baccio broke up at the end of 1512. Albertinelli lacked conviction, and as Vasari ironically recounted, 'prese in odio le sofisticherie e gli stillamenti di cervello della pittura' ('he began to hate the subtleties of painting and the way it taxed his brains'), instead opened an inn so as to devote himself 'a meno faticosa e più allegra arte' ('to a less demanding and more cheerful craft').[5] But I would like to show that the rather unusual composition of the Besançon altarpiece also illustrates something else: namely, a crisis in the conception of the Marian *pala* in Italy around 1510; or, to be more precise, the persistent competition in these years between the free structure (with landscape) and the architectonic structure (with throne). The conflict between the two painters thus appears to reflect a more general problem. But, as it happens, the problem itself is the subject of rather widely differing readings. Sydney Freedberg, for example, compares the composition for Carondelet with that of Raphael's roughly contemporary *Madonna of Foligno* (plate 73), which also shows a large circular motif resting on two lateral groups framing a landscape.[6] But how is such a remarkable coincidence possible? Since Fra Bartolomeo went to Rome only in 1514, is it possible that Raphael owes some debt to our Dominican? But Raphael left Florence in the summer of 1508; and in any case, what is the source of the new Marian iconography of the *Virgo in nubibus*?

Ludovico Borgo, on the other hand, has formulated an argument that deserves comment:

> While the Carondelet painting still bears a resemblance to the works of the 1490s familiar to the Florentine scene, such as Perugino's *Vision of Saint Bernard*, Fra Bartolomeo's other altarpieces of the same period with architectural interiors do not. The source for their key architectonic feature, the spherical niche, must be sought outside of Florence, in Giovanni Bellini's San Giobbe and San Zaccaria altars which Fra Bartolomeo had, almost certainly, studied during his visit to Venice (1508).[7]

I have difficulty in accepting such an interpretation. The reference to Perugino is prompted by the nude figure of St Sebastian on the left, which is clearly drawn from the Umbrian model; but is painted in full light which – as Wölfflin noticed – reminds us rather of the corresponding figure in Bellini's San Giobbe altarpiece. In any case, the reference to Perugino does not hold true for the totality of the composition. May I add that the argument is not an altogether happy one? For when it came to his turn to treat the theme of the *Vision of St Bernard* (Florence, Accademia) in 1507, Fra Bartolomeo marked his distance from Perugino by orchestrating a well-developed landscape, even before he received any encouragement from his Venetian experience to portray views of nature. Was it an interest in landscape and the accidents

[5] G. Vasari, *Le vite de' più eccellenti pittori, scultori ed architettori*, ed. G. Milanesi, vol. 4 (1568; Florence, 1880), p. 222.
[6] S. Freedberg, *Painting of the High Renaissance in Rome and Florence* (Cambridge MA, 1961), pp. 202–3.
[7] Borgo, 'The problem of the Ferry Carondelet altarpiece', p. 371; also L. Borgo, 'Fra Bartolomeo, Albertinelli and the *Pietà* for the Certosa of Pavia', *Burlington Magazine*, 108 (1966), pp. 463–8.

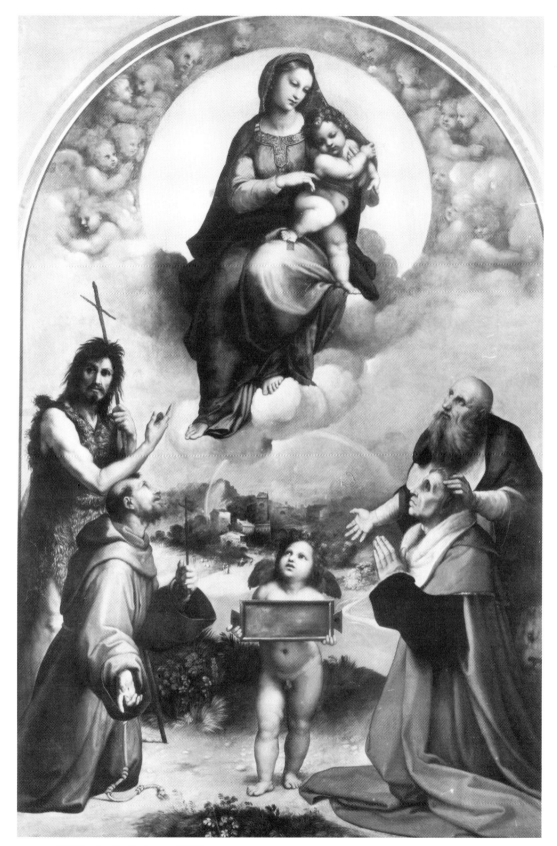

73 Raphael, *Madonna of Foligno*

of light that attracted him to Giovanni Bellini? By contrast, there is no reason why he should have been particularly struck by the latter's use of an architectural envelope for his sacred compositions, since there already existed ample Florentine examples by such painters as Botticelli and Raphael.

I see proof of this special interest in the artist's earliest works, starting with the *Annunciation* in Volterra, the attribution of which to Baccio was so long in coming. This work already shows his favourite device of an opening into the distance in the form of a *veduta inquadrata*, permitting a fine play of shadows on the countryside. From a formal point of view, the surprising landscape of the Carondelet *pala* follows the same layout. I cited the luminous *St Bernard*, so rich in nuances: everything here is organised so that the figures facing one another act as masses framing the tunnel of space, in which the golden undulation of nature in summer unfolds towards the horizon. This work dates from 1507 – at the very time, in other words, when Lorenzo Lotto and Giorgione were searching out novel effects of a similar type. In Tuscany, the original, eccentric Piero di Cosimo – often so close to the Frate, as has been observed – was the only one to have similar preoccupations; but his drawing is more rigid, and his almost grimacing figures have not yet received the delicate anointing of Leonardism.

The most exquisite moment of Fra Bartolomeo's art in this respect is represented by the altarpiece with two saints in Lucca (Museo Nazionale), with 'Santa Caterina da Sienna ratta da terra spirito' (Vasari),[8] together with her less mystical counterpart, Mary Magdalen. The relationship between heaven and earth dominates the whole composition; but the framing pilasters are pushed apart, permitting the horizon to dilate. The moment is one of perfect lyricism; and one is not surprised to learn that Baccio passed the time on the return journey from Lucca in singing: 'per passar tempo usava cantare'. The work dates from 1509, and something of its melodic suppleness remains in the Carondelet *pala*, despite the fact that the latter is a Marian altarpiece, obedient to certain norms. In the grouping of the saints, the painter has played off his responding colours and pools of unifying shadows with a deftness that led John Shearman to term the work a masterpiece of the High Renaissance.[9] But the crucial problem was that of the placement of the Virgin. In giving her a position *in nubibus*, one that had hitherto been reserved for God the Father (as in the Lucca altarpiece), Fra Bartolomeo took an entirely new decision in Florence. For he suppressed the apsidal throne so well illustrated by Botticelli's San Barnaba altarpiece (Florence, Uffizi) and by Raphael's *Madonna del Baldacchino* (Florence, Pitti). By maintaining the rising walls of the apse the painter emphasised – a bit too strongly – that the Virgin carried by the angels occupied the place of the enthroned Madonna; and he was obliged to pierce the back wall so as to insert the *veduta*, which was indispensable if he wanted to display a view of nature under the celestial group.

The precision with which the landscape is painted departs from the Umbrian stereotypes; and the fascinating drawings from the Gabburri collection (plate 74) assure

[8] Vasari, *Le vite* (as in note 5), p. 192.
[9] J. Shearman, 'Le seizième siècle européen', *Burlington Magazine*, 108 (1966), p. 60.

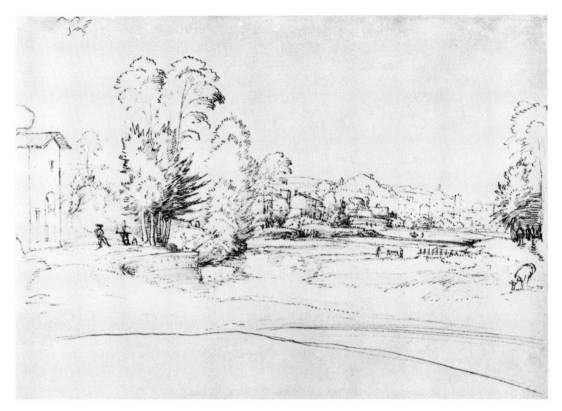

74 Fra Bartolomeo, Landscape drawing

us that when (plate 74) he took up painting again in 1505, Fra Bartolomeo turned, with a curiosity exceptional among the Florentines (Leonardo and Piero di Cosimo apart), to specific aspects of the countryside. The *veduta* of the countryside in the Carondelet *pala* is a product of this curiosity. Instead of the silhouettes of peasants he has introduced nude figures, apparently intended to refer to Eden, and in particular to Original Sin, in line with the representations frequently found in the lower sections of the Marian throne. If I may indulge in a personal appreciation of it, I would call it the postlapsarian human family in a prelapsarian garden.

If the architectural structure had melted away entirely, we would have come very close indeed to the *Madonna of Foligno*, which was completed, as we have seen, at exactly the same moment as this work. But the type of compromise we are witnessing here may be understood better if one considers what had been happening for some time in Emilia. Two works that Fra Bartolomeo may have known (though we cannot be sure) help to clarify the situation. In Lorenzo Costa's Gheddini altarpiece of 1497 for S. Giovanni in Monte, Bologna, the artist has slipped in a deep *veduta* under a raised throne of a strongly articulated Ferrarese type; but the ensemble here is so poorly conceived that the saints, as though indifferent or distracted, do not even look towards the Madonna as convention dictates. Francia's altarpiece of 1499 for S. Martino Maggiore, again in Bologna, marks a curious stage in the expanding of space in the sacred scene, with the *veduta* well in place, and the throne replaced by a strange arcade forming a base. The embarrassment of these and other painters if clearly demonstrated by the awkward solution contrived by a provincial artist such as Macrino d'Alba, who thought it fitting to place the Madonna on a throne made of clouds (plate 75). The more responsible painters of the period clearly understood the necessity of discarding the formula of the throne if the composition was to be given breathing space. But there was an internal difficulty to overcome. It was not, in fact, in Bologna, nor even in Venice, where Cima da Conegliano was so attracted to the open-air *Sacra Conversazione,* that the decisive step was taken of placing the Virgin *in nubibus,* borne aloft by angels in the manner of God the Father.

This was the solution first proposed simultaneously by Fra Bartolomeo and Raphael. Perhaps it was suggested by the former to the latter; or just possibly, the relationship was the reverse. In any case, this solution, once discovered, shattered the architectural armature and the throne of the Quattrocento. Raphael's masterly *Madonna of Foligno,* painted for the church of the Aracoeli in Rome, then engendered by contagion ten years later another masterpiece, Titian's Ancona altarpiece (Museo Civico), the immense posterity of which cannot be described here.

If things happened as we suggested, should we then regard the evolution of the Marian *pala* in terms of a chain of formal schemes proposed by the leading masters in a moment of intense artistic invention – in other words, in terms of a problem or artistic morphology? In a sense the answer is yes. And yet, it is historically correct, it seems to me, to introduce another factor that should help us account for the passage from the static type of the Madonna enthroned to the dynamic type of the *Virgo in nubibus.*

Chris Fischer has noticed that in Fra Bartolomeo's *Mystic Marriage of St Catherine* (Paris, Louvre), completed in 1511, two of the saints embrace affectionately.[10] A preliminary drawing (Lille, Museé) identifies them as Francis and Dominic, and hence they are symbols of a great reconciliation between the friars minor and the preachers. It should be noted that the *pala,* which belonged to the convent of San Marco, was acquired by the Soderini government and offered to Jacques Huralt, the French ambassador, in whose care the painting found its way to the bishopric of Autun in 1512. Fischer thinks that Carondelet was able to interest his compatriot Huralt in the art of the Frate from San Marco. But in fact things happened differently. It was a question rather of competition: since the representative of the Emperor Maximilian had ordered an altarpiece from the atelier of San Marco, the ambassador of Louis XII felt obliged to obtain one too. And thus two *pale* by Fra Bartolomeo crossed the Alps.

Now, why the embrace of the two great rival saints whom Dante had already portrayed in an exchange of reciprocal praise in Paradise? We should remember that the *Mystic Marriage* was a *pala* destined for a conventual church. The theme of the

---

[10] C. Fischer, 'Remarques sur *Le mariage mystique de Sainte Cathérine de Sienne* par Fra Bartolomeo', *Revue du Louvre et des Musées de France,* 22 (1982), pp. 167–80.

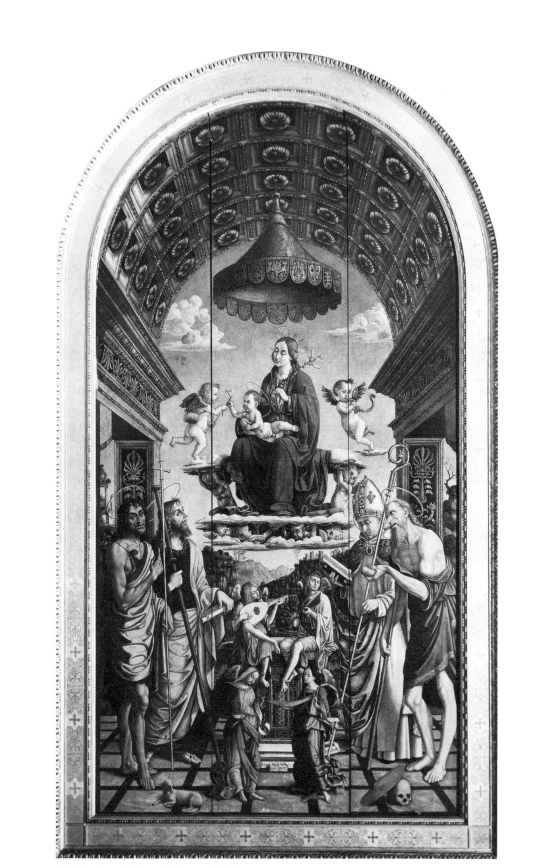

75 Macrino d'Alba, *Virgin and Child with Saints*

embrace is found in the *Golden Legend*.[11] For a period of time, theological discussion had been marked by a lively animosity between the Franciscans, partisans of the Immaculate Conception (The Virgin conceived without sin), and the Dominicans, who held that the Virgin was exempted after her birth. Pope Sixtus IV intervened in 1483 by declaring the Virgin to be situated 'outside impure humanity', and hence worthy of inclusion in the celestial court of the Divinity. The question of a new Marian iconography was, in a sense, timely. Many historians have pondered the implications of the Immaculist dogma. While the enthroned Madonna signified the Church, the *Virgo in nubibus* signified a divine essence, and merited the cult of *hyperdulia*, close to the cult of *latria*, reserved for God alone.

We feel there must have been a moment of great hesitation about the necessity of a new formal arrangement. When we look at the famous altarpiece with six saints (including St Philip Benizzi and St Antonino) by Piero di Cosimo (plate 76), we become aware that 'Nostra Donna ritta che è rilevata da terra con un dado, e con un libro in mano, senza il figluolo' ('Our Lady standing, raised from the ground on a dado, with a book in her hand and without the Child'),[12] is something more than a normal Virgin Annunciate. When Albertinelli tried to imitate it in an altarpiece of 1506 (Toulouse, Museé des Augustins), he clearly did not understand the *sofisticherie* of the new Marian iconography, and put a simple Virgin and Child on a pedestal adorned with the usual emblem of the Fall.

Evidence of the embarrassment that painters could experience when required to represent the dogma may be found in a mediocre altarpiece by Previtali of c.1515 (plate 77).[13] The artist returned to the old system of phylacteria as a means to introduce inscriptions and to make the concept of the work explicit. Thus God the Father presents a banderole inscribed 'Videte matrem filii mei sine originali peccato conceptam' (Behold the mother of my Son, conceived without original sin); while St Augustine (?), one of the two symmetrically disposed doctors, holds a long scroll with obscure theological commentaries that had been obliterated by repaints, but which re-emerged during the recent cleaning. Above the oak-tree painted in the upper right-hand corners of the composition we even find a bird (goldfinch?) with the rather unexpected inscription: 'avis paradisi'. Strangely enough, the Virgin is kneeling on the ground, with her hands joined in prayer; the crown on her head is the emblem of her exalted position, but it did not occur to the painter to place her *in nubibus* above her champions. Neither the usual type of the *Annunciation*, nor the crowning of the Virgin in the skies, were considered appropriate for conveying the meaning of the *Immacolata*; and still less the type of composition known as the *Sacra Conversazione*, with the Virgin enthroned.

It would be of great interest to know if the invention of the Virgin without a throne was due to Fra Bartolomeo or to Raphael,[14] or if it was the fruit of one of those

---

[11] Jacobus de Voragine, *The golden legend*, trans. G. Ryan and H. Ripperger (New York, 1969), pp. 417–18.

[12] Vasari, *Le vite* (as in note 5), pp. 137–8.

[13] See S. Marinelli, ed., *Proposte e restauri: i musei d'arte negli anni ottanta* (Verona, 1987), pp. 83–5.

[14] For a recent study of the iconographic sources of Raphael's *Madonna of Foligno*, see C. Gardner von Teuffel, 'Raffaels römische Altarbilder: Aufstellung und Bestimmung', *Zeitschrift für Kunstgeschichte*, 50 (1987), pp. 1–45.

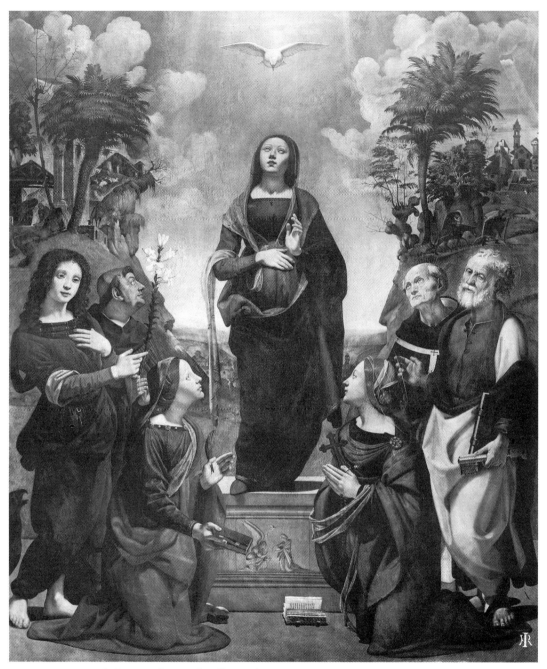

76 Piero di Cosimo, *Immaculate Conception*

operations without precise date or location so frequent in the history of religious symbolism. What is clear is that the composition of the Carondelet *pala* reflects an intense debate currently being pursued in the workshops of the leading Italian painters on the very structure of the church altarpiece.

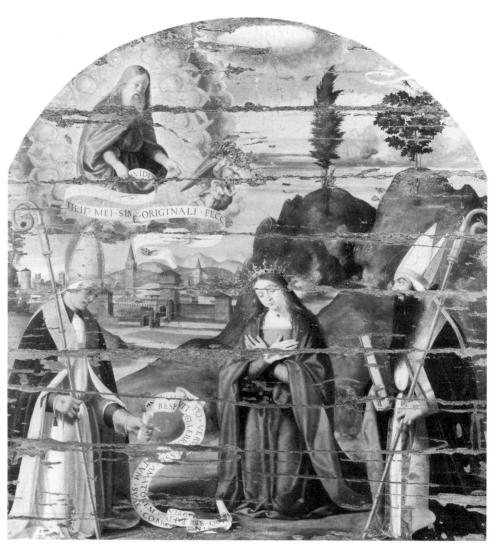

77 Andrea Previtali, *Immaculate Conception*

8 'Divinità di cosa dipinta': pictorial structure and the legibility of the altarpiece

David Rosand

The invitation to participate in a conference on 'the altarpiece in the Renaissance' encouraged speakers 'to address the broader issues relating to the altarpiece as a type ... rather than dwelling too narrowly on art-historical detail'. In this chapter I have taken the invitation rather literally, even at the risk of treating issues so fundamental as to appear obvious. Within the title both of the conference and the present volume, the juxtaposition of the two terms, 'altarpiece' and 'Renaissance', posits certain assumptions as axiomatic. It presupposes the generic status of the altarpiece as a specific pictorial type, and it assumes modification of the type by historical circumscription. That generic status is defined in the first place by a functional constant, which determines not only the special position of the image, over the altar, but its affective role in devotional or liturgical practice. That functional identity, as it were, is subject to formal inflection according to variable circumstances – of time and place, patronage and personality, of the requirements of cult and the contingencies of history, of material and medium.

In this paper I am concerned essentially with the Italian *pala*, a painted image on a single flat surface. In accepting both the invitation and its underlying assumption, we confront a remarkably controlled set of conditions for the investigation of the operations of pictorial structure. Those conditions are determined, on the most basic level, by factors such as format, field, and frame. In considering the shape of the field and the treatment of the plane we confront particular pictorial options, and in attending to them we engage certain fundamentals of the art of painting itself. The issue before us, ultimately, is the degree to which the meaning and function of the altarpiece inhere in its pictorial structure, that is, the degree to which signification depends upon form.

Placed above the sacramental table of the altar, the altarpiece enjoys a privileged position within its sanctified architectural setting; its phenomenological situation is precisely defined, as is its relationship to the viewer/worshipper. The focus that is essential for that relationship suggests certain qualities of the field, especially its dominant verticality (plate 78). Through its vertical axis, the painting participates most directly in the surrounding architecture and its ascent from pavement to vault. Moreover, the particular shape of the field, architecturally derived, confirms that participation: the arched crown of the framing border, whether pointed or round, marks the culminating accent of the vertical axis and its aspiration. Establishing a fundamental polarity of high and low, top and bottom, with its clear, but reversible,

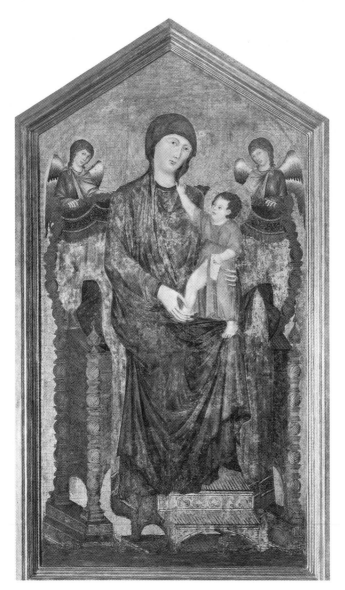

78 Cimabue, *Madonna and Child Enthroned with Angels*

directionality, the dominant vertical axis enables the pictorial accommodation of notions of heaven and earth.

Weighting the vertical axis of the field also establishes the central focus of design, its iconic stasis. Even when the overall field is expanded horizontally (plate 79), ecclesiastical function requires the articulation of that field to focus on the central vertical. What we might call the iconic imperative of the altarpiece enforces that centrality of focus; the lateral forces of the field operate centripetally, with reference to the centre. Such visual dynamics naturally determine the relationship of the viewer/worshipper to the image. In viewing such a field, lateral scansion is rendered irrele-

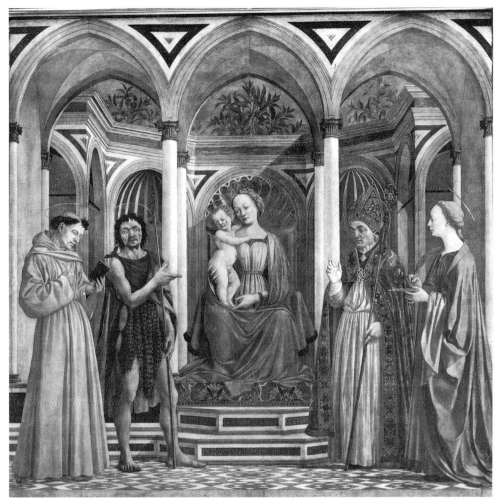

79 Domenico Veneziano, *Madonna and Child Enthroned with Saints*

vant, except as a way toward the centre. The iconic field insists upon direct confrontation – with a divine centre. All eyes are, literally, on the deity (or his surrogate), the functional core of the image.

These, then, may be postulated as some of the constant values that distinguish the altarpiece as a pictorial type. There are, of course, exceptions, but by their own alternative example they tend to confirm the rule. Horizontal extension may indeed be maintained at the expense of the central axis (plate 80); such lateral scansion belongs in effect to a different mode: narrative as opposed to iconic. These alternatives, however, are not mutually exclusive. Often they are held in expressive tension: horizontal narrative representation – especially a votive gesture (plate 81) – may work within and even against a field that strongly preserves the iconic imperative by its framed shape. Under other conditions, the central axis itself might be shifted in

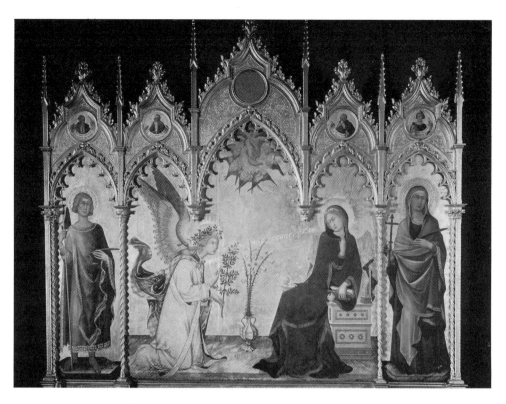

80 Simone Martini and Lippo Memmi, *Annunciation*

the field, leaving a void, as it were, to be filled by the centralising focus of the altar itself.[1]

Viewing an altarpiece is hardly an act of detached aesthetic experience. The act of viewing is – or ought to be – an act of worship. In no other pictorial category is seeing quite so charged with responsibility – and, potentially, with such consequence. What distinguishes the altarpiece functionally from other kinds of devotional imagery is its liturgical situation. Set above the altar table, the painting is transformed by the ceremony over which it visually presides: the celebration of the mass (plate 82). Its own authority as an image is enhanced and validated by its presence at the elevation of the host. That special aura clings to it even, as it were, off hours.

Vertical format and central focus, we understand, involve more than merely formal matters. Their formal dimensions, however, are of special interest, for they permit us to begin measuring the Renaissance inflections of the traditional pictorial type (plate 83). Indeed, just these issues were addressed by Alberti in the first declaration of the new principles of Renaissance painting. Although *De pictura* famously ignores any comment on religious imagery – and in fact quite deliberately sets forth a programme for secular painting that will have proleptic resonance – Alberti's discussion of the art, his exploration of its structural foundations and his expectations of its

---

[1] As, for a prime example, in Titian's *Madonna di Ca' Pesaro*: see David Rosand, *Painting in Cinquecento Venice: Titian, Veronese, Tintoretto* (New Haven and London, 1985), chapter 2, esp. pp. 58–69.

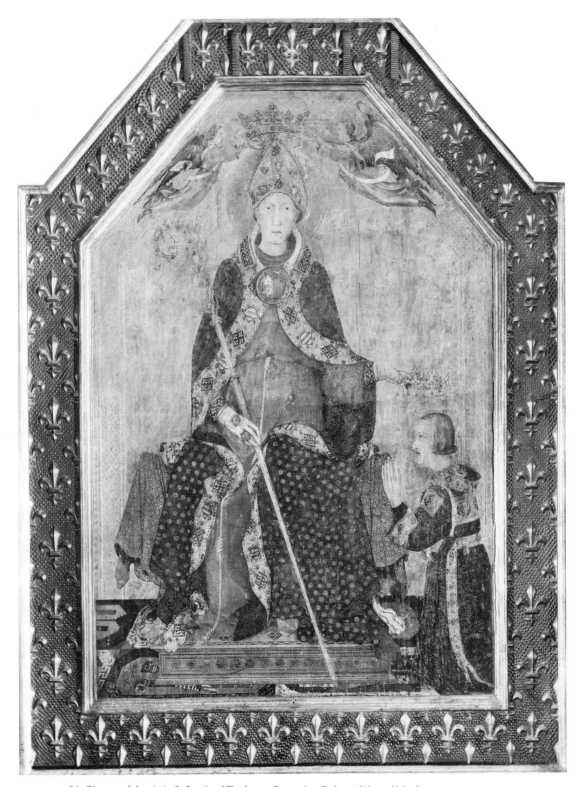

81 Simone Martini, *St Louis of Toulouse Crowning Robert, King of Naples*

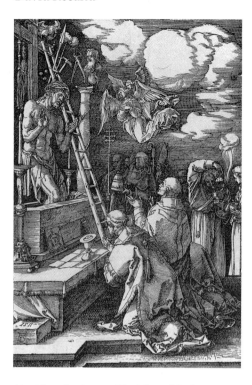

82 Albrecht Dürer, *The Mass of St Gregory*

affective force, can be directly related to a changing conception of the altarpiece.
We might even suggest that it is the altarpiece that serves as the most fruitful model
for the new principles (plate 84). Alberti's presentation of artificial perspective, with
its overt recognition of the picture plane as simultaneously opaque and transparent,
assumes its most weighted consequence in that context. The principle of the inter-
sected pyramid of vision and, especially, the location of the centric point in the field
acknowledge the privileged position of the viewer, at once determined and determining. The viewer is to appear on the same level as the objects pictured on the
plane. If those objects are sacred beings the implications for the viewer are indeed
charged. Perspective construction renders the divine accessible in a special way.
Alberti's injunction, in book two, against the application of gold leaf in painting
effectively affirms that new accessibility.[2] The gold ground, a fundamental value of
the traditional altarpiece, stood for the divine. In the new art it was to be replaced
by the limpid continuum of natural space.

The Renaissance system of artificial perspective places special emphasis on the
mediation between realms on either side of the picture plane. Structurally, the frame
becomes the natural locus of such mediation. Alberti's recommended interlocutor
(para. 42), someone in the picture who directly addresses the viewer and cues him
on proper response, extends that function beyond pictorial structure to the figural
participants in the image, that is, to the *istoria* itself. That concept, the *istoria*, adds

[2] Leon Battista Alberti, *De pictura*, ed. C. Grayson (Rome and Bari, 1975), para 49.

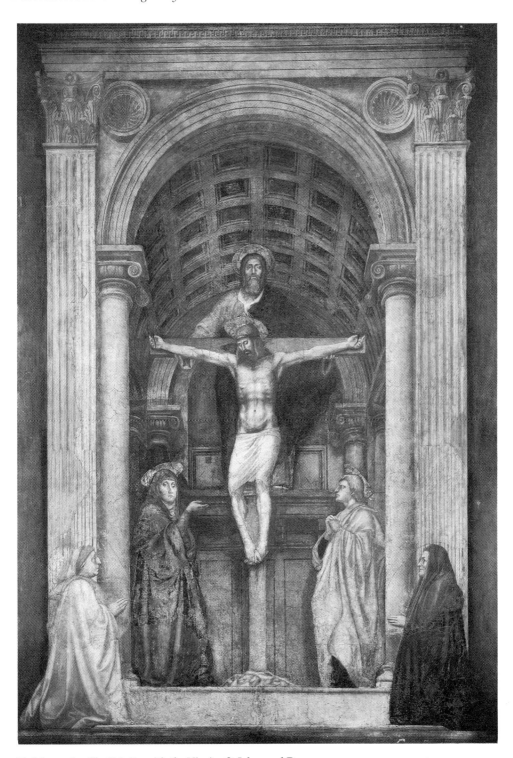

83 Masaccio, *The Trinity with the Virgin, St John, and Donors*

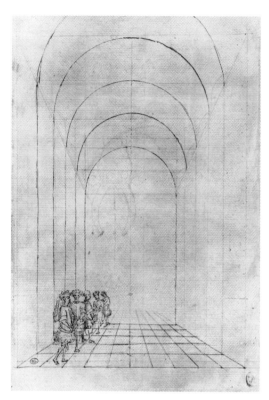

84 Circle of Pisanello, Perspective study

a further Renaissance inflection to the basic type of the altarpiece. Alberti is hardly referring to altarpieces when he declares that the *istoria* worthy of praise should hold the eye of the learned and the unlearned alike, delighting the eye of the beholder as it moves his soul (para. 40).[3] We recognise the rhetorical commonplace. Nonetheless, the mechanics of vision and response that concern Alberti, the affective appeal of the *istoria*, remain especially central to the full functioning of the altarpiece. The viewer's responsibility to the image involves active engagement and interpretation.

To a degree, then, we are locating the altarpiece as a pictorial species within the larger genus of painting in general. The demands and expectations of Renaissance painting, as first articulated by Alberti, apply with special force to the altarpiece: above all, the values of engagement and legibility, inviting interpretation.

At the beginning of the sixteenth century, Leonardo amazed all of Florence when he exhibited the cartoon for an altarpiece intended for the high altar of SS. Annunziata, an image of the Virgin and Child and St Anne (plates 85–6). Vasari recounts that it 'not only amazed all the artists, but, finished as it was, for two days men and women, young and old, continued to crowd into the room where it was exhibited, as if attending a solemn festival, to see the marvels of Leonardo, and all were asto-

---

[3] For recent discussion of the subject, see K. Patz, 'Zum Begriff der ''Historia'' in L. B. Alberti's ''De Pictura'',' *Zeitschrift für Kunstgeschichte*, 49 (1986), pp. 269–87; also D. Rosand, ' *Ekphrasis* and the Renaissance of Painting: Observations on Alberti's Third Book', in *Florilegium Columbianum: Essays in Honor of Paul Oskar Kristeller*, ed. K. -L. Selig and Robert Somerville (New York, 1987), pp. 147–65, with further bibliography.

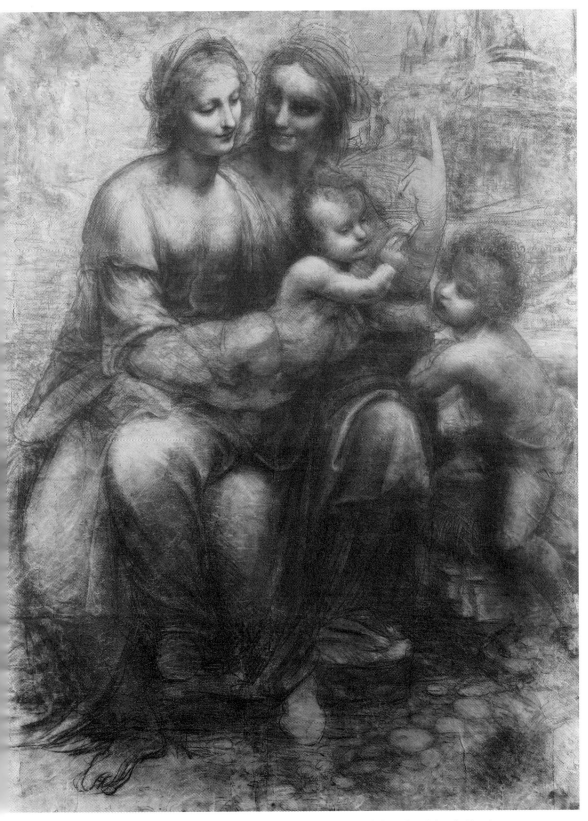

85 Leonardo da Vinci, *Virgin and Child with St Anne and the Infant John the Baptist*

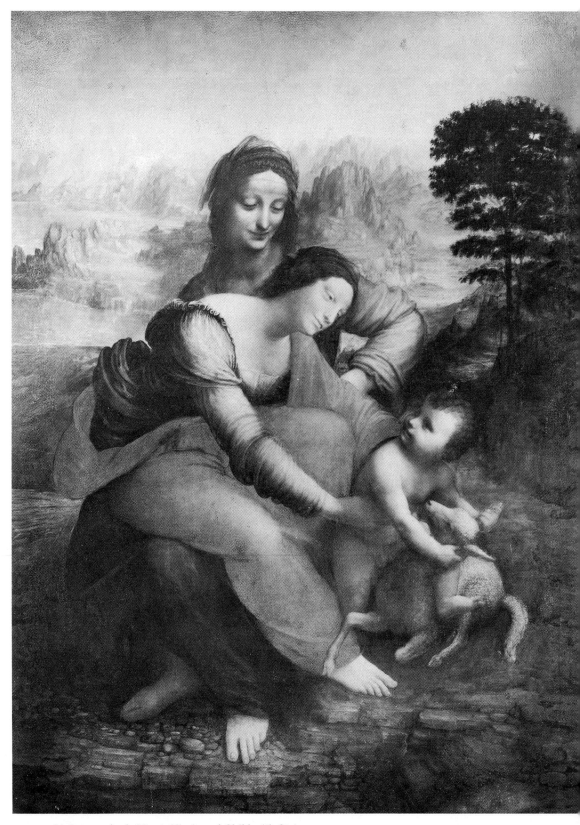

86 Leonardo da Vinci, *Virgin and Child with St Anne*

nished.'[4] The agent of Isabella d'Este, Fra Pietro da Novellara, offered his patron a description of the picture, in which the infant

> almost climbs out of his mother's arms and seizes a lamb which he appears to embrace. His mother, half rising from the lap of St. Anne, is taking the Child to draw it from the little lamb (the sacrificial animal), which signifies the Passion. St. Anne rises slightly from her feet, and it seems as if she would wish to restrain her daughter so that she should not separate the Child from the lamb, which perhaps signifies that the Church did not wish to prevent the Passion of Christ.[5]

In proper ekphrastic response, description and interpretation merge in the friar's account of the picture, which, we must not forget, was conceived as an altarpiece. Its basic iconography – the maternal genealogy of the Child – was well established, and especially in Florentine painting (plate 87). Leonardo's rendering, we might say, is post-Albertian: the theological core of the image has been realised as a narrative to be read, that is, as an *istoria*. Such exploration of the dramatic potential of figural composition in the altarpiece – beyond obviously narrative subjects – is surely a major aspect of its development in the Renaissance. A recognition of the mimetic base of painting, it exploits the rhetorical appeal of the figure as a direct means of engaging the viewer.

The legible action of the *istoria* takes place within a pictorial field that, as we have seen, is hardly neutral. Novellara's understanding of St Anne's restraining gesture appears quite natural to us, his reading in effect confirmed by her indication in the London cartoon. It may seem gratuitously academic to recall the convention that privileges the upper sphere and calls it heaven. But is it precisely this interdependence of figural action and the valorisation of the field that, I am suggesting, we ought not to take for granted.

To gain a clearer perspective on these principles in action, we may shift the discussion out of the chapel, so to speak, and into the papal apartments: specifically to the Stanza della Segnatura and Raphael's *Disputa* (plate 88).[6] Although itself no altarpiece – or perhaps for that very reason – this mural comments upon the essential aims and meaning of the altarpiece with critical clarity. Its own pictorial structure epitomises the operations we have been considering and manifests their fullest significance. Exemplifying the faculty of Theology within the quadripartite programme of the room, the *Disputa* may be the most legible monumental painting of the Renaissance. Vasari, who fully appreciated the legibility of Raphael's work ('le storie sue ... sono simili alli scritti' [IV, p. 12]) – and who was himself visually quite literate – offers us an account of the fresco that performs its ekphrastic function most effec-

---

[4] Giorgio Vasari, *Le vite de' più eccellenti pittori, scultori ed architettori*, ed. Gaetano Milanesi, Vol. 4 (Florence, 1906), p. 38.

[5] On Leonardo's lost cartoon, see Martin Kemp, *Leonardo da Vinci: The Marvellous Works of Nature and Man* (Cambridge MA, 1981), pp. 215–27.

[6] An earlier version of the following discussion was presented at a symposium in honor of Howard McP. Davis at Columbia University: 'Raphael and the Pictorial Generation of Meaning', published in *Source: Notes in the History of Art*, 5:1 (1985), pp. 38–43.

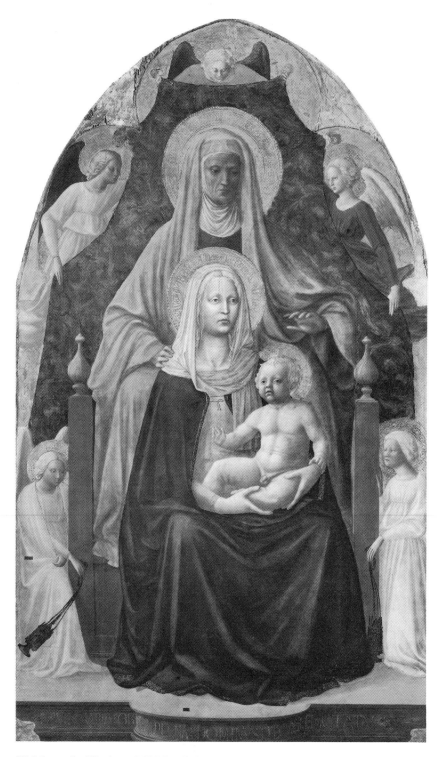

87 Masaccio, *Virgin and Child with St Anne and Angels*

tively, narrating and interpreting as it describes and delights in the picture. Vasari explains that Raphael painted

> a heaven with Christ and Our Lady, St. John the Baptist, the Apostles and the Evangelists and Martyrs on clouds, with God the Father above all, sending down the Holy Spirit, notably to a great assembly of Saints below who are writing down the mass and debating [*disputano*] the nature of the host displayed upon the altar (IV, p. 335f.).

Vasari then proceeds to identify individual members of this saintly throng: the four Doctors of the Church, Saints Dominic, Francis, Thomas Aquinas, Bonaventura, Duns Scotus and Nicholas of Lyra, as well as Dante and Fra Girolamo Savonarola, and, he adds, all the Christian theologians, many of whom are portrayed from life. Then the description turns heavenward:

> Hovering in the air are four little boys holding open the Gospels, and no painter could have created figures more graceful or more perfect. And those Saints seated in a circle in the air are coloured so as to seem alive; they are foreshortened and recede as though they were in high relief. Furthermore, they are dressed variously, their draperies rendered with the most beautiful folds, and their expressions more celestial than human. And so it is with the head of Christ, which displays that divine mercy and compassion which can be revealed to mortal men by the divinity of something painted [*divinità di cosa dipinta*]. For Raphael was endowed by nature with the ability to paint heads of the sweetest and most graceful countenance. This can be further seen in the figure of Our Lady, who, her hands upon her breast, intently contemplates her Son; clearly she can deny no favour [*non possa dinegar grazia*] (IV, p. 336).

Vasari's reading shifts back and forth between art and illusion, what we might distinguish as form and content. The two find a unity, however, precisely in his reading, which fuses both in the experiential richness of response. The critic naturally engages, surrenders to the fiction, then steps back, to observe the effective mechanics of the image, the cause of his response, and then, more knowingly and consciously returns again to the illusion.[7]

Praising the fine sense of decorum that the painter displayed in depicting the antiquity of the Patriarchs, the simplicity of the Apostles, and the faith of the Martyrs, Vasari finally descends to the crowd below. Raphael, he writes,

> showed still more artistry and talent [*molto più arte ed ingegno*] in the holy Christian doctors, who are portrayed in groups of six or three or two debating the subject [*disputando per la storia*]. In the expressions of their faces one sees a certain curiosity and concern to discover the truth of what is in question, all of which is indicated by their actions: arguing with their hands and with other gestures of the body [*faccendone segno col disputar con le mani e col far certi atti con la persona*], inclining their heads to listen, knitting their brows, and showing astonishment in different ways, all varied and truly appropriate. Apart from this are the four Doctors of the Church who, enlightened by the Holy Spirit, unravel and resolve through the holy Scriptures everything in the Gospels held by those *putti* flying in the air above (IV, pp. 336f.).

[7] For further consideration of Vasari's interpretive description, see S. L. Alpers, '*Ekphrasis* and Aesthetic Attitudes in Vasari's *Lives*', *Journal of the Warburg and Courtauld Institutes*, 23 (1960), pp. 190–215.

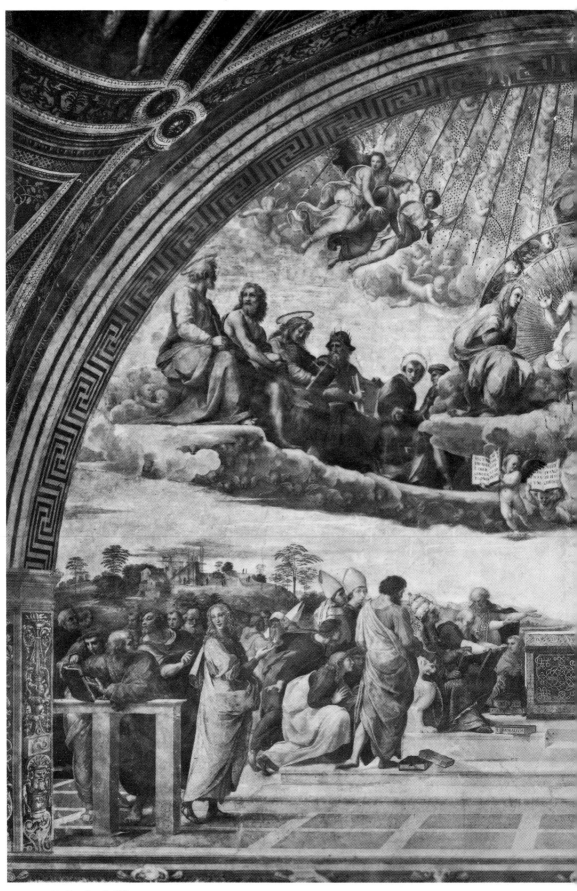

88 Raphael, *Disputa*

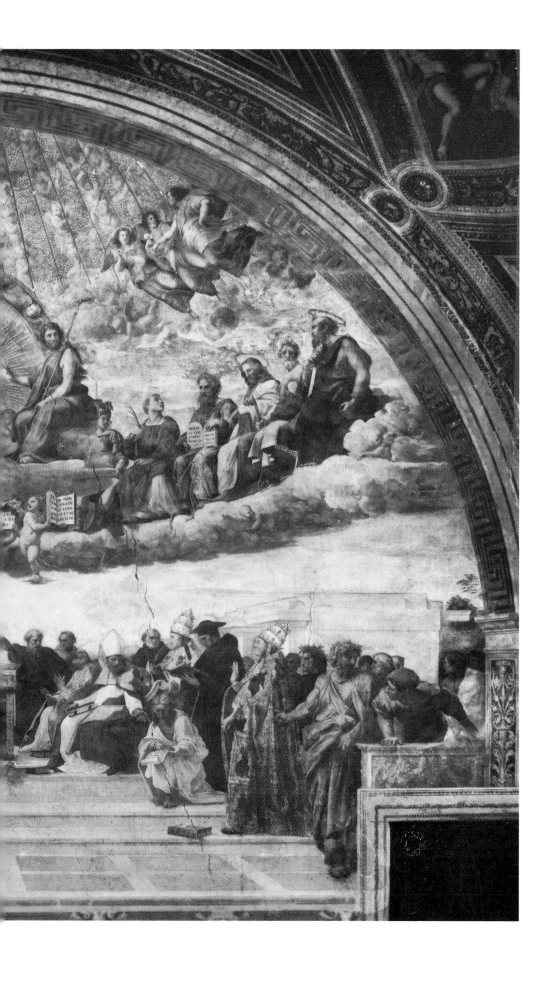

Vasari, who is ultimately responsible for the title by which Raphael's painting is known, had no problems with the meaning of the image, still less about how that meaning was conveyed. His description opens with a declaration of the heavenly setting, establishing its double axes of figural groupings: horizontal, with Christ flanked by Mary and the Baptist; vertical, with the Trinity descending from the Father through the Son and the dove of the Holy Ghost. That descent leads to the altar below with its monstrance and the assembled saints gathered around, who affirm and institutionalise the liturgical presence of the body. No great learning was (or is) required to recognise the doctrine of the Transubstantiation as the inspiring principle of Raphael's composition. Its essential truth is open to 'the learned or unlearned spectator' (Alberti, para. 40).

More interesting is Vasari's focus on figural action, what we might call the mime of meaning. This attention to what theatrical treatises of the Renaissance were to term *l'eloquenza del corpo* extends a concern voiced earlier by Alberti and still more precisely addressed by Leonardo.

We know quite well how much thought and effort Raphael put into just this aspect of the *Disputa*. For no other painting by him do we have so full a documentation of graphic gestation: some forty preparatory drawings record Raphael's evolving conception – and we can only assume that this represents a fraction of the original endeavour. These drawings do indeed concentrate on the figural groupings, the human architecture of the design. Without rehearsing the progress of Raphael's compositional thinking, we need only emphasise that the process is one of constant clarification, of distillation and simplification. As the function of each figure, its individual eloquence and its larger, choral responsibility, is realised, the full composition acquires an increasing perspicuity. The final design exhibits a structural rightness, a geometric simplicity so basic as to seem inevitable. We are tempted to accord it the status of idea, and we cannot but wonder that such purity of form and efficiency of expression ever required so much labour to come into being.[8]

From his earliest preserved design (plate 89), which involved an architectural framework and several more levels of figures – including, most importantly, the female personification on a cloud, hovering between heaven and earth – Raphael moved purposefully and efficiently toward his end. The efficiency is nowhere better attested than in the translation of the enclouded allegory to earth (plate 90). Deprived of intellectual insignia, no longer mediating between viewer and heaven, this figure – now male – nonetheless retains his mediating function, but rather more horizontally now, within a new and more self-consciously dramatic context: what had been an abstraction, a mere gesture of faith, has become a fully responsible human action, appropriate to its mover's *accidente mentale* (to borrow a term from Leonardo); the figure now turns from his companions' gesticulations of vain reason and with that sweet innocence of faith indicates the source of truth. Vasari knew how to read this figural language – and so, of course, do we.

---

[8] For surveys of the graphic preparation of the *Disputa*, see J. Pope-Hennessy, *Raphael* (New York, 1970), pp. 59–68, and F. Ames-Lewis, *The Draftsman Raphael* (New Haven and London, 1986), pp. 72–100.

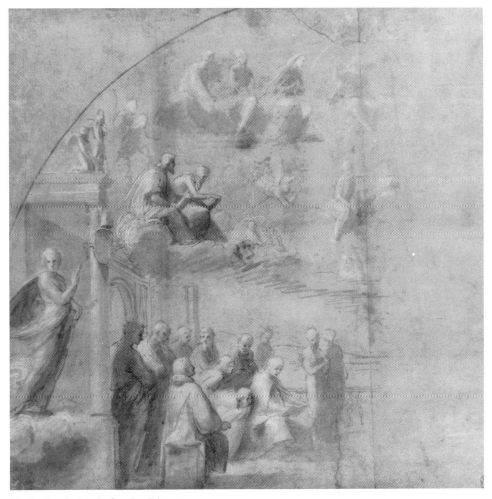

89 Raphael, Study for the *Disputa*

In eliminating an intermediary level of allegorical abstraction, Raphael crystallised the essential binary division of his arched field. Now mediation between heaven and earth is effected at and through a single moment in the composition: through the wafer of the Eucharist upon the altar of the Church.

Vasari's reading of the figures is a persuasive one. But only implicit in his responsive description is an awareness of the larger construct in which these various actions take place, against which they acquire their significance. From lower left and right – the least privileged zones of the field – gestures indicate the way toward the altar, moving horizontally, on earth. The monstrance, we note – like the cross in so many paintings of the Crucifixion – rises above this world's horizon, above the vanishing point of the receding orthogonals of the pavement, and only approaching that central focus do gestures and gazes move determinedly heavenward.

More significant, however – and this Vasari immediately intuited – is the descent that occurs on the central vertical axis: the descent of the persons of the Trinity

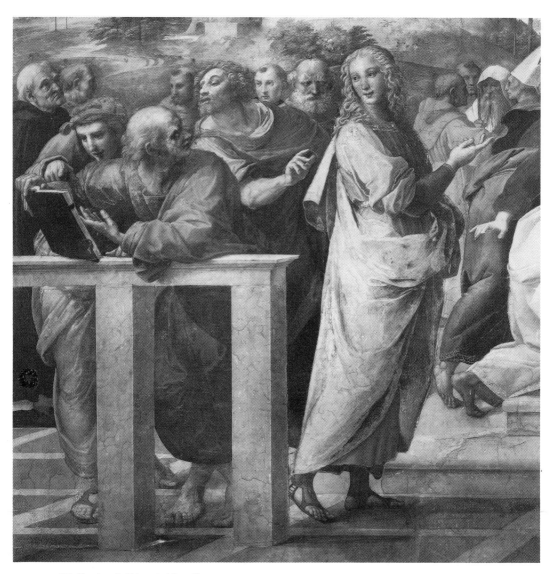

90 Raphael, *Disputa* (detail)

to the host. It is a descent of circles of gold: Father, Son, and Holy Ghost are each set against a tooled circular ground of applied gold leaf; further gold rays fall from the Holy Spirit to the lowest circle of the ladder, the monstrance displaying the wafer. Nothing could be clearer; the geometry of pictorial structure testifies to theological truth, makes manifest the doctrine of Transubstantiation, the ordained presence of the body and the blood in the sacrament. Again, the elegant simplification of the design, its perfect fit of form and content, makes us wonder that Raphael worked so hard to achieve it. It seems so natural.[9] With knowledge of all those preparatory

[9] Cf. Velazquez's simple acknowledgment of the *Disputa* as 'the great painting in which theology is harmonised with philosophy and in the midst of which the Supreme Good stands upon the altar': Carl Justi, *Diego Velazquez und sein Jahrhundert*, Vol. 1 (Bonn, 1888), p. 288.

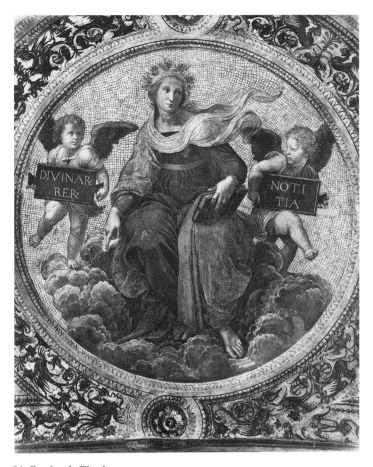

91 Raphael, *Theology*

drawings we more willingly acclaim the *sprezzatura* of his solution – for, as we know, *è arte a nascondere l'arte*.

We must also wonder at the modern assumption of a detailed theological programme elaborated by some adviser at the papal court.[10] The drawings themselves suggest by their collective search the absence of such a precisely prescribed iconographic schedule. Raphael seems to have been given a general, but basic, theological tenet as his subject, a subject that would epitomise theology itself. And his charge would have been its pictorial realisation. 'Knowledge of Things Divine' (*Divinarum rerum notitia*) is the inscription accompanying the personified Theology reigning over the *Disputa* (plate 91). We may imagine that in the course of searching and testing possibilities the painter came to recognise the match of theological truth and axiomatic geometry, the congruence of simple structures.

The *Disputa* makes its statement with the clarity of a Euclidean proposition. Acknowledging the determining control of its lunette field – and purifying the semiotic tra-

[10] Cf. H. Pfeiffer, *Zur Iconographie von Raffaels Disputa: Egidio da Viterbo und die christlich-platonische Konzeption der Stanza della Segnatura*, Rome, 1975, and M. Winner, 'Disputa und Schule von Athen', in *Raffaello a Roma* (Rome, 1986), pp. 29–45.

ditions of Last Judgment scenes with which it evolved – Raphael's composition trans-lates the polarities of heaven and earth into a fundamental geometric contrast between circle and rectangle, and artfully provides the means for exchange between the two. More surely than any architectural theory or practice of the Renaissance, the *Disputa* demonstrates the divinity of the circle.[11] Following the arch of the wall, the circle informs the structure of the upper half of the painting, the spheres of heaven. Presented *in maestà*, in its absolute – that is, unforeshortened – form, it is reserved exclusively for the persons of the Trinity, and for their Eucharistic extension on earth. And the supernatural status of the form is reaffirmed by the gold ground. By deliberately adopting this archaic and, as we have noted, discounselled technique, Raphael quite explicitly puts the circle beyond the reach of pictorial illusion, beyond the realm of nature.

To either side of the divine central axis figuration moves into the temporality of history. Appropriately, the holy court of Adam, prophets, evangelists, apostles, and martyrs is seated upon a less than perfect circle: the angelically corbelled embankment of clouds. Still partaking of the spiritual quality of the ideal geometry, this natural form inflects the circle into space, the ungilded illusionistic space of a lower world, subject to the rules of perspective: foreshortening itself mediates the dual nature of these sanctified beings. Within the heavenly registers of the *Disputa*, then, a hier-archy of spheres is distinguished, measured from the uninflected circles of the central axis. The clouds themselves and the blue sky behind further extend the overlap of humanity and divinity.

The lower, earthly half of the composition is founded solidly upon the four-square geometry of this world of elements and temperaments. Its commensurability is pal-pable in the perspective grid of the pavement pattern. Elevated above this ground, as it should be, the altar stands as an unforeshortened rectangle that responds in its formal perfection and majesty to the pure circles above. Sustaining the Eucharist and descended from the Holy Spirit, this is clearly the Church on earth – and quite explicitly the Church of Julius II, whose name figures so prominently in the golden embroidery of the antependium. Although rectangular, that is, of this world, the altar shares the gilded grace of the Holy circles. Along the vertical axis, a sacred chain of being, the position of the Church in the order of things is declared an integral part of revealed truth. In the focal object of the lower realm there occurs the perpetual miracle of the Transubstantiation, and the sacramental, or institutional, resonance of that divine condescension is manifested as a kind of pictorial squaring of the circle.[12]

Within the vertical exchange of the *Disputa*, its economy of reciprocities, the domi-nant position of the altar below in turn affects our response to the celestial realm

---

[11] On the circle in Renaissance art and architecture, see especially R. Wittkower, *Architectural Principles in the Age of Humanism*, 3rd rev. ed. (New York, 1971), part I: 'The centrally planned church and the Renaissance'.

[12] Within the heavenly circularity of the *Disputa*, however, God the Father is set off by a square nimbus, possibly a declaration of eternal presence: *Ego sum*. See A.-N. Didron, *Christian Iconography*, Vol. 1 (1851; New York, 1965), p. 64f., and G. Ladner, 'The so-called square nimbus', in *Images and Ideas in the Middle Ages* (Rome, 1983), pp. 115–66, esp. p. 141.

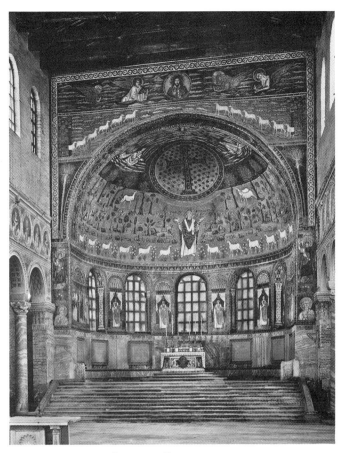

92 Ravenna, S. Apollinare in Classe

above. Set within an arched opening, atop a series of steps, and the focus of a longitu-
dinal perspective, the painted altar evokes the actual experience of which it is the
epitomising ideal: it alludes to real church structures. Part of its sanction to do so
it claims by appropriation of the highest register of the fresco, the segment of celestial
dome behind God the Father. That the incised rays of this golden sphere emanate
from an unseen source above the Eternal already transposes that surface – down,
as it were – to a different realm, one explicitly architectural. Seen together with the
altar, it allusively becomes the half-dome of a church apse – significantly, Early Christian (plate 92). Effected at the upper and lower extremes of the *Disputa* and charging
the entire design, this ecclesiastical allusion grounds the abstract truth of the image
in a certain reality. In this sense, Raphael's mural speaks for all altarpieces.

On its primary level, the eloquence of the *Disputa* resides in its large-scale compositional structure, a dynamic structure that, building upon the semiotic potential
of the field, embodies the essential theme of the image. As Vasari recognised, the
gestures and discourse of the figures on earth serve to articulate and expound this
central truth. As viewers of the painting, we need these notional figures in the same

way that the faithful congregation need their originals: through their guidance we are directed to the knowledge of things divine.

But the truth that we, as viewers, confront in the *Disputa* is a pictorial truth. As historians we will want to locate it within the contexts of High Renaissance Rome, of the papacy of Julius II, of the debates over the Transubstantiation of the host, of the Early Christian revival, of the painting's position within the full decorative complex of the Stanza della Segnatura – not to mention the context of Raphael's own art. When we stand before the fresco, however, we know that there is a meaning more immediate to us, a meaning that lies on, not beyond, the surface, that depends upon and resides in a kind of visual thinking, that is expressed in the operations on the plane. It was, we might say, only in working on the surface – acknowledging the powerful claims of the axes of the field and the determining control of its shape, recognising the dialectic of circle and square, the signifying tension between picture plane and orthogonal recession – that Raphael himself discovered the truth. Theology, we might legitimately argue, becomes a commentary on painting in the *Disputa*. Pictorial structure – directly semiotic rather than mimetic – is meaning.

Of the mural opposite the *Disputa* Walter Pater wrote, 'in Raphael, painted ideas, painted and visible philosophy, are for once as beautiful as Plato thought they must be, if one truly apprehended them'.[13] What then shall we say of Raphael's painted and visible theology? Surely it would be difficult to imagine a clearer demonstration of the central mystery of the Church: we truly apprehend it, *divinità di cosa dipinta*. To the saintly Doctors, then, shall we add the painter?

---

[13] W. Pater, 'Raphael' (1892), in *The Renaissance*, ed. K. Clark (Cleveland and New York, 1961), p. 158.

9   *From cult images to the cult of images: the case of Raphael's altarpieces*

Sylvia Ferino Pagden

By suggesting a progress from 'cult images' to the 'cult of images', I wish to say something about the changing relationship between liturgical function and aesthetic quality in religious art, with specific reference to some of Raphael's altarpieces.[1] If we assume that early Christian and medieval cult images, particularly those thought to be of divine origin, were not venerated primarily for their aesthetic value, we can safely argue that from the Duecento onwards, and particularly in the Renaissance, religious images in general, and especially those painted for public places, had a marked aesthetic character. The 'beauty' of the work became an integral part of the function of an altarpiece, which consisted primarily in the promotion and enhancement of a particular cult and site.

The question of aesthetic quality obviously arose the moment the patron was faced with the need to choose which artist should paint his altarpiece. The choice was, of course, frequently determined by the degree to which the artist had already been successful in creating new visual prototypes for the kind of subject-matter the patron required, and by the extent to which these prototypes were taken up by other artists. Works by painters of the calibre of Raphael and Duccio, for example, allow us to focus more clearly on the potential conflict between religious and aesthetic function because, as I shall argue, these artists created aesthetic prototypes which – and this is particularly true of Raphael – soon became objects of veneration in themselves, partly because of their intrinsic beauty, but more obviously because they were painted by the 'divine Raphael'.[2]

It will be clear that this phenomenon is closely related to the rise of the concept of the artist as a genius and divinely inspired creator. When in 1814, for instance,

[1]   The original title of this paper, 'From Kultbild to Bildkult', as well as some of the following reflections on Raphael's altarpieces, were inspired by H. Belting, *Das Bild und sein Publikum im Mittelalter. Form und Funktion früher Bildtafeln der Passion* (Berlin, 1981). Of the more general literature on altarpieces, I found the following particularly helpful and relevant: J. Burckhardt, 'Das Altarbild', in *Beiträge zur Kunstgeschichte von Italien* (Basle, 1898); E. von Dobschütz, *Christusbilder, Untersuchungen zur christlichen Legende* (Leipzig, 1899; Hager, 1962); M. Warnke, 'Italienische Bildtabernakel bis zum Frübarock', *Münchner Jahrbuch der bildenen Kunst*, 19 (1968); H. W. van Os, *Demut und Verherrlichung Mariens in der sienesischen Malerei 1300–1450* (The Hague, 1969); M. Ingendaay, *Sienesische Altarbilder des sechszehnten Jahrhunderts* (Bonn, 1976); L. Ketzenbacher, 'Das verletzte Kultbild, Voraussetzungen, Zeitschichten und Aussagewandel eines abendländischen Legendentypus', *Sitzungsberichte der Bayrischen Akademie der Wissenschaften, philosophisch historische Klasse*, Jahrgang 1977, Heft 1, (Munich, 1978); and H. W. van Os, *Sienese altarpieces, 1215–1460*, Vol. 1 (Groningen, 1984), and its review by H. Belting in *Zeitschrift für Kunstgeschichte*, 48 (1985), pp. 567–72.
[2]   The veneration of the artist as inspired genius and creator is closely linked to the concept of the rise of the artist from craftsman to intellectual. Accounts of this development are given in E. Zilsel, *Die Entstehung des Geniebegriffs* (Tübingen, 1926); E. Kris and O. Kurz, *Die Legende von Künstler. Ein geschichtlicher Versuch* (rpt. Frankfurt, 1980); R. and M. Wittkower, *Born under Saturn. The character and conduct of artists* (London, 1963); and S. Gohr *Der Kult des Künstlers und die Kunst im 19. Jahrhundert. Zum Bildtypus des Hommage* (Cologne, 1973), with further bibliography on pp. 2–7.

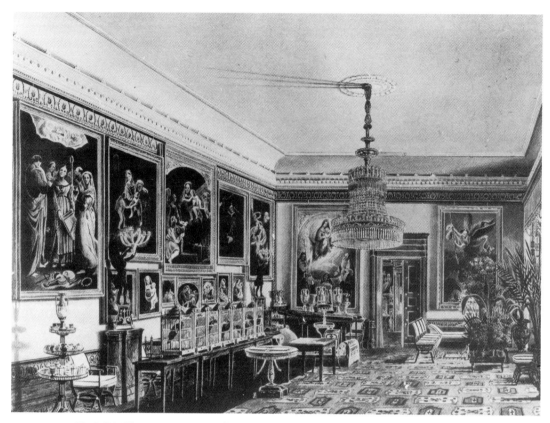

93 F. W. Klose, Apartment of Friedrich Wilhelm III of Prussia at Charlottenburg

Friedrich Wilhelm III of Prussia had the walls of one of his rooms in Charlottenburg covered with copies of Raphael's religious paintings – mainly altarpieces and Madonnas[3] – the effect was strikingly similar to that of a collection of relics and cult items in a reliquary chapel (plate 93).[4] By this time, of course, the cult of Raphael was firmly established, and its devotees often borrowed their methods of display from those of religious veneration. In the Romantic period the 'religious' veneration for the artist expressed itself, as in the room at Charlottenburg, by a clear preference for his religious paintings.[5]

In this paper, however, I will restrict my discussion to the reception of Raphael's altarpieces and their elevation to the status of cult objects in the first century or so after their creation. I shall also try to demonstrate how interest in the aesthetic quality of some of Raphael's altarpieces took over from their religious significance as the cult of the figure of Raphael increased.

Raphael's extraordinary artistic fame led to the collection and veneration of his works even during his lifetime, and this obviously had some effect even on large-scale commissions for public worship. The Umbrian patrons of his earlier altarpieces were

[3] *L'Estasi di S. Cecilia di Raffaello da Urbino nella Pinacoteca Nazionale di Bologna* (Bologna, 1983), pp. 292–3.
[4] See, for instance, the reliquary chapel at S. Paolo fuori le Mura in Rome.
[5] See M. Ebhardt, *Die Deutung der Werke Raffaels in der deutschen Kunstliteratur von Klassizismus und Romantik*, Studien zur deutschen Kunstgeschichte 351 (Baden-Baden, 1972).

still primarily interested in acquiring beautiful works that would be effective at convey-ing a particular religious message. Good examples include the *Crucifixion* for the Gavari chapel in S. Domenico in Città di Castello, and the Colonna altarpiece for the nuns of S. Antonio in Perugia.[6] Raphael's Roman patrons, on the other hand – and I am thinking here primarily of Giulio de' Medici and the *Trans-figuration*[7] – were eager to emphasise the aesthetic character of the works they commis-sioned by the use of artistic competitions. The same general set of concerns – primarily aesthetic rather than religious – also explains the commission from Raphael of large-scale religious paintings intended as diplomatic gifts from the Pope and his family to the King of France and his entourage.[8] I need only mention the large *St Michael* or the large *Holy Family of Francis I* (both Paris, Louvre), the religious function of which we know absolutely nothing, although the subjects represented and the size of the panels would not have been inappropriate for altarpieces. In any attempt at establishing which of Raphael's undocumented large-scale panel paintings might have been destined as public altarpieces, our only source is Vasari, for he appears to make a consistent distinction between *tavola* (i.e. 'altarpiece') and *quadro* (i.e. 'picture').[9] For example, he initially refers to the so-called *Madonna dell' Impannata* (Florence, Pitti), executed for Bindo Altoviti, as a *quadro*; but then, after the confiscation by the Medici of Altoviti's palace and its furnishings, and the placing of the picture over the altar in the Medici chapel in the Palazzo Vecchio, Vasari describes it as a *tavola d'altare*.[10] However, in regard to works such as the diplomatic gifts for France Vasari is unhelpful, as he calls them simply *opere*.

Another particularly interesting case in this context is the cartoon for the large *St Michael*, which was given by Raphael to the Duke of Ferrara as a consolation for his not having painted the long promised *Triumph of Bacchus*.[11] It seems to have been Raphael's failure to paint the *Bacchus* that made the figure of St Michael so popular among Ferrarese patrons and artists in the following century or so.[12] It might be going too far to suggest that the fame of Raphael's cartoon actually contri-buted to the increase in the saint's popularity in Emilia, but we cannot exclude this possibility altogether.

The collecting of Raphael's works, which had already started in his lifetime, conti-nued more intensely after his death. It concentrated primarily, however, on small-scale religious paintings for private devotion; and most of the large-scale panels that had been commissioned for public worship remained *in situ* for another century or

[6] For the *Crucifixion* (now London, National Gallery), see L. Dussler, *Raphael. A critical catalogue of his pictures, wall paintings and tapestries* (London, 1971), pp. 8–9. For the Colonna altarpiece (now New York, Metropolitan Museum of Art), see most recently F. F. Mancini, *Raffaello in Umbria. Cronologia e committenza. Nuovi studi e documenti* (Perugia, 1987), pp. 13–38.

[7] See F. Mancinelli, *Primo piano di un capolavoro: la Trasfigurazione* (Vatican City, 1979); and K. Weil-Garris, *Leonardo and central Italian art: 1515–1550* (New York, 1974).

[8] See S. Béguin in *Raphaël dans les collections françaises* (Paris, 1983), pp. 91–8, cat. nos. 9–11.

[9] G. Vasari, *Le vite de' più eccellenti pittori, scultori ed architetti*, ed. G. Milancsi, Vol. 4 (Florence, 1878ff), pp. 315–86.

[10] Ibid., p. 351.

[11] V. Golzio, *Raffaello nei documenti nelle testimonianze dei contemporanei e nella letteratura del suo secolo* (Vatican City, 1936), pp. 53ff.

[12] *L'Estasi di Santa Cecilia* (as in note 3), pp. 324–6.

so. I shall now turn to discuss some of the various ways in which the worship of Raphael's altarpieces changed from the religious to the aesthetic.

Of particular interest here is the *Madonna del Baldacchino* (plate 94), since it represents one of the earliest examples of the veneration of an altarpiece by Raphael primarily because it was by Raphael. The work was originally commissioned by the Dei family of Florence for their chapel dedicated to St Bernard in S. Spirito; but as is well known, the artist left the work unfinished when he went to Rome in 1508, and he probably never worked on it again.[13] It was acquired by Baldassare Turini, *datarius* of Leo X, and executor of Raphael's will as well as his friend, admirer and patron. Turini had the painting installed in the Cathedral of Pescia, in a chapel dedicated to St Augustine (plate 95).[14] When the Turini chapel was consecrated in 1540, therefore, the picture on the altar wall was still unfinished.

Unfortunately, we have no documents on Turini's acquisition of the painting, nor for the commission of the chapel. But Vasari gives an account that is most illuminating in this context. In the Life of Raphael he says: 'he left his works at Florence and the picture of the Dei unfinished (but so far complete that M Baldassare da Pescia had it put in the Pieve of his native place after Raphael's death), and went to Rome'.[15] This confirms the unfinished state of the work. Then, in the Life of Giuliano di Baccio d'Agnolo, the architect of the chapel, Vasari went on to observe: 'At that time M. Baldassare Turini had to set up a picture by Raphael in the principal church of Pescia, of which he was provost, and for this, comprising a stone ornamentation, as well as an entire chapel and a tomb, Giuliano made designs and models.'[16] On the basis of a comparison of the format of the composition of the preparatory drawing and that of Dandini's copy, which is still *in situ*, we may assume that the format of the painting was not altered to fit an existing space.[17] Vasari's claim that the architect built a chapel around it seems, therefore, all the more plausible.[18]

Baldassare Turini must have given priority to the location of Raphael's altarpiece over those of the family tombs that the chapel was also intended to house.[19] His overriding concern with a proper setting for the picture has recently been confirmed by Claudia Conforti's analysis of the architectural structure of the chapel (plate 96).[20] The opening arch between the main part of the church and the chapel is mirrored

---

[13] See P. A. Riedl, 'Raffaels *Madonna del Baldacchino*', *Mitteilungen des Kunsthistorischen Instituts von Florenz*, 8 (1957–9), pp. 223–46.

[14] E. Nucci, *La Chiesa Cattedrale di Pescia. Note storiche* (Pescia, 1938), pp. 15–16.

[15] Vasari, *Le vite* (as in note 9), p. 329; G. Vasari, *The lives of the painters, sculptors and architects*, ed. W. Gaunt, Vol. 2 (London, 1963), p. 226.

[16] Vasari, *Le vite*, Vol. 5, p. 158; *The lives*, Vol. 3, pp. 57–8.

[17] For the preparatory drawing, see E. Knab, E. Mitsch and K. Oberhuber, *Raphael, die Zeichnungen* (Stuttgart, 1983), no. 257; P. Joannides, *The drawings of Raphael* (Oxford, 1983), no. 176. For Dandini's copy see the very inadequate copy in Riedl, 'Raffaels *Madonna del Baldacchino*', fig. 2.

[18] It is somewhat ironic, therefore, that the format of the *Madonna del Baldacchino* was later drastically altered when it entered the Gallery of Duke Ferdinand de' Medici, with the purpose of making it harmonise with other paintings in the collection. See L. Strocchi, 'Il Gran Principe Ferdinando collezionista e l'acquisizione delle pale d'altare', in *La Galleria Palatina. Storia della quadreria granducale di Palazzo Pitti*, exhibition catalogue (Florence, 1982), pp. 42–9; and *Raffaello a Firenze. Dipinti e disegni delle collezioni fiorentine*, exhibition catalogue (Florence, 1984), pp. 119ff.

[19] T. R. Verellen, 'Raffaello da Montelupo 1504–1566 als Bildhauer und Architekt', Doctoral thesis, University of Hamburg (1981), pp. 95–7.

[20] C. Conforti, 'Architettura e culto della memoria: la committenza di Baldassare Turini datario di Leone X', in *Baldassare Peruzzi. Pittura, scena e architettura nel Cinquecento*, ed. M. Fagiolo and M. L. Madonna, (Rome, 1987), pp. 603–28.

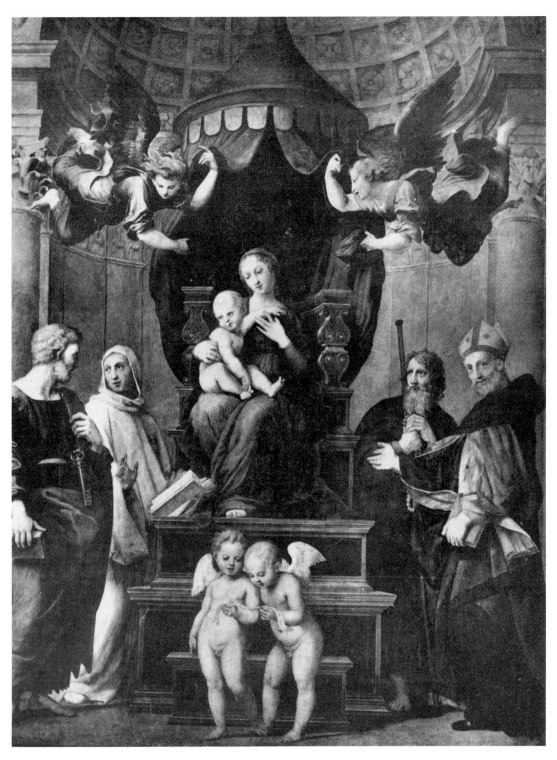

94 Raphael, *Madonna del Baldacchino*

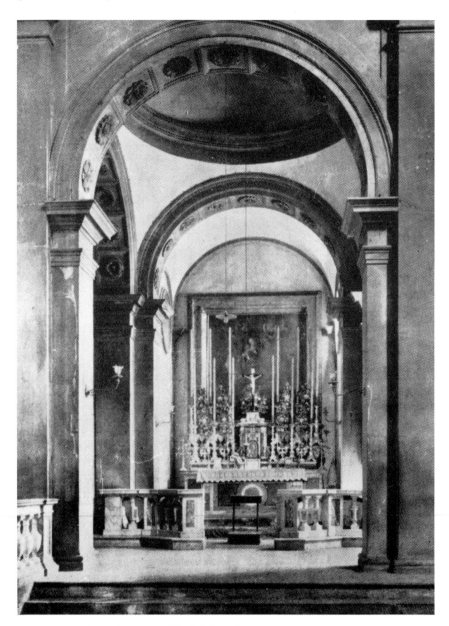

95 Pescia, Cattedrale, view of Turini chapel

in that of the altar wall, the cornices of which would in turn have emphasised the painted cornices. The painting would have been illuminated by two lateral oculi, which were framed in *pietra serena* and set into the walls at a height designed so that they would act as spotlights, which by casting an oblique light would have avoided striking the painted surface directly, and prevented the cornice from casting shadows or reflections over it.

In his concern for the best setting of what was essentially an unfinished work, originally destined for a totally different location with a different chapel dedication,

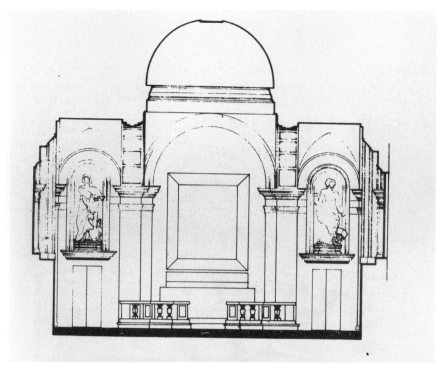

96 Reconstruction of elevation of Turini chapel by C. Conforti

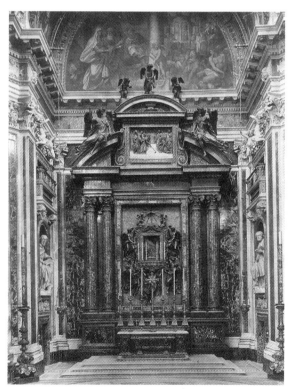

97 Rome, S. Maria Maggiore, altar wall of Paoline chapel

Baldassare Turini's veneration is comparable to that enjoyed by relics of saints or miraculous cult images, since these, too, had appropriate shrines or sanctuaries built around them.[21] One only has to think of the Casa Santa of Loreto,[22] or from a later period, the Paoline chapel at S. Maria Maggiore (plate 97), which was specifically set up and decorated to house and celebrate the image of a Madonna painted by St Luke.[23]

Despite all these considerations we have, of course, only Vasari's account to go by, and this was itself probably heavily indebted to the many well-known legends surrounding medieval cult images. But the sheer fact that such legends were woven round Raphael's altarpieces is a further indication of the extent to which they were transformed into icons of artistic excellence.

These legends derive from earlier accounts of divinely created cult images, and were then translated from a specifically religious into an artistic discourse. A particularly telling example is provided by Vasari's story about the *Spasimo di Sicilia* (plate 98), an altarpiece destined for the church of S. Maria dello Spasimo in Palermo: 'When this picture was finished ... it was nearly lost, because on its way by sea to Palermo a terrible storm overtook the ship, which was broken on a rock, and the men and merchandise all perished, except this picture, which was washed up at Genoa in its case. When it was fished out and landed it was found to be a divine work, and proved to be uninjured ... for even the fury of the winds and the sea respected the beauty (*bellezza*) of such a painting.'[24] Once it was set up in Palermo it was held to be 'more famous than the mountain of Vulcan' – that is, Mount Etna.

This I take to be a reworking of one of the early legends that formed around Christian cult images. According to Von Dobschütz[25] and Kruft,[26] the famous miracle-working Virgin Annunciate of Trapani, believed to be of oriental origin (like all the best and most authentic cult images) and to have been carved by angels, arrived in Sicily in the following miraculous manner.[27] A group of Knights Templar brought the statue with them from the east. When they ran into a storm off the coast of Sicily they made a vow that if they were saved they would leave the Virgin at the first Christian port they entered. This turned out to be Trapani. But the Templars soon forgot their vow, and set out again, taking the Virgin with them. Another storm broke over them and they were forced to throw everything overboard, including the statue, in order to save themselves. The statue floated miraculously back to Trapani, where it was recovered by a fisherman. It became one of the most famous

[21] H. Belting, 'Die Reaktion der Kunst des 13. Jahrhunderts auf den Import von Reliquien und Ikonen', in *Ornamenta Ecclesiae, Kunst und Künstler der Romanik*, exhibition catalogue, Vol. 3 (Cologne, 1985), pp. 173–83.

[22] F. Grimaldi, *La chiesa di Santa Maria di Loreto nei documenti dei secoli XII-XV* (Ancona, 1984); and Grimaldi, *La Basilica della Santa Casa di Loreto* (Ancona, 1986).

[23] See G. Wolf, ' *Salus Populi Romani*: Studien zur Geschichte der Präsentation und Rezeption der Madonna di San Luca von S. Maria Maggiore', Doctoral thesis, University of Heidelberg (1989).

[24] Vasari, *Le vite*, Vol. 4 (as in note 9), p. 328; *The Lives*, Vol. 2 (as in note 15), p. 238.

[25] Dobschütz, *Christusbilder* (as in note 1), pp. 86ff.

[26] H. W. Kruft, 'Die Madonna von Trapani und ihre Kopien. Studien zur Madonnenmythologie und zum Begriff der Kopie in der sizilianischen Skulptur des Quattrocento', *Mitteilungen des Kunsthistorischen Instituts in Florenz*, 14 (1970), pp. 297–322.

[27] This is a simplification and conflation of the various versions given in Dobschütz, *Christusbilder* and Kruft, 'Die Madonna'.

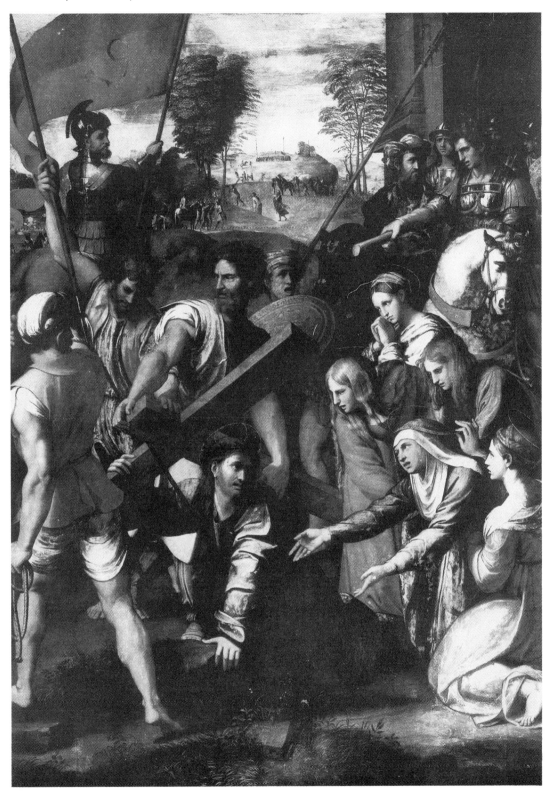

98 Raphael, *Christ carrying the Cross ('Lo Spasimo di Sicilia')*

miracle-working images of the Virgin in Sicily during the fourteenth, fifteenth and sixteenth centuries.[28] Authorised replicas were commissioned, and even today one can buy little plastic copies of it. It is obviously not possible to say whether Vasari's story was intended to be a direct echo of a legend of a type that circulated widely in Sicily, where the sea, of course, figured prominently in most miracle tales.[29] But it is clear that the narrative structure of the two stories is remarkably similar. If we accept, then, that Vasari's story of the *Spasimo* does not record a real event, but rather echoes a traditional miracle tale – and we must not forget that many art historians believe that it does record a real event, partly because of the painting's poor state of preservation[30] – then it becomes highly significant that the emphasis in the attribution of the miraculous power has been radically altered. For while the earlier images were saved because of their religious nature – precisely because they were not made by human hands – Raphael's work was saved because of its artistic worth. It was its *bellezza* (its human origin), not its supposed proximity to the deity, that compelled even the winds and the waves to respect it, and which made it even more famous than Mount Etna.

In this analogy between a religious and an aesthetic image, the power of creation has passed from a literally divine being – in this case the angels – to a metaphorically divine one, the artist. Something similar is happening in the following account, also by Vasari, of Raphael's painting of the *Transfiguration* (plate 99):

> One of the apostles has his head on the ground, one shades his eyes with his hands from the rays of light of the splendour of Christ, who, clothed in snow white, opens his arms and lifts his head, showing the divine essence of the three persons of the Trinity thus displayed in the perfection of Raphael's art. The artist seems to have gathered all his force to worthily present the face of Christ, which was the last thing he did as death overtook him before he again took up the brush.[31]

Although it is not entirely clear to me what model Vasari is drawing on here, the author's suggestion that the painting of the face of Christ effectively killed Raphael, and further, that the artist had some understanding of his own imminent death (which conveniently took place on Good Friday), clearly does have the effect of fusing the notion of divinity with that of the artist as divine creator. The conflation of Raphael the artist with Christ the Redeemer is made even more explicit in a letter from Pico della Mirandola to Isabella d'Este in Mantua: 'Of this death the heavens wished to give a sign, like that which indicated the death of Christ when stones were split. Thus the papal palace opened up so that it seemed about to fall into ruins, and

---

[28] Kruft, 'Die Madonna', figs. 5–27.

[29] It is also the case that a great number of the miraculous images established in Italy in the Middle Ages were claimed to be of eastern origin and to have been transported to the west by ship. One that was better known to Vasari than any of the Sicilian examples was the Volto Santo in Lucca. Of particular interest in this context is a painting pointed out to me by Henk van Os, which was also miraculously saved from the sea, and which despite its obviously Italian origin, was considered to have come from the east. See *The Florentine paintings in Holland 1300–1500*, ed. H. W. van Os and M. Prakken (Maarssen, 1973), p. 73, no. 38.

[30] This seems to have been caused by a fire in the chapel of the Spanish Royal Palace in the eighteenth century. See *Rafael en España* (Madrid, 1985), p. 121.

[31] Vasari, *Le vite*, Vol. 4, p. 372; *The Lives*, p. 243.

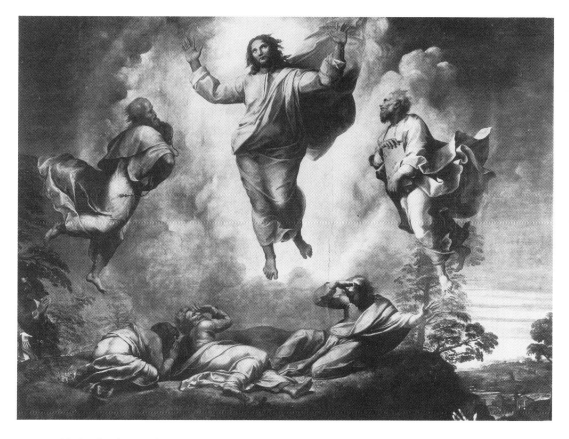

99 Raphael, *Transfiguration* (detail)

His Holiness fled in fear from his rooms.'[32] Still more telling, perhaps, is Tebaldeo's discarded epigram:[33]

> De Raphaele pictore
> Quid mirum si qua Christus tu luce peristi?
> Naturae ille Deus, tu Deus artis eras.
>
> (What wonder if you like Christ should perish by the light – He was the God of Nature, You the God of Art.)

Another indication of the veneration of Raphael's excellence as a painter of altarpieces is their increasing desirability as collectors' items. Initially it was easily moveable works of private origin such as portraits, Madonna panels and drawings that attracted collectors. Most of the large-scale paintings on panel that had been commissioned for public worship remained *in situ* for a century after Raphael's death. But as the passion for collecting increased and the more moveable pictures became ever more difficult to find, cardinals, princes, viceroys and other members of the European upper nobility increasingly turned their attention to liturgical paintings such as altar-

---

[32] Golzio, *Raffaello* (as in note 11), pp. 114–15.
[33] Ibid., p. 119.

pieces. Most of Raphael's altarpieces were painted for chapels of private patrons such as the Baglione in Perugia, the Branconio at L'Aquila and the Dolce in Naples.[34] These pictures remained the property of the patrons' families, and it was the patron's heir who had to agree to the sale or removal of the altarpiece. But even if the family was willing to part with its property, no altarpiece could be removed from a church without ecclesiastical sanction. And even if this was obtained, final authorisation had to come from the papacy, which maintained a watchful eye upon every matter involving the rights and property of the Church.

There are a number of reasons why the actual owners or assumed proprietors of an altarpiece might find it attractive, or at least prudent, to part with it. Only rarely were the motives purely economic ones, as may have been the case with the heirs of the Turini chapel in Pescia, who sold the *Madonna del Baldacchino* for 10,000 scudi.[35] In most cases owners either succumbed to the sheer pressure that the agents of the absolutist states were able to exert, or they hoped to derive political and social advancement by ceding to the wishes of those in power. The patterns of intrigue between the various parties involved, which might include the city councillors, could on occasion become very complex, and might even result in a considerable amount of violence. Some of the events described in Lightbown's essay 'Raphael and the spogliators' read like a modern thriller.

The *Entombent*, for instance (Rome, Galleria Borghese), which Cardinal Borghese wanted for himself and whose ambitions were supported by his uncle, Pope Paul V, had to be taken from the church of S. Francesco by night and lowered over the city walls, so that its removal should not be forcibly prevented by the citizens of Perugia.[36] When, however, they realised that they had been cheated in this manner, their anger almost led to a revolt. And when Scipione Borghese realised that he had probably underrated the Perugians' devotion to their altarpiece, he offered the rather lame explanation that he required it for private devotion, an explanation that interestingly reverses the process I have been describing by offering a religious motive for what was clearly an aesthetic one.[37]

A similar night expedition was necessary when the *Madonna del Baldacchino* was transferred from Pescia to Florence in 1697.[38] In the case of the Borghese *Entombent* the friars of S. Francesco in Perugia had been part of the conspiracy. When, however, the Spanish viceroy of Naples had obtained the consent both of the owners and of the papacy to remove the *Visitation* (Madrid, Prado) from the Branconio chapel in S. Silvestro in L'Aquila, the chapter closed the church in order to prevent its removal. The Spaniards then resorted to pulling down the walls of the building from the outside.[39]

What the Perugians, Aquilans and Pescians tried heroically to resist was the removal

[34] R. Lightbown, 'Princely pressures: I Raphael and the spogliators', *Apollo*, 78 (1963), pp. 98–102.

[35] Ibid., pp. 98ff; *Raffaello a Firenze* (as in note 18), p. 121.

[36] P. della Pergola, *Galleria Borghese, I Dipinti*, Vol. 2 (Rome, 1959), pp. 116ff, no. 170, documents 210–16.

[37] Lightbown, 'Princely pressures' (as in note 34), p. 101.

[38] *Raffaello a Firenze* (as in note 18), p. 121.

[39] A. Leosini, *Monumenti storici artistici della città di Aquila e suoi contorni* (Aquila, 1849), pp. 40–51; Lightbown, 'Princely pressures' (as in note 34), p. 102.

of an object from a public place with which they closely identified themselves. But that identification must itself have been in part due to the aesthetic quality of the work, or at least, to the fact that it had been painted by an artist of the status of Raphael. Clearly religious veneration, although this cannot perhaps be so easily detached from civic pride, was only a part of their reasoning, if at all – for in each case a copy of the original was supplied, which in principle, at least, should have been sufficient for the purposes of worship. Nor were these copies in themselves insignificant: Scipione Borghese, for instance, ordered a copy of Raphael's *Entombment* from Lanfranco, even though it was Cavalier d'Arpino's copy that eventually replaced the original;[40] and the *Madonna del Baldacchino* was copied by Pietro Dandini.[41]

The practice of substituting copies to serve as visual and religious memorials for absent originals may indeed have started on a major scale with Raphael's works.[42] When in earlier periods altarpieces were replaced by new ones, it was because they had become old and shabby, or old-fashioned. The removal of Raphael's works by collectors seems to have had very few precedents in the field of religious painting.[43] It became standard practice thereafter, and it is, of course, still employed today by the conservation offices in the case of particularly popular images that shaped the popular climate of a place or its surroundings, such as Michelangelo's *David*, the horses of S. Marco, and the statue of Marcus Aurelius.[44]

There is only one major exception to this reverence for Raphael's creations. This concerns the fate of the *Madonna of Foligno* (plate 73), the only altarpiece actually executed by Raphael for a Roman church.[45] The painting was described by Vasari as decorating the high altar of S. Maria in Aracoeli and as having been commissioned by Sigismondo de' Conti, Julius II's secretary and the author of a massive history of his times, who in the picture is shown being introduced by St Jerome. Vasari's description of the painting is one of the most successful examples of *ekphrasis* ever dedicated to an altarpiece, and it is clear that he had ample opportunity to study the picture.[46] Although in the second edition of the *Lives* he describes the work as still on the high altar of the church, it had in fact already by 1565 moved to the convent of S. Anna delle Contesse in Foligno by the niece of Sigismondo, and there it remained until it was removed by Napoleon (hence its presence today in the Vatican

[40] Della Pergola, *Galleria Borghese* (as in note 36), p. 213, doc. 43.

[41] Riedl, 'Raffaels *Madonna del Baldacchino*', fig. 2.

[42] Charles Hope has drawn my attention to the parallel case of Titian's *Resurrection* polyptych in SS. Nazaro e Celso, Brescia, part of which was to be immediately replaced by another version made by Titian himself. See R. Pallucchini, *Tiziano* (Florence, 1969), Vol. 1, p. 252.

[43] R. Lightbown, 'Princely pressures: II Francesco I d'Este and Correggio', *Apollo* 78 (1963), pp. 193–9.

[44] While the *David* had already been replaced by a copy in the nineteenth century, the horses of S. Marco in Venice have only recently been replaced. A lively debate is currently being pursued as to whether the original *Marcus Aurelius* should be returned to the Capitol or be replaced by a copy.

[45] H. von Einem, 'Bemerkungen zu Raffaels *Madonna di Foligno*', in *Studies in late medieval and Renaissance painting in honor of Millard Meiss*, ed. I. Lavin and J. Plummer (New York, 1977), pp. 132–42; C. Gardner von Teuffel, 'Raffaels römische Altarbilder: Aufstellung und Bestimmung', *Zeitschrift für Kunstgeschichte*, 50 (1987), pp. 1–45; E. Scroter, 'Raffaels *Madonna di Foligno* ein Pestbild?', *Zeitschrift für Kunstgeschichte*, 50 (1987), pp. 47–88.

[46] Vasari, *Le vite*, Vol. 4 (as in note 9), pp. 341–2.

gallery).[47] Why would an altarpiece such as this be removed from Rome to the provinces? Certainly Sigismondo's niece would never have been able to remove it without the consent of the friars and the papacy.[48] The reasons for the transfer lie in the restoration plans for Roman churches begun by Pope Pius IV and continued under Gregory XIII.[49] A *motu proprio* for the Aracoeli laid down by Pius and reinforced by Gregory orders a number of changes. The nave was to be cleared of all altars, tombs and tabernacles that obstructed free access to the high altar. The original apse-shaped choir was replaced by a rectangular one, the ancient *scola cantorum* was destroyed, and a new high altar was set up.[50] In the course of this restoration, which began with the choir in 1561 and was completed in 1568, it was decided that the ancient cult image that was actually related to the foundation of the church, namely the Madonna supposedly painted by St Luke, should be set up on the high altar, thus replacing Raphael's *Madonna* (plates 100, 101). The Latin wording reads as follows: 'et imaginem B. Mariae Virginis, quae similiter in medio dicti templi consistebat in altari maiori eiusdem templi, ubi decentius videretur, collocari'.[51] In this instance, therefore, Raphael's work fell victim to a Counter-Reformation concern with a return to the early church, for it was precisely at this period that the interest in early Christian monuments and paintings for strictly religious rather than aesthetic reasons led to a return to prominence of those pictures that were thought to date from apostolic times.[52]

If the *Madonna of Foligno* was removed from Rome for reasons of renewed interest in early Christian and medieval cult images, there is another altarpiece by Raphael, which for precisely the same reasons was re-introduced to Rome, and played a vital part in the revival of at least one of these earlier cult figures.

The *St Cecilia* (plate 102) had been commissioned by Bolognese patrons, and it adorned their family chapel in S. Giovanni del Monte outside Bologna until it was brought to Paris by Napoleon, and whence it was later transferred to the Bologna gallery.[53] It was copied throughout the sixteenth century by local artists for various purposes: from exact copies of the whole picture to adaptations of the iconic representation of the main saint who, with her head uplifted and her gaze turned heavenwards, became a model for other female, and even for male saints.

---

[47] Casimiro Romano (Casimiro da Roma), *Memorie istoriche della Chiesa e Convento di S. Maria in Araceli di Roma* (Rome, 1736), p. 142 ('Questa tavola la fece dipingere . . . et sora Anna Conti nepote del ditto missere Gismondo la facta portare da Roma et facta mettere a questo altare nel 1565. A Di 23 De Maggio'); D. Michele Faloci Pulignani, 'Vita di Sigismondo de Comitibus scritta dall'Abate Mengozzi', *Bolletino della R. Deputazione di Storia patria per l'Umbria*, 13 (Perugia, 1907), p. 195, no. XXXII (with a different indication of the day).

[48] The fact that the panel was taken away by a member of the patron's family seems to indicate that Sigismondo actually stipulated in his will that the painting was to be returned to the family to prevent it being removed from its original location.

[49] Casimiro, *Memorie* (as in note 47), 142–3.

[50] R. Malstrom, 'S. Maria in Aracoeli at Rome', Ph.D. dissertation, New York University (1973), pp. 92ff.

[51] Casimiro, *Memorie* (as in note 47), 30.

[52] For the Counter-Reformation concern for medieval cult images, see M. Warnke, 'Italienische Bildtabernakel bis zum Frühbarock', *Münchner Jahrbuch der bildenen Kunst*, 19 (1968), pp. 61–102, 61ff; H. Jedin, 'Entstehung und Tragweite des Tridentiner Dekrets über die Bildverehrung', rpt. in *Kirche des Glaubens, Kirche der Geschichte*, Vol. 2 (Freiburg, 1966), pp. 481ff; S. Mayer-Himmelheber, *Bischofliche Kunstpolitik nach dem Tridentinum, der Secunda-Roma anspruch Carlo Borromeos und die mailandischen Verordnungen zu Bau und Ausstattung von Kirchen* (Munich, 1984).

[53] See Gardner von Teuffel, 'Raffaels römische Altarbilder' (as in note 45), pp. 3–4 for bibliography.

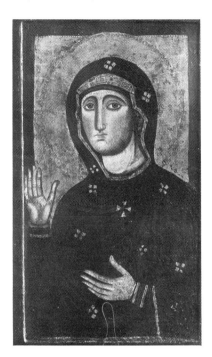

100 St Luke icon

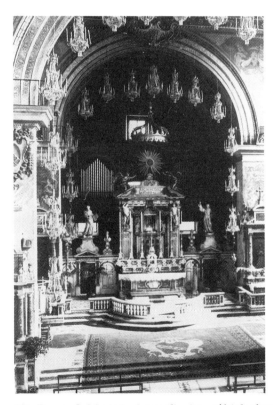

101 Rome, S. Maria in Aracoeli, view of high altar

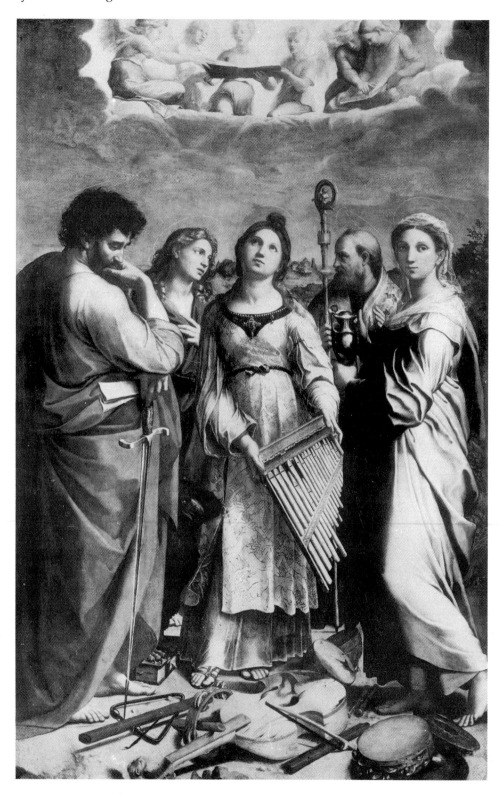

102 Raphael, *St Cecilia*

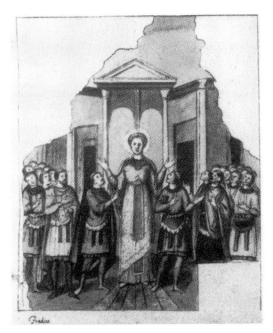

103 Seventeenth-century copy of medieval fresco in S. Cecilia in Trastevere, Rome

The pose, expression and attire of this particular saint, which is specific in meaning and yet allows itself to be adapted for a variety of saintly expressions, came to be thought of as the most perfect representation of the moral attitude of a saint, in whatever frame of mind we may encounter her or him. This is why, for instance, Pomarancio adopted it for his St Domitilla and Rubens for his St Helena.[54]

As is well known, Raphael had carefully studied the visual tradition of images of St Cecilia before he formulated his own vision of the saint; and he may have drawn inspiration from the then still well-preserved medieval frescoes in the Cappella del Bagno in the church of S. Cecilia in Trastevere, to judge from the similarity in dress and hair-style apparent in drawings made after these early frescoes (plate 103).[55] When the body of St Cecilia was unearthed by Cardinal Sfondrato in 1593 and her cult was revived, it was not the early Christian or medieval images of the saint still present in the church but Raphael's translation of them that provided the model for all subsequent representations of her, from iconic portrayals to narratives. Examples include the relief by Maderno, or Guido Reni's illustration of her beheading.[56]

Since Raphael's original painting never came to Rome, the Romans themselves knew it only through an exact copy made by the Bolognese Guido Reni, which was first set up in a chapel in the church of S. Cecilia, until it was moved to the chapel

[54] C. Bernardini, 'Problemi di fortuna postuma: fra maniera e accademia, pittura senza tempo e ideale classico', in *Indagini per un dipinto. La Santa Cecilia di Raffaello* (Bologna, 1983), pp. 141–9, 158–62.

[55] S. Mossakowski, 'Raphael's *St Cecilia*, an iconographical study', *Zeitschrift für Kunstgeschichte*, 31 (1968), pp. 10–11 and figs. 3–4; *L'Estasi di S. Cecilia* (as in note 3), pp. 228–30, figs. 216–18; S. Waetzold, *Die Kopien des 17. Jahrhunderts nach Mosaiken und Wandmalereien in Rom* (Vienna and Munich, 1964), fig. 31, Cat no. 59.

[56] Bernardini, 'Problemi' (as in note 54), pp. 167, 170.

of St Cecilia in S. Luigi dei Francesi, commissioned by the French Cardinal Polet around 1613.[57]

There is a certain analogy between this attitude towards Raphael's altarpiece and the reproduction of medieval cult images such as that of the famous Virgin painted by St Luke. But instead of the authenticity of the cult underlying the image we are presented here with the authority of the visual representation of it. Once more the shift has been brought about by the aesthetic achievement of Raphael's invention of a canonic formulation for a saint.

Another particularly interesting instance of the inter-relatedness of the religious and the aesthetic is provided by the much disputed *Virgin painted by St Luke* at the Accademia di S. Luca in Rome,[58] a copy of which still adorns the high altar of SS. Martina e Luca at the Forum Romanum, which, appropriately enough, is the church sacred to Roman painters (plates 104, 106). In this picture the figure of Raphael stands looking over the shoulder of St Luke, in a prominence generally reserved for saints or figures essential to the narrative. The picture was believed to be by Raphael until the nineteenth century, when it was downgraded to a workshop piece.[59] Until recently this opinion has been more or less widely accepted. Scholars such as Oberhuber believe either that it was begun by Raphael himself around 1511, and was then completed after his death by one of his assistants; or that it was created *ex novo* by one of the assistants after the master's death.[60] The painting, which, it must be stressed, is in a bad state of preservation, has been transferred from panel to canvas, and it has obviously been restored and overpainted a number of times,[61] as will become clear from the reports of c. 1600 that I shall mention later. Its present appearance has led Zygmunt Wazbinski to claim it as a forgery or – to put it more elegantly – an *invenzione* of a Raphael painting created by Federico Zuccari in collaboration with Scipione Pulzone da Gaeta, the man who according to Baglione was instructed by Zuccari to restore the picture.[62] According to Wazbinski, as the new principal of the Academy, Zuccari had felt the need not only for a painting of the appropriate subject-matter, but also for one that had been executed by the 'prince' of painters. Such an image would, Wazbinski believes, have formed an important part of Zuccari's attempts to provide a secure financial and ideological grounding for the Academy. Raphael's image would serve to exemplify the transcendent role of art in general – and of religious art in particular – and the status of the artist as creator. The importance of St Luke had also been reaffirmed during this period by the discovery of ancient paintings in the catacombs that were then generally

---

[57] D. J. S. Pepper, *Guido Reni. A complete catalogue of his works with an introductory text* (Oxford, 1984), no. 11. According to Pepper there is some evidence that Sfondrato actually gave it to Polet for the chapel.

[58] S. Wazbinski, 'San Luca che dipinge la Madonna all'Accademia di Roma: un ''pastiche'' zuccariano nella maniera di Raffaello?', *Artibus et Historiae*, 6 (1985), pp. 27–37, with previous bibliography.

[59] For the history of the attribution of the painting, see H. Wagner, *Raffael im Bildnis* (Bern, 1969), pp. 76–7.

[60] See the letter quoted by Wazbinski, 'San Luca' (as in note 58), p. 33 note 23.

[61] P. Cellini, 'Il San Luca di Raffaello', *Bollettino d'Arte*, 30 (1936–7), pp. 282–8; Cellini, 'Il restauro del S. Luca di Raffaello', *Bollettino d'Arte*, 43 (1958), pp. 250–62.

[62] Wazbinski, 'San Luca' (as in note 58), 33.

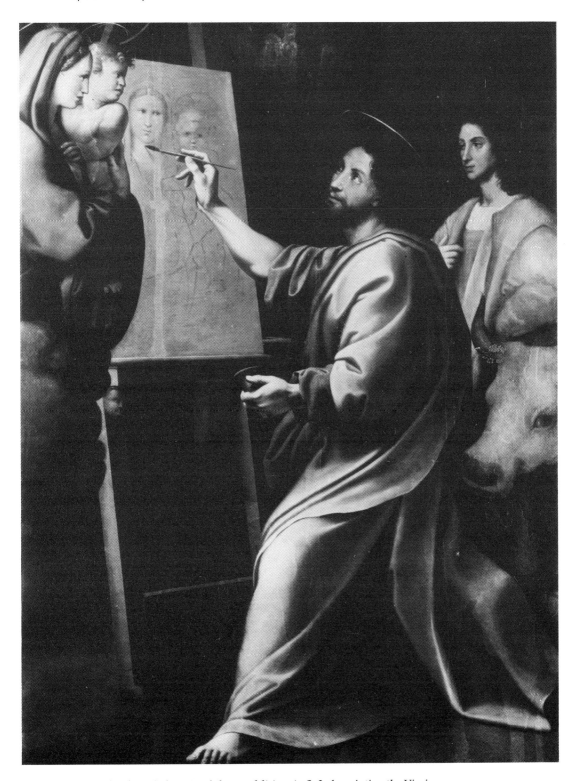

104 Raphael workshop (with later additions), *St Luke painting the Virgin*

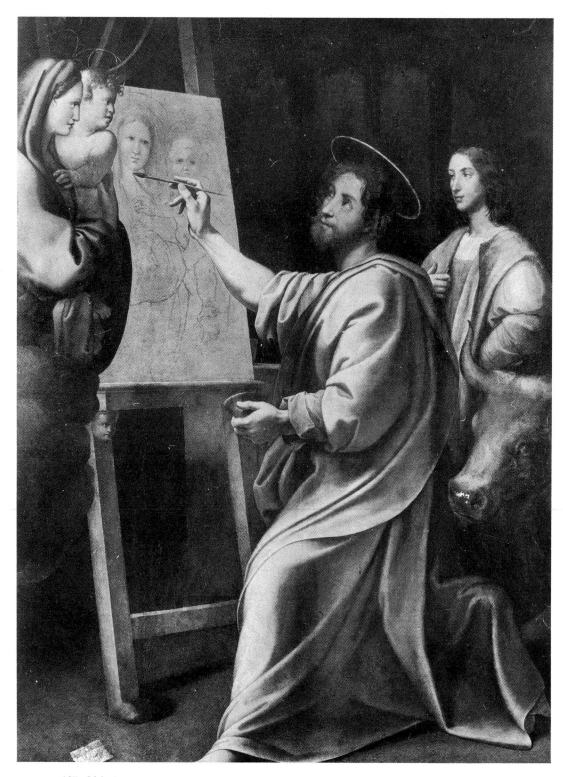

.105 Old photograph of plate 104, showing Pulzone's *cartellino*

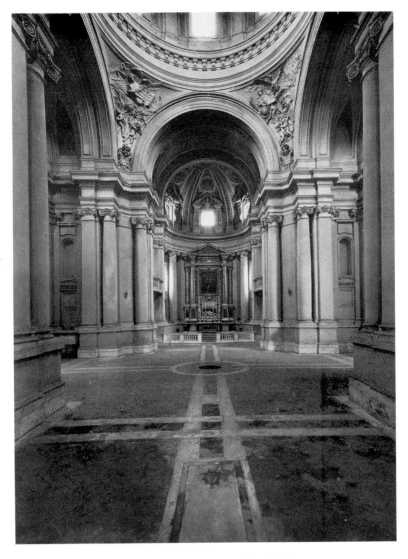

106 Rome, SS. Martina e Luca, view towards high altar

believed to date from the time of the apostles.[63] Raphael, of course, was seen as the embodiment of the concept of the Academy, and Zuccari's decision to forge (or fabricate) this particular painting represents a historical necessity that was to determine the future course of academic development. Although Wazbinski's theory is very attractive and fits my purposes particularly well, his interpretation fails to take into account all the historical facts.

It is true that the painting is not mentioned by Vasari, nor does it appear in any

[63] One famous example is the discovery of paintings in what Cardinal Baronio believed to be the catacomb of St Priscilla near the Via Salaria, which was discovered in 1587 when some workmen fell into it.

document prior to 1593. In a report of a meeting of the Academy for that year,[64] there is a mention of a Virgin painted by St Luke on the altar of the assembly room set up in a former hay-loft near the church of SS. Martina e Luca, where the painters had to move in 1588 after their previous church near S. Maria Maggiore had been sacrificed for the building of the Villa Montalto.[65] At some later point the painting was set up on the high altar of the church itself, where the poor state of repair into which the church had fallen caused serious damage to it.[66] While Antiveduto della Grammatica was principal, it was decided that he should make a copy to replace the original on the high altar.[67] A year later, in 1624, Antiveduto actually proposed to a secret assembly of the academicians to sell Raphael's altarpiece, and to use the money to restore the church and to provide for two masses a month for Raphael's soul. The assembly, however, voted against him.[68] Their reluctance to part with the original also transpires from a correspondence of 1601–2 between Lelio Arrigoni and the Duke of Mantua, who wanted the picture for his collection.[69] In this Lelio singles out the painting of St Luke as a good Raphael, well worth the money and effort required to secure it, but he warns the Duke that it would be difficult to persuade the painters to part with it.[70] And in the end the deal came to nothing.[71] At a later point the Duke of Ferrara also became interested in the piece, but his agents discouraged him from proceeding because of the poor condition of the picture.[72]

The later history of the Academy and its church is well known. Francesco Barberini sponsored the rebuilding of the church.[73] The painting was set up on the new high altar, and was then exchanged at a later date for Antiveduto's copy. This history, and in particular the repeated reports of the poor state of the picture, make it, in my opinion, unlikely that Zuccari and Pulzone forged it *ex novo* (apart from the fact that it does not actually look like a Zuccari or a Pulzone). The fact that Raphael's name does not appear in the reports of the 1593 *sedute* could be interpreted to mean that the painters took Raphael's authorship for granted, and that they believed that it had been donated to the Academy by Raphael himself.[74] It is probably also true that Zuccari paid special attention to the painting and that he had it restored as Baglione said he did. Baglione also tells of how Zuccari reprimanded Scipione for

---

[64] R. Alberti and F. Zuccari, *L'origine e progresso dell'Accademia di S. Luca a Roma* (Pavia, 1604), rpt. in *Scritti di Federico Zuccari*, ed. D. Heikamp (Florence, 1961), p. 14. There is no mention in this text of Raphael as the author, and it is possible to conclude that the picture was prized because it represented St Luke, and also because it incorporated the figure of Raphael. But mention of Raphael's authorship may also have been omitted because it was a well-established fact that had no need of special emphasis.

[65] For the history and movements of the Academy of St Luke, see K. Noehles, *La Chiesa di SS. Luca e Martina nell'opera di Pietro da Cortona* (Rome, 1964), pp. 47ff., 57ff.

[66] Ibid., pp. 47, 334, doc. 9, 20 November 1622 ('tutti assieme congregati . . . fu notato, che il quadro di S. Luca dell'Altare Maggiore fato per mano di Raffaele si debbia copiare, et portar l'originale in Accademia').

[67] Ibid., pp. 57, 335, doc. 11.

[68] Ibid., pp. 57, 335–6, doc. 16.

[69] Wagner, *Raffael* (as in note 59), p. 73.

[70] Ibid., p. 74.

[71] Ibid.

[72] Ibid., p. 75.

[73] Noehles, *La Chiesa* (as in note 65), pp. 97ff.

[74] See above, note 44, and Wagner, *Raffael im Bildnis* (as in note 59), p. 76.

having put his own name on the *cartellino* in the painting (plate 105), which, he said, showed scant reverence for the great artist.[75]

The painting became particularly celebrated in the seventeenth and eighteenth centuries and inspired a number of artists to copy the composition.[76] Two particularly significant examples were provided by Carlo Maratta in a drawing and by Pierre Mignard in a painting.[77] Both of these share the same basic composition with our painting, and also the concept that the self-portrait of the artist is not identical with the figure of St Luke. Rather, either the artist passively observes his patron saint at work, as in Maratta's drawing, or he looks out at the observer, as in Mignard's painting. While Raphael's picture thus started a tradition, it seems to have had no precedents at all.

First, we have to ask whether the inclusion of the portrait of Raphael was planned from the beginning, or whether it was a later addition.[78] This question becomes all the more pressing when we note that it is out of proportion with the other figures, awkwardly squeezed in behind the gigantic bull, and insecurely anchored to the ground. Furthermore, it is different in style and handling, and seems warmer in tone than the rest of the picture. According to Pico Cellini an x-ray of the picture reveals that originally a window was intended to be where the figure now is. Is it possible that the figure of Raphael could have been added? Or at least, superimposed over another figure, an onlooker or an inspiring angel? And if so, when? Two moments seem most likely: the first is immediately after Raphael's death, when the painting may have been completed – or even executed – by one of Raphael's assistants. The second is when it was restored by Pulzone.

It is difficult to imagine that Raphael's assistants would have depicted him as the youth from the Stanza della Segnatura – which had been painted ten years earlier – rather than as he looked at the time of his death, a bearded adult, similar in appearance to St Luke himself.[79] The portrayal of Raphael as he looked around 1510 suggests either that the picture dates from this period, and indeed, Oberhuber has suggested

[75] Ibid., p. 73. G. Baglione, *Le vite de' pittori, scultori et architetti dal Pontificato di Gregorio XIII del 1572 in fino a tempi di Papa Urbano nel 1642* (Rome, 1642), p. 124. While restoring the picture Pico Cellini (as in note 61) found traces of this *cartellino* in the underpainting. However, on an old photograph at the Bibliotheca Hertziana in Rome it is still fully visible. It was probably only removed when the panel was transferred from panel to canvas.

[76] In his work for his doctoral thesis Gerhard Wolf ('*Salus Populi Romani*', as in note 23) discovered the covers for the icon of S. Maria Maggiore, which were executed on the occasion of its famous *translatio* to the Paoline chapel on 27 January 1613. These covers are painted on their inner sides, so that when opened they form a sort of triptych, with the icon at the centre. The left wing shows the Virgin of the icon in full length, and (according to Wolf) in a state of pregnancy; while the right wing shows St Luke in a manner similar to that of his counterpart in Raphael's painting – in other words, seated in front of the easel, on which he paints the Virgin as she appears in the icon. To the right of St Luke there is a standing figure not unlike that of Raphael's portrait in Raphael's painting, and which according to Wolf represents St John the Evangelist in the act of inspiring the painter. Wolf provides a thorough analysis of the meaning of this very interesting work, which constitutes probably the earliest response to Raphael's painting in seventeenth-century Rome. For further examples of the impact of the composition on later painters, see Wazbinski, 'San Luca' (as in note 58), figs. 10–11.

[77] Mignard's painting is reproduced in G. Kraut, *Lukas malt die Madonna. Zeugnisse zum künstlerischen Selbstverständnis in der Malerei* (Worms, 1986), p. 140, fig. 41. Maratta's drawing of St Luke painting the Virgin (Rugby School, Art Museum, inv. no. 17) is reproduced in Wazbinski, 'San Luca' (as in note 58).

[78] This was already questioned by M. Missirini, in *Descrizioni delle Immagini dipinte da Raffaello d'Urbino nel Vaticano e di quelle alla Farnesina di Gio. Pietro Bellori colla vita di Raffaello scritta dal Vasari* (Rome, 1821), s. XIV.

[79] Compare the features of St Luke with those of Raphael in the double portrait in the Louvre. The first to consider St Luke as a possible portrait of Raphael was A. Sartorio, *Galleria di S. Luca* (Rome, 1910), p. ix.

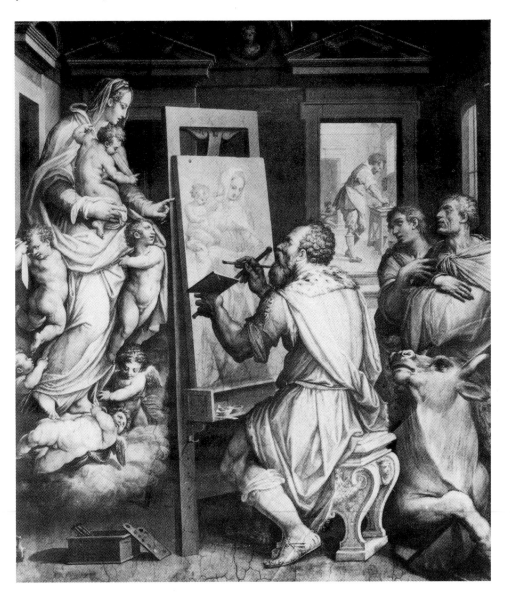

107 Vasari, *St Luke painting the Virgin*

a date of around 1511; or that it is a commemoration done much later, possibly even as part of Pulzone's restoration. But if this were the case, we would have to assume that at least some kind of figure was already present – an apprentice or a simple onlooker – or even the donor of the picture.

This becomes more convincing if we take another painting as a comparison, the one that Vasari painted in the 1560s for the chapel of St Luke in SS. Annunziata in Florence (plate 107).[80] In the way the Virgin, the Evangelist, the bull and the onlookers are arranged, this painting is strikingly similar to our painting. But Vasari

---

[80] Kraut, *Lukas malt die Madonna* (as in note 77), p. 65, fig. 14; p. 72, fig. 16.

has given his own features to St Luke. Did Vasari know Raphael's painting and use it as a model for his own? If so, why then did he not mention it in the *Lives*? Or might it have been his own invention, which then became the model for Pulzone, who retranslated it into a Raphaelesque idiom? Or was Raphael's picture originally intended to portray himself as St Luke, and did part of Pulzone's restoration involve the transformation of the onlooker into the younger image of Raphael? Even though I am inclined to accept this last hypothesis,[81] this is not the place to attempt to offer a definitive answer to this question. What is essential for my purpose is that here on the main altar of a Roman church we have at least one full-length portrait of Raphael, and most likely even two. St Luke is, of course, the mythical painter of the Virgin, the founder father of all Christian art. But watching over his shoulder is the real painter and his heir. The cult of the personality of Raphael has thus been legitimised through a fusion of the sacred and the aesthetic. Goethe on his visit to the Accademia di S. Luca in 1788, after going on at some length about the beauty of Raphael's skull ('a brain-pan of beautiful proportions and perfectly smooth, without any of those protruberances and bumps which have been observed on other skulls ... I could hardly tear myself away'), observed of the picture of St Luke that 'the juxtaposition of the two figures – of the Evangelist and the painter – could not express more charmingly the way in which a man finds himself drawn to a particular vocation'.[82]

---

[81] Although Wazbinski's thesis is a seductive one, and consistent with certain trends in current art-historical thinking, I feel uneasy about attributing intentions of fraud to highly respectable personalities of the past such as Federico Zuccari, who cannot return to defend themselves.

[82] Goethe's *Italienische Reise*, ed. C. Schuchardt, Vol. 1 (Stuttgart, 1862), p. 580 (April 1788); English translation by W. H. Auden and E. Mayer as *Italian Journey* (Harmondsworth, 1970), pp. 490–2.

10 *Co-ordinated altarpieces in Renaissance Venice: the progress of an ideal*

Peter Humfrey

When Vasari undertook in the 1560s and 70s to replace the motley collection of late medieval altar decorations in the aisles of the Florentine churches of S. Maria Novella and S. Croce with a regularly placed series of altarpieces of a co-ordinated design, he was fulfilling an ideal that had long been cherished by Renaissance architects and theorists. As we now know, Brunelleschi had provided a standardised design for the frames of the altarpieces that were to adorn the side-chapels of S. Lorenzo, and probably those of S. Spirito as well;[1] and Alberti in his treatise *De Re Aedificatoria* had spoken of the desirability of restricting the pictorial decoration of churches to framed paintings (in other words, altarpieces as opposed to frescoes) placed at regular intervals.[2] Especially at S. Croce, where the subjects of the new set of altarpieces combine to form a coherent Passion cycle, Vasari's renovations were also consistent with the current spirit of religious reform. In the 25th session of the Council of Trent in 1563, Catholic theologians had reaffirmed Pope Gregory's defence of religious images as the books of the unlettered;[3] and although Vasari's convolutedly Mannerist style in painting did not, perhaps, depict the individual scenes with exemplary clarity, their uniform aspect and orderly sequence, combined with the textual inscriptions carved on their friezes, were well calculated to stress their overtly didactic purpose. Vasari's cycle thus provided a means by which the ignorant laity could receive instruction by the clergy in the story of Christ's Passion, while also providing food for meditation by the more sophisticated devout on the inner significance of these events.[4]

The ideal realised by Vasari at S. Croce, both aesthetic and religious, involved a direct contradiction of the traditional character and function of the church altarpiece. Responsibility for the upkeep and decoration of the great majority of the side-altars in late mediaeval and Renaissance churches had hitherto resided with the respective individual, family or confraternity that owned rights to it. The commissioning of altarpieces thus depended on a large number of different initiatives undertaken by different donors often at different times, and the natural result was a great diversity of shapes, sizes, styles and materials. This diversity was not simply the result of disorganisation, or of a lack of aesthetic will: most donors, in particular the socially

---

[1] C. Gardner von Teuffel, 'Lorenzo Monaco, Filippo Lippi und Filippo Brunelleschi: die Erfindung der Renaissance-pala', *Zeitschrift für Kunstgeschichte*, 45 (1982), pp. 1–30.
[2] L. B. Alberti, *L'Architettura*, ed. and trans. G. Orlandi, Vol. 2 (Milan, 1966), pp. 608–9.
[3] *The canons and decrees of the Council of Trent*, ed. and trans. H. Schroeder (Rockford IL, 1978), pp. 214–17.
[4] For Vasari's cycle at S. Maria Novella and S. Croce, see M. Hall, *Renovation and Counter-Reformation: Vasari and Duke Cosimo in Sta Maria Novella and Sta Croce 1565–1577* (Oxford, 1979).

ambitious, would positively have wanted their contributions to distinguish themselves visually from those of their neighbours. We may also assume that in the highly
competitive world of Italian Renaissance artists portrayed by Vasari himself in his
Lives, many of the painters they employed would similarly have welcomed any opportunity to outshine the work of rivals or predecessors nearby. From the religious point
of view, too, it was important for altarpieces to be distinct from one another. It
was normal for the lay patrons of chapels and side-altars to be permitted to choose
their own dedications, in accordance with their own devotional interests; and these
interests would in turn be reflected in the choice of subject-matter. Before the mid-
sixteenth century, this was usually a question of making a selection from the vast
company of heaven of those saints whom the donor considered to be most effective
as intercessors on his own behalf before God. But even when the subject was a
narrative one, taken from scripture or hagiography, it was chosen in the first place
as a personalised expression of devotion to a particular saint or mystery, and only
secondarily, if at all, as a sermon to the general public on Catholic doctrine or ethics.[5]
In this situation, any thematic relationship between the various altarpieces in a church
would have been one of deliberate contrast rather than of harmonious co-ordination.

Yet Vasari's cycles were not the only ones of their kind, and other Renaissance
examples immediately spring to mind. Among the best known are the group of five by
various Sienese artists enclosed in matching frames, which were installed in Pius II's
new cathedral in Pienza in 1461–3 (see plates 7, 10); the series of eight with hagiological
subjects commissioned from various painters by Cardinal Ercole Gonzaga in 1552
for the newly rebuilt cathedral in Mantua; and the cycles planned in the late sixteenth
century for the Gesù and the Chiesa Nuova (S. Maria in Vallicella) in Rome.[6] The
evidence of these, and of a number of lesser-known examples,[7]
suggests that the ideal of formal unity gradually gained ground during the Renaissance
period, and also that this was increasingly complemented by an ideal of thematic
unity with the progress of the Counter-Reformation. Such an ideal was obviously
consistent with the spirit of the Tridentine pronouncement on the use of images,

[5] I have argued this in closer detail in P. Humfrey, 'The Venetian *scuole piccole* as donors of altarpieces in the
years around 1500', *Art Bulletin*, 70 (1988), pp. 403–4.

[6] For these four sets, see respectively H. W. van Os 'Painting in a house of glass: the altarpieces of Pienza', *Simiolus*,
17 (1987), pp. 23–38; C. Perina in *Mantova: le arti*, ed. G. Paccagnini, E. Marini and C. Perina, Vol. 3 (Mantua,
1965), pp. 340–4; H. Hibbard ' *Ut pictura sermones*: the first painted decorations of the Gesù', in *Baroque Art:
the Jesuit contribution*, ed. R. Wittkower and I. Jaffé (New York, 1972), pp. 29–49; M. A. Graeve, 'The Stone of
Unction in Caravaggio's painting for the Chiesa Nuova', *Art Bulletin*, 40 (1958), pp. 233–5.

[7] To mention a few: the late fifteenth-century series at Cestello (S. Maria Maddalena de' Pazzi), Florence, and
at S. Bartolomeo, Vicenza; the series of marble frames installed in Pisa Cathedral by Stagio Stagi in the 1530s;
the series at S. Barbara, Mantua in 1564–5. Outside Italy: the series by the school of Cranach for the Moritzkirche,
Halle, from the 1520s; El Greco's series for S. Domingo el Antiguo (plate 125), the chapel of St Joseph and the
chapel of the Hospital of St John the Baptist in Toledo. See respectively A. Luchs, *Cestello. A Cistercian Church
of the Florentine Renaissance* (New York, 1977); P. Humfrey, 'Cima da Conegliano at San Bartolomeo in Vicenza',
Arte Veneta, 31 (1977), pp. 176–81; Vasari's *Le vite de' più eccellenti architetti, pittori et scultori*, ed. G. Milanesi (Florence,
1878ff.), 5, p. 27, and Vasari, *The lives of the painters, sculptors and architects*, ed. W. Gaunt, 2, pp. 344–6 (Life
of Sogliani); C. Perina in *Mantova* (as in previous note), pp. 344–8; U. Steinemann, 'Der Bilderschmuck der Stifts-
kirche zu Halle', *Staatliche Museen zu Berlin. Forschungen und Berichte*, 11 (1968), pp. 69–104; A. E. Pérez Sánchez,
'On the reconstruction of El Greco's dispersed altarpieces', in *El Greco of Toledo*, catalogue of exhibition held
in Madrid, Washington, Toledo (Ohio) and Dallas, 1982–3 (Boston, 1982), pp. 149–76, and R. Mann, *El Greco
and his patrons* (Cambridge, 1986).

and with contemporary efforts by the ecclesiastical hierarchy to bring the production of religious art more directly under clerical control; but as far as I know, it was never explicitly advocated by reforming churchmen, and it is not clear to what extent they consciously sought to implement it. The purpose of the present chapter is to trace the progress of the ideal of co-ordinated altarpieces in a single major religious and artistic centre – Venice – in an attempt to assess how far it was recognised as such by church architects and church authorities. As we will see, the history is a patchy one, and few apparent efforts at unity remained undisrupted by the very different interests of lay donors and their painters. Such disruption was especially likely in republican Venice, which lacked absolutist figures such as Vasari's employer, the Grand Duke Cosimo de' Medici, or the various popes and cardinals of Counter-Reformation Rome, who were in a position to impose a single grand design on all the altar decorations in a single church. Yet Venice in the 1580s and 90s achieved one of the most perfect examples anywhere of formal and thematic integration within a group of altarpieces in Palladio's church of the Redentore; and this achievement was foreshadowed by a number of local precedents that seem interesting and instructive for the history of altarpieces in general.

The way in which the Renaissance vocabulary of form was introduced in Venice was not of a kind that would automatically tend to promote unity and symmetry of altarpiece design. Unlike in Florence, where the new style first appeared as an intellectual and structural system governing monumental architecture, and was only later adapted to decorative features such as the frames of altarpieces, it was initially conceived in Venice in terms of a novel repertory of ornament. Thus altarpieces began to receive frames *all' antica* several years before the construction of the first Renaissance-style churches; and in their Gothic surroundings, the earliest Renaissance altarpieces merely added an element of novelty to the existing diversity. The general effect is clearly illustrated by the three altarpieces visible in Carpaccio's view of the interior of the now-demolished church of S. Antonio di Castello (plate 108) in the early years of the sixteenth century, where the mixture of styles and arbitrariness of arrangement are precisely of the kind that Vasari was seeking to reform.

Under these circumstances, it is somewhat surprising to find that a group of four altarpieces of identical format were produced in Venice as early as 1460–4. These are the four triptychs (now in the Accademia; plates 109–10) painted for the newly built church of S. Maria della Carità, which were probably commissioned from Jacopo Bellini and executed by various members of his shop, including his son Giovanni.[8] The church was built in the traditional Gothic style (not unlike that of S. Antonio di Castello), but many of its original furnishings were in the new style, including the original frames of the triptychs, and also the *barco*, or choir-screen, under which

[8] G. Robertson, 'The earlier work of Giovanni Bellini', *Journal of the Warburg and Courtauld Institutes*, 23 (1960), pp. 49–51. The panels are shown in modern gallery frames in Pls. 109, 110 here, but these probably correspond fairly accurately to the lost originals. It should be noted, however, that the panels are shown in an historically incorrect arrangement, and that the pairs of flanking saints in the two plates should be reversed.

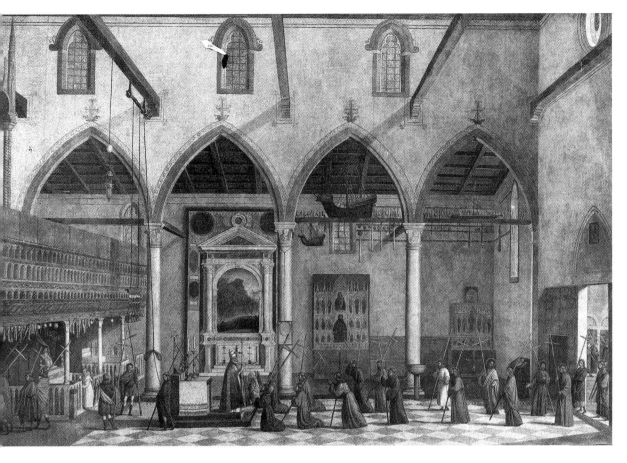

108 Carpaccio, *Vision of Prior Francesco Ottobon*

they were originally placed.[9] This was unfortunately destroyed when the church was closed and gutted in the early nineteenth century; but a ground plan of 1807, together with a letter referring to it as a 'loggietta',[10] make it clear that it would have constituted an updated version of that just visible at the left in Carpaccio's view of S. Antonio di Castello, and would have closely resembled the slightly later *barco* still surviving in Coducci's church of S. Michele in Isola. It would thus have presented the spectator standing in the nave with a view of four identical chapels seen through four identical archways; and it was surely this setting, as opposed to the more normal one down the side-walls, or in apsidal chapels, that prompted the decision by the

[9] See the documents published by G. Fogolari, 'La chiesa del Carità', *Archivio Veneto-Tridentino*, 5–6 (1924), pp. 57–119. Payments for constructing the *barco* were made to one Jacopo da Milano, who is described as working 'al antigua'.

[10] L. De Carli and M. Zaggia, 'Chiesa, convento e Scuola di S. Maria della Carità in Venezia', *Bolletino del Centro di Studi di Architettura 'A. Palladio'*, 16 (1974), p. 428 and fig. 230. The representation of the *barco* in the reconstruction by Fogolari (see preceding note) is not quite accurate.

clergy – Augustinian canons of the Lateran congregation[11] – to have the triptychs commissioned as a matching quartet. As emerges from the account-books, patronage rights to the altars were ceded to laymen in the usual way, in this case four patricians, on the condition that they paid for the decoration themselves.[12] But it is equally clear that while each lay donor was free to choose the dedication of his altar, and also the saints that were to be represented in his altarpiece, each was obliged to follow a common model, and to order it from the same workshop. We have no certain knowledge about how the four donors reacted to these unusual constraints, which effectively prevented them from competing with one another and distinguishing their own contributions. But it is interesting to notice that one applicant for a chapel later withdrew, and that one of the donors, Andrea da Molin, renegotiated his agreement with the canons several times. At one point, he apparently wanted to commission a pentaptych, with five rather than three full-length saints, a more ambitious arrangement that would clearly have disrupted the symmetry of the set. Eventually he must have been persuaded to have two of his saints depicted in half-length in the lunette; but even so, his choice of a narrative *Nativity* in the central panel rather than a standing saint represents a certain break in the uniformity of the series (plate 110). Similar constraints in the interests of an overall harmony also seem to have been felt by the painters. A commission that involved not one but four altarpieces, all to the same design, might have been attractive, easy and remunerative for the head of a workshop; but for the various executants it must have closely resembled drudgery. Indeed, it is precisely the combination of a pictorial style that is evidently close to that of Giovanni Bellini and an execution that is well below his normal standards, that has always made the attribution of the triptychs so problematic. As we will see later at the Redentore, a purist urge towards standardisation brought with it the dangers and penalties associated with mass-production.

We cannot know how far the set of triptychs for the Carità was consciously regarded by artists as an unsuccessful experiment, but it may be no accident that no further deliberately planned series of altarpieces was produced in Venice for many years. One might have expected the greatest Venetian architect of the early Renaissance, Mauro Coducci, with his systematic mind and his feeling for the organic inter-relationship between the various parts of the buildings, would also have been the disciple of Brunelleschi and Alberti in his attitude to altarpieces. But in fact, there is no evidence to show that he was ever directly involved in the design of an altarpiece for any of his churches. On the contrary, we know that even major decorative features, such as the main doorway of S. Michele in Isola, were the work of autonomous

---

[11] The Lateran Canons (until 1444 called after the church of S. Maria di Frigionaia in Lucca) were one of the most important reforming congregations of the fifteenth century: see C.-D. Fonseca, 'Frigionaia', in *Dictionnaire d'histoire et de géographie ecclésiastiques*, Vol. 19 (Paris, 1981), cols. 95–9, with bibliography. We know rather little of their possible humanist or artistic interests, but given their close connections with the Roman curia, they may well have been aware of the Cathedral at Pienza, with its set of five matching altarpieces of a format closely similar to that adopted for the Carità triptychs (see above, note 7; plate 7).

[12] See the documents in Fogolari, 'La Chiesa' (as in note 9 above), supplemented by R. Gallo, 'I polittici già nelle cappelle del coro di Santa Maria della Carità', *Arte Veneta*, 3 (1949), pp. 136–40.

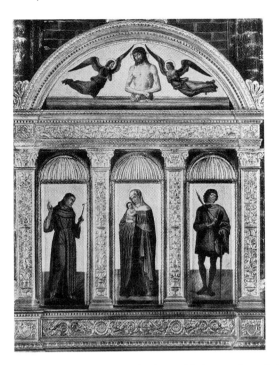

109 Giovanni Bellini and others, *Madonna* triptych from S. Maria della Carità (in modern frame)

craftsmen, employed separately by the clergy;[13] and by the time that most of the altarpieces came to be installed in his churches, Coducci himself had frequently moved to supervise the construction of another building.[14] Nevertheless, the very character of his architecture, which by its internal logic and consistency imposed a symmetrical placing of altars and chapels and related them visually to one another, did sometimes result in the creation of a number of altarpieces that were evidently conceived by their independent creators as mutually complementary. At S. Giovanni Crisostomo, for example, the decoration of only one of the three main chapels, corresponding to the three arms of the Greek Cross plan, was executed in the architect's lifetime, and even this was supervised by Tullio Lombardo rather than by Coducci himself. But the design of Tullio's *Coronation* altarpiece and frame is sympathetically integrated with the architecture of the church, and so too is that of Giovanni Bellini's Diletti altarpiece of 1513 opposite; so although the two works are separated in date by a decade, and were commissioned by separate patrons, they successfully present the appearance of harmoniously co-ordinated pendants. The achievement of this harmony, which probably originally also embraced Sebastiano del Piombo's high altarpiece, was no doubt considerably assisted by the continuous presence of a parish

---

[13] See J. McAndrew, *Venetian architecture of the early Renaissance* (Cambridge MA, 1980), p. 249.

[14] In at least two of Coducci's churches existing polyptychs were installed, presumably transferred by their owners from the previous buildings. Thus F. Sansovino, *Venetia città nobilissima*, ed. G. Martinioni (Venice, 1663), p. 235, records a work by the early fifteenth-century Sienese painter Andrea di Bartolo under the *barco* in S. Michele in Isola; and a triptych by Bartolomeo Vivarini dated 1473 still hangs in S. Maria Formosa.

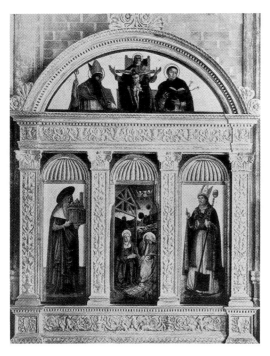

110 Giovanni Bellini and others, *Nativity* triptych from S. Maria della Carità (in modern frame)

priest of enlightened artistic interests.[15] A similar co-ordinating role, with similarly harmonious results, was then apparently played by the parish priest of the post-Coduccesque church of S. Maria Mater Domini only a few years later.[16]

But it is Jacopo Sansovino rather than his predecessor Coducci who may be recognised as the first Venetian architect to provide co-ordinated designs for the altarpieces in his churches, as at S. Francesco della Vigna and the Incurabili. The case of S. Francesco (plate 111) is particularly interesting, because it illustrates many of the tensions already seen at the Carità at a different historical moment. The combination of Sansovino's Tuscan background with the reforming seriousness of his Franciscan Observant employers would seem to be one especially likely to promote a general effect of consistency and discipline within the various side-chapels of the church; and indeed, all the various patrician families who presented themselves as patrons were required to construct their chapels according to a uniform model provided by the architect.[17] Sansovino also seems to have provided a uniform design for the altarpiece frames, since two (and probably originally three) of the ten in the matching side-chapels are identical.[18] The remainder, however, are different, some slightly

[15] For the altarpieces at S. Giovanni Crisostomo in relation to the architecture, see McAndrew, *Venetian architecture* (as in note 13), p. 313; the role of the parish priest, Alvise Talenti, is discussed by S. Tramontin, *San Giovanni Crisostomo* (Venice, 1968), p. 10, and by C. Bertini, 'I committenti della pala di S. Giovanni Crisostomo di Sebastiano del Piombo', *Storia dell'Arte*, 53 (1985), pp. 23–31.

[16] See S. Tramontin, *S. Maria Mater Domini: arte e storia* (Venice, 1962), pp. 19–20.

[17] D. Howard, *Jacopo Sansovino* (New Haven and London, 1975), p. 68.

[18] D. Howard in H. Macandrew *et al.*, 'Tintoretto's *Deoposition of Christ* in the National Gallery of Scotland', *Burlington Magazine*, 127 (1985), p. 507.

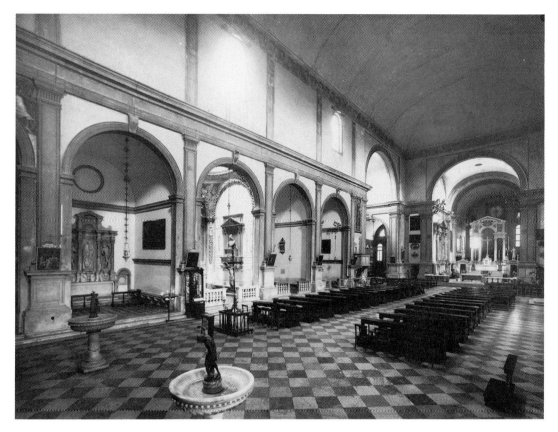

111 Jacopo Sansovino, Church of S. Francesco della Vigna, Venice, interior

and others radically. The most striking departure from the austere norm originally envisaged by architect and clergy is represented by the elaborate and self-consciously Romanising decoration of the first chapel on the left, that of the Grimani family (see plate 140).[19] The Grimani were perhaps exceptional in their display of a particular aesthetic taste to symbolise their pro-Roman political sympathies and grandiose dynastic aspirations; yet it is likely that the various other patrician chapel-owners would similarly have regarded the decoration of their chapels as symbols of their own individuality and prestige, and would similarly have sought to abandon the Sansovinesque norm in the design of their altarpieces. The brothers Lorenzo and Antonio Giustinian, for example, commissioned a frame that afforded a considerably larger field for their altar painting by Veronese than the standard frame in the neighbouring Dandolo chapel would have done (plate 112).[20] This is not to say that Sansovino seriously resisted such attempts to break away from the common pattern. On the contrary, he may well himself have been responsible not only for the Giustinian frame, but also for the even more anomalous frame of the Grimani chapel, together

[19] A. Foscari and M. Tafuri, *L'armonia e i conflitti. La chiesa di San Francesco della Vigna nella Venezia del '500* (Turin, 1983), pp. 137f.
[20] See P. Humfrey, 'La Pala Giustinian: contesto e committenza', in *Nuovi studi su Paolo Veronese* (Venice, 1990), pp. 299–307.

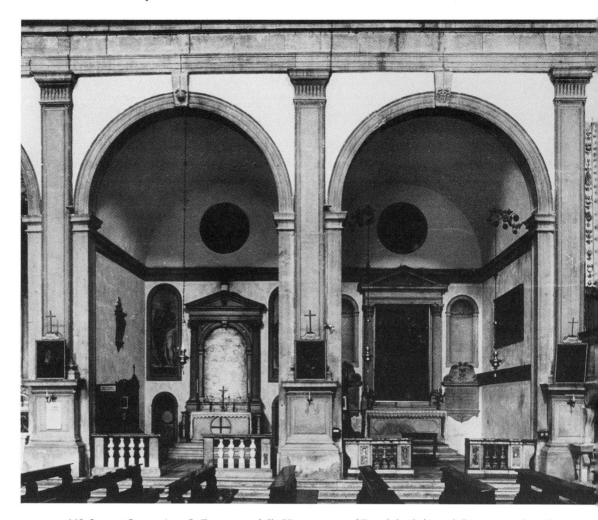

112 Jacopo Sansovino, S. Francesco della Vigna, view of Dandolo (left) and Giustinian chapels

with the appropriately antique-looking coffering on its vault.[21] Unlike that of Palladio, Sansovino's genius was not one that sought the systematic application of an intellectual ideal, but one that instinctively found effective and striking solutions for a variety of different situations. On the one hand, the fact that several of his altarpieces nearly match, yet do not quite do so, is undeniably disruptive of the overall architectural harmony. On the other hand, it could be argued that with their moderate variations in shape and scale, the architectonic frames are better suited to express not only the individuality of their respective donors, but also that of the various paintings and sculptures they contain. Several of these, by such artists as Tintoretto, Vittoria, Veronese, Battista Franco, Giuseppe Salviati and Federigo Zuccaro, are of outstanding quality, and are unlikely to have been improved by being placed within a rigid formal straitjacket.

[21] Howard, *Jacopo Sansovino* (as in note 17), p. 69. Foscari and Tafuri, *L'armonia* (as in note 19), p. 137, on the contrary, describe the decoration of the Grimani chapel as 'antisansoviniana'; but elsewhere (p. 69) recognise the stylistically flexible character of Sansovino's architecture.

In his most important later ecclesiastical commission, that of the hospital church of the Incurabili, Sansovino again seems to have provided a more or less standard aedicular design for the frames of the four main side-altarpieces.[22] But again, there were minor variations in the size and shape of the canvases, variously by Tintoretto, Veronese, Salviati and Hans Rottenhammer,[23] which were apparently executed over a number of years as individual donors presented themselves. The altarpieces in Sansovino's parish churches of S. Giuliano and S. Martino, on the other hand, show little or no formal unity; and nor do those in the great majority of other Venetian churches built, decorated or redecorated around the mid to late sixteenth century, such as S. Sebastiano, S. Maria Maggiore and S. Trovaso.[24]

So far our Venetian examples have consisted of groups of at least four altarpieces, none of which have shown any thematic unity. At S. Francesco della Vigna, as at the Carità, the traditional practice of allowing donors to choose the dedications for their own altars seems to have been generally maintained.[25] But already in the fifteenth century there are a number of examples of twin, or pendant altarpieces, usually on a relatively small scale, which in addition to matching one another formally were clearly intended to embody complementary ideas. Probably the earliest of these is the pair of polyptychs (plates 113–14) executed in a florid late Gothic style in 1443 for the old church of S. Zaccaria (now the chapel of S. Tarasio) by the carver Lodovico da Forlì and the painters Antonio Vivarini and Giovanni d'Alemagna, in conjunction with a much larger polyptych for the high altar. Although the three polyptychs are inscribed with the names of three different donors – the abbess and two of her Benedic-

[22] Howard, *Jacopo Sansovino* (as in note 17), p. 94; Howard, 'Le chiese del Sansovino a Venezia', *Bolletino del Centro Internazionale di Studi di Architettura 'A. Palladio'*, 11 (1977), pp. 49–67.

[23] The first three are now in the church of S. Lazzaro de' Mendicanti, the fourth is lost. The date of Tintoretto's *St Ursula and the ten thousand virgins* is controversial (see R. Pallucchini and P. Rossi, *Tintoretto: le opere sacre e profane* (Milan, 1982), p. 169), but in any case it seems to predate Sansovino's building, and it must therefore have been adapted to a new Sansovinesque frame. None of the donors of the altarpieces is known; but it may be noted here that the presence of a confraternity of Ursulines in the church is recorded by E. Cicogna, *Delle iscrizioni veneziane*, Vol. 5 (Venice, 1842), p. 303, and so it may well have been they who commissioned the work by Tintoretto.

[24] It is, however, worth noting here two campaigns of redecoration that involved the imposition of a new regularity of the placing of the altars, and a corresponding standardisation of the framing of their altarpieces. The first took place from 1562 onwards in the church of S. Maria dei Servi, the interior of which must previously have resembled that of S. Antonio di Castello (plate 108); see J. Benci and S. Stucky, 'Indagini sulla pala belliniana della *Lamentazione*', *Artibus et Historiae*, 8:15 (1987), p. 59. The second, in the church of S. Zaccaria, apparently took place in the 1590s, when the four altarpieces in the nave, together with two flanking portals, were given a unified architectural design. Interestingly, the design itself seems to go back to *c*. 1520, when it was probably devised to be applied to Giovanni Bellini's famous altarpiece above the second altar on the right. The design must then have been extended to the other altars and to the portals in the last decade, in response to the growing desire for aesthetic uniformity. I am grateful to Wendy Stedman Sheard for kindly discussing the dating of the S. Zaccaria altarpiece frames with me.

[25] For the dedications of the chapels at S. Francesco della Vigna, see F. Corner, *Ecclesiae venetae et torcellanae*, Vol. 7 (Venice, 1749), pp. 55–6. The dedications of the first on the right, the fourth on the left and the one to the left of the chancel, respectively in the custody of the Bragadin, Dandolo and Giustinian families, correspond to the Christian names of the chapel founders (or in the first case, to that of his wife). For the first two, see D. McTavish, *Giuseppe Porta called Giuseppe Salviati* (New York, 1981), pp. 290–2, 287–8; for the third, see D. Lewis, 'The sculptures in the chapel of the Villa Giustinian at Roncade and their relation to those in the Giustinian chapel at San Francesco della Vigna', *Mitteilungen des Kunsthistorischen Instituts in Florenz*, 27 (1983), pp. 307–52. On the other hand, the dedications of the third chapel on either side of the nave, to St Joseph and to the Name of God, reflect devotions particularly dear to the Observant Franciscans, and may well have been chosen by the clergy. Further, it is clear that at least some of the altarpieces contain sacramental references in keeping with the spirit of the Counter-Reformation; see chapter 10 by A. D. Wright in this volume, 'The altarpiece in Catholic Europe'.

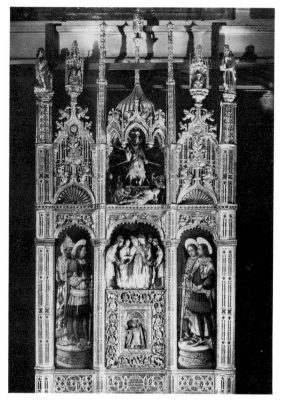

113 Antonio Vivarini and Giovanni d'Alemagna, *Ancona del Redentore*

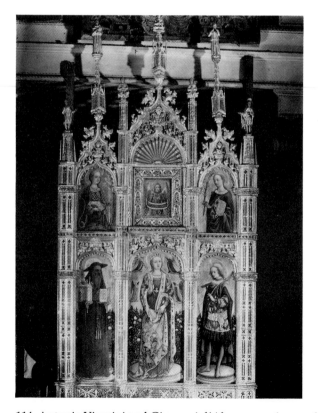

114 Antonio Vivarini and Giovanni d'Alemagna, *Ancona di S. Sabina*

tine sisters[26] – these noblewomen were obviously acting in concert rather than rivalry, and the smaller polyptychs were clearly intended to be placed on either side of the main one as its satellites.[27] It cannot be excluded that votive masses for their respective donors were sometimes performed at the two subsidiary altars; but to judge from the iconography of the altarpieces, their main function was to serve rather as tabernacles, or reliquaries. Thus the presence of carved groups of a *Man of Sorrows* and of the *Resurrection* makes it clear that the so-called *Ancona del Redentore* (plate 113) was commissioned primarily to house the reserved Sacrament,[28] and probably also the relics of the four saints represented in the side panels, identified by inscriptions as the martyrs Nereus, Achilleus, Pancratius and Pope Caius. Similarly, two of the three main panels of the *Ancona di S. Sabina* (plate 114) signal the presence of the venerated relics of Sabina and Lizerius, while a third represents an angel bearing a scroll, explicitly inscribed with the words 'Hic est sanguis Christi'.[29]

A comparable instance of twin altarpieces being commissioned in honour of particular holy objects, the significance of which is stressed by the choice of iconography, is that of Alvise Vivarini's *Resurrection* and Cima's *Constantine and Helena*, which were painted for the chancel of the parish church of S. Giovanni in Bragora between 1497 and 1503. These, too, were commissioned by the local clergy, respectively for an altar of the Sacrament and for a relic-altar (of the Holy Cross); and once again, their related function is emphasised by their originally identical format.[30] A slightly later example of a pair of satellite altarpieces, this time closely related formally and iconographically not only with each other, but also with the principal altarpiece, is represented by the three marble reliefs by Giovanni Battista da Carona installed in the Emiliani chapel at S. Michele in Isola in 1539. In accordance with the will of the donor, made as early as 1427, the chapel was dedicated to the Virgin Annunciate; the subject of the principal altarpiece accordingly represents the Annunciation, while those of the two subsidiary altarpieces represent two further Joys of the Virgin, the Nativity and the Adoration of the Magi.[31]

The extension of coherently planned altar dedications,[32] expressed visually through

---

[26] For dimensions and inscriptions, see R. Pallucchini, *I Vivarini* (Venice, 1962), pp. 99–100.

[27] The main polyptych is double sided; it is likely, therefore, that it was originally placed further forwards than it is now, perhaps with its back facing the nuns' choir. In this case the two matching polyptychs may have been placed against the choir-screen, on either side of the entrance to the choir.

[28] In this sense, the work is a precocious example of a type of altarpiece to become common in Venice only after about 1500. In the fifteenth century it was still customary for the reserved Sacrament to be kept in a small wall-cupboard, usually in the sacristy, rather than on an altar. See H. Caspary, *Das Sakramentstabernakel in Italien bis zum Konzil von Trient* (Munich, 1969), pp. 44ff. and 84ff.

[29] For the relics at S. Zaccaria, and the representation of their corresponding saints in the S. Tarasio polyptychs, see S. Tramontin, *San Zaccaria* (Venice, 1979), pp. 36–45. For documents relating to the polyptychs, see P. Paoletti, *L'architettura e la scultura del Rinascimento in Venezia* (Venice, 1893), p. 63.

[30] P. Humfrey, 'Cima da Conegliano, Sebastiano Mariani and Alvise Vivarini at the east end of S. Giovanni in Bragora in Venice', *Art Bulletin*, 62 (1980), pp. 360–2.

[31] See V. Meneghin, *San Michele in Isola di Venezia*, Vol. 1 (Venice, 1962), pp. 333–9.

[32] R. Goffen *Piety and patronage in Renaissance Venice: Bellini, Titian and the Franciscans* (New Haven, 1986), pp. 20–2, has tried to discern a unifying programme behind the altar dedications in the Franciscan church of the Frari, but this seems a case of special pleading. The dedications of the first two altars on either side of the nave of the Dominican church of SS. Giovanni e Paolo did, by contrast, form a coherent group; but this did not result in any formal unity between their artistically very distinguished respective altarpieces. See Humfrey, 'The Venetian *scuole piccole*' (as in note 5), pp. 405–8.

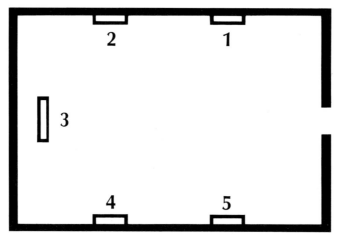

Figure 1 Venice, S. Maria dell'Umiltà. Reconstruction of dedications of altars and of corresponding altarpieces.

1. Apostles Peter and Paul (Jacopo Bassano)
2. Passion (*Crowning with thorns?*) (Palma Giovane)
3. Visitation (Tabernacle of the Sacrament)
4. Circumcision (Marco del Moro) (pl. 115)
5. St Francis (Simonetto da San Canciano)

equally coherent altarpiece iconographies, to all the altars of a single church was to take place in the later sixteenth century in Palladio's churches of S. Giorgio Maggiore and the Redentore. But it is interesting to notice that an intermediary step is represented by the first Jesuit church in Venice, S. Maria dell'Umiltà, which was rebuilt from about 1550 and began to receive its interior decoration from about 1560.[33] This church no longer exists, and our knowledge of its appearance is very incomplete; but from the information provided by Francesco Sansovino and other early sources,[34] it is possible to reach an approximate reconstruction of the arrangement of its four main side-altars and the subjects of their altarpieces (figure 1). Thus the two altars at the left were respectively dedicated to St Francis and to the Circumcision, and carried altarpieces depicting *St Francis* by one Simonetto da S. Canciano (lost or unrecognised), and the *Circumcision* by Marco del Moro, datable to the 1570s (plate 115); while the two altars on the right were dedicated to the Apostles Peter and Paul and to the Passion, and carried altarpieces depicting *Peter and Paul* by Jacopo Bassano (*c.* 1562; Modena, Galleria Estense) and probably a *Crowning with Thorns* by Palma Giovane (*c.* 1580; lost).[35] These dedications and subjects correspond remarkably closely to those of the side-altars in the mother church of the Jesuit order in Rome, where they formed part of a programme carefully devised to reflect the particular

[33] For the history of the church and a discussion of the elaborate tabernacle of the Sacrament made as the principal decoration for the high altar around 1580, see S. Mason Rinaldi, 'Il tabernacolo della chiesa dei "Geisuiti" alla Dogana di Mare', *Arte Veneta*, 36 (1982), pp. 211–16.

[34] Sansovino, *Venetia* (as in n. 14 above), p. 275; *The itinerary of Fynes Moryson*, Vol. 1 (1594; Glasgow, 1907), p. 183; M. Boschini, *Le minere della pittura* (Venice, 1664), p. 347; A. M. Zanetti, *Descrizione di tutte le pubbliche pitture della città di Venezia* (Venice, 1733), pp. 332–3.

[35] The identity of Simonetto da S. Canciano, mentioned by Sansovino, is not clear; Zanetti attributes the *St Francis* to 'a follower of Paris Bordon', evidently meaning to dismiss it as artistically insignificant. For the lost altarpiece by Palma Giovane, see S. Mason Rinaldi, *Jacopo Palma il Giovane* (Milan, 1984), p. 183.

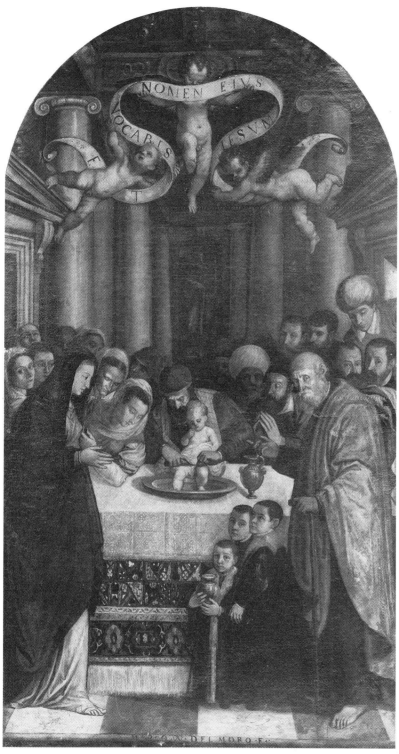

115 Marco del Moro, *Circumcision*

interests of the order.[36] Thus *St Francis*, the archetypal imitator of the person of Jesus, commemorates a special devotion of Ignatius Loyola; the *Peter and Paul* refers to the authority of the Catholic church; the *Circumcision* refers to the naming of Jesus and the first shedding of his blood; and the *Crowning with Thorns* again refers to the shedding of blood by Christ and his martyrs. The four altarpieces on the Umiltà also fall into matching pairs, the first two with hagiological themes and the second two with Christological. All this is entirely in keeping with the post-Tridentine, and specifically Jesuit, stress on preaching, eucharistic devotion, and the dignity of the priesthood.[37] Although the side-altars at the Umiltà were presumably maintained with the help of alms from the pious laity, no particular group of laymen was ever granted special rights to them, and complete control over their usage and decoration was retained by the clergy. Hence the iconography of the altarpieces was not devised to express any one individual's hope for salvation, but to provide a set of linked visual sermons aimed at the faithful at large.

We cannot properly assess how far the thematic co-ordination at the Umiltà may have been complemented by a formal one, since two of the four altarpieces are now missing. But the two survivors, by Jacopo Bassano and Marco del Moro, are quite disparate in pictorial style and artistic quality, and also in shape, dimensions and figure-scale; and this suggests that for the Jesuits, here as elsewhere, the aesthetic programme was of much less importance than the iconological one. For the Benedictines of S. Giorgio Maggiore the iconology of their side-altars was also clearly important; but now the inter-relationship between them was powerfully emphasised by a set of architectonic frames of unprecedented formal coherence. Although the documents show that these were executed after Palladio's death in 1580, it is clear from certain phrases in the payments made to the mason Giangiacomo Comini by the clergy, as well as from the essential role played by the frames in the architectural articulation of the church, that they were designed by the architect himself.[38] The frame designs consist of two main types: one more elaborate, for the single monumental altarpiece in each of the transepts; and the other simpler, for the three smaller (although still very large) altarpieces in each of the aisles and for the one in each of the chapels adjoining the chancel (plate 116; figure 2). Within this second type, the pairs of flanking columns are varied according to the colours of their marble, or according to whether they are smooth or fluted. But unlike at S. Francesco della Vigna, these differences are not, of course, the result of the altarpieces having been commissioned by different donors at different times, but are part of the architect's carefully controlled scheme for creating subtle variety within an overall unity. Also in contrast to the earlier situation at S. Francesco della Vigna, great care was evidently taken by the clergy in choosing the dedications of the altars and in ordering their relationships. Of the ten side-altars, five dedications refer to highly prestigious relics enshrined within them (Stephen, George, Cosmas and Damian, Lucy, James Minor);

---

[36] Hibbard, ' *Ut pictura sermones*' (as in note 6).
[37] See further the chapters by D. Davies and A. Wright in this volume.
[38] G. Zorzi, *Le chiese e i ponti di Andrea Palladio* (Vicenza, 1967), pp. 48–9.

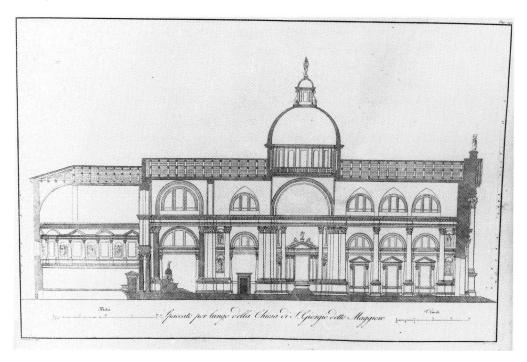

116 Palladio, Church of S. Giorgio Maggiore, Venice, section. From Cicognara, Diedo and Selva, *Le fabbriche . . . di Venezia*

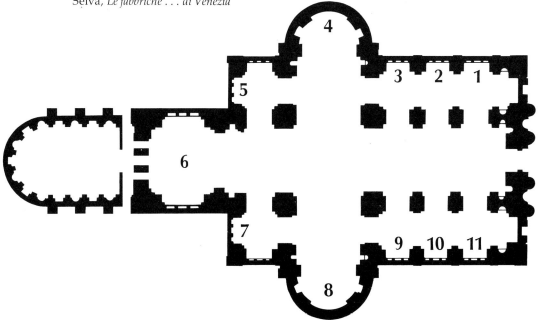

Figure 2. Venice, S. Giorgio Maggiore. Dedications of altars and their altarpieces.

1. St James Minor (Jacopo Bassano: *Adoration of the shepherds*)
2. Crucified (Anon. 15th-century German sculptor: Crucifix)
3. Sts Cosmas and Damian (Shop of J. Tintoretto: *Martyrdom of Cosmas and Damian*)
4. St Benedict (Shop of J. Tintoretto: *Coronation*)
5. Apostles Peter and Paul (?)
6. High altar
7. St Andrew (Shop of J. Tintoretto: *Resurrected Christ*) (pl. 117)
8. St Stephen (Shop of J. Tintoretto: *Martyrdom of St Stephen*)
9. St George (D. Tintoretto: *St George and the dragon*)
10. Virgin (Campagna: *Virgin and Child*)
11. St Lucy (Leandro Bassano: *Martrdom of St Lucy*)

one refers to the founder of the Benedictine order; two refer to princes of the apostles (Peter and Paul, Andrew); and the final two are dedicated respectively to the Virgin and to the Crucified Christ.[39] These dedications are naturally reflected in the iconography of their altarpieces, all but two of which were apparently commissioned by the clergy themselves.[40] In the case of S. Giorgio, this post-Tridentine reassertion of ecclesiastical authority would have been greatly facilitated by the extraordinary wealth of the monastery, which made the clergy generally independent of the need to concede patronage rights to lay donors and to accommodate their devotional tastes. The two exceptions are represented by the pair of chapels dedicated to the apostles on either side of the chancel, which were conceded to the patrician families of the Bollani and the Morosini, probably because these had owned chapels in the previous building, and were in a position to press special claims. Yet it is significant that in both cases the monks made it a condition that neither *stemmi* nor inscriptions indicating ownership were to be displayed.[41] In its form and content, the Morosini altarpiece, painted between 1583 and 1586 by Tintoretto and his son Domenico (plate 117),[42] clearly constitutes a compromise between the separate interests of the donor and the clergy. By showing Vincenzo Morosini together with his family immediately behind his own marble sarcophagus, in the presence of Christ rising from the tomb, the painting directly expresses the donor's personal hope for the salvation of himself and his own. At the same time, the dedication of the altar to the Apostle, as part of a larger programme, is signalled by the presence to the left of St Andrew, towards whom the donor is not known to have had a special devotion; and the painting is duly set within a frame and chapel of the standard Palladian design.

There are a number of other minor anomalies or asymmetries in the pattern of altar dedications and in the iconography of the altarpieces, for reasons that are not always easy to explain. It is not clear, for example, why an *Adoration of the Shepherds* was chosen for the first altar on the right, dedicated to St James Minor. But such anomalies are disguised and regulated by the rhythmical alternation of Palladio's frames, with their subtle variations of design and use of materials; and as a group, the altarpieces contribute to rather than detract from the majestic harmony of the building as a whole. In keeping with the very different context of the Redentore, Palladio's designs for the altarpieces in the six identical side-chapels there show no such variations (plates 118–19). Their absolute uniformity is instead consistent with the fact that for the first time in Venice, the subjects of all seven altarpieces in the main body of the church – including the high altar – cohere to form a true cycle.[43] Beginning with the first altarpiece to the right, Francesco Bassano's *Nativity*, and

[39] For the relics and altar dedications at S. Giorgio, see Cicogna, *Delle iscrizioni veneziane*, Vol. 4 (1834; as in note 23), pp. 248–68.

[40] Documents in ibid., pp. 351–3.

[41] Ibid., pp. 350–1; Zorzi, *Le chiese* (as in note 38), pp. 49, 54.

[42] Pallucchini and Rossi, *Tintoretto* (as in n. 23 above), p. 445.

[43] W. Timofiewitsch, *The Chiesa del Redentore* (University Park and London, 1971), p. 54; A. Niero, 'I templi del Redentore e della Salute: motivazioni teologiche', in *Venezia e la peste 1348–1797*, exhibition catalogue (Venice, 1977), pp. 294–6. The high altar is occupied by a tabernacle of the Sacrament surmounted by a monumental Crucifixion group in bronze by Girolamo Campagna.

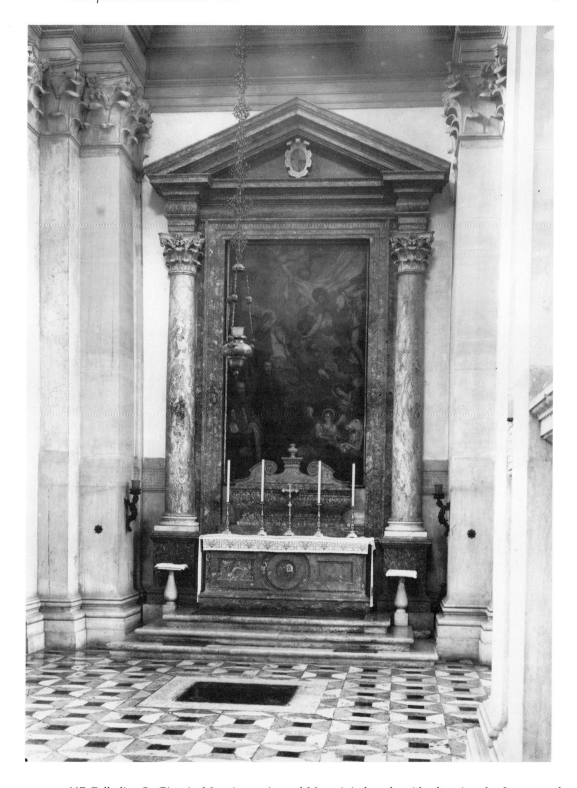

117 Palladio, S. Giorgio Maggiore, view of Morosini chapel, with altarpiece by Jacopo and
Domenico Tintoretto

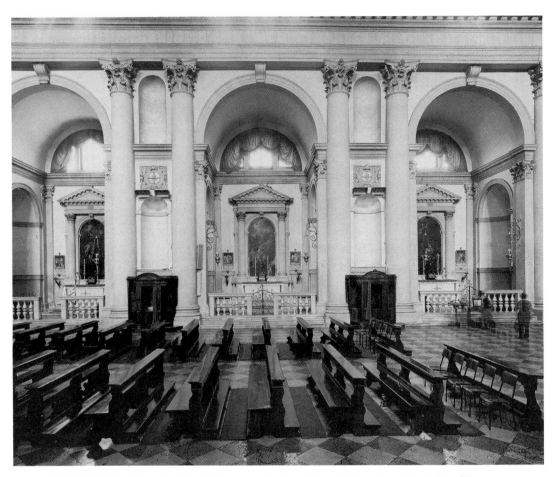

118 Palladio, Church of the Redentore, Venice, view of chapels on the right of the nave

ending with the first on the left, Tintoretto's *Ascension*, they represent successive scenes from Christ's early life, Passion and Resurrection (figure 3). This anti-clockwise sequence is further complemented by thematic correspondences across the nave: thus Christ's descent to earth and ascent to heaven are placed opposite one another, and so are the two Passion scenes. The programme is also intimately linked with the sepulchral and triumphal symbolism of the building as a whole,[44] and explicates the meaning of its dedication to Christ the Redeemer. With much greater clarity and consistency than at the Umiltà, or even than in Vasari's slightly earlier work at S. Croce, the altarpieces together proclaim a central Christian doctrine of relevance to the entire body of the faithful, and not a single one of them contains any reference to individual interests. Since none of the chapels in the Redentore contain tombs or personal insignia, it may be that they were never used for votive masses for the benefit of particular individuals.

The treatment of the altarpieces at the Redentore must have been recognised in

[44] Discussed in detail by S. Sinding-Larsen, 'Palladio's Redentore, a compromise in composition', *Art Bulletin*, 47 (1965), pp. 419–37 (but without reference to the cycle of altarpieces).

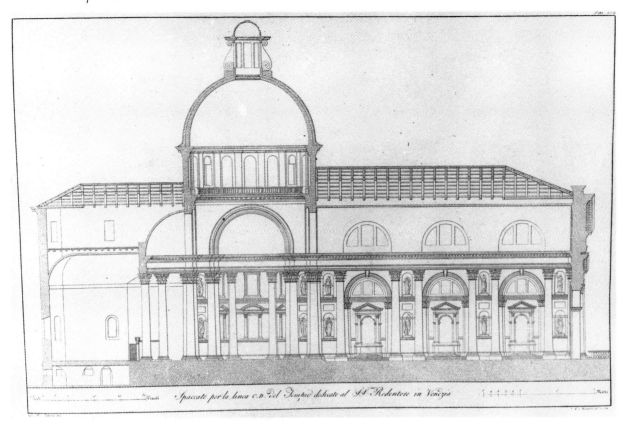

119 Palladio, Redentore: section. From Cicognara, Diedo and Selva, *Le fabbriche . . . die Venezia*

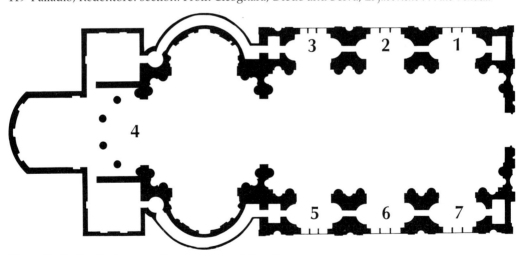

Figure 3 Venice, Redentore. Arrangement of altarpieces.

1. Francesco Bassano: *Nativity*
2. Heirs of P. Veronese: *Baptism*
3. Shop of Tintoretto: *Flagellation*
4. Campagna: *Crucifix*
5. Palma Giovane: *Entombment*
6. Francesco Bassano: *Resurrection*
7. Shop of Tintoretto: *Ascension*

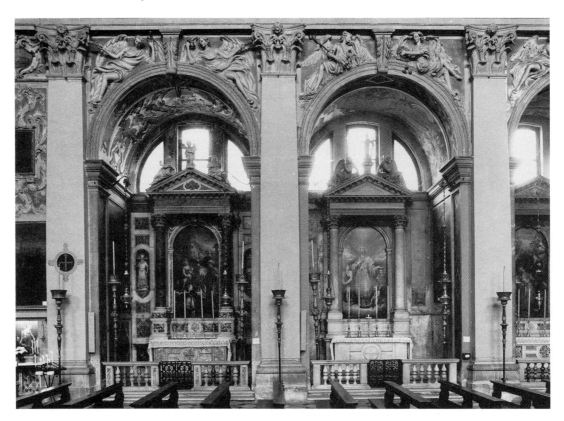

120 Scamozzi, Church of S. Niccolò dei Tolentini, Venice

its day, both by architects and reforming churchmen, as the fulfilment of an ideal that had previously been realised with only partial success. Yet it would always have been easier for both parties to admire the ideal than to imitate it. Its achievement at the Redentore was made possible, in fact, by an almost unique coincidence of three elements: an architect of exceptional intellectual rigour and purism; a clergy of a reformed order (the Capuchins) that took seriously the Tridentine directives that holy images should once again become the books of the unlettered; and most important of all, a patron with the power to carry these architectural and religious ideals into effect, namely the Venetian government itself. Funded from the public exchequer as a token of general thanksgiving to God for release from the terrible plague of 1576, the building of the church could proceed with extraordinary speed and without reference to the wishes of individual benefactors. Thus the foundation stone was laid in 1577, the altarpiece frames had been installed by 1588, and all six altar paintings were complete by the beginning of the new century.[45]

The uniform design of the chapels and altarpiece frames at the Redentore was taken up almost immediately by Scamozzi in his church of the Tolentini, constructed in the 1590s (plate 120); but although the paintings themselves reflect the deep pen-

---

[45] See Timofiewitsch, *The Chiesa* (as in n. 43), especially pp. 13, 17, 54. The last of the six altar paintings was apparently Palma Giovane's *Deposition*, dated by Mason Rinaldi, *Jacopo Palma* (as in n. 35 above), p. 132, to *c.* 1600–5.

etration of Counter-Reformation religiosity, they were funded in the traditional way by individual laymen[46] whose particular interests they accordingly reflect; and there is no question of any thematic co-ordination between them. In the seventeenth and eighteenth centuries further examples of thematic unity between altarpieces do occur, as at the Salute, S. Stae[47] and the Gesuati; but these always remained the exception rather than the rule, and in the case of the first, the same extraordinary circumstances applied as at the Redentore. And since despite the resurgence of ecclesiastical authority in the post-Tridentine era, Baroque donors were just as concerned to celebrate their own piety and individuality as their Renaissance and medieval predecessors had been, homogeneity even of format was to remain elusive.[48] It may also have been recognised that the architectural harmony at the Redentore, as at the Carità more than a century earlier, was achieved at the cost of pictorial interest. As individual paintings, the altarpieces of the Redentore can never have aroused much aesthetic admiration, and even those associated with the eminent names of Tintoretto and Veronese are clearly workshop products. It is true that 1588 was hardly a propitious moment in the history of Venetian painting, and a decade or two earlier, Veronese, for example, might well have come up with a splendid matching set, as indeed he did in 1562 in his trio for S. Benedetto Po.[49] Yet in general, it may be said that the task of producing one or more altarpieces to a strictly uniform prescription can never have been a wholly congenial one for painters; and even the limited flexibility, such as that offered by the commissions at S. Francesco della Vigna, must have proved much more stimulating.

In this chapter I have tried to assess Venice's contribution to the ideal of co-ordinated altarpieces in the Renaissance period on the city's own terms. But the question of how the Venetian experience compares with that of other artistic and religious centres remains an open one. Was Venice, with its stronger local tradition in the practice of painting than in the theory of architecture, and its proud defence of local religious traditions and institutions in the face of growing pressures from the Tridentine Church towards centralism and uniformity, exceptionally resistant to the ideal? Or did the city, on the contrary, make a relatively important contribution towards developing an ideal that was singularly difficult to realise anywhere, and which was only to reach full maturity in the more absolutist period of the seventeenth century? Venice, after all, played a far from insignificant role both in the history of Renaissance architecture and in the early implementation of the Counter-Reformation. To answer the question, we must first reach a clearer idea of the parallel progress of the same ideal in Renaissance and Counter-Reformation Rome, Florence, Milan or Bologna, or for that matter, Toledo or Antwerp.

[46] R. Gallo, 'Vincenzo Scamozzi e la chiesa di S. Niccolò da Tolentino di Venezia', *Atti dell'Istituto Veneto di Scienze, Lettere ed Arti*, 117 (1958–9), pp. 103–22.
[47] Niero, 'I templi' (as in n. 43 above), pp. 296–8; D. Lewis, *The late baroque churches of Venice* (New York, 1979), p. 267.
[48] Lewis, *The late baroque churches*, pp. 150, 363 n. 2.
[49] C. Gould, *National Gallery catalogues: the sixteenth-century Italian schools* (London, 1975), pp. 316–17.

11 *The Relationship of El Greco's altarpieces to the mass of the Roman rite*

David Davies

The purpose of this chapter is to draw attention to the relationship of the iconography and style of El Greco's altarpieces to the Tridentine mass. This may also apply to his designs of the framework of the altarpieces and the tabernacle. To identify and assess the significance of these relationships, it is necessary to consider not only the original setting and liturgical context but also the effect of the Protestant Reformation on liturgical practices and the iconography of altarpieces in the Catholic Church.

The Protestant Reformers dismissed the special sanctity of the mass, the central act of Catholic worship. They denied that the sacrifice of Christ on Calvary was bloodlessly re-enacted on the altar.[1] They rejected the belief that the bread and wine that was co-mingled with water were transubstantiated at the Consecration into the real flesh and blood of Christ, thus mysteriously making real His presence.[2] Yet Luther did accept the co-existence of the Real Presence and the bread and wine.[3] In contrast, Zwingli and Calvin refused to accept that the real flesh and blood of the glorified Christ was offered in Communion. In this connection, the supernatural role of the priest, as a sacramental channel of Grace, to consecrate, to offer the sacrificial victim to God the Father, and to administer the sacrament of the Eucharist was also censured by the Reformers.[4]

They also argued that, after the Fall, man had lost his free will and was radically corrupted by original sin.[5] His justification depended solely on faith in God's mercy to cover up his sins by the extrinsic imputation of Christ's merits.[6] Therefore, neither the invocation of the Virgin and saints nor good works, nor a special priesthood were of any avail to man seeking justification. Furthermore, since faith alone assured justification, man no longer had to be punished in purgatory for his temporal sins. Consequently, the Protestant Reformers also inveighed against the belief in purgatory.

These doctrines threatened to undermine the very nature of the mass. Since the mass is a sacrifice, the intercession of the Virgin and saints in this context is especially efficacious for the salvation of the living and of the souls in purgatory. The Virgin and saints are invoked repeatedly during the ordinary and canon of the mass, as well as in the secret and postcommunion of masses specifically celebrated in their honour. It is hoped that they, as paragons of faith and good works, will intercede

---

[1] *Documents of the Christian Church*, Selected and edited by H. Bettenson, 2nd ed. (Oxford, 1967), p. 198.
[2] Ibid., pp. 197–8.
[3] Ibid., p. 198.
[4] Ibid., pp. 193–4.
[5] Ibid., p. 213.
[6] Ibid., pp. 210, 212.

with God the Father to accept the sacrificial offering and bestow divine grace so that the sins of the faithful will be expiated. After the Consecration, the presence of Christ is mysteriously made real on the altar and, in Communion, union with Christ is consummated and the soul spiritually nourished. In the prayer of postcommunion, the saints are invoked, essentially, to help the faithful to sustain the benefits of this sanctifying grace.

Thus the extra special benefits derived from this fountain of grace and bestowed on the communicants and on those, such as donors, named either in the Commemoration of the Living or the Commemoration of the Departed, or in Masses for the Dead, were now denied by the Reformers. Similarly, the tradition of linking donations, such as chapels or altarpieces, to the saying of masses, often in perpetuity for the souls of the departed, was also repudiated.[7]

In addition, the Reformers sought to reduce the rites of the Church. According to the Confession of Augsburg (article XV), certain rites were to be preserved, 'but men are warned not to burden their consciences in such matters, as if such observance were necessary to salvation'.[8] Although there is no specific reference to the mass in this article, its tenor suggests that its ritual would have been considered excessive. Certainly it was anathema to the Calvinists, who promoted an austere form of worship.

Owing to the denial by Zwingli and Calvin of the Real Presence of the flesh and blood of Christ, it followed that the tradition of revering the Host, placing it in a special receptacle, such as the tabernacle, and displaying it in a monstrance was also cast aside.

Moreover, as a result of the rejection of invocation and intercession, the veneration of holy relics was deemed superfluous.[9] Although this pertained essentially to relics on display, it would also apply to those which are housed within the altar and which are saluted by the celebrant's kissing of the altar table at the beginning of the mass.

As well as these attacks on the mass and liturgical practice, the altarpiece itself was rejected because the Protestants argued that the worship of religious imagery was idolatrous.[10] Indeed, their attitude to the Virgin and saints challenged the very purpose of the altarpiece. Apart from its instructive value, it is essentially an expression of praise, thanksgiving and petition to God. It is intimately associated with prayer. Representations of Christ, the Virgin and saints enable the Catholic to pray to the prototypes in heaven in the hope that they will intercede with God for the bestowal of his blessings, merited by the sacrifice of Christ, which is liturgically re-enacted in the mass.

These Protestant objections were staunchly countered by the Council of Trent. The sacrifice and the sacrament of the Eucharist, liturgically celebrated in the mass, were upheld in the *Decree concerning the Most Holy Sacrament of the Eucharist*[11] and

---

[7] E. Heller, *Das Altniederländische Stifterbild*, PhD. Dissertation, Munich, 1976, pp. 166–8, has noted the Lutheran rejection of images of the donor.

[8] *Documents of the Christian Church*, (as in note 1) p. 211.

[9] Ibid., p. 231.

[10] Ibid., p. 233.

[11] *The Canons and Decrees of the Council of Trent*, trans. and introd. by Rev. H. J. Schroeder (Rockford ILL, 1978), pp. 72–80.

in the *Doctrine concerning the Sacrifice of the Mass*.[12] The sacramental role of the priest was re-affirmed in the *Doctrine concerning the Sacrament of Order*.[13] The need for both faith and good works in the economy of man's justification was spelled out in the *Decree concerning Justification*.[14] In the Twenty-fifth Session, belief in Purgatory and the intercessory role of the Virgin and saints was re-asserted.[15] It is significant that sacred imagery was also treated in the context of the invocation of the saints. In answer to the Protestant charge of idolatory, the Council decreed that sacred images were to be displayed and retained, especially in churches, because the veneration shown to them is referred to the prototypes which they represent. Moreover, they serve to instruct the faithful in the tenets of the Catholic Church and inspire them to 'fashion their own life and conduct in imitation of the saints and be moved to adore and love God and cultivate piety'.[16]

Yet the response of the Catholic Church was, essentially, to re-affirm its hallowed dogmas. No fundamental changes were introduced in either its theology or liturgy. The Tridentine doctrine on Transubstantiation, for example, confirmed that of the Lateran Council and the Council of Florence.[17] In a similar manner, the 'Missale Romanum ex decreto ss. Concilii Tridentini restitutum, Pii V. Pont. Max. iussu editum' was characterised merely by the reduction of saints' feasts and the elimination of 'disturbing accessories'.[18] The most significant innovation was that its use was to be uniform throughout the Catholic Church.[19] Therefore, a comparison between some missals printed before and after the Council of Trent, such as the Missale Romanum, Venice, 1501, the Missale Toletanum, Burgos, 1512, the Missale Romanum, Salamanca, 1587, and the Missale Romanum, Antwerp, 1587, reveals few basic differences, apart from the addition of feast-days particular to Spain in the edition printed at Salamanca.[20]

Furthermore, in his post-Tridentine treatise on the ceremony of the Mass, Iuan de Alcocer frequently cites the medieval liturgist, William Durandus, and acknowledges his debt to the 'Ceremonial Romano' of Paris de Grassis.[21] Likewise, some of the ceremonial practices recorded in St Carlo Borromeo's *Instructiones Fabricae et Supellectilis Ecclesiasticae* (1577)[22] are not very different from those encountered, for example, in the first book of Durandus' *Rationale Divinorum Officiorum*.[23]

Although there were no notable changes either in Catholic theology or liturgy as a result of this religious crisis, it did have the effect of focusing more intensely the

[12] Ibid., pp. 144–52.
[13] Ibid., pp. 160–3.
[14] Ibid., pp. 29–46.
[15] Ibid., pp. 214–17.
[16] Ibid., p. 216.
[17] *The Catechism of the Council of Trent*, trans. with notes by T. A. Buckley (London, 1852), p. 232.
[18] J. A. Jungmann, *The Mass of the Roman Rite* (New York, 1951), vol. 1, pp. 136–37.
[19] Ibid., pp. 135, 138.
[20] D. J. Baudot, *The Roman Breviary. Its sources and history* (London, 1909), p. 166.
[21] I. de Alcocer, *Ceremonial de la Missa* (Madrid, 1614), pp. 215, 224, 231.
[22] St Carlo Borromeo, *Instructiones fabricae et supellectilis ecclesiasticae*, (1577; trans. with commentary and analysis by E. C. Voelker (Syracuse, NY, 1977).
[23] W. Durandus, *The symbolism of churches and church ornaments*, A translation of the first book of the Rationale Divinorum Officiorum, with an introductory essay and notes by J. M. Neale and B. Webb, 3rd ed. (London, 1906).

minds of Catholics on the mass and, by association, the altarpiece. Inevitably, the re-definition of fundamental dogmas attracted more attention to them. Moreover, according to the Tridentine Catechism, Transubstantiation 'was still more explicitly defined' in the Council of Trent than in those of the Lateran and of Florence.[24] Similarly, the ceremonial instructions of the Council of Trent[25] and of St Carlo Borromeo[26] were intended to heighten awareness of the majesty of the Sacrifice and the mystery of the Real Presence. Alcocer, too, stressed the need for reverence, silence, composure and devotion when present at the 'santissimo, y altissimo sacrificio de la Missa'.[27] Pius V gave further emphasis to the ritual by making the elevation of the Chalice obligatory after its Consecration.[28] Accordingly, the mass generally assumed a more dramatic and splendid aura.

The treatment of the tabernacle also conformed to this pattern. It had been placed prominently on the altar table prior to this controversy over the Real Presence, but now it was generally more conspicuous by its increased size.[29] A consequence was that imagery behind it was sometimes obscured. In the retables designed by Becerra (Astorga), Herrera (Escorial) and Gómez de Mora (Guadalupe), for example, the importance of the tabernacle was manifested, and the artistic problems obviated, by its large scale and its isolated position in a central compartment of the retable. When El Greco was commissioned to design a very large tabernacle for the high altar of Sto Domingo el Antiguo, he solved this problem by making the second storey open, so that the *Assumption*, in the retable behind, was visible.[30]

In the same manner, the Tridentine *Decree on Sacred Images* was remarkably similar to some of the definitions and canons of the Seventh General Council, the Second of Nicaea, which was convened in 787AD.[31] In fact this was acknowledged in the Decree.[32] Furthermore, largely in answer to the Protestant Reformation, and in response to the Catholic spiritual reform movements, the didactic and devotional aspects of Catholic art were given a new impetus. The didactic method was advocated in the Decree, and it complemented the exposition of the theological definitions of the Council. The fervent desire for devotional imagery was clearly attested to in Fray José de Sigüenza's description of the pictures in the Escorial. He insisted that 'saints should be painted in a manner which does not hamper the desire to pray in front of them, but which rather excites devotion since this should be the chief effect and aim of painting'.[33]

The iconography of altarpieces also tended to reflect this pattern. Although there

---

[24] *Catechism of the Council of Trent* (as in note 17), p. 232.
[25] *Canon and Decrees of the Council of Trent* (as in note 11), p. 147.
[26] Borromeo, *Instructiones* (as in note 22), pp. 23–4, 26. See also A. Blunt, *Artistic theory in Italy 1450–1600* (Oxford, 1959), pp. 127–8; E. Mâle, *L'art religieux de la fin du XVIe siècle, du XVIIe siècle et du XVIIIe siècle*, 2nd ed. (Paris, 1951), pp. 22, 83.
[27] Alcocer, *Ceremonial* (as in Note 21), p. 84.
[28] *The New Catholic Encyclopedia*, vol. 9, p. 422.
[29] Concerning the renewed emphasis on the importance of the tabernacle, see Borromeo, *Instructiones* (as in note 22), pp. 15, 160ff.
[30] H. E. Wethey, *El Greco and his school*, vol. 2 (Princeton, 1962), p. 4.
[31] *The seventh General Council, the Second of Nicaea*, trans. J. Mendham (London, nd), pp. 253–4, 411–13, 455–7.
[32] *Canons and Decrees of the Council of Trent* (as in note 11), p. 216.
[33] Fray José de Sigüenza, *Fundación del Monasterio de El Escorial* (Madrid), 1963), p. 385.

is scarcely any dogma which does not relate to the mass,[34] because it is the central act of Catholic worship, the subject matter of altarpieces in this period generally reflected those issues which were raised by the Protestants and treated in the theological Canons and Decrees of the Council of Trent.[35]

To counter the denial of the Sacrifice of the mass and the Real Presence, it was explained in the Tridentine Catechism that the Eucharist signified the Passion of Christ, the impartation of Divine Grace, and 'eternal grace and glory'.[36] The Consecration of the Blood, in particular, 'serves to place before the eyes of all, in a more forcible manner, the passion of our Lord, his death, and the nature of his sufferings.'[37] This teaching was congruous to the ideals of the Catholic Spiritual Reformers. Their quest for union of the soul with Christ in contemplative prayer paralleled their adoration of the Sacrament of the Eucharist. This heightened their fervour for the crucified and resurrected Christ, who was present in the sacrament. Striking images are those of St John of Ávila praying before a crucifix that is suspended in a chalice, full to the brim with blood,[38] and St Teresa's visions in which 'almost invariably the Lord showed himself to me in his resurrection body, and it was thus, too, that I saw him in the Host'.[39] Yet it is interesting that St Teresa lamented the use of pictures of Christ during the celebration of the mass: 'You may be in the habit of praying while looking at a picture of Christ, but at a time like this it seems foolish to me to turn away from the living image – the Person Himself – to look at His picture.'[40] Nevertheless, when altarpieces were commissioned, the redemptive and salvific role of Christ figured large in their iconography. Scenes from the Infancy and the Passion, as well as those of the Resurrection and Ascension, appear to be the principal subjects from the life of Christ. Comparatively few are taken from the ministry.

The subjects chosen would seem to relate to the feasts of Christ,[41] notwithstanding the flexible relationship between the title of the altar or subject of the altarpiece and the feast.[42] In spite of the interest in such scenes as the healing of the blind and the purification of the temple, particularly at the time of the Counter-Reformation, none of El Greco's numerous versions, for example, appears to have been an altarpiece.[43] These two events are recorded in the liturgy, in the lesson on Quinquagesima Sunday and on Monday, the Fourth Week of Lent, respectively, but they do not

---

[34] A. A. Parker, *The allegorical drama of Calderón* (Oxford, 1968), pp. 60–1.

[35] Mâle, *L'art* (as in note 26). See especially chapter 2 for a discussion of the manifestation of the Catholic reaction to Protestantism in religious art in general.

[36] *Catechism of the Council of Trent* (as in note 17), pp. 214–15.

[37] Ibid., p. 233.

[38] *Obras completas del P. Mtro. Juan de Ávila*, ed. L. Sala Balust, vol. 1 (Madrid, 1952–3), p. 32.

[39] *The complete works of St Teresa of Jesus*, trans. E. Allison Peers, vol. 1 (London, 1978), p. 188.

[40] Ibid., vol. 2, p. 149.

[41] É. Mâle, *L'Art religieux du XIIIe siècle en France* (Paris, 1910), pp. 211–20. Mâle gave this same explanation for the paucity of scenes from the public life of Christ in thirteenth-century church decoration.

[42] Neither the title of the altar nor the subject of the altarpiece are necessarily determined by the subjects of feasts. 'If the Titular be our Lady under a title that has no special feast, the Titular feast is celebrated on the feast of the Assumption' (J. O'Connell, *Church building and furnishing: the church's way* (London, 1955), p. 20). In some cases, the subject of the altarpiece, such as the Baptism of Christ, will relate to the Titular, St John the Baptist, but not to the feasts of the Titular, which commemorate the birth (June 24th) and death (August 29th) of the Baptist. The Baptism of Christ is celebrated on the Octave of the Epiphany, which is a feast of Christ.

[43] G. Schiller, *Iconography of Christian art*, vol. (Greenwich, CT, 1971), p. 173, records the subject of the Healing of the Blind in the central panel of a fifteenth-century Netherlandish altarpiece.

relate to the title of any feast of Christ. This may have been the reason why the main subjects of altarpieces, as in preceding centuries, seem to be rarely chosen from the ministry of Christ.

A major factor in relation to this phenomenon may have been the omission of the Ministry from the Life of Christ in Jacobus de Voragine's *Golden Legend*. Instead, there is a discussion of the liturgical periods of Septuagesima, Sexagesima, Quinquagesima, Quadragesima and Ember Days. This may well have further reinforced the tendency to concentrate on those events which did have intimate liturgical connections.

In short, those scenes from the life of Christ which are most appropriate for the principal subjects of altarpieces are those directly related to his redemptive and salvific role. Indeed, these are the very subjects alluded to in the Nicene Creed, which is recited at mass on all Sundays, and often on principal feasts during the week.

In addition to these Christological themes, there is a distinct emphasis on the mediation of the Virgin and saints, their faith and charity, and the supernatural purity of the Virgin. Undoubtedly, the representation of these subjects had been encouraged by the Tridentine decisions to uphold the invocation and intercession of the Virgin and saints, to exhort the imitation of their faith and good works and to exclude the 'blessed and immaculate Virgin Mary' from the 'Decree concerning Original Sin'.[44] To a perceptive eye, the presence of the Virgin and saints in the altarpiece would be a reminder also of the sacrifice and sacrament of the Eucharist.

This is indicated, too, by the presence of angels. The triumphal hymn of the angels, the Sanctus, is sung or recited at the end of the Preface. This is an expression of praise and thanksgiving, and heralds the canon or sacrificial part of the mass. After the Consecration, an angel uplifts the sacrificial victim to the altar of God. The sacrament itself is hailed as the bread of angels in the preparatory prayer of St Ambrose and in the Sequence of the Feast of Corpus Christi composed by St Thomas Aquinas. The inclusion of angels in the imagery of the tabernacle and altarpiece has been acknowledged since the time of their inception. In this period, celestial beings abounded in such imagery. They not only signalled the operation of divine grace in the subject represented, but also re-affirmed the triumph of the Eucharist.

In addition, the intimate liturgical and devotional association between the mass, the altarpiece and the donor was strengthened. The Council of Trent re-asserted that the sacrifice of the mass 'is rightly offered not only for the sins, punishments, satisfactions and other necessities of the faithful who are living, but also for those departed in Christ but not yet fully purified'.[45] Consequently, what had been exemplified both in innumerable altarpieces, apse mosaics, stained glass windows in the choir, liturgical vestments and furnishings, diptychs and books placed on the altar, and in the desire to be buried near the altar, was once again vindicated.

Yet some Catholic Reformers, such as St Carlo Borromeo, prohibited the display

---

[44] *Canons and Decrees of the Council of Trent* (as in note 11), p. 23.
[45] Ibid., p. 146.

of personal insignia in sacred places.[46] Probably they were heeding Christ's admonishment 'that you do not do your justice before men, to be seen by them, otherwise you shall not have a reward of your Father who is in heaven'. (Matthew 6:1). Possibly for reasons of 'modestia' and reverence for the sanctity of the altar, the Synod of Seville (1603) banned portraits from the altarpiece and the vicinity of the altar, unless ordered by that synod.[47]

The zealous response of Catholics was also reflected in the proliferation of the devotions to the Holy Sacrament, and the increased non-liturgical worship of the Host, as in the Forty Hours' Devotion. Most telling was the renewed emphasis on the frequent reception of the Eucharist in Holy Communion as the prime sacramental channel of God's grace to fallen man.[48] At the Fourth Lateran Council (1215), it had been decreed that Catholics should receive Communion at least once a year, at Easter.[49] This was upheld in the Tridentine *Decree On the Most Holy Sacrament of the Eucharist* (1551).[50] It is interesting that, later, in the Tridentine *Doctrine concerning the Sacrifice of the Mass* (1562),[51] and, particularly, in the Catechism of the Council of Trent (1566),[52] Catholics were urged to communicate daily. It was this which drew the faithful frequently to mass and intensified their response to the drama of sacrifice and salvation which was ritualistically enacted at the altar.

El Greco's knowledge of these theological disputations, as well as his interest in liturgy, is reflected in the inventory of his library[53] and the learned clerics whose company he frequented.[54] He possessed books dealing with early Christian liturgical practices, for example, the *Apostolic Constitutions*, and the work of Justin Martyr, whose *First Apology* contains information regarding contemporary Eucharistic devotions. He also had in his possession the *Canons and Decrees of the Council of Trent* in Greek translation. His reading of Aristotle's *Metaphysics*, which is also recorded in the inventory of his library, would have made him acutely aware of the theological argument concerning Transubstantiation. Among his learned friends was Antonio de Covarrubias, a former delegate at the Council of Trent.[55]

El Greco's perception of the liturgical function of the altarpiece is manifest in his treatment of iconography and style. In varying degrees of collaboration with his patrons, he eschews narrative schemes in favour of distinct devotional images. These combine to effect a more direct theological statement. In conformity to this pattern, he dispenses with a literal interpretation and seizes the spiritual significance of a subject in relation to the economy of man's redemption and salvation. His altarpieces

---

[46] Borromeo, *Instructiones (as in note 22), p. 450.*
[47] A. Rodríguez G. de Ceballos, 'La repercusión en España del decreto del Concilio de Trento acerca de las imágenes sagradas y las censuras al Greco', *Studies in the History of Art*, 13 (1984), p. 57.
[48] H. O. Evennett, *The spirit of the Counter-Reformation* (Cambridge, 1968), p. 38; Mâle, *L'art* (as in note 26), pp. 82–3.
[49] *Catechism of the Council of Trent* (as in note 17), p. 246.
[50] *Canons and Decrees of the Council of Trent* (as in note 11), p. 80, Can. 9.
[51] Ibid., p. 147.
[52] *Catechism of the Council of Trent* (as in note 17), p. 245, question LVII.
[53] Francisco de Borja de San Román, *El Greco en Toledo* (Madrid, 1910), pp. 195–7.
[54] Wethey, *El Greco*, vol. 1 (as in note 30), pp. 12–15.
[55] C. Gutiérrez, *Españoles en Trento* (Valladolid, 1951), p. 128ff.

are hymns to charity in which the redemptive and salvific role of Christ and the intercession, faith and deeds of the Virgin and saints are extolled.

In addition, in some paintings, thematic and illusionistic motifs relate to specific stages of the mass, thereby enhancing both their meaning, when considered in their original setting, and their relationship with the officiating priest and the congregation. This is manifested in the following sequence of images.

El Greco was commissioned to paint a series of *Apostles* for the Sacristy of Toledo Cathedral.[56] Viewed by the priest as he prepared to celebrate mass, they should have made him acutely aware of the significance of the Sacrament of Holy Orders, which Christ had instituted at the Last Supper and which empowered the priest to consecrate, offer and administer the Body and Blood of Christ, as well as to forgive and retain sins.

For the vestry of the Cathedral sacristy, El Greco painted the rare subject of the *Disrobing of Christ before his Crucifixion* (plate 121).[57] Thus as the celebrating priest donned the liturgical vestments, the picture would have put him vividly in mind of the sacrifice of the mass that he was about to celebrate.[58] A further reference to vesting is reflected in El Greco's polychrome sculpture of the *Virgin presenting a chasuble to St Ildefonso*, which was later displayed at the base of the painting.[59]

Other iconographic motifs in the *Espolio* would seem to relate to the preparation for mass. Novel to this theme are the expression and gestures of Christ. He raises his eyes to heaven and appears to protect or forgive the executioner. This evokes the words which he uttered on the Cross: 'Father, forgive them; for they know not what they do' (Luke 23:34). In the context of the sacristy, Christ's intercession would probably have been viewed as a direct response to the repeated pleas for forgiveness in the preparation for mass, especially in the Antiphon: 'Remember not O Lord, our offences, nor those of our fathers: neither take thou vengeance of our sins'.[60]

The theme of preparation for sacrifice is also implied in another of his pictures, at least one version of which is recorded in a sacristy. This is the unusual subject of *Christ taking leave of his Mother*,[61] the occasion when, according to the Pseudo-Bonaventura, Christ predicted his death to his Mother.[62]

At the start of the mass, the priest mounted the altar steps and moved to the centre of the altar to recite the hymn 'Gloria in Excelsis Deo' in which praise is given to both God the Father and the 'Lamb of God, Son of the Father. Thou who takest away the sins of the world'. El Greco's altarpiece of the *Adoration of the Shepherds*

[56] Wethey, *El Greco* (as in note 30), p. 102–4.

[57] Ibid., vol. 2, pp. 51–4. Two copies of the Espolio have also been recorded in sacristies, vol. 2, pp. 184, 185, no. X-85.

[58] In connection with this picture, it is noteworthy that the fragments of the purple tunic of Christ, which he wore during his Passion, and of the true Cross were among the prized relics of the sacristy. Francisco de Pisa, *Apuntamientos para la II parte de la 'Descripción de la Imperial Cuidad de Toledo'*, ed. J. Gómez-Menor Fuentes (Toledo, 1976), p. 45.

[59] Wethey, *El Greco* (as in note 30), pp. 53, 158, 161.

[60] For the saying of preparatory prayers in the sacristy, see Borromeo, *Instructiones* (as in note 22), p. 363.

[61] Wethey, *El Greco*, vol. 2 (as in note 30), p. 47, no. 70.

[62] *Meditations on the life of Christ*, ed. I. Ragusa and R. B. Green (Princeton, 1961), pp. 308–9.

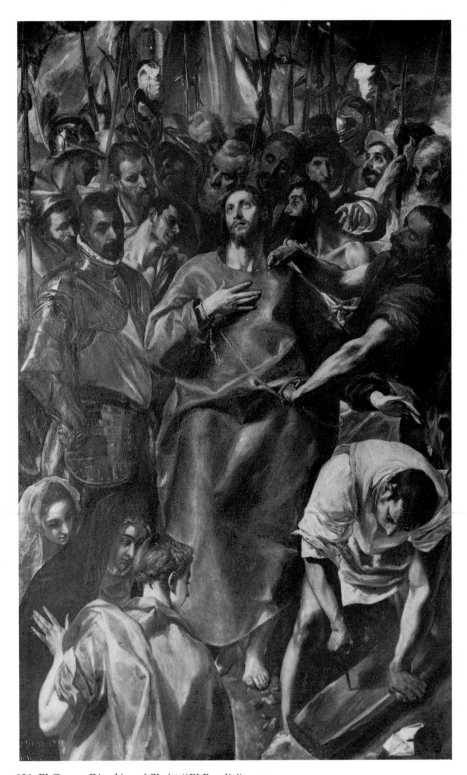

121 El Greco, *Disrobing of Christ* (*'El Espolio'*)

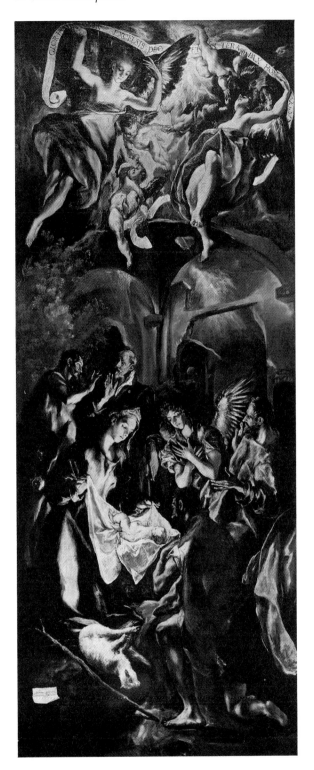

122 El Greco, *Adoration of the Shepherds*

(plate 122),[63] which formed part of the retable in the Colegio do Dña María de Aragón, could have been designed to recall such a moment. Two angels suspend a banderole inscribed with the opening lines of the hymn, while a trussed sacrificial lamb is conspicuously placed near the Christ Child. No reference is made to the lamb in the account of the narrative in the Bible.

After the Sanctus, the celebrant alone and silently entered upon the rite proper to the sacrifice of the mass, the canon. Perhaps El Greco's *Holy Family with St Anne and the Infant Baptist*,[64] which was recorded in a baroque altarpiece in the Hospitalillo de Santa Ana,[65] was originally intended to recall this liturgical stage.[66] As the Baptist approaches the sleeping Christ Child, a figure of sacrifice, he enjoins silence.

El Greco's altarpiece of the *Crucifixion with Donors* (plate 123)[67] obviously relates to the canon of the mass. Whether the artist intended the gesture of the lay donor, similar to that of St Ildefonso in the *Resurrection* in Sto Domingo el Antiguo (plate 129), to relate to the real crucifix on the altar is not known. Nevertheless, such a link would surely have been visualised during the mass, thereby heightening the relationship of the altarpiece to the liturgy.

During the canon, the priest commemorated both the living and the dead. The *Crucifixion with Donors* not only relates to the canon, but also ingeniously recalls the commemoration. The donors are depicted in half-length at the base of the painting so that they relate illusionistically to the officiating priest standing at the altar at approximately their level. Thus the priest was made acutely aware of their presence and their desire to be commemorated in the mass.[68]

In some altarpieces, donors were represented by their patron saints and would have been commemorated, at least, on the patronal feast days. Accordingly, when the priest celebrated mass in front of the *Assumption* (Sto Domingo el Antiguo), the *Annunciation* (Colegio de Nuestra Señora de la Encarnación), the *Visitation* (Capilla Oballe) and *St Martin and the Beggar* (Capilla de San José), it is likely that he would have commemorated, respectively, the donors Dña María de Silva, Dña María de Aragón, Isabel de Oballe, and Martín Ramírez.

---

[63] Wethey, *El Greco*, vol. 2 (as in note 30), p. 10, no. 12.

[64] Ibid., p. 62, no. 93. See also M. del Carmen Garrido and J. M. Cabrera, 'Estudio técnico comparativo de dos Sagradas Familias del Greco', *Boletín del Museo del Prado*, 3:8 (1982), pp. 93–101.

[65] M. B. Cossío, *El Greco* (Madrid, 1908), pp. 31–2, 585.

[66] E. H. Frankfort, 'El Greco's *Holy Family with the Sleeping Christ Child and the Infant Baptist*: an image of silence and mystery?', in *Hortus Imaginum, essays in western art*, ed. R. Enggass and M. Stokstad (Lawrence KS, 1974), p. 105.

[67] It is recorded as an altarpiece in 1800 by J. A. Ceán Bermúdez, *Diccionario histórico de los más ilustres profesores de las bellas artes en España*, vol. 5 (Madrid, 1800), p. 10.

[68] There are precedents for this illusionistic device in Italian painting. See illustrations in A. Chastel, 'Le donateur "in abisso" dans les "Pale '''", in *Festschrift für Otto von Simson*, ed. L. Grisebach and K. Renger (Frankfurt, 1977), pp. 273–83. Titian had experimented earlier with this idea in his altarpiece of the *Annunciation* in Treviso. See Liberali, 'Lotto, Pordenone Tiziano a Treviso. Cronologie, Interpretazioni ed Ambientamenti', *Atti dell' Istituto Veneto di Scienze, Lettere ed Arti*, (Classe di Scienze Morali e Lettere), vol. 33, fascicolo III (Venice, 1963), pp. 97–98, XVII. I am grateful to Elizabeth McGrath for drawing my attention to this interesting document, and to Charles Hope for locating its publication. In this document, reference is made to both the illusionistic presence of the donor and his being commemorated in the mass.

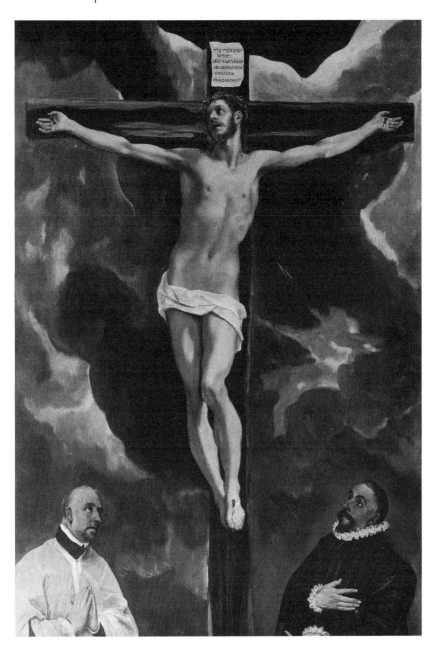

123 El Greco, *Crucifixion with donors*

The sacrificial blood which was made present at the Consecration is vividly evoked in the *Crucifixion with the Virgin and St John the Evangelist* (plate 124)[69] by the predominant red colour. Blood gushes out of the side of the dead Christ and flows freely from the wounds in the palms of his hands. At the foot of the Cross, St Mary

[69] Wethey, *El Greco*, vol 2 (as in note 30), p. 49, no. 75.

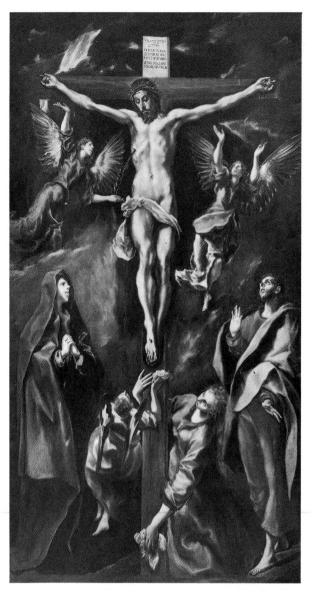

124 El Greco, *Crucifixion with the Virgin and St John the Evangelist*

Magdalene and an angel ardently mop up the precious blood.[70] Above it is eagerly
collected in the open hands of the exultant angels. Their expression of joy, like those
of the dancing angels in Raphael's *Crucifixion* (London National Gallery) signals the
redemption and salvation of man. In contrast to other artists' versions of this subject,
in which the angels are often depicted collecting the blood in chalices, El Greco
here shows them gathering it in their open hands. He may have been inspired by
the text of the missal. After the consecration and elevation of the Host and Chalice,

---

[70] In the opinion of Manuel Trens, the collection of the blood by angels was for distribution to the seven sacraments:
La Eucaristiá en el arte Español (Barcelona, 1952), p. 162. In this connection, the participation of St Mary Magdalene
may have signified the Sacrament of Penance.

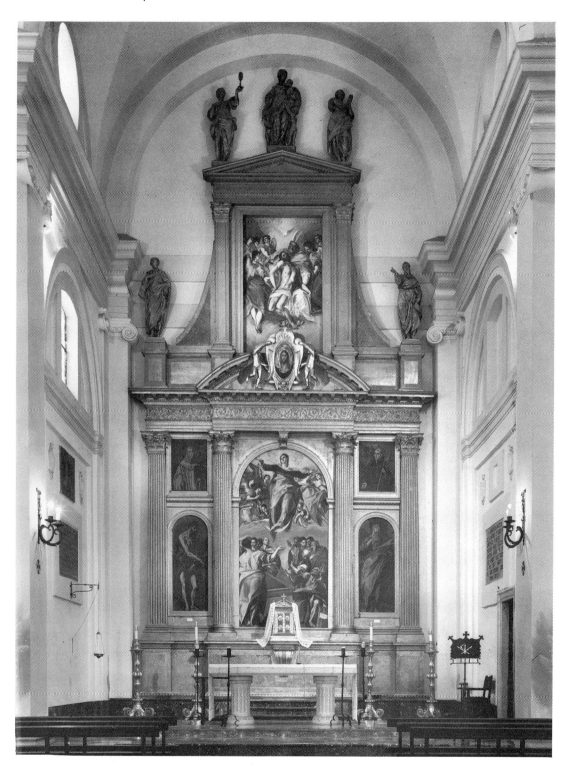

125 Toledo, Sto. Domingo el Antiguo, view of high altar, with copies of the *Assumption* and *Trinity* in place of the originals

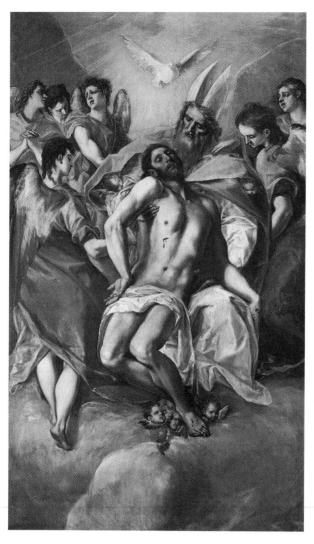

126 El Greco, *Trinity*

the priest bowed down over the altar and prayed thus: 'Humbly we beseech thee, Almighty God, to command that by the hands of thy holy Angel, this our Sacrifice be uplifted to thine Altar on high.'

The priest had already petitioned the Holy Trinity to accept the sacrificial gifts in the prayer of oblation and at the commencement of the canon, and would repeat the petition after the dismissal. His plea is accompanied by the intercession of the Virgin and saints. In the central compartment of the high altarpiece in Sto Domingo el Antiguo (plates 125, 131), the Virgin is depicted ascending into heaven, where she will intercede with God the Father to accept the sacrificial offering and to bestow divine grace to expiate the sins of the faithful. God's acceptance of the sacrificial victim is visualised in El Greco's painting of the *Trinity* (plate 126) in which God the Father holds His dead Son in His arms. Originally this painting was in the upper

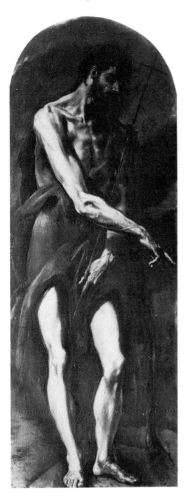

127 El Greco, *St John the Baptist*

register of the high altarpiece in Sto Domingo el Antiguo (plate 125). At its apex stands a sculpted female personification of *Charity*, who symbolises the essence of the Eucharist. Aquinas had called it '''the sacrament of charity'', which is the *bond of perfectness*, as we read in Colossians (3,14)'.[71] 'Ainsi Dieu qui est la force est aussi la bonté, et c'est par amour qu'il se donne aux hommes'.[72] She holds a child in her arms, visually recalling God the Father holding His dead Son in the *Trinity*, and the officiating priest holding the Host.

The sacrifice and the sacrament of the mass are subtly suggested in the *St John the Baptist* (plate 127) (a component of the high altarpiece in Sto Domingo el Antiguo) and *St Joseph and the Christ Child* in the Capilla de San José (plate 128). In the former painting, the Baptist points either to the crucifix or tabernacle on the altar, signifying

---

[71] St Thomas Aquinas, *Summa theologiae*, vol. 58, *The Eucharistic Presence* (3a. 73–78), trans. and ed. by William Barden (Blackfriars, 1965), pp. 12–13.

[72] Mâle, *L'art* (as in note 26), p. 86.

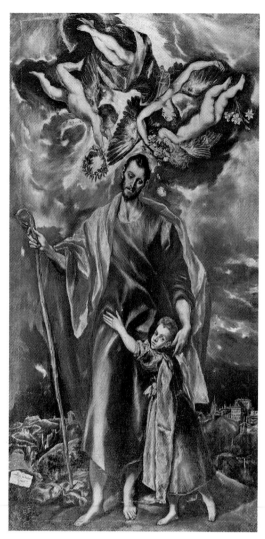

128 El Greco, *St Joseph and the Christ Child*, Modello for high altarpiece in the Capilla de San
José

the sacrificial 'Lamb of God … who taketh away the sin of the world'.[73] In his
altarpiece of *St Joseph and the Christ Child*, El Greco has represented the saint as
a guardian of Christ, for which 'good work' he is rewarded with a victor's crown.
This is in accord with the Tridentine *Decree concerning Justification*,[74] and the Preface
of the Mass of St Joseph: 'and being a faithful and wise servant, was by Thee set
over thine Household, in order that he might be the Guardian, in place of a Father,
of thine Only-Begotten Son'. But instead of depicting the saint with his usual attribute
of a rod in bloom, El Greco has knowingly substituted a shepherd's crook. Here,

[73] Charles Robertson kindly informed me that there are earlier, Italian examples of St John drawing attention to
the crucifix or tabernacle, as in Botticelli's *Madonna and Child with saints* (Uffizi) from the church of S. Barnaba
in Florence.
[74] *Canons and Decrees of the Council of Trent* (as in note 11), p. 41.

St Joseph protects the Lamb of God, clothed in a blood-red garment. These pictures relate not only to the sacrificial element that is already implicit in the consecration but also to the threefold 'Agnus Dei' that is chanted by the clergy and congregation prior to Communion. Moreover, before distributing Communion, the priest held up the host and said, 'Ecce Agnus Dei' (Behold the Lamb of God). In these cases, the priest literally indicated the Lamb of God to which St John the Baptist is pointing, and which St Joseph is protecting.

El Greco seems to refer to the Communion service that follows in his side altarpiece of the *Resurrection with St Ildefonso* in Sto Domingo el Antiguo (plate 129). St Ildefonso is shown half-length at the base of the painting and dressed in white liturgical vestments, as prescribed for Easter Sunday. Illusionistically he mirrors the priest who would officiate at the altar. Christ appears to offer himself to the saint,[75] who reverently responds, thus evoking the reception of the glorified, that is, resurrected, body of Christ in Communion. Indeed, in the office of the Feast of the Assumption, the principal subject of the scheme of decoration in this chapel, it is written: 'Yea in this solemn day of His joy and of the gladness of His Heart, may our Lord Jesus Christ thy son be pleased to make a special out-pouring of His grace through thee, O merciful Queen! upon all who are calling upon the sweet name of Mary.' Affirmation that Christ will bestow his grace would seem to be subtly implied in the *Resurrection*, in which the glorified Christ presents himself to St Ildefonso, who had been presented with a chasuble by the Virgin for having defended her virginity.[76]

In the 'Decree concerning the things to be observed, and to be avoided, in the celebration of Mass', the Council of Trent demanded 'the greatest possible interior cleanness and purity of heart ... [and] that the local ordinaries ... prohibit and abolish all those things which either *covetousness, which is a serving of idols,* or irreverence ... or superstition ... have introduced ... they shall in the first place, as regards avarice, absolutely forbid conditions of compensations ... also, those ... demands ... for alms and other things of this kind which border on simoniacal taint or certainly savor of filthy lucre ... that the house of God may be seen to be and may be truly called a house of prayer'. These words recall those of Christ when he chastised the money traders in the Temple, 'saying to them: It is written: *My house is the house of prayer. But you have made it a den of thieves*' (Luke 19:46).

The association of this subject with the celebration of mass may be significant for an understanding of those versions of the *Purification of the Temple* which El Greco painted in Spain, and in which the theme of Sin and Redemption is woven into their meaning.[77] A late version is in the room of the Confraternity of the Holy Sacra-

---

[75] The gesture of Christ is later repeated in that of the carved statuette of the Risen Christ which surmounted the Tabernacle in the Hospital de San Juan Bautista. For the association of this gesture with libation, see R. Mann, 'The altarpieces for the Hospital of Saint John the Baptist, Outside the Walls, Toledo', *Studies in the History of Art*, 11 (1982), p. 61.

[76] D. Davies, 'El Greco of Toledo' (exhibition review), *The Burlington Magazine* (August 1982), p. 531.

[77] For a discussion of the iconography of these pictures, see E. Harris, *El Greco, the purification of the temple* (London, nd); R. Wittkower, 'El Greco's language of gesture', *Art News*, 56 (1957), p. 54; and D. Davies, 'El Greco and the spiritual reform movements in Spain', *Studies in the history of art*, 13 (1984), pp. 63–6.

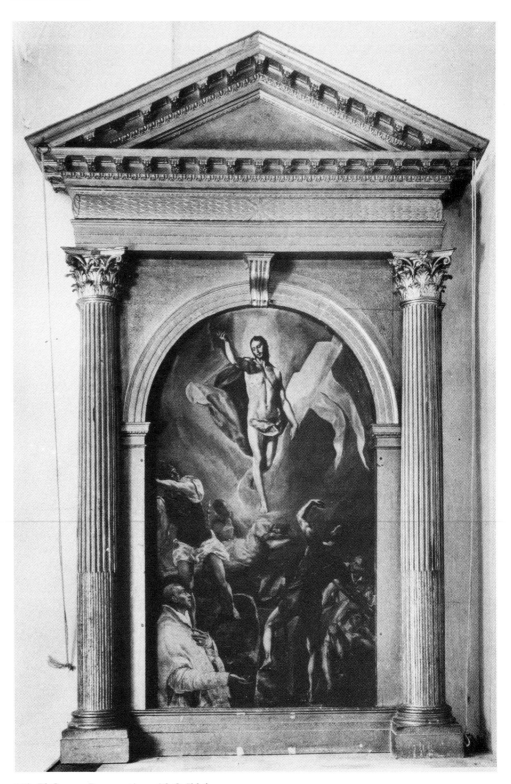

129 El Greco, *Resurrection with St Ildefonso*

ment in the church of San Ginés (plate 130).[78] Whether this was its original destination or not, it was obviously considered, at some time, to be an appropriate subject for such a location.

The relationship of the iconography of the altarpiece to the mass is sometimes elaborated in the Divine Office. It would appear that it is a particularly significant source for some conventual and monastic commissions. For instance, the Common Office for Feasts of the Virgin and, especially, the Office for the Feast-day of her Assumption were of signal importance for the iconography of the scheme of decoration which El Greco executed in the chapel of the Bernardine convent of Sto Domingo el Antiguo (plate 125). The main picture in the high altarpiece was the *Assumption of the Virgin*, the principal subject of Bernardine dedications (plate 131). The Virgin was visualised as soaring upwards to the *Trinity* (plate 126), which was above, in the second storey of the altarpiece. At the apex of the altarpiece stand sculpted personifications of *Faith, Charity* and *Hope*. The two side altarpieces, representing the *Adoration of the Shepherds*, and the *Resurrection* (plate 129), include St Jerome and St Ildefonso respectively. Both saints were ardent defenders of the virginity of the Virgin.

At First Vespers, the ascent of the Virgin to the Trinity is recounted in the hymn, 'Ave, maris stella':

> Through the highest heaven
> To the Almighty Three,
> Father, Son, and Spirit,
> One same glory be.

The splendour of her appearance is evoked, for example, in the Third Responsory of the First Nocturn on her feast day:

> Who is this that cometh up like the sun?
> This, comely as Jerusalem?

In the Lessons of the Second Nocturn on both the Fifth Day within the Octave and the Octave itself, her ascent to Christ in heaven is exultantly recalled and her virginity and charity are extolled. It is significant that these Lessons are taken from St Bernard's sermons on the 'Assumption of the Virgin'.[79]

In addition to these subtle inter-relationships, El Greco elicits a more dramatic and spiritual response, a quickening of the spirit, to the majesty of the Sacrifice and the mystery of the Real Presence, through his handling of light, colour and form. As his style gains in intensity, light is incandescent, increasingly white, and seems to emanate from within the form. Colours are pure and luminous. The application of broken colour to suggest the illusion of physical reality has been rejected in favour of startling contrasts and harsher brilliance. Forms are increasingly two-dimensional, animated by zig-zag accents, and elongated so that they assume flame-like shapes. Verticality is also emphasised by the reflections of light, which taper

---

[78] Wethey, *El Greco*, vol. 2 (as in note 30), p. 70, no. 110.
[79] Davies, 'El Greco' (as in note 76), p. 531, notes the relationship of St Bernard's sermons on the Assumption to this scheme of decoration.

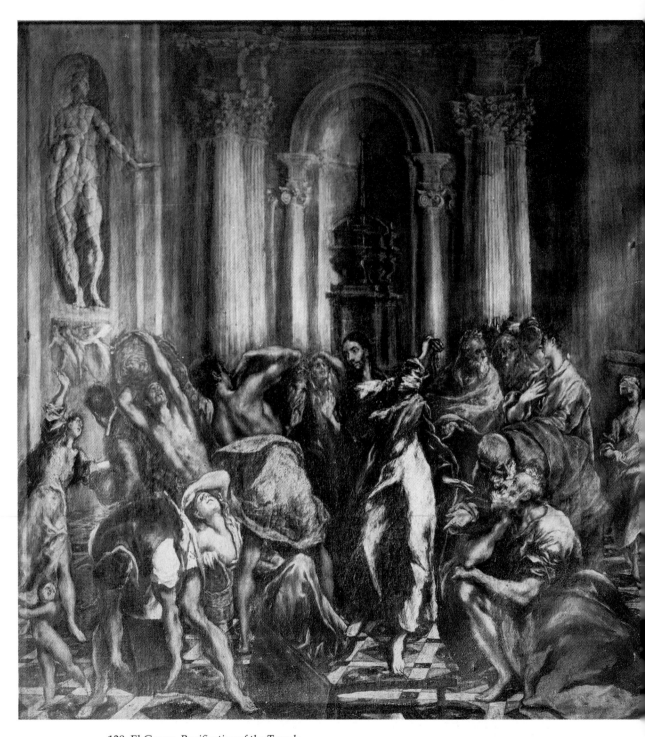

130 El Greco, *Purification of the Temple*

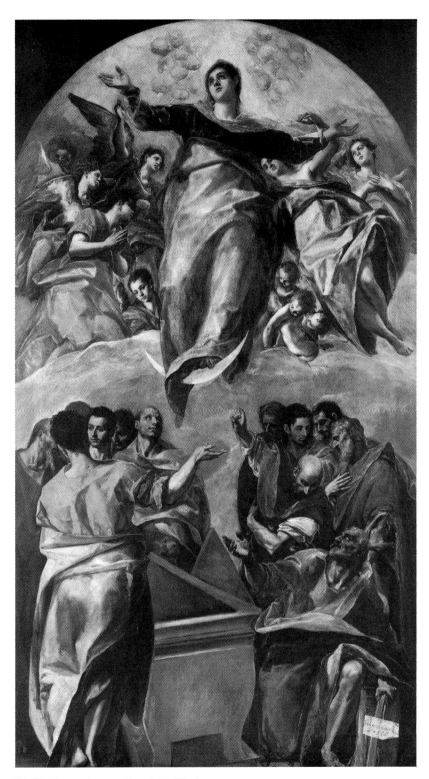

131 El Greco, *Assumption of the Virgin*

upwards, irrespective of the configuration of the forms, and by the design, in which the vertical axis and steep diagonals force the attention of the beholder to its apex. The vertical format of many of his religious paintings, particularly his altarpieces, is increasingly attenuated. The observation of natural phenomena has been forsaken for the creation of conceptual images that transcend the physical world.

Such imagery would seems to complement both the visual splendour of the ritual and the figurative language of the mass. In response to Protestant objections to the special sanctity of the mass, Catholic Reformers rekindled the splendour of its ritual and stressed its symbolic import.[80] The Council of Trent decreed that: 'since the nature of man is such that he cannot without external means be raised easily to meditation on divine things, holy mother Church has ... made use of ceremonies, such as mystical blessings, lights, incense, vestments and many other things of this kind, whereby both the majesty of so great a sacrifice might be emphasised and the minds of the faithful excited by those visible signs of religion and piety to the contemplation of those most sublime things which are hidden in this sacrifice'.[81] This mystical approach is also manifest in the works of medieval writers such as Abbot Suger and Bishop Durandus. The former extolled the properties of the precious stones with which he decorated the altars and crucifixes of the Abbey church of St Denis: 'Thus, when – out of my delight in the beauty of the house of God – the loveliness of the many-colored gems has called me away from external cares, and worthy meditation has induced me to reflect, transferring that which is material to that which is immaterial, on the diversity of the sacred virtues: then it seems to me that I see myself dwelling, as it were, in some strange region of the universe which neither exists entirely in the slime of the earth nor entirely in the purity of Heaven; and that, by the grace of god, I can be transported from this inferior to that higher world in an anagogical manner.'[82]

A contemporary of El Greco, Fray José de Sigüenza, adopted a similar interpretation. In his description of the consecration of the high altar of the Escorial, he referred to the practice of anointing the twelve crosses in front of which candles were burning. These he perceived as the twelve doors which St John saw in his vision of the heavenly Jerusalem.[83]

El Greco, too, shared this anagogical approach. He treated light in a metaphysical way to suggest spiritual illumination. This is evident from the inscription in his *View and Plan of Toledo* (Toledo, Museo del Greco), in which he refers to the Virgin and Angels as celestial bodies, and implies that they emit light. This idea is derived from the *Celestial Hierarchy* of Pseudo-Dionysius the Areopagite, a Greek edition of which figures in the inventory of El Greco's library. Significantly, it was the same source to which Suger referred for his theories of light metaphysics.[84]

[80] See note 26.
[81] See note 25.
[82] *Abbot Suger on the Abbey Church of St Denis and its art treasures*, ed., trans. and annotated by Erwin Panofsky (Princeton, 1946), pp. 62–5.
[83] Sigüenza, *Fundación* (as in note 33), p. 159.
[84] Davies, 'The influence of philosophical and theological ideas on the art of El Greco in Spain', *Actas del XXIII Congreso Internacional de Historia del Arte*, vol. 2 (Granada, 1977), pp. 242–9.

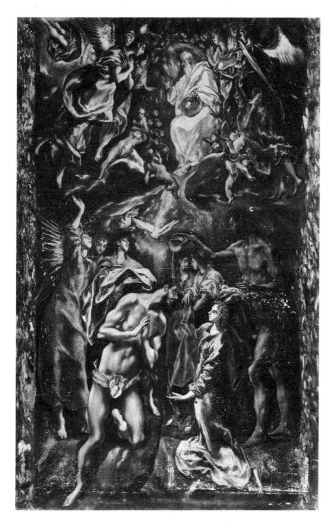

132 El Greco, *Baptism of Christ*

Such light imagery is found not only in contemporary spiritual literature to suggest the reception of grace in mystic union of the soul with the divine, but also in the mass. As well as containing a plethora of light metaphysical images, it is significant that after the blessing, the priest recited the first verses of the Gospel of St John: 'In him was life and the life was the light of men: and the light shineth in darkness, and the darkness did not comprehend it. . . .'

It is illuminating to note that in El Greco's altarpiece of the *Baptism of Christ* in the Hospital de San Juan Bautista (plate 132), the burst of incandescent light that emanates from God the Father contrasts mysteriously with the surrounding darkness. There is no scriptural source for the scene taking place at night. Probably El Greco is alluding to the early Christian practices in which baptism took place on the vigils of Easter and Pentecost in order to express the concept of spiritual illumination.[85]

[85] Davies, 'El Greco' (as in note 76), p. 532.

Since

Since it is demonstrable that the light in El Greco's religious paintings is to be interpreted mystically, it is conceivable that his colour and form should be similarly interpreted. The crystalline colours recall the precious stones which embellished the altars and altar furnishings in St Denis, and those which formed the heavenly Jerusalem: 'The Gates of Jerusalem shall be built of sapphire, and of emerald, and all the walls thereof round about of precious stones' (Tobias 13:21).

The sensation of ascent is sometimes heightened by the visual translation from naturalistically described forms at the base of his paintings to conceptually conceived ones above. Since this parallels the disposition of earth and heaven in the paintings, as well as in the contemporary mind,[86] it would seems that he relates form to content in order to signify the ascent from the physical world to that of the transcendental. Such a method recalls that of the spiritual illumination of the mind and its ascent to God as described by the Pseudo-Dionysius.[87] The idea of ascent to heaven also figures large in the Mass: 'May this incense, blessed by thee, ascend before thee, O Lord, and may thy mercy descend upon us. Let my prayer be directed, O Lord, as incense in thy sight; the lifting up of my hands as an evening sacrifice' (Ordinary of the Mass).

Indeed, the image of both spiritual illumination and ascent is vividly conjured up in the preface of masses celebrated from Christmas day to Epiphany, and on the Feasts of Corpus Christi and the Transfiguration: 'It is truly meet and just . . . to give thanks to thee, O Lord . . . because by the Mystery of the Word made flesh, from they brightness a new light hath risen to shine on the eyes of our minds, in order that, God becoming visible to us, we may be borne upward to the love of things invisible'. It is no wonder that El Greco's religious imagery, which was indebted to the heady stuff of Christian Neoplatonism and the ideas of the Spiritual Reformers in Spain,[88] should also have had such a wide appeal.

The relationship of El Greco's altarpieces to the mass may not be confined to the actual paintings. The profusion of gilded framework reflects the light from the altar candles and lamp, and glows in the dim light of the church, thus enhancing the sense of majesty and mystery. It is striking, too, that El Greco's design of the framework is distinctly architectural, and is reminiscent of church façades, portals or frontispieces.[89] For example, in Sto Domingo el Antiguo (plate 125), the design of the entire framework of the retable is, basically a reduced adaptation of Vignola's plan for the facade of the Gesù in Rome.[90] The design of the frames of the side altarpieces in Sto Domingo and the Capilla de San José is derived from standard Venetian forms of portals and altarpiece frames.[91] The frames of the high altarpieces

[86] E. M. W. Tillyard, *The Elizabethan world picture* (Harmondsworth, 1972), p. 45ff.
[87] Dionysius the Areopagite, *Mystical theology and the celestial hierarchies*, trans. and ed. The Shrine of Wisdom Press (Fintry, Surrey, 1965), p. 21.
[88] Davies, 'El Greco' (as in note 77), pp. 57–74.
[89] The application of the architectural term, 'frontispiece', to the title-page is recorded in the English Language by 1682. *Shorter English Dictionary*, vol. 1, p. 811. I am grateful to John Bury for information about the frontispiece.
[90] D. Davies, *El Greco* (Oxford, 1976), p. 6. For an illustration of Vignola's project, see L. H. Heydenreich and W. Lotz, *Architecture in Italy 1400–1600* (Harmondsworth, 1974), plate 285.
[91] Wethey, *El Greco*, vol. 1 (as in note 30), p. 68.

in the Capilla de San José and the chapel of the Hospital de la Caridad (plate 139), as well as that of the altarpiece in the Oballe Chapel in San Vicente, are ingeniously based on the design of the title-page in Palladio's *Quattro Libri dell'Architettura*.[92] Such designs conform to a long established if uneven tradition in Spain, Italy and the north.[93] They provide both a convenient and an ornamental setting for images, and, occasionally, a harmonious relationship with the church façade, as in the Escorial. Is it possible that they signified entrance into an inner, heavenly sanctuary, a figure of the Holy of Holies or the heavenly Jerusalem?[94]

A brief examination of the ciborium lends some support to this interpretation. The ciborium is a special canopied structure, often free-standing, which covers the altar. Visually, it is similar to an inner temple or sanctuary.[95] When the altar was set against a wall, the ciborium was structurally connected, occasionally, with the altarpiece frame, as in the Ciborium of the Sudarium, formerly in the Old Basilica of St Peter in Rome.[96] Perhaps this architectural association of ciborium and altarpiece frame was illusionistically implied in Giovanni Bellini's *San Zaccaria* altarpiece.[97] Possibly it conveys to the congregation and to the celebrant as he approaches the altar, the idea of an inner, heavenly sanctuary associated with sacrifice and salvation. Could it be that these associations were transferred, consciously or unconsciously, to the framework of the altarpiece?

Certainly, the idea of entrance into heaven and the Holy of Holies is prominent in the liturgy and in liturgical commentaries. In the Office for the Dedication of a Church, it is repeated that 'this is none other but the house of God, and this is the gate of Heaven'. Durandus wrote that 'the door of the church is Christ: according to that saying in the Gospels, "I am the door" (John 10:9)'.[98] From the main door to the sanctuary, there is a conscious succession of entrances, indicating stages of increasing sanctity. The association of the sanctuary with the Holy of Holies or 'sancta sanctorum' is found in the writings of St Jerome,[99] Suger,[100] Durandus[101] and Aquinas.[102]

It is notable that, at the beginning of mass, the celebrating priest stood at the

[92] Ibid., pp. 69, 71. Palladio's title-page may also have inspired El Greco's choice of subjects for the attic of two of these altarpieces. The crowned female figure (Regina Virtus) has been replaced by the *Coronation of the Virgin* in the Capilla de San José, and by the *Virgin of Charity*, the highest form of the theological virtues, in the Hospital de la Caridad.

[93] For numerous examples, see the illustrations in J. Braun, *Der Christliche Altar in seiner geschichtlichen Entwicklung*, vol. 2 (Munich, 1924).

[94] For Halldor Soehner, too, the framework of the high altarpiece in the Capilla de S. José suggested the idea of a portal, and evoked the illusion of an entrance into heaven. *La capilla de San José de Toledo* (Madrid, 1901), p. 21.

[95] See illustrations in Braun, *Der Christliche Altar*, vol. 2.

[96] Giacomo Grimaldi, *Descrizione della basilica antica di S. Pietro in Vaticano*, ed. di Reto Niggl (Rome, 1972), p. 123, fig. 40. I am grateful to Brendan Cassidy for this reference.

[97] For an illustration of the altarpiece in its original frame, see G. Robertson, *Giovanni Bellini* (Oxford, 1968), plate LXVII. Peter Humfrey has kindly drawn my attention to the possibility of a similar connection between Bellini's lost altarpiece from SS. Giovanni e Paolo and the ciborium in the Basilica of San Marco.

[98] Durandus, *The symbolism* (as in note 23), p. 21.

[99] Jungmann, *The Mass of the Roman Rite*, vol. 1, p. 311, no. 82.

[100] Suger, *St. Denis*, pp. 98–9, 134–5.

[101] Durandus, *The Symbolism* (as in note 23), pp. 56–7, 61, 163.

[102] Aquinas, *Summa Theologiae* (as in note 71), p. 23.

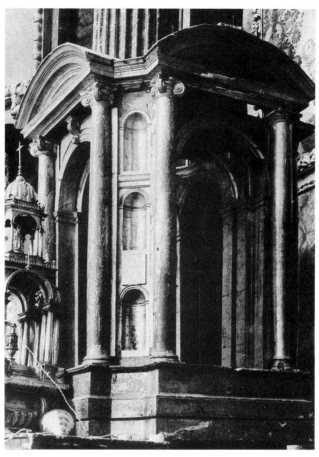

133 Tabernacle

foot of the altar steps, and pronounced on three separate occasions: 'Introibo ad altare Dei': 'I will go into the altar of God'. Going up to the altar, the priest prayed silently: 'Take away from us our iniquities, we beseech thee, O Lord; that, being made pure in heart, we may be worthy to enter into the Holy of Holies. Through Christ our Lord'.

Whatever the symbolism, if any, of the framework, it is likely that the design of El Greco's tabernacle in the Hospital de San Juan Bautista (plate 133) signifies sacrifice and salvation.[103] It is centrally planned, recalling the rotunda of the Holy Sepulchre,[104] and in the form of a temple, providing an appropriate chamber for the Real Presence. Originally, its dome was surmounted by El Greco's carved statuette of the risen Christ.[105] Such a design was common. In the centrally planned tabernacle

[103] It is illustrated in Wethey, *El Greco*, vol. 1 (as in note 30), plate 379.
[104] Richard Krautheimer indicated the relationship of centrally planned ecclesiastical monuments to the Holy Sepulchre, and the association of this design with sacrifice and salvation: 'Introduction to an ''Iconography of Medieval Architecture''', *Journal of the Warburg and Courtauld Institutes*, 5 (1942), pp. 1–33. Cornelia von der Osten Sacken reached similar conclusions in her discussion of the tabernacle on the high altar of the Escorial, *El Escorial estudio inconologico* (Bilbao, 1984), p. 61.
[105] Wethey, *El Greco*, vol. 2 (as in note 30), p. 161.

which Juan de Herrera designed and Jacomo da Trezzo executed for the high altar in the Escorial, the symbolism may have extended to the materials. The gold and precious stones, such as jasper, crystal, topaz, emerald and sapphire,[106] call to mind the very fabric of the 'tabernacle of God', the lustrous 'holy city of Jerusalem', which was revealed to St John (Apocalypse 21). Since few centrally planned ecclesiastical buildings were newly constructed in this period, partly for liturgical reasons,[107] it would seem that the diffusion, splendour and increased size of the centrally planned tabernacle reflected a conscious desire to suggest the sacrifice of the mass and the Real Presence.

It is fitting to end this discussion of El Greco's altarpieces with one of his last and most stunning examples. For the Oballe Chapel in San Vicente, he painted an altarpiece of the *Assumption of the Virgin* (plate 134).[108] Above, in the vault, there was to be the *Visitation* (plate 135). Its inclusion was a reference to the foundress, Isabel de Oballe;[109] its position was undoubtedly El Greco's invention. At the bottom of the canvas of the *Assumption* there is a cluster of naturalistically painted lilies and roses. They relate to the flowers which were discovered in the empty sepulchre of the Virgin. In Spanish liturgical drama there are references to the sepulchre of the Virgin as being represented by the altar on the Feast of the Assumption.[110] The painted flowers are to the right of centre, presumably to avoid being masked by the crucifix or tabernacle on the altar; illusionistically, they would have mirrored real flowers which were probably placed on the altar during her feast-days.[111]

From the realm of the naturalistic flowers, heavenly beings flare upwards illuminating the dark night. Amidst the flickering light of the candles on the altar and the clouds of incense, they would have appeared to soar to the real light from the window

---

[106] Sigüenza, *Fundación* (as in note 33), pp. 342–7.

[107] Heydenreich and Lotz, *Architecture in Italy* (as in note 90), p. 306.

[108] In 1576, Luis Hurtado de Toledo, a priest at San Vicente, recorded the titles and patronal names of chapels in that church. The title of the Cisneros family chapel was the 'Assumpcion de Nuestra Señora'. No reference ws made to Isabel de Oballe concerning this or any other chapel. (*Relaciones histórico-geográfico-estadisticas de los Pueblos de España hechas por iniciativa de Felipe II*, Reino de Toledo, Tercera parte, ed. Carmelo Viñas and Ramón Paz (Madrid, 1963), p. 530).

From the researches of R. Ramiréz de Arellano, (*Las Parroquias de Toledo* (Toledo, 1921), pp. 283–94), Cossío, *El Greco* (as in note 65), pp. 663–6, San Román, 'De la vida del Greco', *Archivo Español de arte y arqueología*, 9 (Madrid, 1927), pp. 278–80 and Fernando Marías, *La arquitectura del Renacimiento en Toledo (1541–1631) – III* (Madrid, 1986), pp. 32–4, it would appear that the title and patronal name of this chapel were unchanged in 1590. Later, the patronage of this chapel passed to Isabel de Oballe. Renovations were begun in 1597, presumably funded by Isabel de Oballe, who is referred to as 'fundadora', and supervised by the city council. By 1601, the council had assumed patronage of this chapel. Until further documentation appears, there is no reason to suppose that the title was ever changed. The title of the chapel/altar would determine the subject of the altarpiece: see M. Carmichael, *Francia's masterpiece* (London, 1909), p. xxii. The inclusion of Immaculist symbols in paintings of the Assumption of the Virgin is not unprecedented. See Agustin-Marie Lépicier, *L'Immaculée Conception dans l'art et l'iconographie* (Spa, 1956), pp. 206–10. Their inclusion would suggest that this special privilege accorded to the Virgin was affirmed by her Assumption.

[109] San Román (as in previous note), p. 278.

[110] R. B. Donovan, *CSB, The Liturgical drama in medieval Spain* (Toronto, 1958), p. 97. In the Rovere chapel in Sta. Trinità in Rome, Daniello da Volterra painted an *Assumption* and made it appear as if the altar were the sepulchre. Vasari, *Le vite*, ed. G. Milanesi, vol. 7 (Florence, 1878–85), pp. 60–1.

[111] O'Connell, *Church building* (as in note 42) p. 197. A similar illusionistic motif is present in the *Annunciation* (Madrid, Prado), which was painted for the high altar of the Colegio de Doña María de Aragón. The flames of the Burning Bush, which was painted at the base of the picture, would have related illusionistically to the real flames of the candles burning on the altar table.

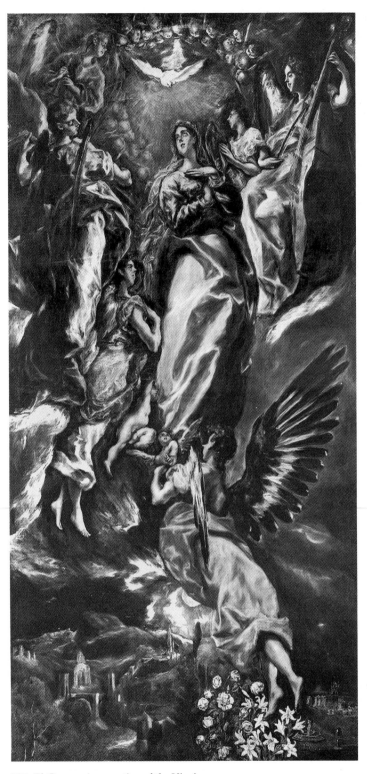

134 El Greco, *Assumption of the Virgin*

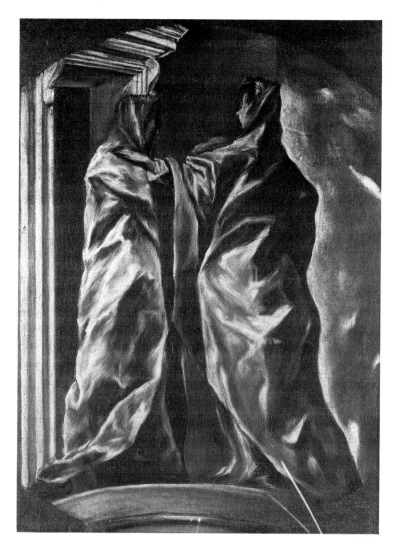

135 El Greco, *Visitation*

and to the heavenly sphere above, where the two celestial bodies, the Virgin and St Elizabeth, are fused in a burst of incandescent, metaphysical light.

Such a vision seems to have been inspired by the poetic imagery of the Office for the Feast of the Assumption of the Virgin.[112]

> Maiden most wise, whither goest thou up, like the dawn gloriously rising? O daughter of Zion, thou are all beautiful and pleasant, fair as the moon, clear as the Sun. (First Vespers, Antiphon).

> Who is this that cometh out of the wilderness like a pillar of smoke, perfumed with myrrh and frankincense? (First Nocturn, Verse)

---

[112] Reference to the Visitation in the context of the Assumption is made specifically, in the Fourth Lesson of the second Nocturn on the Fifth Day within the Octave of the Feast of the Assumption.

And about her it was as the flower of roses in the spring of the year, and lilies of the valley. (First Nocturn, Answer).

In this manner, El Greco has conjured up a vision of an ascent from the physical to the transcendental. Anagogically, he expresses the 'ascent of the mind to God' (St John Damascene) by both the brilliance of light and colour and the ascending forms. They spiritually illuminate and elevate the mind of the believer 'to the contemplation of those most sublime things which are hidden in this sacrifice'.

In response to a re-vitalised liturgy, El Greco relates art to ritual and wondrously evokes in the mind of the faithful the drama of sacrifice and salvation, the meeting of Heaven and Earth.[113]

[113] I wish to dedicate this chapter to Dr Angel García Gómez, a valued friend and teacher. I owe a special debt of gratitude to him and to Mrs Enriqueta Frankfort, Professor John White, Dr Elizabeth McGrath, Dr Ronald Cueto, Dr Paul Donnelly and Philip Troutman. As a result of their constructive criticisms, numerous revisions have been made to the text since it was first read at the University of London Golden Age Seminar in January 1986. I have also benefited much from the help of Dr Ronald Truman, Dr Gordon Kinder, Christa Gardner von Teuffel, Professor Howard Burns, Dr Brendan Cassidy, Fr John Arnold and Timothy McFarland. Alison Whittle's clerical assistance has been a boon.

I also wish to thank the editors for their extraordinary patience and their encouragement to extend my research in order to consider, generally, the influence of the theological polemics between Protestants and Catholics on the liturgy and the altarpiece. I hope that this focus of attention will serve as a pale shadow to Emile Mâle's magisterial study of post-Tridentine religious art in general.

12 The altarpiece in Catholic Europe: post-Tridentine transformations

A. D. Wright

The decrees of the Council of Trent, in the face of Protestant criticism, reasserted the special sanctity of the mass. Veneration of the saints and respect for the visual representation of sacred subjects were also defended at the Council. The distinct authority of the priest was moreover stressed, again in response to Protestant attack. In the post-Conciliar Church, as a result, the Catholic hierarchy renewed attention to the altar and its fittings, just as to vestments, vessels, and other liturgical equipment. The ideal, furthermore, was that laity should be entirely excluded from the sanctuary and from proximity to the altar. What has perhaps been less noted hitherto is that such preoccupations sometimes had a specific influence, in the immediately post-Tridentine Church, on altar paintings and adjacent decorations or sculpture. The didactic implications of even seeming details were no more overlooked than was the need to preserve the most solemn and sacred sections of the mass as a priestly mystery, not audible to non-clerical ears. Yet the Tridentine Council also underlined the Real Presence of Christ not only during the celebrations of mass but, therefore, wherever the Sacrament was reserved. Fear of disrespect or worse sacrilege towards the Reserved Sacrament led to post-Tridentine practice increasingly confining reservation to a tabernacle on the altar, as opposed to the variety of locations used in different parts of the Medieval Western Church. But even on altars where there was no tabernacle and no reservation, the doctrine of the mass and the sacramental role of the priest, reaffirmed at Trent, could be permanently represented in visual form. Orthodox teaching could thus be maintained, whether or not mass was being celebrated and whether or not the decoration of the altar had a tabernacle as its focus. As more generally in the implementation of Conciliar reform after Trent, Italian and Iberian prelates were particularly prominent in imposing and encouraging new standards. Their concerns were reflected in the care which patrons, whether clerical or not, exercised in commissioning new altarpieces. This meant that on occasion at least artists gave less prominence than before to visual references which were not integral to the sacred subject depicted. In some instances therefore figures of donors, patrons, or other un-canonised persons were made distinctly subordinate, if included at all. For the post-Tridentine papacy was also intent on preventing the cult of any but officially recognised saints. Yet even in Italy and Spain, in the later sixteenth and early seventeenth centuries, such developments in the form of the altarpiece were never absolute nor were they universally found. To assess the nature of these developments as far as they did occur is the purpose of this chapter.

The first point which perhaps needs to be made in relation to the sixteenth-century evolution of the altarpiece is the apparently obvious one of the liturgical space involved. Liturgical and not just proprietary, for both post-Tridentine bishops and new orders of the Counter-Reformation attempted from the later sixteenth century onwards to extend at least some control over the use and décor even of side chapels.[1] The insistence of Carlo Borromeo on the exclusion of laity from the chancel, and on the railing of side altars, is well enough known. But the long contests at Milan cathedral itself over the exclusion from the chancel of a throne for the Spanish governor, as opposed to that of the archbishop himself, did not end with Borromeo's death. His two immediate successors continued the struggle to exclude even such highly placed representatives of the Catholic monarchy from the chancel.[2] In these disputes learned reference was made to other areas of Catholic Europe, as for example the choir of Toledo cathedral (where the distinct *coro* not chancel was involved, but where royal representatives at provincial councils were certainly seated adjacent to the high altar).[3] In Spain after the Council of Trent there was conflict over the exclusion of laity from the chancel, with royal insistence that the right of lay patrons as well as of the knights of Military Orders must be respected; the presence of wives of patrons or of female patrons, however, continued to exercise Jesuit and other purists.[4] The contest in the Hispanic world was indeed such that in Sicily, where the Spanish Crown after Trent continued to assert the legatine rights of its viceroys, ceremonial as well as jurisdictional, the place in church claimed by the viceroys was defended with reference to the arrangements at Naples as well as at Milan.[5] The Venetian world after Trent presents an obvious contrast: the present chancel of S. Marco, screened with Byzantine exclusiveness from the body of the basilica still between the Council of Trent and the Revolution, was indeed the Doge's chapel *par excellence*, within the wholly ducal church.[6] This essentially liturgical presence

[1] The classic study of E. Mâle, *L'Art religieux de la fin du XVIe siècle, du XVIIe siècle et du XVIIIe siècle* (Paris, 1951) should be complemented by the approach of F. Haskell, *Patrons and painters*, rev. ed. (New Haven and London, 1980); cf. also the study of S. Sinding-Larsen, *Iconography and ritual* (Oslo, 1984). In Italy older religious orders were also involved, as at Florence and Venice, and ducal or oligarchic as well as episcopal influence: M. Hall, *Renovation and Counter-Reformation: Vasari and Duke Cosimo in Sta Maria Novella and Sta Croce 1565–1577* (Oxford, 1979); R. Goffen, *Piety and patronage in Renaissance Venice* (New Haven, 1986). Spain has been treated in works of varying quality: S. Sebastián, *Contrarreforma y barroco. Lecturas iconográficas e iconológicas* (Madrid, 1981); F. Cañedo Argüelles, *Arte y teoría: la contrarreforma y España* (Oviedo, 1982). See also V. Gerard-Powell, 'Notes sur la diffusion de l'iconographie de saint Charles Borromée en Espagne', in *San Carlo e il suo tempo. Atti del Convegno Internazionale, Milano 1984*, vol. 2 (Rome, 1986), pp. 1021–31; Gerard-Powell, 'Les Annales de Baronius et l'iconographie religieuse du XVIIe siècle', *Baronio e l'arte*, ed. R. De Maio *et al.* (Sora, 1985), pp. 473–87.

[2] Carlo Borromeo, 'Instructiones Fabricae et Supellectilis Ecclesiasticae', in *Trattati d'Arte del cinquecento*, ed. P. Barocchi, vol. 3 (Bari, 1960–62), pp. 1–113; 31–2. Biblioteca Apostolica Vaticana (BAV), MSS Barb. Lat. 5484, fos. 61v – 62r; 7819, fo. 85r; Biblioteca Vallicelliana, Rome, MS N.13, fos. 340r ff., 346r-v, 350v – 351v, 404r; Biblioteca Nazionale, Rome, MS Fondo Gesuitico 627, fo. 7v; Biblioteca Ambrosiana, Milan (BA), MS G.258 inf., 3 June 1595; Archivio della Curia Arcivescovile, Milan, Carteggio Ufficiale, vol. 12, Q.11 (fo. 3r); vol. 56, no.5; vol. 68, A 1–5; 1588–1629; Archivo General de Simancas, Spain (AGS): Consejo de Italia, Secretaría Provincial de Milán, Consultas, Legajo 1796; C. Bascapè, 'Commentarii de Ecclesia Mediolan. ab obitu Sancti Caroli ad annum 1613' in *Documenti spettanti alla storia della S. Chiesa Milanese*, ed. C. Annoni (Como, 1838), sect. 4, pp. 43ff.; P. P. Bosca, *Decadis Quartae historiarum Mediolan. Ecclesiae Sive de Pontificatu Gasparis Vicecomitis* (Milan, 1682), pp. 44ff., 54–6; *Storia di Milano*, 10, 314, Fondazione Treccani degli Alfieri (Milan, 1957); C. Marcora, 'Il diario di G. B. Casale', *Memorie storiche della Diocesi di Milano*, 12 (1965), pp. 209ff., p. 369; C. Beretta, 'Jacopo Menochio e la controversia giurisdizionale milanese degli anni 1596–1600', *Archivio Storico Lombardo*, 103 (1977), pp. 47–128.

[3] Bosca, *Decadis*, p. 49; Biblioteca Nacional, Madrid (BNM), MS 13044, fo. 18v; cf. MS 6148, fos. 32r ff.

[4] BNM, MSS 13019, fos. 13r ff.; 6148, fos. 24r ff., 103r ff.; 5788, fos. 123r ff.; Archivo Histórico Nacional, Madrid (AHN), Inquisición: Leg. 4511, fo. 79v; cf. R. Mann, *El Greco and his patrons* (Cambridge, 1986), p. 3.

[5] AGS: Estado: Sicilia: Leg. 1164, fos. 22, 47; 1610.

[6] B. Boucher, 'Jacopo Sansovino and the Choir of St Mark's', *Burlington Magazine*, 118 (1976), pp. 552 ff.

of the Doge, facing the centre of the high altar, contrasts with the relative discretion of the lateral view of the sanctuary and high altar obtained at the Escorial from the chamber of Philip II. The contrast of lateral royal monuments there or at Guadalupe, flanking the high altar, should not be too rashly made *vis-à-vis* the sacramental or saintly scenes of Venetian *laterali*.[7]

Thus whatever the partial success of post-Tridentine prelates, inspired by Borromean example, in prohibiting burials of lay persons – at least within the sanctuary – and by implication the juxtaposition of tombs and altars, the ideal remained clear: Trent's reassertion of the uniquely priestly powers involved in the sacrament of the altar should lead to the exclusion of laity from the sanctuary, in life as in death.[8] The political argument of the pre-Tridentine image in the Vatican *Stanze*, Raphael's *Expulsion of Heliodorus*, – though not an altarpiece – could be understood after the Council in a wider sense, both ecclesiological and, in practical implications, liturgical. Thus Venice and other Catholic powers protested over the perfection of reform at the post-Conciliar papal court, when the seating at papal ceremonies in the Sistine Chapel itself was revised to emphasise liturgical, and hence clerical, precedence at the expense of courtly or diplomatic representation.[9] It is not surprising, by the seventeenth century, to find papal celebration of a Counter-Reformation victory, that of the Battle of the White Mountain, concentrated in a church re-dedicated to Our Lady of Victories; where a chapel enshrining the mystic consummation of St Teresa, at the heart of the other arena of Habsburg Catholicism, is visibly in the patronage of the Venetian Cornaro family, in Bernini's famous masterpiece (plates 136–7).

The relative triumph of post-Tridentine clerical programmes in this case is demonstrable from the lateral décor of the chapel. Although the reliefs on the side walls form a collective or family monument of a kind, the clerics represented in sculpture are properly attendant on the mysteries enacted on and above the altar, as their attitudes demonstrate. Only one secular figure, a Doge, is allowed a glimpse over the shoulder of one of the seven cardinals represented; and he, in life, had resigned his own political dignity before the claims of his clerical relation.[10] This later example is important in any case as a crucial reminder of the second major consideration in approaching post-Tridentine altarpieces. Such pieces were, to contemporaries, first and foremost a part of the altar furnishings: not primarily a painting or a sculpture, or a mixture of these, located in one place rather than another. Thus in the notorious contest over payment between El Greco and the brothers of the Hospital of Charity, Illescas, the archiepiscopal Council, sympathetic enough to the artist, could still accept the

[7] J. M. Brown, *Images and ideas in seventeenth-century Spanish painting* (Princeton, 1978), pp. 116 f.; P. Hills, 'Patronage and piety in Cinquecento Venice: Tintoretto and the Scuole del Sacramento', *Art History*, 6 (1983), pp. 30–43.

[8] Ibid.; cf. K. B. Hiesinger, 'The Fregoso Monument: a study in sixteenth-century tomb monuments and Catholic reform', *Burlington Magazine*, 118 (1976), pp. 283–93; AHN, Inquisición, Leg. 4511, fo. 78r.

[9] Fondazione Cini, Venice: Microfilm: Archivio Segreto Vaticano: Segreteria di Stato: Nunziatura in Venezia: filza 266 (fo. 96) (1575); cf. Archivio di Stato, Venice [AS Ven.]; Capi del Consiglio dei Dieci, Lettere di Ambasciatori, Roma, busta 26, nos. 9, 17 (1574); cf. A. Chastel, *The Sack of Rome, 1527* (Princeton, 1983), pp. 50–4, 186–8. For the continued question of the secular clergy's beards, see M. Smith O'Neil, 'The patronage of Cardinal Cesare Baronio at San Gregorio Magno: renovation and innovation', *Baronio e l'Arte*, pp. 145–71, 158–60; A. Melloni, 'History, pastorate, and theology: the impact of Carlo Borromeo upon A. G. Roncalli – Pope John XXIII', in *San Carlo Borromeo. Catholic reform and ecclesiastical politics in the second half of the sixteenth century*, ed. J. M. Headley and J. B. Tomaro (Washington DC, 1988), pp. 277–99, 280–1, 293–4.

[10] I. Lavin, *Bernini and the unity of the visual arts*, vol. 1 (New York, 1980), pp. 75–157, 98–103.

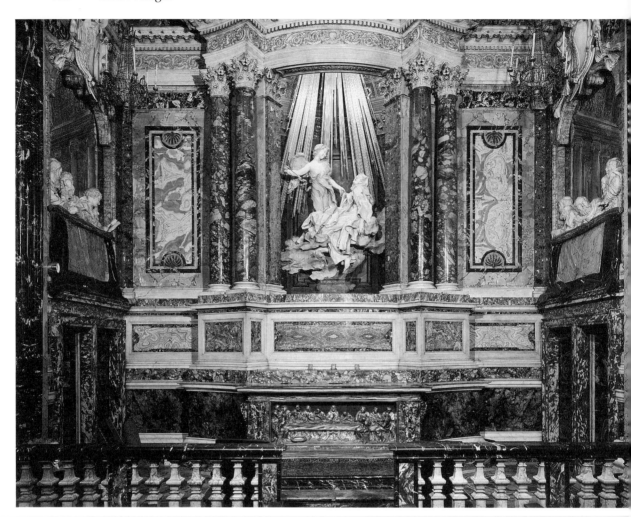

136 Bernini, *Ecstasy of St Teresa*

brotherhood's assertion that 'the main reason why the altarpiece was made was so that the holy image of Our Lady could be dressed with the greatest decency' (plate 139). A later submission equally mentioned the dressing of the image and its lowering to the ground for processions, such as the one which had been intended to precede the inauguration of the *retablo* on the original completion date.[11]

Post-Tridentine episcopal caution in Spain, both within and beyond the Toledan ecclesiastical province, over the dressing of sacred images does not contradict the essential point.[12] Altarpieces, even if in Italy, not Spain; even if involving only painting, without attendant sculpture or relief, are most usefully thought of as *retablos*,

[11] R. Enggass and J. Brown, *Italy and Spain 1600–1750* (Englewood Cliffs NJ, 1970), pp. 205 ff.; cf. S. J. Barnes, 'The decoration of the Church of the Hospital of Charity, Illescas', *Studies in the History of Art, XI, Figures of Thought: El Greco as Interpreter of History, Tradition and Ideas*, ed. J. Brown (Washington DC, 1982), pp. 45–55; R. L. Kagan, 'El Greco and the law', *ibid.*, pp. 79–90. For the structure of Toledan archiepiscopal councils: Archivio Segreto Vaticano (ASV): S. Congregatio S. Concilii: Visita ad limina: 805 A: Toletan. (I): Relatio 1614; 1630.

[12] BNM, MS 5788 (Plasencia Diocesan Synod, 1624), fo. 41r; cf. AHN, Inquisición, Leg. 4511 (Cuenca Synod, 1602), fo. 91r.

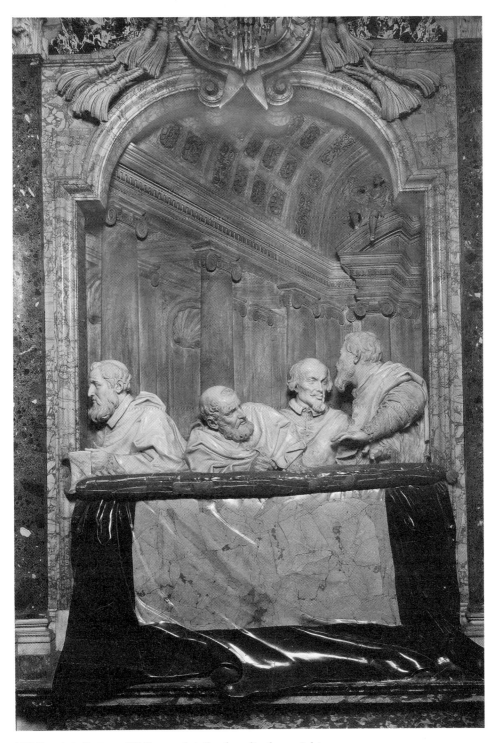

137 Bernini, *Ecstasy of St Teresa*, details of cardinals on right

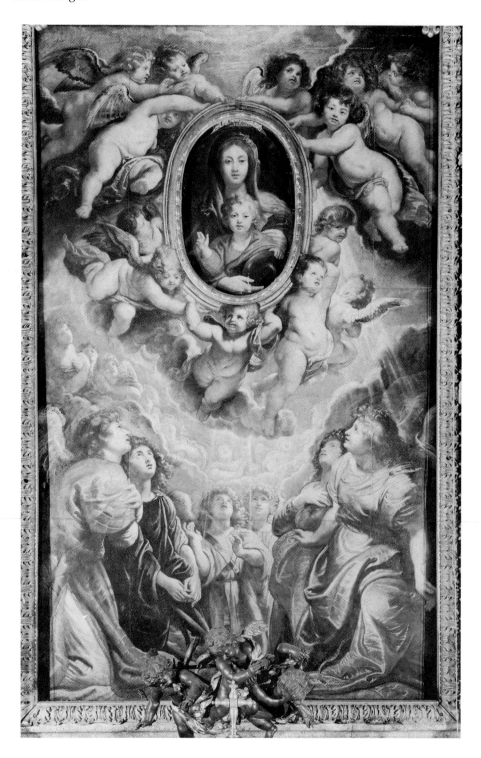

138 Rubens, *Virgin and Child with angels*

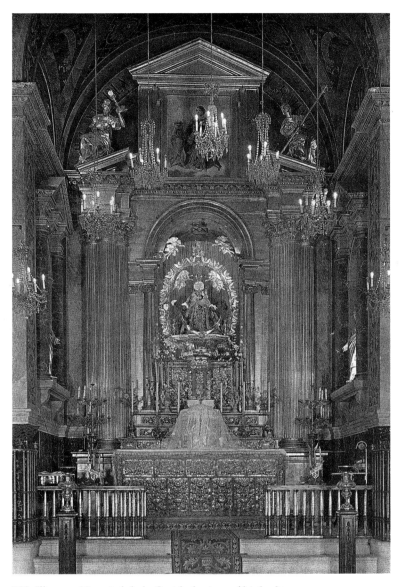

139 Illescas, Hospital de la Caridad, view of high altar

as reredoses. The commission to as great an artist as Rubens, for the high altar of the Chiesa Nuova in Rome, after all required him to fit his canvas around the ancient image of the Madonna, venerated not for its aesthetic but for its miraculous properties. The need to recommission Rubens, to repeat the work on the less reflective surface of slate (plate 138), is equally a reminder of the didactic purpose chiefly involved in such commissions.[13] This Oratorian concern was accepted as natural by those who contributed to the original decoration of the Chiesa Nuova. The contributions of a clerical art patron and theorist such as Federico Borromeo, friend of Neri and

[13] *Corpus Rubenianum Ludwig Burchard*, 8, ii (London, 1973), pp. 44–50. See recent discussion of the Oratorian tradition in relation to the theological and cultural milieu of the Rome of Caravaggio: T. Buser, 'The supernatural in Baroque religious art', *Gazette des Beaux-Arts*, 108 (1986), pp. 38–42.

Baronius, as well as of Barberini and Bosio, were intended, like Baronius's own donations, to mark out the high altar by the demonstrative deployment of marble and
of altar plate, where reliquaries had liturgical use. This much remains true, whatever
the precise turns of recent historical debate on the original balance of colour and
whitewash at the major Roman churches, such as the Gesù.[14]

But such didactic clarity was in any case not simply a Roman or a Borromean
preoccupation alone. In the litigation with El Greco the Illescas brotherhood stated
that 'the paintings are done in such a manner that they cannot be seen at a distance'.
Such an allegation had to be countered, not ignored, as a more sympathetic evaluation
allowed: 'if they cannot be seen clearly it is because they are set in a recessed chapel'.[15]
Similarly the purity of iconography, so much stressed by commissioning patrons
as well as by theorists, whether Paleotti, Federico Borromeo or others, involved the
need to distinguish sufficiently between saints depicted for veneration and emulation,
according to Tridentine teaching, and any other figures who might have cause to
be represented in the sanctuary or altarpiece.[16] Thus the notorious allegation of
the Illescas brotherhood that El Greco had included his nephew in the figures of
supplicants sheltered beneath the cloak of the Virgin of Charity, as well as the more
accurate observation that the supplicants wore ruffs, in contemporary fashion, con-
cluded that the 'other identifiable persons . . . should be completely eliminated from
this painting, because they steal attention from everything else . . . It was for this
reason that the original appraisers declared that they should be removed as
indecent'.[17]

The accusation of indecency was serious, and not confined to the area of physical
morality. The objections of Federico Borromeo to aspects of Michelangelo's *Last Judgment* included concern at the pagan and unscriptural intrusion of Charon, ferryman
of the dead; but the cardinal found consolation in the fact that liturgical requirements

[14] AGS: Estado: Negociación de Roma: leg. 978, fo. 123r; Sicilia: Leg. 1161, fo. 111 (1604); BA, MS G. 173 bis
inf., fo. 225r (1596); G. Calenzio, *La Vita e gli scritti del Card. Cesare Baronio* (Rome, 1907), p. 934; cf. pp. 477-8;
F. Rivola, *Vita di Federico Borromeo* (Milan, 1656), p. 140; E. Strong, *La Chiesa Nuova* (Rome, 1923), p. 73; L. von
Pastor, *The history of the Popes*, XXV (London, 1937), 21; B. A. V., MS Barb. Lat. 7819, esp. fos. 59r, 61r (1624);
C. Marcora, 'Il cardinal Federico Borromeo e l'archeologia cristiana', *Studi e Testi*, 235, Mélanges Eugène Tisserant,
5, ii (Vatican City, 1964), pp. 115-54; cf. E. D. Howe, 'The Church of Il Gesù explicated in a Guidebook of 1588',
Gazette des Beaux-Arts, 106 (1985), pp. 195-202; M. M. Byard, 'A new Heaven : Galileo and the artists', *History
Today* 38 (February 1988), pp. 30-8. For recent illustration of the theme of Jesuit building outside Rome involving
both the Society's central approval of plans and local direction of work by Jesuit lay-brothers: R. Turtas, *La
Casa dell'Università. La politica edilizia della Compagnia di Gesù nei decenni di formazione dell'Ateneo sassarese (1562–1632)*
(Sassari, 1986). Cf. M. Jaffé, *Rubens and Italy* (Oxford, 1977), pp. 86-7. The archiepiscopal control (not that of
the society) of the creation of the Jesuit church of San Fedele in Borromean Milan influenced even the design
of certain other North Italian Jesuit churches, as opposed to the more common influence on such churches elsewhere, as approved by the central authorities of the Society, of the Roman Gesù. Note also the handing of
newly established university education at Salzburg – where Baroque reconstruction as at the cathedral was introduced with Borromean inspiration and the employment of North Italian artists – not to the Jesuits but to the
Benedictines: *Regole della Congregatione della Fabrica della Chiesa, e Casa di S. Fedele* (Milan, 1605); cf. G. Galbiati,
Un manipolo di lettere degli Altemps al Card. Federico Borromeo (Rome, 1940). ASV: S. Congr. S. Conc.: Visita ad
limina: Milano, 1597: fo. 416r; cf. Rivola, *Vita*, p. 721; L. Welti, *Graf Kaspar von Hohenems 1573–1640* (Innsbruck,
1963), pp. 148, 160, 419, 430.

[15] Enggass and Brown, *Italy and Spain* (as in note 11), pp. 205 ff.

[16] Gabriele Paleotti, 'Discorso intorno alle imagini sacre e profane', in *Trattati d'Arte del cinquecento*, ed. P. Barocchi,
vol. 2 (1961), pp. 117-509; Federico Borromeo, *Musaeum* (1625; Milan, 1909); *De Pictura Sacra* (Rome, 1754); cf.
C. Eire, *War against the idols. The Reformation of worship from Erasmus to Calvin* (Cambridge, 1986).

[17] Enggass and Brown, *Italy and Spain* (as in note 11), pp. 205 ff.

caused the altar canopy to obscure the lowest parts of the fresco.[18] So too at Toledo the archiepiscopal council could sympathise with the more favourable evaluation of El Greco's *retablo*: 'The ruff collars . . . are acceptable, since they are usually worn these days. In fact it is more realistic to have them since it makes the figures look like supplicants. Otherwise they could be images of other saints and not portraits of ordinary men.'[19] The care here to observe the post-Tridentine rigour in the matter of a cult to be attributed only to recognised and official saints, something as important in the territories of the Spanish Inquisition as in the Italian states subject to the more immediate exercise of papal authority, can be seen also in El Greco's *Burial of the Count of Orgaz* (Toledo, San Tomé).[20] The officially cultivated saints, Saints Augustine and Stephen, are participants distinct from the contemporary company of mere mortals, clerics or laity, attendant on the figure of the count, whose reputation was essentially local.[21]

When laity featured in altarpieces or immediately lateral décor, then, their function must be absolutely necessary and precisely distinguished. Even the royal figures at the Escorial and Guadalupe, flanking the altar, are featured as supplicants, kneeling before both priest and altar. The earlier kneeling figures of donors or patrons might have entered the register of painted altarpieces, supplicants before the raised, if painted steps leading up to the Madonna or the patron saint. But such inclusion in the canvas itself, over the very altar, was arguably less suitable, as the central focus of at least some altarpieces changed. The Borromean insistence on the reservation of the Sacrament in a permanent tabernacle and on the location of such tabernacles on the high altar of parish churches at least (cathedrals and pilgrimage churches could pose different problems) meant that more often, after Trent, the scene of even a painted reredos had in practice to be subordinate to the focal point of the tabernacle. In Spain indeed the devotion to the tabernacle could eventually demand an altar backing on to the high altar, with a secondary view of the tabernacle: in plans for Guadalupe as well as in the climax of Toledo's *trasparente*, the high altar at the Escorial, or the famous double approach, more and less veiled, to the *Sagrada Forma* there.[22]

Venetian resistance to removal of the Reserved Sacrament to the high altar in some cases naturally arose from a political desire to maintain traditional ecclesiology in the city. The confraternities of the Blessed Sacrament might not be of the same social and economic importance as the *Scuole Grandi*, but they still involved lay funds and officers, as well as parochial organisation. The chapels of the Blessed Sacrament managed by confraternities were quite literally more accessible to laity than were

---

[18] *De Pictura Sacra*, p. 13. [Original edition, Milan 1624].

[19] Enggass and Brown, *Italy and Spain* (as in note 11), pp. 205 ff.

[20] BNM, MS 5788, fo. 41r; AHN, Inquisición, Leg. 4511, fo. 91r.

[21] S. Schroth, 'Burial of the Count of Orgaz', *Studies in the History of Art*, 11 (1982), pp. 1–17. The Saints' vestments are cloth of gold; the human officiant is in the black cope of the Funeral Rite.

[22] Borromeo, 'Instructiones', pp. 22–4; Brown, *Images and ideas* (as in note 7), pp. 116 f. and fig. 29; C. von der Osten Sacken, *El Escorial. Estudio iconológico* (Madrid, 1984), pp. 60–4 and fig. 1; G. Kubler, *Building the Escorial* (Princeton, 1982), p. 117 and figs. 109 A–B; cf. R. Mulcahy, 'Federico Zuccaro and Philip II : the reliquary altars for the basilica of San Lorenzo de el Escorial', *Burlington Magazine*, 129 (1987), pp. 502–9, 503–4.

the clerical enclaves of the sanctuary before the high altar.[23] Yet the relative devaluation of high altar paintings, *vis-à-vis* precisely liturgical requirements, could go further still outside Venice. If laity, in paint or in the flesh, were excluded from the sanctuary, the didactic priorities of the clergy in the use of the reredos could demand yet more. The seasonal changing of the high altar painting at the Jesuits' main church in Paris is well enough known.[24] But at the patriarchal seminary founded at Valencia after Trent by Archbishop Juan de Ribera, the dedicated chapel of Corpus Christi understandably had an altar painting of the Last Supper. Yet as often as once a week, and not only in Holy Week itself, Friday devotions meant the lowering of the painting, to reveal a life-size crucifix.[25]

In post-Tridentine Portugal, at Braga, archiepiscopal authority was directly asserted over the functions of a lay confraternity of the Blessed Sacrament, as the cult of the reserved sacrament was freshly regulated.[26] Eucharistic devotion could also be specifically associated with other post-Tridentine altars, and not only during the specially theatrical displays created for the solemn exposition of the Host in the *Quarant'Ore*, the Milanese devotion regulated and promoted by Carlo Borromeo. Even at the Cornaro chapel, where there was not eucharistic reservation, the Last Supper was explicitly recorded in the altar front, above the vestigial references to mortuary themes and monumental celebration in the marble pavement.[27] At Venice itself, of course, the peculiar traditions of the Republic survived, but even so in modified form, as exemplified by the evolutionary stages of completion and re-ordering at S. Francesco della Vigna. Though the quasi-sacral role of ducal as well as patriarchal families was still represented by the Gritti monuments flanking the high altar, these were still monuments rather than figurative tombs. The architectural enlargement of the altar of the Badoer-Giustinian chapel avoided personal or family representation, while the Trevisan monuments were placed above doors not altars; just as the projected Grimani tombs for the interior West façade would face the high altar, but at the whole length of the church. In any case the decorative schemes for the altarpiece and chapels of Barbaro and Grimani, related in the fraught patriarchal succession at Aquileia in the Tridentine and post-Conciliar era, avoided directly personal representations in the altar paintings themselves. The sacramental, though not eucharistic, doctrine of baptism, reaffirmed at Trent, appeared in the Barbaro altar painting of Christ's Baptism by Battista Franco. The aspect of the kneeling king at the feet of the infant Christ in the Grimani altarpiece, the *Adoration of the Magi* by Federico Zuccari, may intend an indirect reference to the troubled patriarch. But the altar

---

[23] Hills, 'Patronage and piety'; B. Pullan, *Rich and poor in Renaissance Venice* (Oxford, 1971), pp. 121, 253, 344; cf. P. Prodi, 'The structure and organization of the Church in Renaissance Venice: suggestions for research', in *Renaissance Venice*, ed. J. R. Hale (London, 1973), pp. 409 ff.; R. Mackenney, *Tradesmen and traders. The world of the guilds in Venice and Europe, c. 1250 – c. 1650* (London, 1987), pp. 60, 71, 170–1, 177, 198–9, 202.

[24] J. Evans, *Monastic iconography in France from the Renaissance to the Revolution* (Cambridge, 1970), p. 48.

[25] R. Robres Lluch, *San Juan de Ribera* (Barcelona, 1960), pp. 255–6; P. Boronat y Barrachina, *El B. Juan de Ribera y el R. Colegio de Corpus Christi* (Valencia, 1904).

[26] ASV: S. Congr. S. Conc.: Vis. ad limina: 141: Bracharen. : Relatio 1594; 1615.

[27] Lavin, *Bernini*, vol. 1 (as in note 10), pp. 87–137; cf. R. Krautheimer, *The Rome of Alexander VII, 1655–1667* (Princeton, 1985), p. 115.

painting itself fits as a lower stage beneath the crowning fresco of the Resurrection (plate 140). The whole wall is truly a reredos, and if allusion to the patriarch's Conciliar absolution from suspicion of heresy and resurrection of his reputation is indeed intended, the scheme is nevertheless directly Christocentric, complete with a lateral fresco of the resurrection of Lazarus, not a personal tomb. Trent reasserted the doctrine of the mass, and Tridentine altarpieces were properly ordered in relation to the altar, whether or not there was a tabernacle.[28]

It may be suggested that the final arrangement by Rubens of the high altar paintings at the Chiesa Nuova provided a model for the lateral, clerical not saintly, witnesses of the main subject in the Cornaro chapel sculptures. Apparently at the centre of Rubens's main panel at the Chiesa Nuova the cover painting of the Madonna and Child had to be removable, to reveal at certain seasons the miraculous and crowned icon of the Virgin. There was, in other words, at certain liturgical moments, a sense of recess, mysteriously behind the ostensible surface of the painted figures: perhaps this may have contributed to the dramatic revelation which Bernini set into the Cornaro altar niche, with its miraculous lighting.[29] If Rubens was otherwise more often associated with Jesuit than Oratorian commissions and patrons the priorities of the liturgical seasons could still dominate. Thus the original plan at the Jesuit church in Antwerp was to display above the high altar the two paintings of the Miracles of St Ignatius and those of St Francis Xavier in alternation.[30] St Ignatius indeed is represented, within the painting, as himself in mass vestments, before an altar; as with the Chiesa Nuova depiction of Neri's levitation while celebrating mass by Pietro da Cortona. Even when mass was not in fact being celebrated on an altar, the altarpiece or adjacent decoration could reflect the focal point of the mass; even if such reassertions are not without partial precedents in later medieval altarpieces depicting eucharistic miracles.[31]

At Santo Domingo el Antiguo, at Toledo, the original plan for the paintings by

[28] AS Ven.: Capi, Lettere, Roma, b.25, nos. 11 ff. (1566–73), esp. no. 82 (1569); B. 26, nos. 6 ff. (1574–8); *Nunziature di Venezia*, ed. A. Stella, vol. 9 (Rome, 1972), nos. 56 ff. (1569–70); ibid., ed. A. Buffardi, vol. II, nos. 14 ff. (1573–6); B. Cecchetti, *La Republica [sic] di Venezia e la Corte di Roma nei rapporti della religione*, vol. 1 (Venice, 1874), pp. 86 f., 339, 365; P. B. Gams, *Series episcoporum* (Ratisbon, 1873), p. 774; A. Foscari and M. Tafuri, *L'Armonia e i conflitti. La chiesa di San Francesco della Vigna nella Venezia del '500* (Turin, 1983), figs. 79, 81, 91–3; cf. M. Tafuri, *Venezia e il Rinascimento. Religione, scienza, architettura* (Turin, 1985), and G. Trebbi, *Francesco Barbaro, patrizio veneto e patriarca di Aquileia* (Udine, 1984); cf. also G. Benzoni, *Gli affanni della cultura. Intellettuali e potere nell'Italia della Controriforma e barocca* (Milan, 1978); G. Geiger, *Filippino Lippi's Carafa chapel* (Kirksville, 1986).
[29] M. Warnke 'Italienische Bildtabernakel bis zum Frühbarock', *Münchner Jahrbuch der bildenden Kunst*, 19 (1968), pp. 61–102; *Corpus Rubenianum*, 8, ii, p. 50; cf. M. Rooses, *L'oeuvre de P. P. Rubens*, vol. 1 (Antwerp, 1886–92; Soest, 1977), p. 270; cf. Jaffé, *Rubens and Italy* (as in note 14), p. 102; C. White, *Peter Paul Rubens. Man and artist* (New Haven and London, 1987), pp. 38–51.
[30] T. L. Glen, *Rubens and the Counter Reformation* (New York, 1977), pp. 177, 247.
[31] Lavin, *Bernini*, vol. 1 (as in note 10), p. 119; vol. 2, fig. 241; cf. J. Connors, *Borromini and the Roman Oratory: style and society* (New York, 1980); cf. P. Cannon-Brookes, *Lombard paintings c.1595 – c.1630. The age of Federico Borromeo* (Birmingham, 1974), pp. 128–9, 248–9. It may be noted that within the Milanese ecclesiastical province St Carlo Borromeo was also depicted in pontifical vestments, on the model of St Ambrose, and not only in cardinal's choir dress: ibid., pp. 122–3, 154–5, 164–5, 168–9, 180–1, 190–1; cf. pp. 118–19, 130–1. This is an important corrective to the unqualified implications in P. Prodi, 'Charles Borromée, archevêque de Milan et la papauté', *Revue d'histoire ecclésiastique*, 62 (1967), pp. 379 ff.; cf. Mann, *El Greco*, pp. 139, 145 and fig. 38.

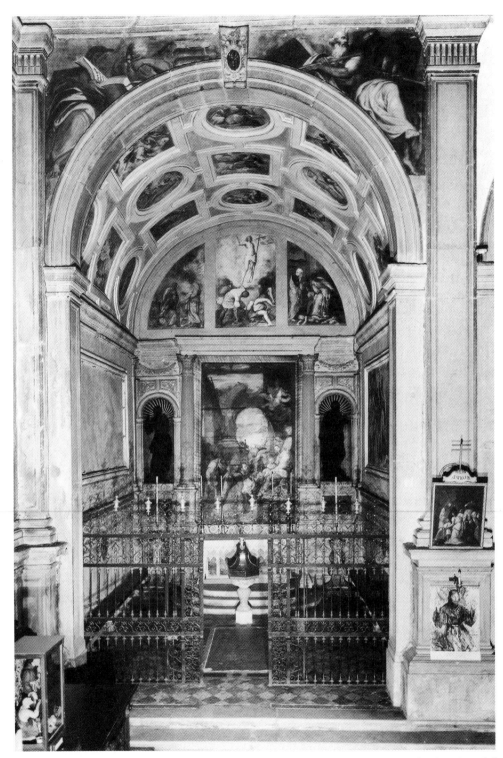

140 Venice, S. Francesco della Vigna, view of Grimani chapel, with copy of *Adoration of the Magi* by Federico Zuccari

El Greco of the high altar and two side altars demonstrated similar concerns (plate 125). The saints who mediate between the priest and faithful before the altar and the mysteries within the scenes for the two side altars (the *Adoration of the Shepherds* and the *Resurrection*) point to a completely Tridentine theology of the mass. Moreover, the figure of St Ildefonso in the *Resurrection* (plate 129) is in mass vestments, like St Ignatius in the painting for Antwerp or St Philip Neri at the Chiesa Nuova. The miraculous origin of the chasuble bestowed on St Ildefonso by the Virgin was, further, here alluded to, in defence of the Toledan saint. For in addition to the contemporary Spanish polemics over the doctrine of the Immaculate Conception, in which the authority of Rome was already involved, the Italian Oratorian Baronius had attacked the reputation of Ildefonso, as well as the historicity of St James's presence in Spain, which the monarchy asserted in support of its jurisdictional claims in relation to the papacy.[32] If an allusion to the figure of Carranza, the archbishop of Toledo perse-cuted by the royally supported Inquisition in Spain but to a degree sheltered by Roman authority, is intended in the person of Ildefonso, the reference does not inter-rupt the primary meaning here.[33] For in the mediating figure of St Jerome, pointing to the Adoration in the other side altarpiece, a secondary representation of the commis-sioning patron, Don Diego de Castilla, may equally be intended. But the authority of this Dean of Toledo cathedral was certainly asserted in support of the Tridentine standards associated with the incarcerated archbishop, whatever the failings of the *ancien régime* typified in the Dean's own person and dynasty. His own and his putative mistress's tombs at either side of the high altar were visually subordinated, in the same way, to the didactic display of the three altars. The tombs of the Dean and of his son and successor as Dean took the liturgically more dignified, or Gospel side of the main chancel; as clerics their proximity, in death, to the altar did not necessarily clash with the major post-Tridentine objective (still pursued in the Toledan province following the work of Carranza's successor, Archbishop Quiroga) of exclud-ing proprietary monuments from such locations. The royal exceptions, in any case,

[32] AGS: Estado: Roma: Leg. 1857, fo. 39r-v (1604); Sicilia: Leg. 1161, fo. 97 (1604); cf. fo. 271 (1605); J. Pérez Villanueva, 'Baronio y la Inquisición Española', in *Baronio Storico e la Controriforma*, ed. R. de Maio *et al.* (Sora, 1982), pp. 3–53; it should be noted, however, that the Jesuit Cardinal Bellarmine was regarded as an even more prominent critic of aspects of the cult of St James: J. L. González Novalín, 'Baronio y la cuestión jacobea. Manipulaciones en el sepulcro compostelano en tiempo del Cardenal', *Baronio e l'Arte*, pp. 173–88; Mann, *El Greco*, pp. 1–45, esp. pp. 29, 39; cf. R. L. Kagan, 'Pedro de Salazar de Mendoza as collector, scholar, and patron of El Greco', *Studies in the History of Art, XIII, El Greco: Italy and Spain*, ed. J. Brown and J. M. Pita Andrade (Washington DC, 1984), pp. 85–93; cf. A. Fliche and V. Martin, *Histoire de l'Eglise*, vol. 18 (Paris, 1960), p. 410 n.3; R. Otero Pedrayo, *Síntesis Histórica do Século XVIII en Galicia* (Vigo, 1969), p. 57; cf. D. Davies, 'The relationship of El Greco's altarpieces to the mass of the Roman Rite', in the present volume.

[33] Mann, *El Greco*, p. 30; Mann, 'The altarpieces for the Hospital of Saint John the Baptist, Outside the Walls, Toledo', *Studies in the History of Art*, 11 (1982), p. 58; see also pp. 67–9; Kagan, 'Pedro de Salazar', (as in note 32), pp. 88–9; D. Davies, *El Greco* (Oxford, 1976), pp. 4–10, 16; Davies, 'El Greco and the Spiritual Reform Movements in Spain', *Studies in the History of Art*, 13 (1984), pp. 57–75, esp. p. 71; J. Rogelio Buendía, 'Humanismo y simbología en El Greco: el tema de la serpiente', ibid., pp. 35–46. The arrest of Carranza and the subsequent long interregnum in his absence raised acutely questions of Toledo's primatial precedence *vis-à-vis* the sees of Santiago (Pérez Villanueva, 'Baronio'), Burgos (J. I. Tellechea Idígoras, *Fray Bartolomé Carranza y el Cardenal Pole* (Pamplona, 1977), p. 289), Córdoba as well as Burgos (BNM, MS 13044, fos. 1r ff., 43r-v), and also Braga (fos. 163r ff.; MS 6148, fos. 85r ff.).

to such exclusion, were to be obvious in Spain, quite apart from any implicit claims represented by the Dean to ancient royal lineage. Orthodoxy, legitimacy in all senses and even assimilation to patristic authority were asserted in the figures of Jerome and Ildefonso.[34]

The two side altars may not have supported tabernacles for the Reserved Sacrament, but the painted manger in the one altarpiece, and the tomb in the other, above which Christ rises, are themselves types of the altar itself, in an extended metaphor of Christ's incarnate presence. The image of the Throne of Mercy incorporated in the depiction of the *Trinity* (plate 126), originally the crowning glory of the high altar – even subordinating the 'Veronica' or true icon of Christ's human face – continues a similar reference, as well as illustrating again the theology of the mass. Immediately above the high altar, however, the painting of the *Assumption* (plates 125, 131) made a parallel reference, in the empty tomb of the Virgin, which rises above the three-dimensional altar, while at the same time asserting the dignity and authority of St James, and also alluding to the doctrine of the Immaculate Conception.[35] Furthermore, the placing of an *Assumption* over the tabernacle of a high altar, as at Santo Domingo el Antiguo, suggested the role of the Virgin Mother in carrying the Word to be made Flesh in her own body. Marian imagery, becoming officially recognised from more popular devotion in the post-Tridentine Catholic world, especially in Italy (rather than in Spain with its concentration on the disputed doctrine of the Immaculate Conception – and hence veneration of St Jerome not confined to Hieronymites and their royal patrons) included the epithets 'House of gold' and 'Ark of the Covenant'.[36]

Patristic authority and sculptural representation of the Risen Christ would seem to have complemented the tabernacle on the high altar of the Tavera Hospital, in the original plan for that altar and the related side altars. This remains clear enough, whatever the precise intentions for the paintings in this programme. El Greco, as at the chapel of St Joseph in Toledo, was attempting to re-order the conventional

[34] Mann, *El Greco*, pp. 1–30, esp. pp. 19, 27–9, 37–9; Kagan, 'Pedro de Salazar' (as in note 32), p. 90; Davies, *El Greco* (as in note 33), pp. 3–5, 10, 16; Davies, 'El Greco and the Spiritual Reform Movements' (as in note 33), pp. 60–2. For the special importance of Saint Jerome as witness to the Immaculate Conception, see also E. F. Rice Jr, *Saint Jerome in the Renaissance* (Baltimore, 1985), pp. 147, 150–1; cf. AHN, Inquisición, Leg. 4511, fo. 78r; BNM, MS 5788, fos. 18r ff. (Plasencia too).

[35] Mann, *El Greco*, pp. 28–45, esp. pp. 37–41; J. J. Martín González, 'El concepto de retablo en El Greco', *Studies in the History of Art*, 13 (1984), pp. 115–19.

[36] Rice, *Saint Jerome* (as in note 34), pp. 57, 68–78, 147; G. Sánchez Meco, *El Escorial y la Orden Jerónima* (Madrid, 1985); cf. J. R. L. Highfield, 'How much did it cost to found a Jeronimite monastery in late medieval Spain?', in *Studies in Medieval History Presented to R. H. C. Davis*, ed. H. Mayr-Harting and R. I. Moore (London, 1985), pp. 271–81; Highfield, 'The Jeronomites in Spain, their patrons and success, 1373–1516', *Journal of Ecclesiastical History*, 34 (1983), pp. 513–33. For the visual relation to other Marian themes, such as the Annunciation, Assumption or Coronation, of the precise doctrine of the Immaculate Conception, contested still before and after Trent by Catholic theologians, particularly between Franciscans and Dominicans, compare Goffen, *Piety and Patronage in Renaissance Venice*, esp. pp. 73–118, and Geiger, *Filippino Lippi's Carafa chapel*, esp. pp. 135–50; cf. M. F. Mellano, 'Aspetti del Culto Mariano nella Diocesi di Milano all'epoca di S. Carlo', *Atti della Accademia di San Carlo*, 6 (1983; Milan 1984), pp. 19–53, 33; C. Marcora, 'L'istituzione della Compagnia del Santo Rosario eretta da S. Carlo', ibid., pp. 111–19, 115–16.

elements of the Spanish *retablo*, painted and sculpted, arguably in a more Italian manner, but certainly better to demonstrate the teachings of Tridentine Catholicism.[37] The reasserted value of indulgences and of intercession for the dead, above all the Requiem, was specifically involved in the indulgenced masses celebrated in the Tavera Hospital chapel (even if many patients also relied on the popular indulgence of the Crusade Bull, still widely purchased in post-Tridentine Spain).[38] The Resurrection surmounted the tabernacle with particular propriety in this altarpiece: the sculpted Risen Christ above the place where His sacramental body lay. Such a combination was indeed uncomplicated by the concern on occasion shown at Venice to preserve an existing *pala d'oro* above an altar, in addition to any new altarpieces.[39] Yet even in France the Gallican tradition of Amiens cathedral could preserve a sacramental focus in a later reredos, where the peculiar reservation of the Sacrament inside a suspended metal dove remained the centre of attention above the high altar. Peculiar liturgical traditions should not be overlooked in their effect on altarpieces. The Ambrosian Rite at Milan and the primatial Rite of Braga in Portugal both survived the Tridentine and post-Conciliar papal imposition of a uniformly Roman liturgy in the rest of the western Catholic world. The Ambrosian regulations revived by Carlo Borromeo and the equivalent prescriptions in the cathedral of Braga required that throughout Lent the reredos of the altar should be veiled in such a way as to leave only the crucifix visible; quite apart from the Braga tradition of a Lenten veil suspended before the whole chancel.[40] More generally the Tridentine insistence on hierarchical approval for new or unusual images of sacred subjects, repeated in Toledan and other Spanish episcopal regulations after the Council, led to such ambiguous orders as that to place iron gates at the entrance to the chapel containing the tomb of the Count of Orgaz, in Santo Tomé at Toledo. El Greco's painting of the Count's burial was not placed over an altar, as its present location might suggest, but on a lateral wall, with an epitaph beneath, and – in the original intention – a painted sepulchre alluding to the actual tomb of the Count. The contemporary

[37] Mann, *El Greco*, pp. 111–46, esp. p. 144; Mann, 'The altarpieces' (as in note 33); Martín González, 'El concepto', pp. 116–17; Davies, 'The relationship of El Greco's altarpieces'; Davies, *El Greco* (as in note 33), pp. 15–16; Davies, 'El Greco and the Spiritual Reform Movements' (as in note 33), p. 67; Kagan, 'Pedro de Salazar' (as in note 32), pp. 86–8; J. Brown and R. L. Kagan, 'View of Toledo', *Studies in the History of Art*, 11 (1982), pp. 19–30, 24, 27–8.

[38] Mann, *El Greco*, pp. 119, 123; Mann, 'The altarpieces', pp. 58, 65, 73; cf. L. Martz, *Poverty and welfare in Habsburg Spain. The example of Toledo* (Cambridge, 1983), pp. 71, 178, 221 and n. 34. It should also be noted in this context that the relatively frequent communion of lay patients at the Tavera Hospital represented a distinctive position in an issue still much contested in Spain after Trent: ibid., p. 180; cf. Mann, *El Greco*, p. 118; Mann, 'The altarpieces', p. 36; cf. also AGS, Comisaria de Cruzada, Leg. 516; and note also the connection of the Bull's sales in the Spanish realm with the funding of the Escorial: Sánchez Meco, *El Escorial*, pp. 128–30; and AGS; J. Goñi Gaztambide, *Historia de la Bula de la Cruzada en España* (Vitoria, 1958).

[39] Mann, *El Greco*, p. 124; Mann, 'The altarpieces', p. 61; cf. Hills, 'Patronage and piety'.

[40] A. A. King, *Liturgy of the Roman Church* (London, 1957), p. 96; King, *Liturgies of the Primatial Sees* (London, 1957), pp. 209–10, 215–17, 223–4, 337, 347; cf. p. 388. The distinctive liturgies of ancient religious orders also of course survived Trent, despite conflicts within some orders after the Council, and this should not be overlooked in relation to the altars of such orders: King, *Liturgies of the religious orders* (London, 1955); ASV: S. Congr. S. Conc.: Vis. ad limina: 141: Bracharen: Relatio 1594; 1615; 1625; cf. BNM, MS 13019, fos. 2r ff.

portraiture effectively included in El Greco's composition was thus not part of an altar painting; though the references to the liturgy of the Funeral Rite are not confined to the vesture of the clerical participants in the scene, but more generally emphasise the Tridentine theology of salvation and intercession.[41]

If at Illescas side altars did indeed provide a complement to the Marian focus of the high altar and chancel decoration provided by El Greco and contested by the Brothers of the Hospital, it is striking that the putative side altar painting of St Ildefonso does not show the archbishop in his famous chasuble, dressed for mass, but in episcopal choir dress. (The colour of the mozzetta may refer to the monastic origin of the archbishop, but the rochet is arguably episcopal not conventual, and the colour of bishops' choir dress was in any case contested in the Spain of Philip II.)[42] Yet the reference to his defence of Marian virtues, intended by the internal allusion to the miraculous statue over the high altar itself and his seat at a study table, once again assimilate his authority to patristic dignity, specifically that of St Jerome (again allowing for a necessary distinction from Jerome's common depiction in cardinal's red).[43] El Greco's portrait of the saint, even if completed after the death of the reforming Quiroga, Carranza's successor as archbishop of Toledo, may surely also refer to more recent reassertion of hierarchic authority at Toledo. The Illescas institution was precisely asserting its role as a pilgrimage shrine, not just a hospital, arguably altering the emphasis of its founder, the earlier reforming monastic and archbishop of Toledo, Cisneros. But this was in the context of disputes in post-Tridentine Spain not only over episcopal regulation of pilgrimage, but also over such charitable brotherhoods and the demand for their subjection to episcopal oversight and regularisation,

[41] Ibid., fos. 9r ff.; MS 5788, fo. 41r; cf. fo. 155r; AHN, Inquisición, Leg. 4511, fo. 91r; A. Rodríguez G. de Ceballos, 'La repercusión en España del decreto del Concilio de Trento acerca de las imágenes sagradas y las censuras al Greco', *Studies in the History of Art*, 13 (1984), pp. 153–9; Schroth, 'Burial' (as in note 21), pp. 5–6, 15.

[42] Barnes, 'The decoration' (as in note 11), pp. 47–8; ASV: Segr. Stato: Spagna, vol. 34, fos. 220r ff., 588r ff.; cf. vol. 35, fo. 26r (conflict over bishops' dress in the Armada year itself, 1588). See also note 31 above for the iconography of St Carlo Borromeo. For the importance of such apparently trivial details of ecclesiastical dress, note later objection by contemporaries to an incongruously 'Italian' surplice (and in fact biretta?) in a depiction of the Spanish secular priest, the Venerable Juan de Avila: R. Cueto Ruiz, 'The Politics of Sanctity. "The Blessed John of Avila" by Pierre-Hubert Subleyras (1699–1749)', in *Catholic tastes and times. Essays in honour of Michael E. Williams*, ed. M. A. Rees (Leeds, 1987), pp. 57–79, 76; cf. *Subleyras* catalogue, ed. O. Michel and P. Rosenberg (Paris, 1987), pp. 40–1, 325–7.

[43] Barnes, 'The decoration' (as in note 11); cf. Mann, *El Greco*, p. 29. For Jerome and the evolution of cardinals' habits: Rice, *Saint Jerome* (as in note 34), pp. 106–8. That El Greco, not least after his Italian experience, was familiar with the conventions of cardinals' dress is clear: J. Brown and D. A. Carr, '*Portrait of a Cardinal*: Niño de Guevara or Sandoval y Rojas?', *Studies in the History of Art*, 11 (1982), pp. 33–42. Since depictions of post-Tridentine cardinals, including El Greco's paintings ('St Jerome as cardinal' and the 'portrait' of Cardinal Tavera), often show the mantellettum worn as well as the mozzetta, this detail is surely hardly surprising (cf. p. 42). Cardinals *in Urbe* (though presumably not in their titular churches) are shown thus, and this Roman image of a cardinal would have been familiar to El Greco. In any case while Madrid was within the diocese of Toledo, the royal Court itself (still not permanently fixed in location moreover) was within the distinct jurisdiction of the royal Chaplain General. (Cf. ASV: S. Congr. s. Conc.: Vis. ad lim.: 246A: Compostellan. (I): Rel. 1590). If the prelate depicted were Inquisitor General or member of the Council of State the supposed setting (whatever the actual place of painting) would arguably be the royal Court: hence the mantellettum in addition to the mozzetta, whether the sitter were archbishop of Toledo or Seville; cf. L. Puppi, 'Il soggiorno italiano del Greco', *Studies in the History of Art*, 13 (1984), pp. 133–51; cf. Mulcahy, 'Federico Zuccaro' (as in note 22), p. 505, fig. 17.

on the lines of universally recognised religious orders.[44] Moreover the defence of the Illescas brothers against the ambitions of the royally patronised Hieronymites (parallel to similar questions at Granada for example) came after the secular control of Illescas would seem to have passed from the Church of Toledo to that of the Crown, presumably during Philip II's extended exploitation of the Toledan possessions and revenues, following Carranza's arrest.[45] If at the Tavera Hospital at Toledo the original programme for the high altar *retablo* was intended to include not only the tabernacle and the figure of the Risen Christ, but also sculpted representation of the patristic witness of the Latin Fathers and, possibly, the painted climax of the Resurrection of the Just, a further reference to the eternal justification of the unfortunate Carranza has been suggested.[46] In any case there is a striking evolution to the later *Cathedra Petri* of Bernini at St Peter's, Rome, as a distanced reredos to the papal altar. The presence there of the Fathers of the Church has often been commented on, but it should be noted that the illumination of the Petrine Office by the Holy Spirit in the form of the stained glass window above the altar clearly reflects a concept of papal authority formulated in terms of the 'special inspiration of the Roman See'. Such a concept – as opposed to one of a more pronounced or personal infallibility of the papacy, of a kind bitterly disputed at Trent – would have been accepted even in post-Tridentine Spain.[47]

The evolution of the Tridentine altarpiece was of course never universal nor absolute. At Toledo the *Crucifixion* by El Greco for Las Jerónimas de la Reina, if originally placed over an altar, introduced a supplicant lay donor, even though accompanied by a cleric in choir dress.[48] In his canvas for the altar of the Oballe chapel in San Vicente, Toledo (plate 134), there are no donors; the mystic roses and lilies at the foot of the canvas are not simply Marian images but possibly suggest the transcendence of earthly constraints of time and space, particularly if the decoration of the

[44] Barnes, 'The decoration' (as in note 11), pp. 45–6; cf. Brown and Carr, '*Portrait*' (as in note 43), p. 39. Note the characteristic appeal of the Illescas brotherhood, in the dispute with El Greco, to the royal Chancillería as well as to the papal nuncio in Spain: Enggass and Brown, *Italy and Spain*, pp. 205 ff. Cf. ASV: S. Congr. S. Conc.: Visita ad limina: 263A: Corduben. (I): Relatio 1608; 1628; 1630; 370A: Granaten. (I): Relatio 1596; 1614; 394: Hispalen.: Relatio 1612; Martz, *Poverty and welfare* (as in note 38), pp. 19 f., 39 f., 49 f., 54 f., 57 ff., 77 ff., 150 ff.; AGS: Patronato Real: Leg. 22; AHN: Inquisición: Leg. 4511, fos. 83v ff.; BNM, MS 6148, fos. 103r ff.; MS 13019, fos. 5v; MS 5788, fos. 154r ff., 156r, 173v; cf. W. A. Christian Jr., *Local religion in sixteenth-century Spain* (Princeton, 1981), esp. p. 104.

[45] Barnes, 'The decoration' (as in note 11), pp. 54–5; Kagan, 'Pedro de Salazar' (as in note 32), p. 89; Martz, *Poverty and welfare* (as in note 38), p. 42; AGS: Patronato Eclesiástico: Leg. 147; Estado: Roma: Legs. 925, 930; 929, fo. 16 (1575–7); BNM, MS 13019, fo. 112r; cf. ASV: Segr. Stato: Spagna, vol. 31, fos. 254r ff., 1585 onwards.

[46] Mann, *El Greco*, pp. 122–44, esp. p. 137; Mann, 'The altarpieces', pp. 59–70, esp. p. 67.

[47] Lavin, *Bernini*, vol. 1 (as in note 10), pp. 35, 40, 44, 71, 105; vol. 2, figs. 58, 128; Krautheimer, *The Rome* (as in note 27), pp. 70, 74, 138–9, 175; ASV: S. Congr. S. Conc.: Visita ad limina: 785A: Tarraconen. (I): Relatio 1598; Segr. Stato: Spagna, vol. 320, fo. 179r (1594); H. Jedin, *Crisis and closure of the Council of Trent* (London, 1967); A. Marín Ocete, *El Arzobispo Don Pedro Guerrero y la política conciliar española en el siglo XVI*, vol. 1 (Madrid, 1970); Marín, 'El Concilio Provincial de Granada en 1565', *Archivo Teológico Granadino*, 25 (1962), pp. 23–178.

[48] Davies, *El Greco* (as in note 33), p. 13 and fig. 12; Davies, 'El Greco and the Spiritual Reform Movements' (as in note 33), p. 69; I. Mateo Gómez, 'Consideraciones iconográficas sobre la *Crucifixión con donantes* del Greco, para la Iglesia de las Monjas Jerónimas de Toledo', *Studies in the History of Art*, 13 (1984), pp. 121–3.

altar itself included flowers as well as candles.[49] At the Hieronymite and royal Escorial his *Martyrdom of St Maurice* did not find its intended place over the relevant side altar, but was relegated to the Chapter House, allegedly for failing to inspire the necessary devotion demanded by Tridentine prescription. Royal as opposed to directly clerical commission apparently produced a confusion of intention in the work of even El Greco, so personally conscious of the letter and spirit of the Tridentine decrees.[50]

From even these few examples it can thus be seen that the reassertion of Catholic orthodoxy at Trent did have some visible effects on the development of the altarpiece in post-Tridentine Italy and Spain. Even in such confirmedly Catholic societies, however, the implementation of Conciliar reform was generally neither universal nor instantaneous. It is therefore hardly surprising that the transformation of the altarpiece was equally not an absolute phenomenon. The meticulous care of the Venetian-trained El Greco in his Spanish commissions makes an interesting contrast to the preservation of distinctive local traditions at Venice itself in any assessment of the evolution of the altarpiece.

[49] Davies, 'The relationship of El Greco's altarpieces'; Davies, *El Greco* (as in note 33), p. 16 and figs. 43–4; Davies, 'El Greco and the Spiritual Reform Movements' (as in note 33), p. 72; Brown and Kagan, 'View of Toledo' (as in note 37), p. 28. Note that El Greco's depiction of St Ildefonso in full pontifical Mass vestments was also possibly intended for this chapel: Davies, *El Greco*, p. 16 and fig. 47; cf. Mulcahy, 'Federico Zuccaro' (as in note 22), p. 506.

[50] Davies, *El Greco* (as in note 33), p. 13 and figs. 4, 6, 8; A. Cloulas-Brousseau, 'Le Greco à l'Escurial: *Le Martyre de Saint Maurice*', *Studies in the History of Art*, 13 (1984), pp. 49–54; Rodríguez G. de Ceballos, 'La repercusión', pp. 153–4. For the ambiguities of Philip II's art patronage see A. Blunt, 'El Greco's "Dream of Philip II" : an allegory of the Holy League', *Journal of the Warburg and Courtauld Institutes*, 3 (1939–40), pp. 58–69; cf. Davies, *El Greco*, p. 13 and fig. 5; cf. J. C. Nash, *Veiled images. Titian's mythological paintings for Philip II* (Philadelphia, 1985); Mulcahy, 'Federico Zuccaro' (as in note 22), p. 509. (Compare the ambiguous alteration of Bernini's intended equestrian statue of Louis XIV with the accepted equestrian statue of Charles I of England by the French artist Le Sueur; see R. Wittkower, *Bernini's bust of Louis XIV* (Oxford, 1951); Wittkower, *Gian Lorenzo Bernini. The sculptor of the Roman baroque*, rev. 2nd ed. (London, 1966), pp. 24, 254–6; plates 111, 113).

Select bibliography

Baxandall, M. *Painting and experience in fifteenth-century Italy*. Oxford, 1972.
  The limewood sculptors of Renaissance Germany. New Haven and London, 1980.
  Patterns of intention. On the historical explanation of pictures. New Haven and London, 1985.
Belting, H. *Das Bild und sein Publikum im Mittelalter. Form und Funktion früher Bildtafeln der Passion*. Berlin, 1981.
Blum, S. N. *Early Netherlandish triptychs: a study in patronage*. Berkeley, 1969.
Borsook, E. 'Cults and imagery at Sant'Ambrogio in Florence', *Mitteilungen des Kunsthistorischen Institute in Florenz*, 25 (1981), pp. 147–202.
Borsook, E. and F. Gioffredi Superbi (eds). *The Italian altarpiece 1250–1550: history, technique, style* (forthcoming).
Boschloo, A. *Annibale Carracci in Bologna: visible reality after the Council of Trent*. 2 vols. Maarsen, 1974.
Braun, J. *Der christliche Altar in seiner geschichtlichen Entwicklung*. 2 vols. Munich, 1924.
  'Altarretabel', in *Reallexicon zur deutschen Kunstgeschichte*. Vol. 1, Stuttgart, 1937, cols.529–64.
Burckhardt, J. 'Das Altarbild', in *Beiträge zur Kunstgeschichte von Italien*. Basle, 1898. Trans. as *The altarpiece in Renaissance Italy*. ed. P. Humfrey, Oxford, 1988.
Cannon, J. 'Simone Martini, the Dominicans and the early Sienese polyptych', *Journal of the Courtauld and Warburg Institutes*, 45 (1982), pp. 69–93.
Carmichael, M. *Francia's masterpiece. An essay on the beginnings of the Immaculate Conception in art*. London, 1909.
Chastel, A. *Le grand atelier d'Italie 1460–1500*. Paris, 1965. Trans. as *Studios and styles of the Renaissance*. London and New York, 1971.
  'Le donateur "in abisso" dans les "Pale"', in *Festschrift für Otto von Simson*, ed. L. Grisebach and K. Renger. Frankfurt, 1977, pp. 273–83.
Christensen, C. *Art and the Reformation in Germany*. Athens OH, 1979.
Dearmer, P. *Fifty pictures of Gothic altars*, Alcuin Club Collection, 10. London, 1910.
Decker, B. *Das Ende des mittelalterlichen Kultbildes und die Plastik Hans Leinbergers*, Bamberger Studien zur Kunstgeschichte und Denkmalpflege, ed. R. Suckale and A. Hubel, vol. 3, Bamberg, 1985.
  'Die spätgotische Plastik als Kultbild', *Jahrbuch für Volkskunde*, n.s. 8 (1985), pp. 92–106.
Ehresmann, D. 'Some observations on the role of liturgy in the early winged altarpiece', *Art Bulletin*, 64 (1982), pp. 359–69.
Ferino Pagden, S. 'Iconographic demands and artistic achievements: the genesis of three works by Raphael', in *Raffaello a Roma*. Rome, 1986, pp. 13–27.
Ferretti, M. '"Con l'ornamento, come l'aveva esso acconciato": Raffaello e la cornice della "Santa Cecilia"', *Prospettiva*, 43 (1985), pp. 12–25.
Freedberg, D. *Iconoclasm and painting in the Revolt of the Netherlands*. New York and London, 1988.

'The representation of martyrdoms during the early Counter-Reformation in Antwerp', *Burlington Magazine*, 118 (1976), pp. 128–38.

Freuler, G. 'Bartolo di Fredis Altar für die Annunziata-Kapelle in S. Francesco a Montalcino', *Pantheon*, 43 (1985), pp. 21–39.

Gardner, J. 'The Stefaneschi altarpiece: a reconsideration', *Journal of the Warburg and Courtauld Institutes*, 37 (1974), pp. 57–103.

'The Louvre *Stigmatization* and the problem of the narrative altarpiece', *Zeitschrift für Kunstgeschichte*, 45 (1982), pp. 217–47.

'Fronts and backs: setting and structure', in *La pittura nel XIV e XV secolo: il contributo dell'analisi tecnica alla storia dell'arte*, ed. H. W. van Os and J. R. J. van Asperen de Boer, Atti del XXIV Congresso Internazionale di Storia dell'Arte, 1979, Vol. 3. Bologna, 1983, pp. 297–308.

Gardner von Teuffel, C. 'Masaccio and the Pisa polyptych: a new approach', *Jahrbuch der Berliner Museen*, 19 (1977), pp. 23–68.

'Lorenzo Monaco, Filippo Lippi und Filippo Brunelleschi: die Erfindung der Renaissance-pala', *Zeitschrift für Kunstgeschichte*, 45 (1982), pp. 1–30.

'From polyptych to pala: some structural considerations', in *La pittura nel XIV e XV secolo: il contributo dell'analisi tecnica alla storia dell'arte*, ed. H. W. van Os and J. R. J. van Asperen de Boer, Atti del XXIV Congresso Internazionale di Storia dell'Arte, 1979, Vol. 3. Bologna, 1983, pp. 323–30.

'Raffaels römische Altarbilder: Aufstellung und Bestimmung', *Zeitschrift für Kunstgeschichte*, 50 (1987), pp. 1–45.

Geiger, G. *Filippino Lippi's Carafa chapel*. Kirksville, 1986.

Gilbert, C. 'Peintres et menuisiers au début de la Renaissance en Italie', *Revue de l'Art*, 37 (1977), pp. 9–28.

Glasser, H. *Artists' contracts of the early Renaissance*. New York, 1977.

Goffen, R. *Piety and patronage in Renaissance Venice: Bellini, Titian and the Franciscans*. New Haven, 1986.

Hager, H. *Die Anfänge des italienischen Altarbildes: Untersuchungen der Entstehungsgeschichte des toskanischen Hochalterretabels*. Munich, 1962.

Hall, M. *Renovation and Counter-Reformation: Vasari and Duke Cosimo in Sta Maria Novella and Sta Croce 1565–1577*. Oxford, 1979.

Harbison, C. 'Visions and meditations in early Netherlandish painting', *Simiolus*, 15 (1985), pp. 87–118.

Hibbard, H. '*Ut picturae sermones*: the first painted decorations of the Gesù', in *Baroque Art: the Jesuit Contribution*, ed. R. Wittkower and I. Jaffé. New York, 1972, pp. 29–49.

Hills, P. 'Patronage and piety in Cinquecento Venice: Tintoretto and the Scuole del Sacramento', *Art History*, 6 (1983), pp. 30–43.

Hirst, M. 'The Chigi Chapel in S. Maria della Pace', *Journal of the Warburg and Courtauld Institutes*, 24 (1961), pp. 161–85.

Hood, W. and C. Hope. 'Titian's Vatican altarpiece and the pictures underneath', *Art Bulletin* 69 (1977), pp. 34–52.

Hope, C. 'Altarpieces and the requirements of patrons', in *Christianity and the Renaissance*, ed. T. Verdon and J. Henderson. Syracuse NY, 1989.

Hueck, I. 'Stifter und Patronatsrecht. Dokuments zu zwei Kapellen der Bardi', *Mitteilungen des Kunsthistorischen Institute in Florenz*, 20 (1976), pp. 263–70.

Humfrey, P. 'The Venetian altarpiece of the early Renaissance in the light of contemporary business practice', *Saggi e Memorie di Storia dell'Arte*, 15 (1986), pp. 65–82.

'Il dipinto d'altare nel quattrocento', in *La pittura in Italia: il quattrocento*, ed. F. Zeri. Milan, 1987, pp. 538–50.

'The Venetian *scuole piccole* as donors of altarpieces in the years around 1500', *Art Bulletin*, 70 (1988), pp. 401–23.

Huth, H. *Künstler und Werkstatt der Spätgotik*. New ed., Darmstadt, 1968.

Ingendaay, M. *Sienesische Altarbilder des sechszehnten Jahrhunderts*. 2 vols. Bonn, 1976.

Jacobs, L. 'The marketing and standardization of south Netherlandish carved altarpieces: limits on the role of the patron', *Art Bulletin*, 81 (1989), pp. 208–29.

Jungmann, J. A. *Missarum Sollemnia*. Vienna, 1948. Trans. as *The Mass of the Roman Rite*. 2 vols. New York, 1951.

Keller, H. 'Der Flügelaltar als Reliquienschrein', in *Geschichte der europäischen Plastik: Festschrift Theodor Müller zum 19, April 1965*. Munich, 1965, pp. 25–44.

Keydel, J. H. 'A group of altarpieces by Giovanni Bellini considered in relation to the context for which they were made'. Ph.D. dissertation, Harvard University, 1969.

Koller, M. and N. Wibiral. *Der Pacher-Altar in St Wolfgang*. Vienna, 1981.

Kurz, O. 'A group of Florentine drawings for an altar', *Journal of the Warburg and Courtauld Institutes*, 18 (1955), pp. 35–53.

Lane, B. *The altar and the altarpiece: sacramental themes in early Netherlandish painting*. New York, 1984.

Lavin, M. A. 'The altar of Corpus Domini in Urbino: Paolo Uccello, Joos van Ghent, Piero della Francesca', *Art Bulletin*, 49 (1967), pp. 1–24.

Piero della Francesca's 'Baptism of Christ'. New Haven and London, 1981.

Luchs, A. *Cestello. A Cistercian Church of the Florentine Renaissance*. New York, 1977.

Mâle, E. *L'Art religieux de la fin du XVIe siècle, du XVIIe siècle et du XVIIIe siècle. Etude sur l'iconographie après le Concile de Trente*. 2nd ed., Paris, 1951.

Mann, R. 'The altarpieces for the Hospital of Saint John the Baptist, Outside the Walls, Toledo', *Studies in the History of Art*, 11 (1982), pp. 57–76.

El Greco and his patrons. Cambridge, 1986.

Matthew, L. C. 'Lorenzo Lotto and the patronage and production of Venetian altarpieces in the early sixteenth century'. Ph.D. dissertation, Princeton University, 1988.

Miller, J. I. 'Major Florentine altarpieces from 1430 to 1450'. Ph.D. dissertation, Columbia University, 1983.

Paatz, W. *Süddeutsche Schnitzaltäre der Spätgotik*. Heidelberg, 1963.

Philip, L. B. *The Ghent altarpiece and the art of Jan van Eyck*. Princeton, 1971.

Preiser, A. *Das Entstehen und die Entwicklung der Predella in der italienischen Malerei*. Hildesheim, 1973.

Purtle, C. *The Marian paintings of Jan van Eyck*. Princeton, 1982.

Rasmussen, J. *Die Nürnberger Altarbaukunst der Dürerzeit*. Hamburg, 1974.

Retables italiens du XIIIe au XVe siècle. Catalogue of exhibition at Musée du Louvre, 1977–8. Paris, 1978.

Riedl, P. A. 'Raffaels *Madonna del Baldacchino*', *Mitteilungen des Kunsthistorischen Instituts von Florenz*, 8 (1957–9), pp. 223–46.

Rosand, D. *Painting in Cinquecento Venice: Titian, Veronese, Tintoretto*. New Haven and London, 1982.

Schindler, H. *Der Schnitzaltar*. Regensburg, 1978.

Shearman, J. 'The Chigi Chapel in S. Maria del Popolo', *Journal of the Warburg and Courtauld Institutes*, 24 (1961), pp. 129–60.

Andrea del Sarto. 2 vols. Oxford, 1965.

Pontormo's altarpiece in S. Felicita. Newcastle-upon-Tyne, 1971.

Sinding-Larsen, S. 'Titian's *Madonna di Ca' Pesaro* and its historical significance', *Acta ad archaeologiam et artium historiam pertinentia*, 1 (1962), pp. 39–69.

Iconography and ritual: a study of analytical perspectives. Oslo, 1984.

Smith, M. T. 'The use of grisaille as a Lenten observance', *Marsyas*, 8 (1957–9), pp. 43–54.

Stirn, M. *Die Bilderfrage der Reformation*. Quellen und Forschungen zur Reformationsgeschichte, 45. Gütersloh, 1977.

Van Os. H. W. *Sienese altarpieces, 1215–1460*. Vol. 1. Groningen, 1984.

  'Paintings in a house of glass: the altarpieces of Pienza', *Simiolus*, 17 (1987), pp. 23–38.

Vloberg, M. *L'Eucharistie dans l'art*. Grenoble and Paris, 1946.

Wackernagel, M. *Der Lebensraum des Künstlers in der florentinischen Renaissance: Aufgaben and Auftraggeber, Werkstatt und Kuntsmarkt*. Leipzig, 1938. Trans. as *The world of the Florentine Renaissance artist*. Princeton, 1981.

Warnke, M. 'Italienische Bildabernakel bis zum Frühbarock', *Münchner Jahrbuch der bildenden Kunst*, 19 (1968), pp. 61–102.

Zimmermann, E. *Der spätgotische Schnitzaltar*. Liebighaus Monographie, 5. Frankfurt, 1979.

Index